Experiential Verbs in Homeric Greek

Brill's Studies in Language, Cognition and Culture

Series Editors

Alexandra Y. Aikhenvald (*Cairns Institute, James Cook University*)
R.M.W. Dixon (*Cairns Institute, James Cook University*)
N.J. Enfield (*University of Sydney*)

VOLUME 27

The titles published in this series are listed at *brill.com/bslc*

Experiential Verbs in Homeric Greek

A Constructional Approach

By

Silvia Luraghi

BRILL

LEIDEN | BOSTON

Cover illustration: Detail of an Ionic capital. Courtesy Isabella Bossolino.

Library of Congress Cataloging-in-Publication Data

Names: Luraghi, Silvia, 1958- author.
Title: Experiential verbs in Homeric Greek : a constructional approach / Silvia
   Luraghi.
Other titles: Brill's studies in language, cognition and culture ; 27.
Description: Boston : Brill, 2020. | Series: Brill's studies in language, cognition and
   culture, 18795412 ; 27 | Includes bibliographical references and index.
Identifiers: LCCN 2020036167 (print) | LCCN 2020036168 (ebook) |
   ISBN 9789004442481 (hardback) | ISBN 9789004442528 (ebook)
Subjects: LCSH: Homer–Language. | Greek language–Verb.
Classification: LCC PA349 .L87 2020 (print) | LCC PA349 (ebook) |
   DDC 883/.01–dc23
LC record available at https://lccn.loc.gov/2020036167
LC ebook record available at https://lccn.loc.gov/2020036168

Typeface for the Latin, Greek, and Cyrillic scripts: "Brill". See and download: brill.com/brill-typeface.

ISSN 1879-5412
ISBN 978-90-04-44248-1 (hardback)
ISBN 978-90-04-44252-8 (e-book)

Copyright 2021 by Silvia Luraghi. Published by Koninklijke Brill NV, Leiden, The Netherlands.
Koninklijke Brill NV incorporates the imprints Brill, Brill Hes & De Graaf, Brill Nijhoff, Brill Rodopi,
Brill Sense, Hotei Publishing, mentis Verlag, Verlag Ferdinand Schöningh and Wilhelm Fink Verlag.
Koninklijke Brill NV reserves the right to protect this publication against unauthorized use. Requests for
re-use and/or translations must be addressed to Koninklijke Brill NV via brill.com or copyright.com.

This book is printed on acid-free paper and produced in a sustainable manner.

Contents

Preface IX
Abbreviations XI
List of Figures and Tables XIII

1 Introduction 1
1.1 The Construal of Situations 3
1.2 A Construction-Based View of Homeric Greek 6
1.3 Embodiment and Domains of Experience 11
1.4 Homeric Greek 13
1.5 Outline of the Book 15

2 Experiential Situations 20
2.1 Experiential Situation Types 20
2.1.1 *Bodily Sensations* 23
2.1.2 *Perception* 24
2.1.3 *Cognition* 28
2.1.4 *Emotions* 33
2.1.5 *Volitionality* 34
2.2 Semantic Roles of Participants in Experiential Situations 35
2.2.1 *Experiencer* 36
2.2.2 *Stimulus* 38
2.3 The Encoding of Experiential Situations Cross-linguistically 41
2.4 Discussion 46

3 Argument Structure Constructions in Homeric Greek 48
3.1 Properties of Constructions 49
3.1.1 *Different Argument Structures with the Same Verb* 49
3.1.2 *Polysemy of Constructions* 53
3.1.3 *How to Recognize Argument Structure Constructions* 55
3.2 Constructions and Construction Variation with Two-Place Verbs 57
3.2.1 *The Sub-system of Local Cases* 58
3.2.2 *Argument Structure Constructions with Verbs Requiring Spatial Specifications* 61
3.2.3 *Frequency of Nom-first Constructions across Verb Classes* 64
3.2.4 *The NomAcc Construction: Non-spatial Functions* 67

VI   CONTENTS

       3.2.5   *The NomDat Construction: Non-spatial Functions* 69
       3.2.6   *The NomGen Construction: Non-spatial Functions* 75
       3.2.7   *Two-Place Verbs with Dative Experiencers* 79
       3.2.8   *Summary* 81
  3.3   Complementation in Homeric Greek 82
  3.4   Discussion 88

4   The Ancient Greek Verb 89
  4.1   Aspect and Tense 89
  4.2   Voice 95
  4.3   Discussion 98

5   At the Edges of the Experiential Domain: Bodily Sensations and Volition 100
  5.1   Bodily Sensations 101
  5.2   Volitionality and Need 106
  5.3   Discussion 113

6   Perception 115
  6.1   Visual Perception 115
  6.2   Aural Perception 127
  6.3   Other Types of Sensory Perception 139
  6.4   From Perception to Evidentiality 142
  6.5   Discussion 146

7   Cognition 150
  7.1   Think 152
       7.1.1   *Thought, Opinion, Awareness* 153
       7.1.2   *Aspects of Mental Activity* 161
  7.2   Know / Learn 169
       7.2.1   *Cognitive States and Skills* 169
       7.2.2   *Learn, Understand, Recognize* 175
  7.3   Remember / Forget 187
  7.4   Discussion 194

8   Emotions 200
  8.1   Verbs of Emotion with the NomDat Construction 201
       8.1.1   *NomDat Construction with Human Stimuli* 201
       8.1.2   *Verbs of Rejoicing* 209
  8.2   Verbs of Emotion with the NomGen Construction 215

CONTENTS VII

8.2.1 *Love as (Sexual) Desire* 216
8.2.2 *Love as Care and Affection* 220
8.3 Verbs of Emotion with the NomAcc Construction 225
8.3.1 *Wonder* 225
8.3.2 *Fear, Shame and Grief* 229
8.4 Alternating Constructions 238
8.4.1 *NomDat / NomAcc* 238
8.4.2 *Constructions Expressing Empathy* 239
8.5 Dative Experiencer Constructions 241
8.6 Discussion 245

9 **Causative Verbs** 250
9.1 The (Anti)causative Alternation 250
9.2 Animate Verbs 253
9.3 Inanimate Verbs 261
9.4 Discussion 263

10 **Concluding Remarks** 266
10.1 The Meaning of Construction Variation with Experiential Verbs 266
10.1.1 *The Role of the NomAcc and the NomGen Construction* 267
10.1.2 *The NomDat Construction* 271
10.1.3 *The Distribution of Constructions across the Experiential Domain* 272
10.2 Embodiment and Social Setting 279
10.3 The Encoding of Experiential Situations in Homeric Greek 281
10.4 Constructions' Productivity 283
10.4.1 *NomAcc as Default Construction* 283
10.4.2 *The Productivity of the NomDat and NomGen Construction* 285
10.4.3 *The Two-Place+P Construction* 286
10.5 Verbal Voice 287
10.6 Outlook 289

References 291
Index of Greek Verbs 304
Author Index 307
Index of Subjects 310

Preface

This book is the outcome of several years of research, in which I have endeavored to cast a fresh look on the construction of two-place verbs in Homeric Greek, focusing on the experiential domain. Through an exhaustive investigation of verbs and constructions in this domain, I believe that I have been able to present some long-debated issues from a different vantage point and give a new and more compelling answer to some long-standing questions. Comparing all verbs belonging to the experiential domain with each other has led me to change my mind on the conclusions I had reached in some earlier publications in which I considered only limited groups of experiential verbs in isolation. The research carried out for this book, instead, has made me realize that experiential verbs feature patterns of construction that can be understood only if one approaches the whole domain as a set of interconnected sub-domains. For this reason, I hope that my work will offer a useful and insightful starting point for new research on various facets of argument structure constructions and related issues at various stages in the history of Greek. In the meantime, I think that extensive exemplification and analysis of the Greek passages may make them accessible to non-specialists, who can profit from a comprehensive overview and a thorough discussion of the experiential domain in a language that provides engaging evidence and insights into the effects of embodiment on the construal and on the encoding of experience. Accordingly, I am confident that this book will appeal to a wide audience of typologists, historical linguists, and other readers interested in the relationship between language and cognition.

Friends, colleagues and institutions have supported my work in various ways over several years. I started writing the book during a research stay at the University of Jena in the fall of 2017, which was funded by the Alexander von Humboldt Foundation. I would like to thank all members of the Seminar of Indo-European Studies (Seminar für Indogermanistik) in Jena for offering their hospitality during that period. The bulk of my research was carried out in the framework of the project *Dipartimenti di Eccellenza* 2018–2022 (Ministry of University and Research) and was funded by the Italian Ministry of Education and Research grant n. 20159M7X5P Prin 2015 *Transitivity and argument structure in flux*. Various parts of the book have been presented at conferences and lectures over the years: I thank all those who have attended my talks and stimulated my thoughts by providing comments and discussion. I am indebted to Valentina Apresjan, Eystein Dahl, Thanasis Georgakopoulos, Eitan Grossman, Masha Ovsjannikova, William Short, Åke Viberg, Carlotta Viti and Chiara

Zanchi for their inputs, criticism and suggestions on all or parts of the present work. Finally, I would like to express my deep gratitude to Sasha Aikhenvald and Bob Dixon for encouraging me to submit the book to Brill and accepting it into this series.

Abbreviations

Abbreviations Used in the Glosses

The glosses follow the *Leipzig glossing rules* (https://www.eva.mpg.de/lingua/resourc es/glossing-rules.php). For the sake of simplification, I have omitted some categories: in particular, gender of nouns, pronouns and adjectives is never specified in the glosses of Greek examples, number is specified only when it is plural or dual, and verbal mood is indicated only for non-indicative moods. Concerning the lexical meaning, I have tried in principle to always give the same English equivalent in the interlinear translation for each given word, irrespective of the contextual meaning that is reflected in the running translation.

1	first person
2	second person
3	third person
A	agent-like argument of canonical transitive verb
ABL	ablative
ACC	accusative
ADESS	adessive
AOR	aorist
ART	article
CONN	connective
DAT	dative
DEM	demonstrative
DU	dual
F	feminine
FUT	future
GEN	genitive
IMP	imperative
IMPF	imperfect
INDF	indefinite
INF	infinitive
INSTR	instrumental
INT	interrogative
M/P	medio-passive
MID	middle
NEG	negation
NOM	nominative

O	patient-like argument of canonical transitive verb
OPT	optative
P	predicative participle
PASS	passive
PIE	Proto-Indo-European
PL	plural
POSS	possessive
PPF	pluperfect
PREV	preverb
PRF	perfect
PRS	present
PST	past
PTC	particle
PTCP	participle
QUOT	quotative
REFL	reflexive
REL	relative
SBJV	subjunctive
SG	singular
VOC	vocative

Authors and Works Cited In the Examples

Cic. *Att.*	Cicero, *Epistulae ad Atticum*
Hdt.	Herodotus, *Histories*
Il.	Homer, *Iliad*
KUB	*Keilschrifturkunden aus Boghazköi*
KBo	*Keilschrifttexte aus Boghazköi*
Od.	Homer, *Odyssey*

Figures and Tables

Figures

1 The experiential situation   2
2 The symbolic structure of constructions   7
3 The modality hierarchy   24
4 The lexicalization hierarchy   25
5 The double nature of the experiencer-stimulus relationship   40
6 The productivity of constructions and the correlation between type frequency and semantic coherence   65
7 Features of participants in the NomDat construction   74
8 NomDat constructions as a prototypical category   74
9 The partitive meaning of the genitive   75
10 The meaning of the NomGen construction   79
11 The mapping of control onto the domain of experience   147
12 Thought and memory   195
13 Constructions across experiential sub-domains   198
14 Emotions in the NomDat construction with human stimuli   248
15 Emotions in the NomGen construction   248
16 Emotions in the NomAcc construction   248
17 Two dimensional verb type hierarchy   269
18 Correspondence analysis: verb groups and constructions   279

Tables

1 The cross-linguistic association of sight verbs with cognition and attention   27
2 The cross-linguistic association of hearing verbs with cognition and attention   27
3 Features of participants and roles   38
4 Frequency of constructions   66
5 Distribution of complements across verb groups   87
6 Vendler's classification of actionality   90
7 Constructions of hearing verbs   128
8 Occurrences of hearing verbs with different argument structure constructions   129
9 Distribution of aspectual stems   151
10 Constructions of cognitive verbs   152

11	Occurrences of *punthanómai* and *peúthomai* in different argument structure constructions 181
12	Cognitive states and acquisition of knowledge 197
13	Plain-induced verb pairs in Nanai and in Russian 251
14	Token frequency of active *vs.* middle forms 254
15	Distribution of constructions across verb groups 273

CHAPTER 1

Introduction

The domain of experience is extremely wide and diverse, as it comprises a disparate set of situations including bodily sensations, perception, cognition, emotions, and volitionality. Participants in experiential situations have different properties, depending on the conceptualization of individual situations or even on different conceptualizations of the same situation, and this makes their encoding more complex and less uniform as compared to the encoding of other, less polymorphic participants. For this reason, experiential verbs have received much attention in recent research, and have been the subject of both language-specific and cross-linguistic studies.

Research from different fields has pointed out that experiential situations constitute a matter of special concern for humans. In a corpus study of conversational English, Thompson and Hopper (2001) have found that people tend to talk about their subjective views of events rather than about what is actually happening: in other words, people are most interested in what they feel or think about situations. In her book about emotions, Wierzbicka (1999: 1) quotes the biologist Charles Birch (1995: ix), who states that "feelings are what matter most in life". Wierzbicka herself noted, in an earlier publication, that "the speaker regards himself as the quintessential 'victim' or the quintessential experiencer." (1981: 46)

If it is true that experiential situations are of great interest to human beings, then the Homeric poems are no exception. The first word of the *Ilias* is *ménin* (accusative of *ménis*) 'wrath': the whole poem is presented as taking as its topic the emotional response of Achilles, the strongest among the Greek heroes, to a wrong he felt he had suffered. The *Odyssey* takes Odysseus as its topic of narration. In the first line, he is described as *anèr polútropos* 'a man of many devices', referring to his renowned cleverness and shrewdness, the cognitive qualities that allowed him to return to his homeland in spite of the numerous obstacles encountered during his long and adventurous journey. Thus, the encoding of experiential situations in the Homeric poems offers a promising and challenging field for research, worthy of being investigated: indeed, in spite of the sizable number of studies devoted to specific issues in this domain of the Homeric language, no comprehensive coverage is available to date.

Based on Verhoeven's (2007) thorough discussion concerning types of experiential situations and the semantic roles of participants involved, I regard the experiential situation as entailing one main participant, the experiencer, and a

© SILVIA LURAGHI, 2021 | DOI:10.1163/9789004442528_002

content that is experienced, the expertum. In example (1), Paul represents the experiencer, while the state of being hungry is the content of the experience, or expertum.

(1) *Paul is hungry.*

In most types of experiential situations, a second participant is also involved as the trigger of the experience, such as Mary in (2). This participant is called stimulus (Fillmore 1971; Blansitt 1978).

(2) *Paul loves Mary.*

Verhoeven (2007) further notes that the experiential situation can be focused on a specific part of the experiencer, be it a body part, or an 'immaterial' entity such as the mind, as in (3) and (4).

(3) *I feel pain in my head.*

(4) *He was meditating a plan in his mind.*

Following Verhoeven (2007), the components of an experiential situation can be represented as in Figure 1 (from Verhoeven 2007: 52).

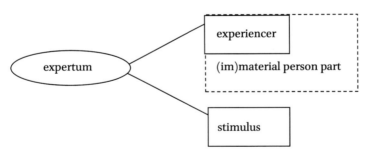

FIGURE 1   The experiential situation

The main participant of experiential situations, the experiencer, is necessarily sentient and hence animate (most often human). Being typically animate, experiencers share an important feature of agents. Notably, however, they also share features of patients, especially in certain types of situations (e.g. bodily sensations), as they undergo the effects of a state of affairs, rather than bringing it about.

As noted above, most types of experiential situations also feature a second participant, the stimulus, which is the trigger of the experience. Stimuli display

INTRODUCTION

a wider range of referential variation than experiencers, as they can be animate or inanimate. Often states of affairs can also function as stimuli. Further properties of experiencers and stimuli as well as features typical of experiential situations will be discussed in Chapter 2.

1.1 The Construal of Situations

Even before finding the linguistic means to encode a specific state of affairs, human beings need to conceive it, and by doing this they crucially introduce a specific perspective (Langacker 1999: 203). The conceptualization of a given situation is here called its construal (Croft 2012: 13; cf. Langacker 1999: 206–212), and mirrors our understanding of the world and our way of presenting events under a given vantage point. Let us consider examples (5)-(8).

(5)   *Mary is Paula's mother.*

(6)   *Paula is Mary's daughter.*

(7)   *The three-story house is next to the church.*

(8)   *The church is next to the three-story house.*

In (5) and (6) the same situation is construed differently, profiling the parental relationship between a mother and a daughter either by taking the mother as the starting point, or the other way around. The term profiling refers to the aspect of a certain situation that is highlighted by the speaker over a certain domain, which constitutes the base (Croft 1991): in (5) and (6) the base is the same, and consists in the specific type of parental relationship that holds between a mother and a daughter, but it is profiled in different ways. Examples (7) and (8) also refer to the same situation, but differ in Figure-Ground alignment (Talmy 1974) or trajector-landmark alignment, following the terminology of Cognitive Grammar (Langacker 1987). In both examples, an entity, the trajector, is located taking a landmark as reference point, but they differ as to which entity is chosen as landmark and which as trajector. In both pairs of examples, the same situation is construed differently, depending on the vantage point taken by the speaker.

Situations can also be construed differently based on their temporal dimension. Croft (2012: 13–14) discusses examples (9) and (10), and notes that "the very choice of participants and the aspectual character of the situation are subject to construal."

4 CHAPTER 1

(9) *John was sick.*

(10) *The virus attacked John's throat, which became inflamed, resulting in laryngitis, until the immune system succeeded in destroying the infection.*

While in (9) the situation in which John was involved is construed as a single event with only John as participant, in (10) the same situation is construed as a sequence of causally connected events, with several participants involved. In addition, while (9) refers to a state, that is, an atelic situation, in (10) the process of getting ill and then healing is described as a sequence of telic events in which the state of the person involved undergoes a number of changes. Similarly, experiential situations may be atelic, either states or activities unfolding over time as in (11), or have an inchoative nature, thus implying a change of state as in (12).

(11) *Mary was meditating whether she should go back.*

(12) *Mary realized that it was time to go back.*

As the examples discussed show, speakers can choose to construe a situation in different ways depending on their intention to profile a specific component of the situation. This depends on the nature of conceptualization itself, and is true for speakers of any language. However, languages may differ in the type of options that are normally adopted by speakers, hence are more readily available. In Homeric Greek, for example, experiencers are most often encoded as nominative subjects, as I will argue in the next Section.

Depending on the construal of experiential situations, experiencers can be more agent- or more patient-like, even in similar situations. For example, emotions can be construed as uncontrolled (notably, according to popular wisdom, love is blind) or they can be construed as controlled and intentional, as shown by the occurrence of the corresponding verbs in the imperative, hence in orders, as in (13).

(13) *Love thy father and mother!*

Moreover, various types of experiential situations can be conceived as being spontaneous, though triggered by a stimulus, or as being caused by an external agent. As an example let us consider the verb pair *remember* and *remind* in English, and their Greek equivalent, instantiated by middle and active forms of the verb *mimnéskomai/mimnéskō* in (14) and (15).

INTRODUCTION

(14) *tôn*   *mnêsai*
DEM.GEN.PL remember.IMP.AOR.MID.2SG
'Remember these things!' (*Il.* 15.375)

(15) *tôn*   *s'*   *aûtis mnḗsō*
DEM.GEN.PL 2SG.ACC again remind.FUT.1SG
'I will remind you again of these things.' (*Il.* 15.31)

While (14) features two participants, the experiencer-subject (not overtly realized with imperative verbal forms either in Greek or in English) and the stimulus, here the genitive second argument *tôn* 'these things', in (15) we find an additional participant, the agent-subject (the speaker, realized as *I* in the English translation but again not overt in Greek). The experiencer is the direct object-causee in the accusative case (*s(e)* 'you'), and the stimulus a genitive third argument, again *tôn* 'these things'.

In general, besides taking the perspective of the experiencer, and accordingly choosing it as subject, experiential situations can be presented taking the stimulus as a starting point. In this case, the experiencer functions as direct object. For example, the same situation of fearing can be indicated by the English verbs *fear* (experiencer subject) or *frighten* (experiencer object), or by the corresponding Greek verbs *deídō* 'fear' as in (16) or *deidíssomai* 'frighten' as in (17).

(16) *mála dè Trôes*   *dedíasin*
much PTC Trojan.NOM.PL fear.PRF.3PL
'The Trojans were greatly scared.' (*Il.* 24.663)

(17) *mēdé tí*   *pō*   *deidísseo*   *laòn*
NEG INDF.ACC at_all frighten.IMP.PRS.M/P.2SG host.ACC
Akhaiôn
Achaean.GEN.PL
'Do not, by any means, frighten the host of the Achaeans.' (*Il.* 4.184)

In (16) fear is viewed as rising spontaneously in the Trojans, while in (17) the addressee is warned not to induce fear in the Achaeans. Fearing is one among numerous events that can be conceived in this two-fold way, as are many other experiential situations, for example remembering as shown in (14) (spontaneous) and (15) (induced).

These occurrences instantiate the so-called (anti)causative alternation (see Haspelmath 1993), which can be variously encoded even within the same language. In the two pairs of Greek examples, we find morphological means (voice alternation) in (14) and (15) and lexical means (derivation) in (16) and (17). This type of alternation, which has been the matter of numerous language-specific and cross-linguistic studies, will be thoroughly discussed in Chapter 9.

All areas of human experience, and especially emotions, are often encoded through metaphors or metonymies (Verhoeven 2007: 87–93): thus, besides expressions such as (16), one often finds metaphorical expressions such as (18).

(18) *mála gàr khlōròn déos haireî*
much PTC pale.NOM fear.NOM seize.PRS.3SG
'Pale fear seizes (them) greatly.' (*Il.* 17.67)

Such metaphorical expressions are frequent both in ancient and in modern Indo-European languages, as the English translation in (18) shows. As we will see in Section 2.3, in Homeric Greek they have been argued to be connected with negatively evaluated experiences.

1.2 A Construction-Based View of Homeric Greek

The vast majority of experiential verbs in Homeric Greek consist of two-place verbs with experiencer subject, with stimuli second arguments encoded by different cases: indeed, an important feature of the Homeric language is its strong tendency to show nominative alignment in the encoding of experiential situations. Accordingly, the bulk of my discussion will be devoted to one specific issue concerning the encoding of experiential situations, that is, case variation with such verbs. Contrary to a well-established tradition in Greek grammatical descriptions, I will take a vantage point that does not consider cases in isolation, but views case-marked arguments as parts of constructions. I will follow the approach of Construction Grammar, as illustrated below, and accordingly I will discuss case variation as variation among three constructions: NomAcc, NomGen and NomDat.

It must be stressed that this is not simply a terminological issue: considering construction variation does not boil down to replacing the name of a case, say the genitive, with the name of a construction, in this case NomGen. Much to the contrary, taking a construction-based approach implies assuming a meaning for the whole construction, which in turn has reflexes not only on the construal of the second participant, for example as being affected to a higher or lower extent, but also on the construal of the first participant, who can then be viewed as being more or less agent-like, and as exerting a higher or lower degree of control on a situation. This point constitutes a cornerstone of my view of Homeric Greek construction variation, and will be further elaborated in Chapter 3.

Of course, other constructions do exist and will not be ignored. In particular, constructions featuring dative experiencers will also be discussed (Section 3.2.7 and 8.5). However, I hasten to add that such constructions, though cross-linguistically quite prominent in the experiential domain, are remarkably limited in Homeric Greek, and often feature agent-like stimuli, thus conforming to the semantics of NomDat constructions with other verb classes, as I argue in Section 8.5.

In Construction Grammar, argument structure constructions are viewed as being constituted by the set of arguments with which verbs may co-occur (see Goldberg 1995). Following a constructionist approach, there is no sharp distinction between syntax and the lexicon. Any combination of morphemes is considered a construction, that is, a holistic unit consisting of a pairing of form and meaning. In the case of argument structure constructions, this means that a verb with its arguments constitutes a unit of meaning. The structure of constructions can be represented as shown in Figure 2 (from Croft 2001: 18).

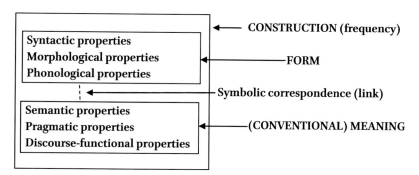

FIGURE 2   The symbolic structure of constructions

Over the last few decades, different strands have emerged in Construction Grammar, which are based on quite different assumptions. In this book, I adopt the view point of what can be called 'Cognitive Construction Grammar' and follow the approach to constructions fleshed out by Goldberg (1995, 2006) and Hilpert (2014) among others. As argued by Boas (2013) and Broccias (2013), this strand of Construction Grammar is closely connected to Cognitive Grammar and to Radical Construction Grammar (Croft 2001) in various respects.

In her book on argument structure in English, Goldberg (1995) challenges the idea that verbs may have different meanings. This latter position has been traditionally argued for by various scholars. Levin (1985: 35), for example, writes: "there is evidence that when the verb *slide* is found in the double object construction, ... its sense is not the purely physical transfer sense of slide but rather a transfer of possession sense." Commenting on this quote, and on Levin's further arguments, Goldberg (1995: 13) remarks that, while "the semantics of (and constraints on) the full expressions are different whenever a verb occurs in a different construction ... these differences need not be attributed to different verb senses; they are more parsimoniously attributed to the constructions themselves."

Following this approach, one cannot speak of the meaning of a verb in isolation that is added to the meaning of its arguments. To the contrary, both the verb and the argument set (a specific argument structure) express their meaning when they are coupled with each other. Constructions, and more specifically the argument structure constructions of verbs, typically have slots that must be filled by the verb's arguments. To put it with Bybee (2010: 9), they are understood as "a direct form-meaning pairing that has sequential structure and may include positions that are fixed as well as positions that are open." The open positions are the slots taken by possible fillers, that is, possible arguments in a construction.

Constructions can be polysemous in the same way as lexemes can be. This has also been acknowledged in the literature on argument structure constructions. Goldberg (1995: 31–35) discusses the polysemy of dative shift in English. She remarks that, even though this construction typically occurs with verbs of transfer, such as *give*, which require a recipient participant, it typically extends to verbs with beneficiaries, which do not imply that the participant ever receives the entity that is intended for him/her. Compare (19)-(20).

(19) *Chris gave Jan a cake.*

(20) *Chris baked Jan a cake.*

While in example (19) Jan is a recipient, and gets hold of the cake as a result of Chris giving it to him, in (20) there is no such implication: as Goldberg (1995: 34–35) remarks, it may well be Chris' intention that Jan receives the cake, but Jan may not receive it eventually, and indeed he might not even know that Chris baked it for him. The states of affairs that result from the two events are different, but there is a common feature, the agent's intention, which accounts for the possible polysemic extension of the construction. Goldberg further discusses the advantage of a polysemic approach over an approach that posits a single abstract meaning for a construction (1995: 37–39). She considers con-

INTRODUCTION

structions as "typically associated with a family of closely related senses rather than a single, fixed abstract sense." (1995: 31).

In recent years, Construction Grammar has also been applied to language change (see among others Bergs and Diewald 2008, Bergs and Diewald 2009; Hilpert 2013; Traugott and Trousdale 2013; Barðdal et al. 2015). Diachronic Construction Grammar has been shown to account for various developments in the field of constructions, among which constructional merger: constructions with multiple origins have been shown to give rise to dynamic constructional networks whose structure may change at different stages (see for example Torrent 2015 on Brazilian Portuguese and Luraghi et al. 2020 on Modern Standard Russian). Notably, as I will argue in Chapter 3, diachronic factors can only partly account for synchronic polysemy of Homeric Greek constructions surveyed in this book. On the other hand, polysemy patterns result from the restructuring of relations among constructions that do not necessarily reflect their original connections.

Goldberg (2006: 38) also acknowledges the possibility of homonymy, and stresses the relevance of the verb's meaning, along with the meaning of co-occurring arguments (see Section 3.1.3 on this latter issue). She writes:

> In fact, there do exist instances of constructional homonymy: a single surface form having unrelated meanings. In order to identify which argument structure construction is involved in cases of constructional ambiguity, attention must be paid to individual verb classes. In fact, in order to arrive at a full interpretation of any clause, the meaning of the main verb and the individual arguments must be taken into account.

In practice, this amounts to saying that, in spite of the fact that non-compositionality is considered a trademark of constructions (as Hilpert 2014: 10 notes, "non-compositional meaning is perhaps the most widely used diagnostic to identify constructions"), some degree of compositionality does exist that explains how homonymous constructions are disambiguated in conjunction to the verb's meaning and the meaning of the NPs that function as fillers. Hence, it seems reasonable to assume that weak compositionality may explain the global meaning of a construction, a view advocated by Goldberg (1995: 16): "By recognizing the existence of contentful constructions, we can save compositionality in a weakened form: the meaning of an expression is the result of integrating the meanings of the lexical items into the meanings of constructions." I will show how such a view may partly explain the distribution of constructions in Homeric Greek in Chapter 3.

In order to capture the attitude of individual verbs to co-occur with one or more arguments, I use the widely employed notion of valency, in spite of some problematic aspects, see the discussion in Aldai and Wichmann (2018: 255–256), and in spite of the fact that this notion has sometimes been viewed as being at odds with the tenets of Construction Grammar. As discussed above, in Construction Grammar argument structures are stored as independent form-meaning pairs: in other words, they are not projected by verbs. Rather, they are in principle independent of verb semantics. However, as highlighted by Stefanowitsch and Herbst (2011), the two approaches may be seen as complementing each other: this has implicitly been acknowledged by Goldberg as well, when she discusses constructional homonymy (see the quote from Goldberg 2006 discussed above).

The issue raised by the relation between valency and constructions has been addressed among others by Perek (2015), who tries to answer the question "if constructions bear most of the burden of argument realization, what role is there left for verbs to play in a constructional approach?" (2015: 27). Perek argues that the notion of valency may incur in inconsistencies when a verb occurs in different constructions in which different arguments may or may not be overtly realized. This leads to the more specific question how many elements in the frame evoked by a verb must be included in its valency (2015: 31). In order to gauge the valency of a verb in a non-arbitrary fashion, Perek proposes the "usage-based valency hypothesis", viewing frequency as a crucial factor, and writes that "the cognitive status of a valency pattern of a verb is related to the frequency of occurrence of that valency pattern with that verb in usage." (2015: 45)

In this book, I tentatively follow Perek's usage-based approach, in spite of the problems encountered when working with a limited corpus such as the one offered by the Homeric poems. I view as included in the verbal valency elements that fill in syntactic slots, based on their frequency of occurrence with specific verbs and with semantically related verb classes. I view valency as the tendency for a verb to occur with a certain number of arguments; accordingly, I speak of one-, two- or three-place verbs depending on their valency, and of first, second, and third argument not only based on case marking, but also on the prominence of the participants encoded. Whenever there is a conflict between prominence and case marking, I try to avoid the term 'subject', and simply speak of 'first argument' (see further Section 2.3).

Following a usage-based approach, constructions emerge as a result of chunking in the encoding and decoding of linguistic units by speakers. Chunking is responsible for the conventionalization of constructions as well as for the emergence of formulas and idioms, which constitute a special case of constructions that allow for a more limited number of fillers, often for a single one. Hence, according to Bybee (2010: 36), "constructions are sequential chunks of

INTRODUCTION   11

language that are conventionally used together and that sometimes have special meanings or other properties." Chunking accounts for the emergence of 'prefabs' (prefabricated expression Bybee 2010: 35) or formulas: as we will see in Section 1.4, this process is crucial for the understanding of the formulaic structure of the Homeric language.

In this perspective, the speakers' knowledge is represented as a "structured inventory" (Langacker 1987: 73), that is, a hierarchical network with multiple levels of abstraction, ranging from concrete representations of individual morphemes, to abstract schemas that represent complex constructions, including syntactic relations (Hilpert 2013: 2). Constructions are stored in very much the same way as lexical items, and vary in terms of symbolic complexity, idiomaticity or specificity, and schematicity. High idiomaticity entails a limited choice of fillers for a construction's slots. For example, in *kick the bucket*, the NP *the bucket* is the only possible filler of the construction. On the opposite side are highly schematic constructions, which allow for a high, and often heterogeneous, number of fillers. For example, the transitive construction in English allows for virtually any type of NP as filler of the direct object slot (Broccias 2013: 150). I will return to this important property of the transitive construction, and to the role of frequency in determining a construction's degree of schematicity and entrenchment, when discussing the distribution of constructions in Homeric Greek, see especially Sections 3.2.3 and 10.4.

1.3   Embodiment and Domains of Experience

Among the tenets of cognitive linguistics, the notion of embodiment plays a central role, and reflects the idea that there is no sharp separation between our bodily and mental capacities. Following Johnson and Rohrer (2007: 27) "human physical, cognitive, and social embodiment ground our conceptual and linguistic systems." Indeed, as argued in Johnson (1987), the structure of our conceptual system is conditioned by properties of our body, and meaning, which in turn derives from our conceptual system, is also embodied.

Experiential verbs constitute a very fruitful field of research on embodiment at various levels, as they provide evidence for reflexes of human experience on lexical and grammatical encoding. Thus, the linguistic expression of bodily sensations is crucially connected with embodiment. Reference to sensations such as pain, heat or cold, hunger or thirst is based on human experience. This can be easily illustrated with the way in which 'normal' temperature is conceptualized and referred to in several languages. The concept of 'normal' temperature is variously construed based on pleasant and unpleasant bodily sensations: in

Russian, for example, a personal feeling of heat is expressed differently depending on the body temperature, with a special encoding in the case that heat is a symptom of fever (Koptjevsaja Tamm 2015). In Italian, intermediate terms in temperature terminology are defined with respect to ambient (cold side) or to body temperature (warm side; Luraghi 2015).

Embodiment also plays a crucial role in other domains of experience. A case in point is constituted by perception verbs, which are often polysemous in referring not only to the physical senses, but also to knowledge. In ancient Indo-European languages, the standard example is the verb 'know' as instantiated by Ancient Greek *oîda* and Sanskrit *veda*. These are forms of the perfect tense from the root **wid-* 'see', and indicate knowledge as the result of having seen something (see Section 4.1 and 7.2). The metaphorical extension of seeing to knowing reflects embodiment, as does the connection with the resultative meaning of the perfect: cognition is a mental state, which results from sensory perception. The extension of perception verbs to cognition has been discussed in the framework of cognitive linguistics, and has been explained as connected with the 'MIND-AS-BODY' metaphor: following this approach, knowledge is metaphorically understood as mental vision (Sweetser 1990: 38).

Studies on evidentiality have shown that verbs referring both to visual and to aural evidence are frequent sources for evidentials (Aikhenvald 2004: 273–274). In this framework, visual perception seems to have a special status in the encoding of sensory evidentials, with hearing often merging with other senses. On the one hand, information acquired from hearing seems to be less perspicuous than information acquired from sight. On the other hand, evidence from Homeric Greek suggests that information acquired from hearing is multifaceted, as it can be direct or indirect. In the latter case, it is often contrasted as uncertain with information from sight, which is a source of unquestionable knowledge, and is always direct (Luraghi and Sausa 2019 and Section 6.4). In Homeric Greek, this contrast is reflected in the argument structure construction of sight verbs, which, contrary to verbs that refer to other perception modalities, always take the construction of highly transitive verbs, thus profiling control over the situation (see Chapter 6).

Verbs of emotion have been the object of numerous studies in Cognitive Linguistics and in lexical typology, as their constructions and the packaging of meaning in specific lexical items may vary, based on beliefs of humans about emotions (Verhoeven 2007: 44). In addition, as emotions have a social and interactive basis, their construal may be culture-specific (Wierzbicka 1999). In Homeric Greek, the interactive dimension of emotions has a special bearing on the choice of construction in which different verbs occur (see Chapter 8).

INTRODUCTION

Emotions are an interesting field for research on embodiment, as often bodily reactions metonymically refer to the emotion that typically triggers them, as for example blushing for shame, or trembling for fear (Pinelli 2015). Embodiment is also responsible for the possible extension of verbs of bodily sensations to emotions, based on a metonymy PHYSICAL EXPERIENCE STANDS FOR THE EMOTION (Kövecses 1990), thus supporting a construal of the experiencer as lacking control over the situation. In Homeric Greek, as in many other languages (cf. e.g. Pinelli 2015), trembling and chilling are associated with fear. As I show in Section 8.3.2, for example, the verb *phríssō*, whose etymological meaning is 'chill', 'shiver', only refers to a state of fear in the Homeric poems.

On a more general plane, I aim to show that the distribution of argument structure constructions across verbs in different experiential sub-domains reflects embodiment in Homeric Greek, as well as a complex social and cultural construal of situations in the sub-domain of emotions (see especially Section 10.2).

1.4 Homeric Greek

The corpus I used for this book consists of the two Homeric poems, the *Iliad* and the *Odyssey*. While the size of the two poems is limited (the total number of tokens is 199,047; data from *Perseus Digital Library*), it offers enough evidence for verbs referring to different types of situations, and has the advantage of being easily manageable.

Homeric Greek is a composite language, with forms from different dialectal traditions and even several idiosyncratic ones (Horrocks 1997, Hackstein 2010). It is also a poetic language, composed in meter: one might wonder whether these characteristics do not make it too artificial to reflect any 'real' language use. In fact, the poems, which were written down between the 8th and the 6th century BCE, represent a notable early example of oral poetry (Parry 1971). Their composition was the collective enterprise of numerous early oral poets, who toured the country reciting the deeds of the heroes in live performances before popular audiences. This accounts for the formulaic nature of the Homeric language (Bakker 1988), and for the structure of the Homeric verse, the hexameter, which tends to reproduce the syntax of the spoken language in order to be easily understood in the specific situations in which it was recited (Nagy 2010). This latter characteristic also contributes to making the Homeric language a suitable field for linguistic research.

When the Homeric poems were given a written form, many features of their grammar had already become obsolete in the spoken dialects, and are not attested in the earliest written forms of literary Ionic, the dialect which is closest to the Homeric language. For this reason, and in light of the enormous prestige of the texts, the Homeric poems have been the matter of grammatical commentaries ever since. In the 3rd–2nd century BCE, the poems were revised by the philologists working at the Library of Alexandria, who, among other things, are responsible for adding diacritics to the text, thus introducing their own interpretation of Homeric prosody. In more recent times, the Homeric poems have been studied by linguists and philologists from several perspectives, and there are hardly any aspects of the Homeric language, ranging from the interpretation of individual lexemes to the interpretation of whole constructions, that have not been the subject of some investigation. In practice, when approaching the Homeric poems one has to reckon with centuries, or even millennia, of scholarly tradition.

In the field of the experiential situations, much has been done especially in the last two centuries concerning some groups of verbs; however, comprehensive studies are limited (cf. e.g. Bertolín Cebrián 1996 on verbs of thinking; Latacz 1966 on verbs of rejoicing), and most often insightful discussions are to be found in lexicons or grammars. Studies on construction variation with semantically homogeneous groups of verbs are quite numerous; they range from construction-specific studies to chapters in grammars. However, no extensive study of construction variation encompassing all types of experiential verbs has been accomplished to the present.

A distinctive feature of the Homeric language that deserves special attention is formulaicity. As I mentioned above, formulaicity is a direct consequence of orality, and studies on contemporary oral poetry have provided extensive evidence for the use of formulas in techniques of oral composition. Lord (2000: 130) goes so far as to consider formulaicity a trademark of oral poetry, and writes: "Formula analysis, providing, of course, that one has sufficient material for significant results, is ... able to indicate whether any given text is oral or 'literary'."

Recent research on the linguistics of formulas has shown that Homeric formulas share features commonly ascribed to constructions (Bozzone 2010, 2016). Formulas are prefabs as defined in Bybee (2010: 35), that is, multi-word expressions (constructions) that are stored in the speakers' knowledge. The use of such prefabricated expressions is pervasive in everyday speech and writing. In much the same way as constructions, Homeric formulas show different degrees of schematicity, and may display features typical of idioms: they may, for example, preserve archaic forms. Similar to other prefabs, formulas may provide the basis out of which new exemplars of constructions develop (Bybee 2010: 28). This may account for occurrences that can at first sight look seman-

INTRODUCTION

tically odd. As Bakker (1988: 19) remarks: "A given phrase, which has a function as a formula in the diction, may at times be used by a poet, under formular pressure in oral performance, under semantic and syntactic circumstances for which it was not devised originally." Indeed, there are passages in which a construction occurs with an unexpected filler, as in cases that feature "standard formular enumeration" in the sense of Bakker (1988: 189), "whose integration in the context is less than perfect" because one of the items does not fit the context (see further Luraghi 2012: 384).

Besides considering the peculiarities of constructions mentioned above, when engaging in a linguistic study of the Homeric language one must also keep in mind the fact that the frequency of constructions may reflect a lower number of actual attestations. So for example, if a certain construction occurs ten times, but then it turns out that these are ten occurrences of the same formula, a number of considerations must necessarily follow. On the one hand, ten identical occurrences do not have the same statistical weight as ten different occurrences. On the other hand, repetition indicates the formulaic nature of a prefabricated expression, and may hint at an archaic character of the construction and of its meaning. In the course of the book we will see several such cases, in which a meaning that is preserved only in a formula is arguably archaic, based on the etymology of a certain lexeme and the meanings and constructions of cognates in other ancient Indo-European languages (see e.g. Section 9.3).

1.5   Outline of the Book

This book is divided into ten Chapters. Following this first introductory Chapter, in Chapter 2 I provide a description of experiential situations, of their components, and of cross-linguistic variation in their encoding. After reviewing different types of experiential situations, including bodily sensations, perception, cognition, emotions, and volitionality (Section 2.1), in Section 2.2 I discuss the prototypical properties of the main participants of experiential situations, the experiencer and the stimulus. I argue that both types of participant can show different characteristics, depending on the construal of a specific situation, which is subject to a wide range of variation in the domain of experience. Variation in construal is reflected in variation in coding, both within the same language, and cross-linguistically, as I show in Section 2.3.

In Chapter 3, I discuss argument structure constructions in Homeric Greek. As I have already pointed out at the beginning of this Introduction, my main focus is constituted by constructions of two-place verbs that take a phrasal second argument: they are the matter of an in-depth treatment in Section 3.2. I argue that the NomAcc, NomDat and NomGen constructions must be viewed as covers for different sub-constructions, in particular a spatial and a non-spatial one for each of them, with the NomDat construction being the most complex one in terms of constructional polysemy. I find support for my claims in the frequency of constructions and in the semantic coherence exhibited by groups of verbs that take each construction in the Homeric poems, which I take as a reflex of their entrenchment. I then turn to the use of the DatNom construction, which occurs with a limited number of mostly experiential verbs. As experiential verbs may take a sentential complement rather than a phrasal second argument, I briefly illustrate Homeric Greek complementation in Section 3.3. In this Section, a construction emerges as especially relevant in the encoding of experiential situations, that is, the Two-place+P construction, consisting in a set of two arguments, including NomAcc, NomDat and NomGen, with a predicative participle that agrees in case with the second argument and encodes an event. This construction, which is cross-linguistically frequent with perception verbs, extends to cognitive verbs and to some verbs of emotion in Homeric Greek.

Chapter 4 offers a brief survey of Homeric Greek verbal categories that play a crucial role in the construal of situations: tense and aspect (Section 4.1), voice (Section 4.2), and their interplay (Section 4.3). This Chapter serves as a preliminary to the discussion in the remainder of the book, as it provides background information that will be then further elaborated in the discussion of specific passages.

Chapters 5 to 8 constitute the bulk of my research, as they explore the semantics and the constructional patterns of individual experiential verbs in Homeric Greek, divided into the different sub-domains of experience. Chapter 5 is devoted to two of these sub-domains: bodily sensations, discussed in Section 5.1, and volition, discussed in Section 5.2. Some words of explanation are in order to clarify my decision to group together two sub-domains that can appear quite disparate in terms of possible control by the experiencer over the situation. Bodily sensations are the most uncontrolled type of situation, with the experiencer sharing properties of prototypical patients, while volitionality is often construed as controlled, and accordingly experiencers in such situations can be conceived as being closer to agents. For this reason, they can be viewed as constituting the edges of the experiential domain, and, as we will see, they do so in constructional terms as well. Remarkably, these two sub-domains often tend not to be encoded by two-place verbs, but rather by one-place ones (most bodily sensations) or by verbs with sentential complements, most often infinitives (volition). Still, as I argue in Section 5.3, when

INTRODUCTION

verbs of bodily sensation and volition occur with two-place argument structures they reveal very insightful information on the semantics of construction variation with other experiential verbs, as they show a clear-cut opposition between the NomGen (bodily sensations) and the NomAcc (volition) construction.

In Chapter 6 I discuss verbs of perception. I follow the Modality Hierarchy (Viberg 1984), and start with verbs of sight (Section 6.1), followed by verbs of hearing (Section 6.2). I show that while the former only feature the NomAcc construction, the latter allow for construction variation, with the NomAcc construction virtually limited to inanimate stimuli and the NomGen construction extending to both animate and inanimate ones. Due to its inherent limits, the Homeric corpus offers little evidence for other perception modalities. In spite of this, as I argue in Section 6.3, a constructional pattern emerges whereby verbs of touch, taste and smell consistently take the NomGen construction. In a cross-linguistically common extension, sight and hearing verbs are a possible source for evidentials in Homeric Greek (Section 6.4). I compare construction variation across perceptual modalities in Section 6.5, and argue that construction alternation with verbs of hearing, that has long puzzled linguists, is in agreement with their position on the Modality Hierarchy. In this framework I also discuss voice distribution and possible distinctions among verbs based on intentionality and control.

Chapter 7 is devoted to cognition verbs. In this Chapter, I especially highlight the role of verbal aspect and its interplay with lexical aspect as reflected in the distribution of aspectual stems. As I point out, most verbs in this sub-field tend to show preferences for the specific aspectual stems. This is especially true for verbs of thinking (Section 7.1) and of knowing and learning (Section 7.2), while memory and forgetfulness are indicated by a smaller number of verbs that show a more versatile behavior (Section 7.3). In Section 7.4 I draw some conclusions on the distribution of the NomAcc and the NomGen construction with verbs in this sub-field as compared to the sub-fields analyzed in the preceding two Chapters.

Chapter 8 tackles the most complex sub-field of experience, emotions. Emotions are multi-faceted, and their construal crucially depends on social and cultural factors; in addition, the same emotion can be variously evaluated even inside the same social group. Not surprisingly, verbs of emotion show the widest range of constructional patterns and variation: in Homeric Greek they are the only sub-group of experiential verbs to feature the NomDat construction along with the NomAcc and the NomGen constructions, and the only ones that includes a sizable number of verbs that take dative experiencers. In Section 8.1, I discuss two groups of verbs that take the NomDat construction, and show how the occurrence of this construction with emotion verbs reflects the construal of certain situations as potentially interactive. Section 8.2 is devoted to verbs that indicate positive feelings such as love and affection, which mostly allow for variation between the NomGen and the NomAcc construction. Verbs that indicate experiencer-centered, mostly negative feelings such as fear are surveyed in Section 8.3. They consistently feature the NomAcc construction. I explain this peculiarity as based on the extension of the construction of sight verbs through verbs of wonder to verbs that denote emotions triggered by a stimulus that raises a state of high attention in the experiencer, as it is conceived as a threat. Section 8.4 is devoted to verbs that allow for construction variation, while verbs that take dative experiencers are discussed in Section 8.5. In Section 8.6 I discuss the findings from construction variation with verbs in this sub-domain.

In Chapter 9 I discuss causative verbs. I focus especially on voice variation with verbs belonging to all the sub-domains of experience with which the middle/active alternation encodes the (anti)causative alternation, as *mimnéskomai* and *mimnéskō* in (14) and (15). I argue that neither voice can be considered as the older one for all verbs. Much to the contrary, based on semantic, distributional, etymological and morphological considerations, I show that with some of these verbs the active voice is a late development and the middle voice must be viewed as original, while with others voice opposition is an original feature that points toward the basicness of the active voice.

Chapter 10 contains the conclusion. In this Chapter, I summarize the findings and provide a general discussion of construction variation in the framework of other variables analyzed in the book, such as verbal categories, referential features of stimuli, and the construal of the experiencer role. I show how construction variation, far from being random, singles out semantically neighboring groups of verbs that cluster within the space of each construction with the NomAcc construction typically connected with sight, volition, consciousness, awareness and attention, while the NomGen construction shows a link to bodily needs and sensations, low awareness, and uncontrolled craving. The NomDat construction, which is basically restricted to the field of emotions, encodes potentially interactive situations, in which not only the experiencer, but often also the stimulus is a human being, possibly reacting and showing an active involvement (Section 10.1). On the evidence surveyed in my study, I show that the distribution of constructions is largely based on embodiment, with the sub-domain of emotions also pointing to the relevance of the social setting (Section 10.2). I then summarize the types of construction that contribute to the encoding of experiential situations in addition to the three Nom-first constructions (Section 10.4), and provide evidence for construction productivity

(Section 10.4). After reviewing the evidence discussed in the book concerning the role of voice with experiential verbs (Section 10.5), I conclude by indicating some directions for further research (Section 10.6).

CHAPTER 2

Experiential Situations

In this Chapter, I describe different domains of experience and specific types of experiential situations. The delimitation of such domains is sometimes quite difficult and even arbitrary, as they often overlap. This is reflected in the types of construction occurring with experiential verbs. For example, a situation such as that of desiring something indicates an emotional state, but it also involves will and in certain cases intentionality. Similarly, caring for someone entails thinking about the same person, keeping this person in one's mind, hence remembering. Verbs of bodily sensation or perception can often extend to other domains, and this is often connected with their effects and their symptoms, as I will discuss below.

In Section 2.1 I briefly review the characteristics of different types of experiential situations, and show how they can be more or less closely related to each other, either by metonymical or metaphorical extension, or by virtue of sharing some specific features. Section 2.2 contains a discussion of the semantic roles of participants involved in experiential situations, the experiencer (Section 2.2.1) and the stimulus (Section 2.2.2). I show that their properties may vary extensively depending on the type of situation and on its construal. In Section 2.3, I take a cross-linguistic perspective on the encoding of experiential situations, on the distribution of argument structure constructions, and on their possible variation depending on the way in which the situation and its participants are construed.

2.1   Experiential Situation Types

Experiential situations are often regarded as being mainly states, but this is an over-simplification: clearly, predicates such as 'feel cold', 'be afraid', 'love', 'know' are atelic and indicate states, but the same situations are also often referred to at their onset, implying a change of state. Hence, they can be construed as telic events, as in 'get cold', 'get scared', 'fall in love', 'learn'. As Verhoeven (2007: 17) remarks, the fact that states lack a temporal dimension results in them often being encoded as nouns or adjectives, rather than verbs, as is also partly the case in English.

Especially in the field of cognition, several atelic situations are construed as activities, with varying degrees of control, as 'think' or 'meditate'. While bodily

© SILVIA LURAGHI, 2021 | DOI:10.1163/9789004442528_003

sensations, even when construed as inchoative situations, are always uncontrolled, other types of experiential situations besides mental activities can be construed as controlled, notably emotions, often depending on social and cultural factors. They, too, can be atelic, mostly stative, as 'be happy', 'be angry', or inchoative, as 'fall in love', 'get upset'.

An important feature of experiential situations, which has been very often highlighted in the literature, is low transitivity. Since Hopper and Thompson's (1980) seminal paper, transitivity has been viewed as a scalar notion, determined by various factors related both to grammar and to discourse (see among others Tsunoda 1985, Kittilä 2002, Næss 2007, and Dahl and Fedriani 2012 with an exhaustive list of references). Kittilä (2002: 110) defines a prototypical transitive event as "a dynamic, concrete event in which a volitionally acting agent acts on a patient that is directly and in a perceptually salient way affected (or effected) as a result of this event." Following this approach, the aspectual features of experiential situations illustrated above, along with frequent lack of control and the absence of a change of state intentionally brought about by an agent and affecting the second participant, are consequences of low transitivity.

Bossong (1998: 259–260) compares action verbs, which he considers the prototype of two-place verbs, or bivalent verbs in his terminology, with experiential verbs, and argues that the latter entail an 'inversion of the verb's semantic vector' (*vecteur sémantique verbal*), as the main participant rather than being the origin of the event (*point de départ*) is its target (*point d'arrivée*). He argues that languages can accommodate the differences between these two types of verbs following either the 'principle of abstraction' or the 'principle of specification'. With this terminology, Bossong indicates the tendency for experiential situations to be encoded as actions (abstraction: the action schema is generalized to other types of events) or to be encoded differently (specification: specific differences have reflexes on the morphosyntactic encoding). As we will see in Section 2.3, the choice between the two options may reflect different construals of the same (type of) experiential situation.

Concerning different degrees of transitivity of experiential situations, there is general agreement on attributing the lowest degree of transitivity to events involving bodily sensations (which accordingly are often denoted by monovalent verbs or by adjectives). For example, Malchukov (2005) discusses the manifestation of (degrees of) transitivity based on construction or case pattern variation with different verb types. Elaborating on the transitivity hierarchy proposed in Tsunoda (1985), he suggests that, among experiential predicates, perception ranks the highest, followed by cognition, emotion, and sensation. Tsunoda (1985) also views perception and cognition as more transitive than a third group, feeling, in which he conflates emotions and sensations.

Malchukov (2005) also makes a very important point when he points out that transitivity with experiential verbs cannot be viewed in the same way as with other groups of verbs, like action verbs. When comparing highly transitive, change-of-state verbs or verbs of 'effective' action in his terminology, he notes that they are distinct, for example, from pursuit verbs (e.g. *look for*) in that "while O [i.e. the second participant or proto-patient] is affected (undergoes some change) in the former case, it is not affected in the latter case, as an action is merely intended but not realized." (2005: 80). Hence, these verbs rank differently on a cline of decreasing patienthood. On the other hand, as Malchukov remarks, with experiential verbs things are more complex, as differences crucially relate to properties of A (the 'proto-agent' or more prominent participant; in the case of experiential verbs, the experiencer). Similar conclusions are reached in Aldai and Wichman (2018), who remark that "experiential verbs, vary along a dimension of agentivity of proto-agents" (2018: 275), and see a reflex of decreased agentivity in the frequency by which such verbs occur in non-canonical constructions, e.g. with non-nominative experiencers. This last tendency appears to be especially relevant for emotion verbs, at least in European languages, as pointed out in Haspelmath (2001). For this reason, according to Malchukov (2005: 78), emotions in these languages rank the lowest on the transitivity scale.

As insightful as these observations may be, the view of transitivity they contribute to sketch is not sufficient to the understanding of the rationale that stands behind construction variation with verbs that take nominative experiencers in Homeric Greek, and some adjustment needs to be made before transfering the notion of decreasing agency to all domains of experience. Indeed, at first sight, one might be tempted to see a straightforward connection between a high degree of transitivity as described above and the NomAcc construction, which could then be taken as indicating an agent-like construal of the experiencer, with other constructions pointing to decreased agentivity. Such an interpretation is supported, for example, by the fact that verbs of seeing always only occur in this construction (see Section 6.1), while other verbs of sensory perception tend to take the NomGen construction, as illustrated in Chapter 6. However, as I discuss in depth in Chapter 8, the relation between transitivity and construction variation is not so clear-cut, as shown by the fact that, among verbs of emotion, the only ones that consistently take only the NomAcc construction are verbs that indicate negative feelings directed toward the experiencer, such as 'fear' (see Section 8.3.2). In fact, these are verbs with which it is doubtful that the experiencer can be considered especially agent-like, and a more complex explanation is needed for this pattern, to which I will return in Section 3.1.1. Moreover, verbs that take the NomDat construction high-

EXPERIENTIAL SITUATIONS

light different aspects of the experiencer-stimulus relation, and do not focus on degrees either of decreasing affectedness or of decreasing agentivity (see Sections 3.2.5, 8.1.1 and 8.1.2).

In general, the literature on non-canonical constructions points toward a wider range of construction variation with emotion verbs with respect to other types of experiential verbs (see e.g. Onishi 2001, Verhoeven 2007 among many others and cf. the two transitivity hierarchies discussed in Aldai and Wichman 2018). However, this should not be taken as an overall index of low transitivity: rather, as I argue in Section 2.1.4 and especially in Chapter 8, greater construction variation points toward a wide range of variation throughout the transitivity spectrum for this type of verbs, and indicates that situations involving emotions are subject to different construals to a higher extent than other types of experiential situations, which look in this respect more 'objective'.

2.1.1 *Bodily Sensations*

The domain of bodily sensations includes feeling of body temperature, physical needs such as feeling hunger or thirst and their opposite, more general states such as feeling well or feeling bad. There are reasons to believe that the construal of bodily sensations as states is cognitively basic, as cross-linguistic evidence points to a widespread tendency for languages to encode states with morphologically simpler means than inchoative situations, as pointed out by Verhoeven (2007: 43).

Bodily sensations are conceived as uncontrolled, and the single participant is similar to a patient. Indeed, these are likely the most uncontrolled among experiential situations, as argued by Bossong (1998: 261). However, the experiencer of bodily sensations crucially differs from a patient as being necessarily sentient. Accordingly, Wierzbicka (1988) points out that one should distinguish between the state in which a living being can be, and his or her feeling: as she remarks, one can be sick without feeling sick. Only the second situation, she argues, can be regarded as involving an experiencer. Verhoeven (2007: 43) discusses the difference between bodily states such as 'be cold' and bodily sensations, such as 'feel cold', and points out that bodily states cannot be considered part of the domain of experience. In the same way, following Verhoeven (2007: 44) bodily functions such as 'sleep' cannot be included among bodily sensations. Notably, sleeping is sometimes considered an experiential situation even though the single participant of this type of situation is not normally understood as perceiving anything from it. In fact, sleeping is better regarded as a bodily function. On the other hand, the situation of falling asleep may be construed as a sensation, associated to a feeling of drowsiness (see further Section 2.3).

The subdomain of bodily sensations provides the source for an embodied conception of other subdomains of experience, as often bodily reactions are metonymically understood as standing for an experience (chilling for fear, for example; see Section 8.3.2). It borders with the sub-domain of perception: especially touch, taste and smell can be associated with the ensuing sensations. The encoding of bodily sensations and perception in Homeric Greek provides evidence for some overlap, as I show in Chapter 6.

2.1.2 *Perception*

Perception verbs refer to the senses through which living beings perceive the exterior: sight, hearing, touch, taste and smell. According to Viberg (1984), the order in which I have listed the senses also represents a scale of lexicalization. In particular, the data assembled by Viberg from a sample of 53 languages, and later supported by evidence from a bigger number of languages, attests to a primacy of sight over other sensory modalities that results in the 'modality hierarchy' shown in Figure 3.

$$\text{Sight} \;>\; \text{hearing} \;>\; \text{touch} \;>\; \left\{ \begin{array}{l} \text{smell} \\[1em] \text{taste} \end{array} \right.$$

FIGURE 3   The modality hierarchy

Viberg (1984: 136–137) offers the following interpretation for this hierarchy: "a verb having a basic meaning belonging to a sense modality higher (to the left) in the hierarchy can get an extended meaning that covers some (or all) of the sense modalities lower in the hierarchy." As we will see in Chapter 6, Homeric Greek attests to a split in the distribution of constructions that separates sight from other sensory modalities, with hearing partly patterning with sight but most often with the other senses. Hence, polysemy does not concern verbal lexemes, but rather whole constructions.

Viberg (1984) classifies English perception verbs based on three parameters: besides sense modality discussed above, he also considers subject/topic selection, and dynamic system. The parameter of subject/topic selection classifies verbs based on their tendency to select either the experiencer or the stimulus as their subject, thus assigning either participant a higher degree of topicality: experiencer-based verbs have experiencer subjects, such as *see* and *hear*, while phenomenon-based verbs have stimulus subjects, such as *look* and *sound*. Notably, part of English perception verbs can be constructed both as experiencer- and as phenomenon-based: this is true for *feel*, *taste* and *smell*. In the case of *look* it is the activity verb that can also be constructed as phenomenon-based.

The dynamic system parameter combines control with actionality (or lexical aspect), and singles out two groups of situations, uncontrolled states, experiences in Viberg's terminology, such as *see* or *hear*, and controlled activities, such as *look* and *listen*. In fact, the latter are on the border between experiential situations and actions: as Croft (2012: 156) points out, while *see* and *hear* are genuine experiential predicates (mental state verbs in his terminology), verbs that highlight the condition of attending to a stimulus such as *listen to* or *watch* are closer to actions even though they do not imply a change of state. Croft calls these and other verbs that indicate controlled but atelic situations 'inactive actions' (see also the definition of 'positions' in Dik 1997: 114).

It further needs to be pointed out that Viberg (1984) considers controlled events of perception as being connected with a specific lexical aspect: he calls them 'activities', so implying that these are ongoing, atelic events. This may be true for English *look at* and *listen to*; however, as I will show in Chapter 6, it is not always the case in Homeric Greek. In the first place, even in English verbs indicating controlled events can refer to sudden, though intentional, perception, as in (21) (compare example (183)).

(21) *She turned and looked at him.*

Based on how uncontrolled and controlled situations are lexicalized in the languages in his sample, Viberg (1984: 135) proposes another hierarchy, shown in Figure 4.

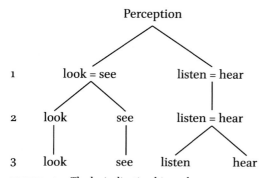

FIGURE 4   The lexicalization hierarchy

According to Viberg, this hierarchy is meant to indicate what meanings are more easily lexicalized, and predicts, among other things, that languages that distinguish between 'hear' and 'listen' also distinguish between 'see' and 'look at'. As I will argue in Chapter 6, Homeric Greek does not clearly lexicalize the distinction for any perceptual modality, even though at first sight one might have the impression that the domain of hearing shows a higher lexical elaboration than the domain of sight. Partly, however, the hierarchy is reflected in the distribution of argument structure constructions.

Another field in which primacy of sight has been advocated is the tendency for perception verbs to extend to cognition. According to Sweetser (1990), only the verb 'see' can extend to 'know' or 'think' cross-linguistically, while 'hear' cannot. This view has been challenged by Evans and Wilkins (2000) who, based on data from Australian languages, have shown that the tendency for either 'see' or 'hear' to extend to cognition may well be culture-specific. In any case, the primacy of sight over other senses is well rooted in Ancient Greek culture, as witnessed by Aristotle, who, at the beginning of his *Metaphysics*, remarks:

> All men naturally desire knowledge. An indication of this is our esteem for the senses; for apart from their use we esteem them for their own sake, and most of all the sense of sight. Not only with a view to action, but even when no action is contemplated, we prefer sight, generally speaking, to all the other senses. *The reason of this is that of all the senses sight best helps us to know things, and reveals many distinctions.* (emphasis added)
> ARIST. *Met.* 1.980a

It is also noteworthy that San Roque et al. (2018) in a cross-linguistic study of thirteen languages found an association between sight and cognition and sight and attention in all the languages in their sample, while only part of them show the same association for hearing, as shown in Table 1 and Table 2. (Limited data in San Roque's et al.'s study do not allow significant generalizations for verbs of other sensory modalities, while multi-modal verbs occurring in about half of the languages in their sample pattern similarly to verbs of hearing. Duna and Tzeltal do not appear in Table 2 because relevant data is not available.)

The association of sight with attention, which is often neglected in favor of the association with cognition, deserves to be highlighted. According to San Roque et al. "items concerning focused attention" include "scrutiny, assessment, and careful attentiveness—for example, to potential danger" (2018: 380). Such items show associations with sight in all languages under scrutiny, whereby "a common context for attentional meaning was in guarding against hazards" (2018: 383). I will return to the relevance of this association for the distribution of argument structure constructions in Homeric Greek in Section 8.3.2.

The relation between perception and cognition is reflected in the frequent use of perception verbs as evidentials. Evidentiality consists in the indication by the speaker of the source of evidence for a statement (Aikhenvald 2004). In

EXPERIENTIAL SITUATIONS

TABLE 1   The cross-linguistic association of sight verbs with cognition and attention

	Avatime	Cha'palaa	Chintang	Duna	English	Italian	Lao	Mandarin	Semai	Siwu	Spanish	Tzeltal	Whiteshands
Cognition													
Attention													

ADAPTED FROM SAN ROQUE ET AL. 2018: 384

TABLE 2   The cross-linguistic association of hearing verbs with cognition and attention

	Avatime	Cha'palaa	Chintang	English	Italian	Lao	Mandarin	Semai	Siwu	Spanish	Whiteshands
Cognition											
Attention												

ADAPTED FROM SAN ROQUE ET AL. 2018: 387

this respect, it is worth introducing the four-fold distinction made by Dik and Hengeveld (1991: 237) relative to types of states of affairs to which verbs of perception may refer. Even though Dik and Hengeveld do not provide a list of the verbs for which their discussion is relevant (they only remark that they do not consider verbs such as *witness*; 1991: 256), their remarks hold for *see* and *hear* rather than for verbs that refer to other perception modalities. The four types of states of affairs are quite different: while (i) immediate perception of individuals as in (22) and (ii) immediate perception of states of affairs as in (23) refer to concrete perception, (iii) and (iv) refer to acquisition of knowledge.

(22) *I heard Luciano Pavarotti several years ago.*

(23) *I heard him singing at Carnegie Hall.*

In (22), the experiencer is depicted as directly perceiving a human stimulus, in this case a singer, while in (23) the experiencer is referred to as perceiving the event of singing. Notably, in (23) the state of affairs described in the complement must be simultaneous to the event of perception. This is not the case when perception verbs refer to type (iii) or type (iv) situations, as in (24) and (25). (Examples (22)-(24) are from Luraghi and Sausa 2019.)

(24) *I heard that Mary had been crying* (e.g., I realized from the sound of her voice).

(25) *I hear he went up to London. / I hear he's going up to London.*

Here, the experiencer acquires knowledge, either through an inference based on his/her own perception (type (iii)), or from a third party (type (iv)), through reception of the propositional content of a speech act. The verb *hear* in both cases indicates a cognitive process, rather than perception, and shows the channel for the shift from perception to evidentiality.

Note that I have given two versions of (25). The first one, with different tenses in the main and in the subordinate clause, is from Dik and Hengeveld (1991): here, the indirect nature of the acquisition of knowledge indicated by the perception verb is highlighted by the use of verbal tense, which shows that the two events are not simultaneous. The second version, with the same tense in both clauses, allows for two interpretations: it can indicate acquisition of knowledge from a third party, but it may as well indicate immediate perception. This second reading would usually correspond to a participial construction such as the one in (23) in English. Crucially, however, this is not the case in Homeric Greek.

In Homeric Greek, a special type of construction involving a predicative participle occurs in cases in which the object of perception is a state of affairs as I will describe in Section 3.3. In most cases, even when perception is clearly not direct, and reference is made to the acquisition of knowledge from a third party, the encoding is the same as the encoding of direct perception. This means that the event that is being learned about is presented as simultaneous with the perception event, as I discuss in Section 3.3. Cases like (25) contain a different type of construction, as they show a full shift in perception verbs, mostly from hearing verbs to evidentiality. I will further elaborate on this in Section 6.4.

2.1.3 *Cognition*

Among the subdomains of experience, cognition is certainly the one that is most typical of human beings. This especially holds true for thinking, which is often construed as a controlled activity: animals can certainly feel bodily sensa-

EXPERIENTIAL SITUATIONS

tions or perceive the external reality, they are also viewed by humans as subject to some basic emotions, such as fear or anger, but the fact that thought implies self-awareness has long been recognized as specifically human. Verbs of cognition include two main semantic areas, those of thought and of knowledge, and border with verbs of perception and with verbs of emotion. According to Halliday (2004: 208), cognition verbs are distinct from the latter two groups of verbs based on the presence/absence of a perceptual input or an emotion of some kind. The border between them is quite flexible though, as we have already seen in Section 2.1.2 discussing the evidential use of perception verbs.

According to Fortescue (2001: 20) the domain of thinking is "subject to fine-grained lexical subdivision—and the territory covered by a single polysemous verb such as English *think* is concomitantly broad." Indeed, patterns of polysemy cross-linguistically point toward a disparate variety of construal for thinking. According to Vendler (1967: 110–111) 'think' refers to two different situations, that is, an activity, as in 'thinking about', and a state, as in 'thinking that'. Goddard (2003) argues that English 'think' in fact refers to a wider variety of situations, as it can for example indicate an achievement, as in (26) (an "occurrent" thought in their terminology, see Goddard 2003: 113 and fn. 4).

(26) *For the first time I thought that we had a chance.*

The verb *think* in (26) indicates a sudden change in one's state of awareness, and 'I thought' here can be paraphrased as 'I realized' or 'it occurred to me'.

Goddard (2003: 112) proposes a set of more fine-grained distinctions, which also accounts for their construction, as shown in a-d.

a.   X thinks about Y [topic of thought]
b.   X thinks something (good/bad) about Y [complement]
c.   X thinks like this:———[quasi-quotational complement]
d.   X thinks that [———]S [propositional complement]

Goddard further singles out three semantic areas that account for frequent compositional polysemy or motivated homonymy, by which a semantic prime can also express meanings associated to another semantic prime: "thinking about someone or something, and feeling something bad because of it; [...] 'count' or 'calculate' [...]; 'intend' or 'would like to'" (2003: 116). Based on these polysemies, four configurations appear to be cross-linguistically frequent according to Goddard (2003: 120), who summarizes them as in i–iv.

i.   thinking about what can happen and feeling something because of it (propositional attitudes), e.g., *hope, expect, look forward to, dread*

ii.   thinking about something for some time, so as to sustain a feeling ("active" emotions), e.g., *rejoice, grieve, worry, fret*

30 CHAPTER 2

iii. thinking good or bad things about someone and feeling something because of it (interpersonal attitudes), e.g., *love, admire, respect, hate, despise*

iv. feelings associated with thinking (emotions), e.g., *happy, jealous, surprised, disgusted.*

The four configurations in i–iv indicate a possible overlap of thinking with various types of emotions. Homeric Greek offers ample evidence for overlap. As an example, let us consider the verb *phronéō*, which, as we will see in Section 7.1, is among the most frequent verbs of mental activity. This verb is most often accompanied by an attitudinal adverb, as in (27), in which the adverb *eú* 'well' indicates a positive attitude of the speaker toward the addressee.

(27) *hó   sphin   eù phronéōn   agorḗsato*
DEM.NOM 3PL.DAT well think.PTCP.PRS.NOM address.AOR.MID.3SG
kaì metéeipen
and speak.AOR.3SG
'He with good intent addressed them and spoke among (them).' (*Od.* 2.228)

Fortescue (2001) discusses a number of cross-linguistic polysemies of cognitive verbs, with a view to diachrony and to their possible etymology. Concerning thinking, Fortescue (2001: 29) lists four main semantic areas, including thinking as weighing, as in French *penser* from Latin *pondero* 'think' based on *pondus* 'weigh', thinking as observing, as in English *regard*, thinking as wanting as in German *glauben* (cf. English *believe*, from the same root with a different prefix), and thinking as calculating, as in English *reckon* and Russian *sčitat'* 'calculate, count, consider, reckon'. As we will see in Sections 7.1, 7.1.1 and 7.1.2 basic verbs of thinking in Homeric Greek are often denominal, and connected with different words that indicate the mind. Polysemy of thinking and measuring that can be considered a variant of thinking and weighing is also attested.

'Know' also constitutes a semantic prime in Natural Semantic Metalanguage (NSM). This theory, first proposed in Wierzbicka (1972), views meaning as decomposable in a number of semantic primes, which are held to be universal based on empirical cross-linguistic evidence (see Goddard 2010 for a brief overview). Similar to verbs of thinking, verbs of knowledge often display compositional polysemy or motivated homonymy. Goddard (2012: 713) mentions as 'mental predicates' that can show this type of polysemy among them KNOW, THINK, WANT, FEEL, SEE, and HEAR. In a similar vein, though not in the framework of NSM, Fortescue (2001: 23) mentions three main patterns of lexicalization, again with a view to possible etymology: knowing as having seen as in Ancient Greek *oîda* that I discuss further on, knowing as having learnt, a polysemy attested in Eskimo languages (West Greenlandic *ilisima-* 'know' from Proto-Eskimo **əlit-* 'learn'), and knowing as feeling, as in Italian *sapere* from Latin *sapio* 'taste'. Fortescue argues that the patterns of polysemy reviewed point toward a construal of knowing "as an internally experienced state, at least potentially conscious, which is the result of recognizing or learning something of which one was ignorant before, much like by seeing or touching an object." (2001: 24).

Fortescue (2001: 20–23) devotes a separate discussion to verbs of understanding. Clearly, understand is a more complex concept than think or know, as it implies different components, partly connected to acquiring and processing knowledge, along with a final result. In addition, other mental events relate to understanding, such as becoming aware, realizing and recognizing, as will become apparent in Section 7.2.2 in the discussion of the Greek verb *gignóskō*, a verb based on the Proto-Indo-European root **gnō-* 'know', which frequently indicates understanding. This is likely the reason why Fortescue finds many more transparent etymological sources for 'understand' than for 'think' and especially 'know'. In addition, events of understanding are telic, rather than stative, similar to events of learning. Languages may vary as to the extent to which the same verb can construe a situation as a state or a change of state, see the discussion of Italian *sapere* and *conoscere*, both meaning 'know' but used to indicate change of state in examples (123) and (124) in Section 4.1.

The concept of 'memory', 'remembrance' seems to be more complex than those of thinking and knowing, as argued in Wierzbicka (2007). As noted above, in the framework of NSM, Goddard (2003) and Wierzbicka (2007) regard the concepts 'think' and 'know' as semantic primes, that is, concepts that are not further decomposable into more basic concepts. Wierzbicka then discusses the universality of the concept of remembering, and highlights its close connections with other mental activities. She argues that "'remember' is a complex concept, which stands for a language-specific configuration of simpler concepts (including THINK and KNOW)" (2007: 21), and concludes that "linguistic evidence indicates that while 'think' and 'know' are indeed universal human concepts, 'remember' is not." (2007: 38). Indeed, cross-linguistic evidence seems to point to a culturally conditioned construction of this concept, as several languages do not have a verb that corresponds to English *remember* which keeps this type of mental state clearly distinct from thinking, reflecting or knowing (see Wierzbicka 2007: 20–21 with reference to various Australian languages). As we will see in Sections 7.3 and 7.4, Homeric Greek also attests to a sharp distinction between memory and other types of cognitive situations.

Remarkably, remembering refers to situations that can be differently construed. Van Valin and Wilkins (1993: 511) observe that English *remember* can have three different interpretations in connection with lexical aspect. It can indicate an achievement, as in (28), an activity, as in (29), or a state, as in (29).

(28) *John suddenly remembered the faucet he left on.*

(29) *John consciously remembered the names of all of the linguists that he met at the party.*

(30) *John remembers his first day at school very vividly.*

In (28) *remember* indicates an inchoative situation, a change of state in which some thought is suddenly activated in the experiencer's mind. In (29) the adverb *consciously* indicates that the situation is controlled; also, the ongoing character of the situation is highlighted by reference to all items in a series. Finally, (30) describes a state of the experiencer's consciousness. As Amberber (2007: 4) notes, remembrance can also be conceptualized as an accomplishment, and corresponding verbs can have a causative meaning, as English *remind* in (31).

(31) *He would have forgotten his birthday, if you hadn't reminded him.*

Interestingly, *remind* can also express the meaning of causing someone to think of something/someone because of resemblance, as in (32).

(32) *His fierce stare reminded her of an owl.*

Examples (28) and (29) can also be viewed as being based on two different concepts, which contrast involuntary to voluntary memory. Many languages have constructions that imply low transitivity in connection with involuntary, or spontaneous memory, as French *il me souvient*, in which the experiencer is encoded as a patient, or Russian *mne vspomnaetsja* with a dative experiencer and a middle-reflexive form of the verb (Wierzbicka 2007: 25–26; Zalizniak 2007: 107–110).

As I have already remarked above, the association of various perception modalities, in particular seeing and hearing, with cognition is quite frequent. However, knowledge cannot only be acquired from an external source: the event of remembering can indicate a state of consciousness reached through recollection from one's internal mental resources. As we will see in Section 6.4

EXPERIENTIAL SITUATIONS

and 7.3, Homeric Greek offers evidence for sudden recollection as contrasting both with the inchoative situation of learning something new, and with the stative situation of having acquired some stable knowledge.

Cognition can also overlap with emotions. Not only can thinking be construed as implying an emotional orientation, as I have shown in example (27), but often the situation of keeping in mind, remembering can extend to caring (see Section 7.3). The implication is not necessary though, and must be inferred from the context, as remembering can also have a negative implication.

2.1.4 *Emotions*

Emotions constitute the widest and more variegated sub-field of experience. As pointed out by Wierzbicka (1999), emotions are, among experiential situations, those whose construal is most culture-dependent. In addition, they have a social dimension and are often interpersonal. Emotions have been the topic of in-depth research, both on specific languages and in a cross-linguistic perspective, and it is impossible to review the extant literature here (see among others the collections in Niemerier and Dirven 1997, Harkins and Wierzbicka 2001, Athanasiadou and Tabakowska 2010).

Emotions can be viewed as divided into positive and negative, largely depending on the experiencer's attitude toward the stimulus. Generally speaking, joy, affection, appeasement are regarded as positive emotions, while hate, envy or fear are regarded as negative. The relation between the experiencer and the stimulus with emotions has a more causal character than with other experiential predicates. In general, as I will discuss in Section 2.2.2, the stimulus is regarded as the trigger of the experiential situation, but with emotions it can be construed as a cause or reason. The difference between emotions and other types of experiential situations can be illustrated with examples (33)-(35).

(33) *Mary heard the music. / ??The music caused Mary's hearing.*

(34) *I am thinking about last night. / ??Last night caused my thinking.*

(35) *Paul got angry at Joan. / Joan caused Paul's anger.*

Given the complex nature of the relation between the experiencer and the stimulus, causality has been widely studied in relation to emotions. Dirven (1997) approaches emotions both as causes for the experiencer's reaction and as brought about by some other cause or reason. As I will argue in Chapter 8, expressions of cause or reason with verbs of emotion in contexts similar to (35) show that the stimulus they encode is construed as a matter of concern for the experiencer in a situation. I will elaborate on this issue further in Section 2.2.2.

2.1.5 *Volitionality*

As argued in Verhoeven (2007: 47–49), the field of volition overlaps to a large extent with the fields of cognition and emotion. Indeed, verbs such as 'plan' on the one hand, and 'desire' on the other, are associated with the other two fields: planning is a more conscious and controlled way of thinking, while desire has a crucial emotional component. Verhoeven (2007: 47) further points out that, owing to its overlap with neighboring domains, the domain of volition is narrower than the other domains of experience; however, it easily extends to modality, and from modality to other domains, such as tense and aspect, thus potentially covering a very broad semantic area.

Will entertains a complex relation with intentionality, and hence control. Will and desire are not in themselves states of affairs that are intentionally brought about by an experiencer/agent: in fact, desire is often depicted as not liable of being controlled. On the other hand, the inference that if someone wants to engage in an activity then he or she has the intention to do so is quite frequent. Verhoeven (2007: 48) remarks that conscious and unconscious forms of will are often encoded by the same verb. However, this does not seem to be the case in Homeric Greek, in which the verb *ethélō* 'want' largely coincides with conscious will, while unconscious manifestations of will are indicated by verbs of desiring (see Section 5.2).

Another feature connected with volitionality is its degree of realisness. In this perspective, Noonan (2007) distinguishes between three classes of verbs, instantiated by English *want*, *wish/desire*, and *hope*. The three classes are distinct by different types of modalities: "*hope*-class predicates ... express an emotional attitude toward a proposition whose status is ... unknown, but which could turn out to be true", *wish*-class predicates "are normally given a contrafactive interpretation." (2007: 132) In turn, *want*-class predicates take complements that "express a desire that some state or event may be realized in the future." (*ib.* 133) I return to this three-fold distinction and its encoding in Homeric Greek in Section 5.2.

Among verbs of volition, Verhoeven includes verbs of (bodily) needs (2007: 48), following Reh and Simon (1998: 42), and argues that "a bodily need can be understood as a will (concerning the realization of a situation) based on person-immanent physical necessities." This view is not without problems. As a bodily need is based on a sensation, and bodily needs are hardly distinguishable from certain types of bodily sensations: 'be hungry' can be seen as equal to 'need food'. In fact, as I will argue in Section 5.1, evidence from the types of construction in which predicates of bodily need occur in Homeric Greek suggest that such situations are construed as more similar to bodily sensations, rather than to volitionality.

2.2 Semantic Roles of Participants in Experiential Situations

Semantic roles are generalizations meant to capture the roles of participants in events (Kittilä, Västi and Ylikoski 2011: 7; see the discussion in Luraghi and Narrog 2014 and Primus 2011 on the relation between case marking and semantic roles). As events are potentially an infinite number, and may all differ to various extents from one another, even the types of involvement of participants in events are potentially infinite. For this reason, semantic roles must be understood not only as generalizations, but also as conceptually structured along the lines of prototypical categories, as argued in Schlesinger (1989) and Nishimura (1993) among others, rather than be defined based on a closed set of necessary and sufficient features (cf. e.g. Radden 1989). This is especially true for the experiencer role that, as we will see in Section 2.2.1, can be construed in different ways, as closer or less close to several other semantic roles.

In the description of semantic roles, participant properties are usually kept distinct from role properties. Participant properties are referential features that can characterize participants, as for example animacy, abstractness/concreteness, (non-)manipulation (Luraghi 2003a: 17–48), and so on. Such properties remain stable in all event types. Role properties, conversely, vary depending on the type of situation: actions, for example, normally require that the agent is not only animate, but also that s/he acts intentionally.

As argued in Daniel (2014: 206–209), approaches to semantic roles and to semantic roles encoding may be verb- or argument-centered. In this book, I follow an argument-centered approach. I also take formal encoding as evidence for relatedness between semantic roles. In this way, I follow the semantic maps approach (Haspelmath 2003), and consider cross-linguistic regularity in semantic structure to be mirrored by coding regularities. This allows me to capture similarities between experiencers and other participants that explain the different types of encoding used for experiencers within the same language as well as across languages.

As I have already mentioned in Chapter 1, experiential situations entail one main participant, the experiencer, and often a second participant, the stimulus. I will survey their properties in Sections 2.2.1 and 2.2.2. Further discussion of these roles can be found in Verhoeven (2007), who also offers a survey of the literature; see also Fedriani (2014: 20–33).

2.2.1 *Experiencer*

As noted in Chapter 1, the basic participant property of experiencers is animacy. The experiencer must be able to experience a situation; hence, it must be a sentient being, endowed with perception. This certainly holds for bodily sensations and perception, while other types of experiential situations may require other properties typical of human beings. Mental activities are usually construed as implying rationality, while emotions display a more varied situation: some of them, fear for example, are easily also attributed to animals, while others, such as envy, are typically human, as they require a more complex elaboration of the stimulus that also comprises some conscious mental activity such as comparing and evaluating and may entail volitionality (Verhoeven 2007: 55–56). Volitionality may be attributed to animals inasmuch as it does not imply intentionality, which again is typically human.

Role properties partly depend on the type of situation, and partly on the way in which a specific situation is construed. Bodily sensations require a patient-like experiencer. Based on our knowledge of the events, we know that bodily sensations, such as hunger, thirst, being warm or being cold, feeling ill or other similar situations can hardly be controlled. One who feels hunger cannot avoid feeling the effects of hunger, unless he or she can remove it by eating something. It is thus a consequence of embodiment if the experiencer in such situations is construed as a patient, and is attributed a relatively high degree of affectedness and low or no control.

Verhoven correctly points out that bodily sensations differ crucially from bodily states, and writes that "it is possible *to feel sick* without *being sick*, and *to be sick* without *feeling sick*" (2007: 43). In other words, a participant who is in a certain bodily state must be conscious of it in order to qualify as an experiencer. The relevance of consciousness is also highlighted by D'Andrade, who writes that "the *perceiving self* not only observes things in the world, it also perceives that it is perceiving—that is, it is *conscious*" (1995: 163). Consciousness entails awareness and a certain degree of possible control, which can be viewed as scalar notions. On the one hand, the experiencer as a participant who acts prompted by an irrational emotion can be construed as being characterized by a lowered level of awareness: one may, for example, react out of angerness without being aware of the consequences. On the other hand, cognition and rational mental activity presuppose a higher level of awareness. To put it with D'Andrade "The perceived self in the folk model has an onion-like character with many layers which can be peeled away. That is, one can say 'I want a cigarette'; here the center of awareness and agency includes the desire. Or, one can say 'I'm going crazy for a cigarette.' Here the desire is treated as outside the self; acting on the self." (1995: 164). Awareness is a key notion for the understanding of the construal of experiential situation types and their encoding in Homeric, as I will argue especially in Chapter 8 when discussing argument structure variation with emotion verbs.

In Homeric Greek, as we will see in Chapter 3, impersonal constructions, or constructions that do not contain a nominative experiencer are infrequent. There are however dative experiencers, both with verbs of emotion, such as *mélō* 'care for', and with verbs of mental activity, such as *dokéō* 'think'. Examples are (36) and (37) (see further the discussion in Section 3.2.7).

(36) *ê   nú   toi   oukéti   págkhu metà   phresì*
PTC PTC 2SG.DAT nevermore totally among heart.DAT.PL
mémblet'   Akhilleús?
care.PRF.M/P.3SG Achilles.NOM
'Don't you anymore care for Achilles in your heart?' (*Il.* 19.343)

(37) *ho   xeînos   mála   moi   dokéei*
DEM.NOM stranger.NOM much 1SG.DAT seem.PRS.3SG
pepnuménos   eînai
be_wise.PTCP.PRF.M/P.NOM be.INF.PRS
'This stranger seems to me a very wise man.' (*Od.* 8.388)

Different construals of the experiencer role account for its notoriously missing a specific coding that keeps it distinct from other basic semantic roles cross-linguistically (Luraghi 2014a: 111; see Luraghi and Narrog 2014 on possible exceptions reported from languages of the Caucasus). As I remarked above, even within the same language experiencers can be encoded as subjects of transitive verbs, hence as agents, or as objects of transitive verbs, hence as patients. In addition, dative experiencers are cross-linguistically quite frequent (Luraghi 2014a: 111–113): in this way, experiencers also receive the typical coding of recipient/beneficiaries.

In fact, experiencers share, or may share, features of all three roles. They are human, as are prototypical agents and recipients/beneficiaries; similar to patients, they are affected by the situation. In stative situations, their degree of affectedness is somewhat lower, as they do not undergo a change of state: this makes them more similar to recipients/beneficiaries, who are affected by the situation to a lower extent than patients, as they do not undergo a change of state.

However, since experiential situations can be inchoative, experiencers may be even more patient-like, and undergo a change of state, as in (38).

(38) *Prince Harry fell in love with Meghan Markle.*

In addition, depending on the type of event and on the way in which we construe it, experiencers can exert some degree of control on the situation. For this reason, they can be similar to agents, and partly also to recipients, which as final possessors of an entity that undergoes a transfer event, may be taken as being prospective controllers.

Shared features of the experiencer and other semantic roles are summarized in Table 3. Shared features of the experiencer with the semantic roles of agent, recipient/beneficiary, and patient account for its being possibly encoded as one of these three roles cross-linguistically. I will elaborate further on this point in Section 2.3.

TABLE 3   Features of participants and roles

	Experiencer	Agent	Recipient/beneficiary	Patient
Humanness	+	+	+	+/−
Control	+/−	+	(+)	−
Volition	+/−	+	−	−
Affectedness	+	−	(+)	+
Change of state	+/−	−	−	+

ADAPTED FROM LURAGHI 2014A

2.2.2 *Stimulus*

Stimuli are much more diverse than experiencers as to their referential properties, and do not display any special feature that can be generalized over all types of experiential situations, as is animacy for experiencers. Rather, groups of experiential verbs or, more often, specific verbs may require that the stimulus bears a certain feature.

Among verbs of emotions, which have an important social dimension, animacy can be relevant for stimuli. I have already pointed out in Section 2.2.1 that an emotion such as envy is normally not attributed to animals, but is construed as a feeling typical of human beings. In fact, in a situation of envy not only are experiencers typically human, but also stimuli are virtually always human beings. This is an obvious consequence of the fact that if a participants feels envy toward another participants, this means that the first participant— the experiencer—compares his/her status with the status of the second participant—the stimulus—and wishes to be in the place of the stimulus. Human

EXPERIENTIAL SITUATIONS

beings typically compare themselves with other human beings, and may feel envy for properties of other human beings: hence, envy is a very good example of a socially conditioned emotion that involves an interpersonal relationship.

Even situations that apparently concern similar emotions can be construed differently as regards possible stimuli. In English, the emotion denoted by the verb *love* can target both animate and inanimate stimuli, but the emotion denoted by the predicate *feel affection* is not normally directed toward inanimate entities: compare (39) with (40).

(39) *Mary loves Charlie/chocolate.*

(40) *Mary feels affection for Charlie/??for chocolate.*

Some cognition verbs may require states of affairs as their stimuli and only admit other types of participants to a limited extent. In Italian for example the verbs *sapere* and *conoscere* both correspond to English *know*, but while the former most often takes sentential complements, and indicates a situation in which an experiencer is aware of a certain state of affairs, the latter rather indicates acquaintance between two participants, as shown in (41) and (42).

(41) *Non sapevo   che tuo fratello lavorasse   a Roma.*
     not know.IMPF.1SG that your brother work.SBJV.PST.3SG at Rome
     'I didn't know that your brother worked in Rome.'

(42) *Tuo fratello conosce   mia cugina.*
     your brother know.PRS.3SG my cousin
     'Your brother knows my cousin.'

(There are of course cases in which the two verbs can overlap, as in *Conosco/so la risposta a questa domanda*, 'I know the answer to this question'.)

Role properties of stimuli also depend on the type of experiential situation. Stimuli are triggers of the experiential situation, but given the wide variety of situations there is no special feature that is generally required (see Blansitt 1978). Especially with verbs of emotion, stimuli have often been described as being either goal- or source-like (Croft 1993). Discussing *at* stimuli in English, as in *get angry at*, Dirven (1993: 70–71) writes that they "evoke a double direction in the chain of emotional causality", as they are conceived both as triggers of emotions, and as targets of the experiencer's reaction. Croft (1993) represents the complex relation between the experiencer and the stimulus as in Figure 5.

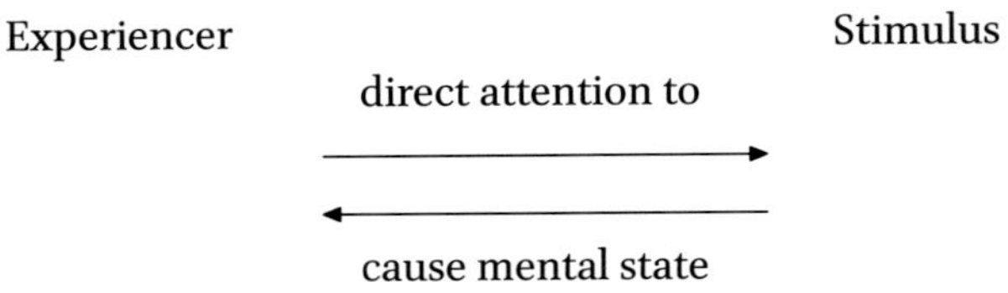

Experiencer   Stimulus

                    direct attention to

                    ────────────────────▶

                    ◀────────────────────

                    cause mental state

FIGURE 5   The double nature of the experiencer-stimulus
            relationship

In certain cases, an emotion can be described as brought about by more than just one stimulus. Consider (43).

(43) *Paula envies her sister for her new ring.*

In (43), Paula is the experiencer and her sister is the stimulus. However, there is one more participant, her new ring, that constitutes the reason why Paula's sister triggers Paula's envy. In cases such as this, Verhoeven (2007: 63–64), following Klein and Kutscher (2002) speaks of split stimuli. She discusses German occurrences such as (44) and (45).

(44) *Ich   gönne   dir   den   Sieg   / dass*
     1SG.NOM begrudge.PRS.1SG 2SG.DAT ART.ACC victory   that
     du   siegst.
     2SG.NOM win.PRS.2SG
     'I don't begrudge you the victory/that you win.'

(45) *Die   Arbeit beeindruckt   vor   allem   durch*
     ART.NOM.F work   impress.PRS.3SG before all.DAT through
     ihren   Umfang / aufgrund/ wegen ihres   Umfangs.
     POSS.3SG.F.ACC size   because   for   POSS.3SG.F.GEN size.GEN
     'The work impresses above all by its size/ because of its size.'

(See also Grimshaw 1990: 23, who speaks of second stimulus or cause in occurrences such as *The article angered Bill by its content*.)
    Possible Greek parallels are (46) and (47).

(46) *hoí   te   theaîs   agáasthe   par' andrásin*
     REL.NOM.PL PTC goddess.DAT.PL envy.PRS.M/P.2PL near man.DAT.PL
     eunázesthai
     lie.INF.PRS.M/P
     '(You) who envy the goddesses because they lie beside men.' (*Od.* 5.119)

EXPERIENTIAL SITUATIONS

(47) *málista dè   Pēnelopeíēi   héndane   múthoisi*
greatly PTC Penelope.DAT please.IMPF.3SG word.DAT.PL
'He greatly pleased Penelope with his words.' (*Od.* 16.397–398)

In (46), envy is said to be directed toward the goddesses because of their sleeping with humans. The inanimate trigger, in this case a state of affairs, causes a conscious emotion, which in Homeric Greek is construed as a matter of concern, and shares the construction of verbs of caring (see Sections 8.1.1, 8.2.2 and 8.6). Example (47) features an occurrence of the verb *handánō*, which takes a stimulus subject and an experiencer dative. This verb will be discussed in Sections 3.2.7 and 8.5. In the occurrence in (47), the stimulus is a human being, portrayed as acting intentionally. The NP *múthoisi* 'with words', then, can well be conceived as having an instrumental function, as also suggested by the encoding (compare the discussion of example (78) in Section 3.1.3).

2.3   The Encoding of Experiential Situations Cross-linguistically

Given the diverse nature of experiential situations, the fact that they are heterogeneously encoded, both cross-linguistically and within individual languages, is not surprising. Within the same language, it may be the case that experiencers are coded differently depending on whether they are more agent- or more patient-like. In many languages, this difference is often paired by the occurrence of nominative vs. so called non-canonical subjects.

As an example, let us consider the domain of bodily sensation. Experiencers in this type of situation are often construed as more patient-like than other experiencers. Consider for example German (48) and (49).

(48) *Mich   friert.*
1SG.ACC be_cold.PRS.3SG

(49) *Ich   friere.*
1SG.NOM be_cold.PRS.1SG
'I'm cold.'

The sentences in (48) and (49) both mean 'I'm cold', but they feature different constructions. In (48), we find an accusative experiencer. No other constituent is available to trigger verb agreement; hence the verb shows the default third singular form (also called impersonal). This type of construction, in which an accusative experiencer is treated as a direct object of an impersonal transitive verb, is called transimpersonal in typological literature (see the discussion in Malchukov 2008). The accusative is the case of the direct object of transitive verbs in German: accusative encoding thus points toward a patient-like construal of the experiencer. Notably, the experiencer can also receive nominative encoding and accordingly trigger agreement, as it does in (49): this is because in German the nominative case is the default case for subjects of any type of verbs, no matter their role.

Emotions are also often construed as having patient-like experiencers. A well know case is constituted by a group of Latin verbs that take accusative experiencers and genitive stimuli (Fedriani 2014), such as the verb *paenitet* 'regret' in (50).

(50) *qua   re   voluntatis me   meae   numquam*
REL.ABL thing.ABL will.GEN 1SG.ACC POSS.1SG.GEN never
paenitebit,   consili   paenitet
regret.FUT.3SG plan.GEN regret.PRS.3SG
'For this reason, I will never regret my decision: what I do regret is my plan of procedure.' (Cic. *Att.* 11.6.2)

In (50), there is no nominative-marked NP that can trigger verb agreement. For this reason, the verb is inflected in the third person singular, but does not give any information as to which of the two arguments functions as grammatical subject or agreement trigger. The experiencer *me* 'me' is inflected in the accusative, while the stimulus, *voluntatis meae* 'my will, my decision' and *consili* '(my) plan' are in the genitive. As the experiencer is typically more salient than the stimulus, it is usually considered the first argument: hence the label of AccGen construction (see the extensive discussion in Fedriani 2014).

Croft (1993), discussing competing constructions of verbs of emotion cross-linguistically, connects experiencer coding with the way in which the relation of the experiencer with the stimulus is construed. As already noted, the relation between the two has a double nature, as the stimulus can be both the source and the target of the experiential situation. Croft shows that in many languages even quite similar emotions can be encoded by different constructions, such as the verb pair *ljubit'* 'love' that takes a nominative experiencer and an accusative stimulus, and *nravit'sja* 'like' with a dative experiencer and a nominative stimulus in Russian. Similarly, in Italian we find the verb pair *amare* 'love', and *piacere* 'like', as in (51) and (52).

EXPERIENTIAL SITUATIONS

(51) *(Io)   amo   Giovanna.*
     1SG.NOM love.PRS.1SG Giovanna
     'I love Giovanna.'

(52) *Mi   piace   Giovanna*
     1SG.DAT like.PRS.3SG Giovanna
     'I like Giovanna.'

Notably, the construction in (52) is generally referred to as DatNom construction; however, as the two participants can both be human, it is not completely clear that the stimulus is always less prominent than the experiencer (see Holvoet and Nau 2014: 24 on experiencers and stimuli in Baltic languages). Apparently, prominence can vary depending on various factors, among which word order, as can also be shown by other syntactic properties (cf. Primus 2011: 200 on the relevance of word order for possible subjecthood of non-nominative experiencers). In (53) the dative *a Giovanna* governs the null subjects of the coordinate clause. This would be the same if one paraphrases *piacere* with *essere simpatico* as in (54).

(53) *A   Giovanna piace   Maria e   la   vede   sempre*
     to Giovanna like.PRS.3SG Maria and 3SG.ACC see.PRS.3SG always
     volentieri.
     gladly

(54) *A   Giovanna Maria è   simpatica e   la   vede*
     to Giovanna Maria be.PRS.3SG nice   and 3SG.ACC see.PRS.3SG
     sempre volentieri.
     always gladly
     'Giovanna likes Mary, and is always happy when she sees her.'

Let us now consider (55). In this sentence, the stimulus participant, *Giovanna e Paola*, might well be considered more prominent than the experiencer *tutti* 'everybody', both because of referential properties (individuation), and because it clearly governs the null subject in the coordinate clause (see further the discussion of the verb *handánō* 'please' in Section 3.2.7).

(55) *Giovanna e   Paola piacciono   a   tutti e   hanno*
     Giovanna and Paola like.PRS.3PL to all.PL and have.PRS.3PL
     molti   amici.
     many.PL friend.PL

'Everybody likes Giovanna and Paola, and they [i.e. Giovanna and Paola] have many friends.'

Languages often vary in the preferred alignment they take for (groups of) experiential predicates. In the case of emotion verbs, for example, English tends to prefer the experiencer-subject / stimulus-object alignment for basic emotions such as love and hate, but the experiencer-dative / stimulus nominative alignment is by no means infrequent cross-linguistically. An example is Hittite, as shown in (56) and (57).

(56) *nu=*   *kan*   ᵈGAŠAN-*li*   [*k*]*uit*   É-*er*   *pukkan*
     CONN PTC Ištar.DAT   INDF.NOM house.NOM hateful.NOM
     'Whatever household Ištar hates [lit.: (is) hateful to/for Ištar], ...' (KUB 24.7 i 24–25; Luraghi 2010a)

(57) *uk=*   *wa*   *at*[*ti*]=   *mm*[*i*   *natt*]*a assus*
     1SG.NOM QUOT father.DAT POSS.1SG.DAT NEG   good.NOM
     'My father doesn't like me.' (KBo 22.2 rev. 4–5; Luraghi 2010a).

In addition, experiencers may be encoded as spatial roles, in particular locations or directions. Lakoff (1993: 27) discusses metaphorical expressions such as English (58) in which, as he rightly points out, the experiencer is conceived as a destination. In some languages the encoding of experiencers as local roles is not as limited as in English, and constitutes the standard, as is the case with the adessive (locative) case in Estonian, as shown in (59) (see the discussion in Luraghi 2014a: 112–113).

(58) *That idea came to me.*

(59) *Mul*   *on*   *häbi/*   *piinlik*
     1SG.ADESS be.3SG shame.NOM/ embarrassing.NOM
     'I am ashamed/I feel embarrassed.' (from Erelt and Metslang 2006)

Experiencers can also often be encoded as possessors. This is common in the case of bodily states or sensations and of some emotions, such as fear, in the Romance languages, as shown in example (60) from French, but it is also cross-linguistically quite frequent (Luraghi 2014a: 113).

(60) *J'*   *ai*   *faim /*   *froid / peur.*
     1SG.NOM have.PRS.1SG hunger cold   fear
     'I am hungry / cold / afraid.'

EXPERIENTIAL SITUATIONS

Even though these expressions are completely lexicalized in French, they also originate from a metaphor, according to which experiencers are possessors, and feelings and sensations are things possessed (see Luraghi 2014a: 113–114).

A factor that may be at play in the choice of a specific type of construction for the encoding of experiential situations is the positive or negative evaluation of the experience. According to Dahl (2014a), for example, the DatNom construction with a dative experiencer and a nominative stimulus in Vedic Sanskrit is limited to verbs that indicate positive experience. Viti (2017) argues that in Ancient Indo-European languages constructions with non-nominative experiencers occur based on an implicational scale on which the verb 'like' ranks the highest, followed by verbs of negative experience, predicates of positive experience other than like, cognitive verbs, and other types of experiential verbs.

Concerning Ancient Greek, Viti (2017: 397–398) further claims that metaphorical expressions with the verb *hairéō* 'take, seize' as in example (18) appear with negative, rather than positive experiential situations. However, a careful scrutiny of the data shows that considering such metaphorical expressions limited to negative experience is unwarranted. Notably, the verb *hairéō* also occurs several times with *hímeros* 'lust, desire', as in (61). Note that the positive evaluation of this feeling is specified by the adjective *glukús* 'sweet'. Even a sensation such as that of falling asleep can be positively evaluated, and occur with *hairéō* as in (62), in which *húpnos* 'sleep' is again qualified as *glukús*.

(61) *hōs séo   nûn éramai   kaí me   glukùs*
     as   2SG.GEN now love.PRS.M/P.1SG and 1SG.ACC sweet.NOM
     hímeros   haireî.
     desire.NOM seize.PRS.3SG
     'As much as I now love you, and sweet desire seizes me.' (*Il.* 14.328)

(62) *kaì gàr dè̀ koítoio   tákh' éssetai   hēdéos   hṓrē,*
     and PTC PTC rest.GEN soon be.FUT.MID.3SG sweet.GEN time.NOM
     hón   tiná   g' húpnos   héloi   glukerós,
     REL.ACC INDF.ACC PTC sleep.NOM seize.OPT.AOR.3SG sweet.NOM
     kaì kēdómenón   per
     and afflicted.PTCP.PRS.M/P.ACC PTC
     'It soon will be time for a sweet rest, for him whom sweet sleep can seize, in spite of his cares.' (*Od.* 19.510–511)

It is true that *déos* 'fear' is the most frequent word occurring as subject in this collocation with 11 occurrences, followed by *húpnos* 'sleep' that occurs five times, and *khólos* 'anger' and *hímeros*, both occurring four times. However, the data does not seem to support the conclusion that "negative experiences such as sorrow, illness or fear are conceptualized as external forces that affect the speaker against his will, while this is not implied for predicates of positive experience." (Viti 2017: 397). Rather, various types of experiences, including positive ones, are often construed as uncontrolled. This is true for fear, but it is most often also true, for example, for love (see Section 8.2). Note further that higher frequency of negative experiences with this specific metaphor in Homeric Greek may be connected with the meaning of the verb *hairéō* 'seize, capture', which is often used when referring to some hostile activity.

It is interesting to observe, in any case, that *hairéō* is the only verb that occurs frequently to indicate experiential situations in metaphorical sense. Other metaphorical expressions abound, as one may expect given the poetic nature of the poems, but they do not look as idiomatic as do expressions containing this verb. An example can be found in (457), in which the verb *kikhánō* 'meet' describes the rise of bodily sensations (thirst and hunger): notably, it is the only occurrence in which *kikhánō* refers to an experiential situation in the Homeric poems, as other metaphorical usages refer to death. The wider context of example (61), discussed below as (358), contains the verb *amphikalúptō* 'enwrap' referred to (sexual) pleasure. This verb also occurs in a similar context in another passage, more often it refers to death.

2.4   Discussion

Experiential situations are of many disparate types, and it is not easy to generalize on them. Their multifaceted nature is reflected in the variety of constructions that can encode experiential situations cross-linguistically. In this perspective, Homeric Greek may appear at first sight quite exceptional, as it shows a clear tendency toward a consistent nominative alignment with respect to the encoding of the experiencer. In particular, as will be discussed in detail in the next Chapters, different constructions with nominative experiencers show clear affinities with specific verb classes. To the contrary, constructions with dative experiencers are not only limited as to their distribution, they also occur with verbs of different classes, and do not seem to be connected with any verb class (see especially Section 3.2.7).

In this framework, one important point needs to be highlighted: even though most experiential situations involve two participants, there is a fundamental asymmetry between the experiencer and the stimulus, possibly more significant than the asymmetry between proto-agents and proto-patients in other types of situations (see Primus 2011 on the properties of proto-roles, in particular of proto-agents and proto-patients). This might look like an obvious fact, but it must be kept in mind when accounting for construction variation in a language, such as Homeric Greek, in which the experiencer is virtually always encoded in the same way, that is, as a nominative subject, while the stimulus is subject to variation. Still, the experiencer is much more prominent than the stimulus, and, being mostly a human being, much more interesting for speakers than the stimulus, which is often inanimate. Consequently, even if it is the coding of the stimulus that varies, one needs to ask oneself how this type of variation affects the construal of the experiencer role. I will go deeper into this issue in Section 3.1.1.

CHAPTER 3

Argument Structure Constructions in Homeric Greek

This Chapter is devoted to argument structure constructions, their general properties, and their distribution and meaning in Homeric Greek. In Section 3.1, I provide a brief survey of various properties of constructions especially relevant when discussing argument structure with Ancient Greek verbs, partly anticipated in Section 1.2, and illustrate the discussion with examples from the Homeric poems. I then proceed to discuss construction variation in Homeric Greek. As most experiential situations typically involve two participants, they are most often encoded by two-place verbs, that is, they occur in constructions that include a set of two arguments. For this reason, as pointed out in Chapter 1, I focus especially on constructions of two-place verbs, which, as I show in Section 3.2, allow for a wide range of variation. Verbs of volition and, to varying extents, verbs of cognition and perception may take sentential complements (see Sections 5.2 and 7). Even though Homeric Greek complementation remains outside the scope of this book, it will be briefly treated in Section 3.3.

Bodily sensations, which are mostly conceived as involving only the experiencer, are encoded by one-place verbs. In Homeric Greek, this group of situations is typically encoded by intransitive verbs with nominative experiencers, as *dipsáō* in (63) (more occurrences will be discussed in Chapter 5). One-place verbs that take non-nominative arguments of the type illustrated in the German example (48) are not attested in Homeric Greek.

(63) *steûto*   *dè   dipsáōn,*   *piéein*
     appear.IMPF.M/P.3SG PTC be_thirsty.PTCP.PRS.NOM drink.INF.AOR
     d'   ouk   eîkhen   *helésthai*
     PTC NEG have.IMPF.3SG take.INF.AOR.MID
     'He looked thirsty, but couldn't take a drink.' (*Od.* 11.584)

The causative verb *mimnéskō* 'remind' is a three-place verb, and takes the NomAccGen construction, with an accusative second argument and a genitive third argument, as shown in (64).

(64) *mēdé me*   *toútōn*   *mímnēsk'*
     NEG 1SG.ACC DEM.GEN.PL remind.IMP.PRS.2SG
     'Don't remind me of this.' (*Od.* 14.168–169)

© SILVIA LURAGHI, 2021 | DOI:10.1163/9789004442528_004

ARGUMENT STRUCTURE CONSTRUCTIONS IN HOMERIC GREEK 49

This and other causative verbs are discussed in Chapter 9.

3.1 Properties of Constructions

In this Section, I tackle a number of issues raised by Construction Grammar and its implications when one applies it to specific verbs and argument structures in Ancient Greek. I start by discussing how construction alternation affects the meaning of a verb (Section 3.1.1). I then address the issue of construction polysemy and homonymy (Section 3.1.2), and show how known diachronic processes underlie the synchronic distribution of constructions in Homer. Finally, I show how NPs that bear the same type of morphological encoding are understood as belonging or not to a specific construction based on lexical meaning (Section 3.1.3).

3.1.1 *Different Argument Structures with the Same Verb*

In Section 1.2, I compared Levin's (1985) approach to verbal semantics, which views verbs as having different meanings that enable them to occur in different constructions, with Goldberg's (1995) approach, which highlights the crucial contribution of different argument structures to the global meaning of a whole construction, built up by the verb and the argument structure.

Let us illustrate this latter view with some Greek examples. The verb *orégomai* 'reach, aim at, hit' in Homer may indicate two different types of situations in which an agent hits or tries to hit another participant. Depending on the construction, and in particular on whether the second argument is an accusative or a genitive NP, the latter participant is depicted as being reached or simply aimed at, as shown in examples (65)-(67) with the accusative and (68) and (69) with the genitive.

(65) *orexámenos*   *prumnòn*   *skélos*
     reach.PTCP.AOR.MID.NOM extreme.ACC leg.ACC
     'Hitting (him) upon the base of the leg.' (*Il.* 16.314)

(66) *hoppóterós ke phthêisin*   *orexámenos*
     which.NOM PTC precede.SBJV.AOR.3SG reach.PTCP.AOR.MID.NOM
     khróa   *kalón, psaúsei*   *d' endínōn*
     flesh.ACC fair.ACC touch.SBJV.PRS.3SG PTC interior.GEN.PL
     'Which of the two will first reach the other's fair flesh and touch the inward parts.' (*Il.* 23.805–806)

(67) *toû*   *d'*   *antítheos*   *Thrasumédēs*   *éphthē*
DEM.GEN PTC godlike.NOM Thrasymedes.NOM overtake.AOR.3SG
orexámenos   *prìn*   *outásai,*   *ou*   *d'*
reach.PTCP.AOR.MID.NOM before wound.INF.AOR NEG PTC
aphámarten,   *ômon*
miss.AOR.3SG shoulder.ACC
'But godlike Thrasymedes was quicker to hit his shoulder before he could wound (him). He did not miss.' (*Il.* 16.321–323)

(68) *hṑs eipṑn*   *ou*   *paidòs*   *oréxato*
so speak.PTCP.AOR.NOM NEG child.GEN reach.AOR.MID.3SG
phaídimos   *Héktōr*
glorious.NOM Hector.NOM
'So saying, glorious Hector could not reach his boy.' (*Il.* 6.466)

(69) *Aías*   *d'*   *hormēthéntos*   *oréxato*
Aias.NOM PTC rush.PTCP.AOR.PASS.GEN reach.AOR.MID.3SG
dourì   *phaienôi*   *Héktoros*   *all'*   *oú*   *pēi*   *khroòs*
spear.DAT bright.DAT Hector.GEN but NEG PTC flesh.GEN
eísato
reach.AOR.MID.3SG
'But Aias aimed with his bright spear at Hector as he rushed, yet in no wise did he reach (his) flesh.' (*Il.* 13.190–191)

In example (65), in which the argument structure contains an accusative second argument, the referent of the NP, the hero's leg, is actually reached. An accusative NP also occurs in (66), in which the event of hitting/reaching, in spite of being located in the future, is envisaged as inevitable. In (67), the accusative NP indicates that the enemy's shoulder has been reached, as is also made clear in the following clause that emphasizes the information that Thrasymedes' stroke did not miss. In example (68), we find a genitive NP as a second argument co-occurring with a negation: here Hector is said to try to reach his child, who shrinks back in fear of his father's armor. Similarly in (69) Aiax is described as hurling his spear at Hector and failing to reach him. However, the genitive does not necessarily imply that the target is not reached: it simply indicates that the situation ensuing from the hurling is not specified.

Notably, when used without a second argument, the verb has no clear implication of reaching or missing a destination, as shown in (70).

ARGUMENT STRUCTURE CONSTRUCTIONS IN HOMERIC GREEK

(70) *tris   mèn oréxat'   ión,   tò   dè*
Thrice PTC reach.AOR.MID.3SG go.PTCP.PRS.NOM DEM.NOM PTC
tétraton híketo   tékmōr
fourth   reach.AOR.MID.3SG goal.ACC
'Three times he made a stride as he was going, and with the fourth he reached his goal.' (*Il.* 13.20)

Example (70) shows that it is one of the specific argument structures, either containing an accusative or a genitive second argument that completes the verbal semantics, giving a certain meaning to the resulting construction built up by the verb plus the argument structure. These are occurrences of the NomAcc and of the NomGen construction, in which the subject (the first argument or proto-agent) is always in the nominative case.

Another verb that occurs with both constructions is *epimaíomai*. Let us consider the meaning of the complex constructions resulting from the occurrence of this verb with either argument structure construction in (71)-(74).

(71) *Hḗrē   dè mástigi thoôs epemaíet'   ár'*
Hera.NOM PTC lash.DAT swiftly strive.IMPF.M/P.3SG PTC
híppous
horse.ACC.PL
'And Hera swiftly touched the horses with the lash.' (*Il.* 5.748)

(72) *hòs ára min   phaménē   rhábdōi*
SO PTC 3SG.ACC say.PTCP.PRS.M/P.NOM wand.DAT
epemássat'   Athḗnē
strive.AOR.MID.3SG Athena.NOM
'So saying, Athena touched him with her wand.' (*Od.* 13.429)

(73) *autàr Odusseùs   kheír'   epimassámenos   phárugos*
but   Odysseus.NOM hand.DAT strive.PTCP.AOR.MID.NOM throat.GEN
lábe   dexiterêphi
take.AOR.3SG by_right
'But Odysseus, feeling for the woman's throat, seized (it) with his right hand.' (*Od.* 19.479–480)

(74) *toi   megálōn   dṓrōn   epemaíeto   thumós*
2SG.DAT great.GEN.PL gift.GEN.PL strive.IMPF.M/P.3SG heart.NOM
'Your heart strived for magnificent gifts.' (*Il.* 10.401)

Similar to *orégomai*, only in conjunction with the NomAcc construction does *epimaíomai* indicate a situation in which a participant touches another participant, as shown in examples (71) and (72). In example (73), Odysseus tries to touch the nurse's throat, and only thereafter gets hold of it. In example (74), the subject *thumós* 'heart, soul' suggests reference to an experiential situation: the verb and its arguments indicate a strong desire to get possession of some goods, but there is no information about the actual getting hold of the goods by the experiencer.

Summing up, comparison of the two verbs and the different constructions shows that it is the NomAcc construction that adds the meaning of reaching a certain target. With the NomGen, and in the case of *orégomai* with the Nom (monovalent) construction, both verbs indicate a situation in which a participant aims, or tries to reach or get hold of an entity. Whether the target is reached or not can be specified in the subsequent context, while in case the NomAcc construction occurs no further specification needs to be added, and the target is necessarily reached. We can thus conclude that the NomGen and the NomAcc constructions are contentful, as the English constructions discussed in Goldberg (1995).

How do these constructions contribute to the verb's meaning? This question will be thoroughly discussed in Section 3.2, but for the time being some remarks concerning the meaning of the two constructions are worth anticipating. The NomAcc construction is typical of change-of-state verbs, and implies a highly transitive interpretation of the complex verb plus arguments. The NomGen construction has a complex meaning that I will illustrate in Section 3.2. Among other things, it occurs with verbs of displacement and verbs that mean 'miss', such as *hamartánō* in (67) and (108), see the discussion in Sections 3.2.2 and 3.2.6. Crucially, however, it does not have the implication of high transitivity brought about by the NomAcc construction. It sporadically occurs with change-of-state verbs, but in this case it indicates that only a part of a referent is affected by the action and actually undergoes the change of state (see Section 3.2.6). Hence, it does not necessarily add information as to the result of the action ensuing from the attempt to reach a target or get hold of an object, but may leave the situation open.

In general, it is the partitive meaning of the genitive (see Section 3.2.6) which is assumed to be at play here: by indicating partial or low affectedness, the genitive implies a lower degree of transitivity, as in cases in which an intended result is depicted as not having been reached. While this is certainly the case, the meaning of the whole construction has implications not only on the construal of the second participant, or proto-patient, as being subject to a lower degree of affectedness when it occurs in the NomGen construction than when occurring in the NomAcc construction.

Importantly, as pointed out by Malchukov (2005), constructions that imply low affectedness in the proto-patient also imply lower agentivity for the first participant, or proto-agent. Indeed, an occurrence such as (68) in which the verb *orégomai* 'reach' occurs with the NomGen construction and implies that the first participant tried to reach the second, but could not, construes the proto-agent as less agentive than the proto-agent in (65), with the NomAcc construction implying that the proto-patient is actually reached. The first participant in the latter occurrence has full control over the state of affairs, which is depicted as accomplished, while in (68) the first participant has a lower degree of control, as the result is not achieved.

This part of the meaning of the construction that focuses on the first participant is the channel that allows the extension of the construction of highly transitive verbs to experiential situations, in which it is normally not the case that one can speak of degrees of affectedness for the proto-patient, which functions as stimulus with experiential verbs. On the other hand, experiencers are variously construed in terms of possible control, which in the domain of experience is reflected by awareness, attention and by the type of mental involvement of the experiencer in different types of experiential situations, as I will argue in connection with construction variation across sub-domains of experience.

3.1.2 Polysemy of Constructions

As I have discussed in Section 1.2, Goldberg (1995) makes a point for viewing constructions as polysemic, rather than positing a single abstract meaning from which more specific meanings are derived. Goldberg illustrates her point with examples from synchronic polysemy of constructions in English but, as I have already mentioned, knowledge from diachronic processes can shed light on the structure of specific patterns of polysemy. In addition, as I pointed out in Section 1.2, Goldberg (2006) also acknowledges the possibility of constructional homonymy, that is, of the occurrence of formally identical structures that instantiate different constructions with different meanings, and highlights the importance of verbal semantics to discriminate among them. In this Section, I will show how the synchronic distribution of constructions in Homeric Greek resulted from well-known diachronic changes that took place before this stage of the Greek language, and how the occurrence of formally identical argument structures with different classes of verbs can better be accounted for either in terms of polysemy or in terms of homonymy.

Let us start by considering some occurrences of the NomDat construction, such as (75)-(77).

(75) hōs d' hót' anèr híppoisi kelētízein eù
as PTC when man.NOM horse.DAT.PL ride.INF.PRS well
eidṓs
know.PTCP.PRF.NOM
'As a man well-skilled in riding horses.' (*Il.* 15. 679)

(76) péphnon laòn áriston, amúnōn Argeíoisin
slay.AOR.1SG host.ACC best.ACC protect.PTCP.PRS.NOM Argive.DAT.PL
'I slew the best of the host in defense of the Argives.' (*Od.* 11.500)

(77) stê dè mésēi agorêi
stand.AOR.3SG PTC middle.DAT assembly.DAT
'He stood in the middle of the assembly.' (*Od.* 2.37)

As I will discuss further in Section 3.2, verbs such as 'ride', 'defend' and 'stand' take the NomDat construction for reasons that are best explained on the diachronic plane. Indeed, the NomDat construction occurs with classes of verbs that are semantically quite distant because it historically results from the merger of three earlier constructions that we can reconstruct as NomDat, *NomLoc, and *NomInstr. This merger is due to case syncretism, by which the dative merged with the locative case and later with the instrumental case inherited from Proto-Indo-European, as illustrated in detail in Sections 3.2.1 and 3.2.2. It brought about a cross-linguistically infrequent polysemy involving the dative, which indicates semantic roles typical of human beings, such as recipient and beneficiary, and the instrumental. Even though semantic motivations can be found for this development, such motivations were hardly available to speakers and, as we will see in Section 3.2, new patterns of polysemy emerged, partly at odds with the diachronic origin of specific argument structures. Often, polysemy of the NomDat construction can be disambiguated only in association with specific groups of verbs and specific lexemes. In other words, it is not the construction alone that adds its meaning to the verb, but the verb that selects one of the meanings of the construction, often in association with lexical features of the NPs that function as fillers in the construction.

Especially in the case of verbs that require spatial specifications, such as *hístēmi* 'stand' in (77), the three argument structures of two-place verbs, that is, NomAcc, NomDat and NomGen, acquire their meaning only in connection with specific verbs. This issue will be illustrated and discussed at length in Section 3.2.1, in which I will argue that in such cases we must reckon with constructional homonymy, rather than polysemy.

ARGUMENT STRUCTURE CONSTRUCTIONS IN HOMERIC GREEK

3.1.3 *How to Recognize Argument Structure Constructions*

Lexical meaning, based on referential features of participants, can indicate whether NPs coded in the same manner instantiate a specific argument structure construction or not. Let us consider the dative NPs in example (78).

(78) *kaí   ken   egṑ   epéessi   kaì   athanátoisi*
  even PTC 1SG.NOM word.DAT.PL even immortal.DAT.PL
  makhoímēn,   égkheï   d'   argaléon
  fight.OPT.PRS.M/P.1SG sword.DAT PTC hard.ACC
  'I too with words could fight even the immortals, but with the spear it would be hard.' (*Il.* 20.367–368)

The passage in (78) features three dative NPs, *epéssi* and *égkheï* that I translated as instrumental 'with/by words' and 'by spear', and *athanátoisi* 'the immortals' that I took as the second argument of the verb *mákhomai* 'fight'. This verb is part of a sizable group of verbs that take the NomDat construction, with human (or divine) second arguments, and indicate various types of situations in which human beings interact with each other: inherently reciprocal situations such as fighting, situations featuring asymmetrical relations such as helping, and so on (see Sections 3.2.3 and 3.2.5). I call these verbs 'verbs of social interaction', as they refer to situations that necessarily involve at least two human beings. (Note that the verb *mákhomai* can also refer to an activity, and occur without a second argument: in this case, it takes the Nom (monovalent) construction.)

From the point of view of the semantic frame of the verb, more information can be added, including the place and time of the fight and, importantly for the present discussion, the instrument used for fighting. In Ancient Greek, the default way of encoding the instrument role is the dative case (Luraghi 1989, 1996, 2003a). Remarkably, this does not create ambiguity with possible second arguments of verbs of social interaction, as the animacy feature fulfills a disambiguating function: our common knowledge about the structure of events and the properties of participants tells us that instruments are typically inanimate and most often concrete. Note that in (78) we find a concrete instrument, the sword, typically used for fighting, and an abstract one, words. A common metaphor by which discussion is understood as a fight (Lakoff and Johnson 1980) ensures our proper understanding of the situation.

When non-prototypical instruments occur, notably human beings, Homer offers two options. Either we find some special type of groups of humans that are typically manipulated, such as soldiers. In this case, dative encoding can also be used. Such pluralities of human beings are subordinated to some other superior human being, and used for the purposes of the latter: accordingly, they can be conceived as instruments. Or we can find individual human beings. In this latter case, the participant is conceived as a secondary agent, and, in Homer, it is encoded in the same way as a passive agent (Luraghi 2003a: 228). Hence, no confusion can arise between non-prototypical human instruments and third argument datives. Verbs such as *mákhomai* show that properties of participants can be specified in the meaning of the construction, and that fillers with specific features are requested, in order to fill in a construction's slots.

Some more words deserve to be spent on the functions of the instrumental dative as a syntactic adjunct. Depending on the type of situation, mainly on its controlled or uncontrolled nature, and on the type of NP, whether it refers to a manipulated entity or not, dative adjuncts can encode not only the semantic roles of instrument or means, but also other types of related semantic roles, such as reason as in (79) and cause, as in (80) (see Chantraine 1977: 76–77; De La Villa 1989, Luraghi 1989, 2003a: 68–72).

(79) *ou   mèn gàr philótētí   g'   ekeúthanon*
     NEG PTC PTC friendship.DAT PTC hide.IMPF.3PL
     'Not even for friendship would they have hidden (him).' (*Il.* 3.453)

(80) *pántes   mèn stugeroì   thánatoi   deiloîsi*
     all.NOM.PL PTC horrible.NOM.PL death.NOM.PL wretched.DAT.PL
     brotoîsi   limôi   d'   oíktiston   thanéein
     mortal.DAT.PL hunger.DAT PTC most.pityable.NOM die.INF.AOR
     'All types of death are horrible for the wretched mortals, but to die of hunger is the most pitiful.' (*Od.* 12.341–342)

In (79), the verb refers to a controlled situation, and the dative *philótētí* 'friendship' is an abstract noun that encodes the reason for the first participant to refrain from performing a certain action. Note that an interpretation of the dative NP as functioning as reason rather than as instrument or means is supported by its lexical meaning. In (80) *limôi thanéein* 'die of hunger (dat)' is an uncontrolled situation, hence the interpretation of the dative NP as encoding cause.

This wide semantic spectrum covered by the dative is relevant for the construction of verbs of rejoicing, as argued in Section 8.1.2.

3.2 Constructions and Construction Variation with Two-Place Verbs

Homeric Greek (and Ancient Greek in general) shows nominative, rather than dative alignment for the experiencer (see the extensive discussion in Viti 2017). Experiential verbs that feature dative experiencers and nominative stimuli exist, but they are a small minority. With such verbs, the context of individual occurrences may point toward a higher prominence of either participant, as argued in Section 3.2.7.

Constructions with non-nominative experiencers and non-nominative stimuli do not occur in Homeric Greek. They are attested in later authors, though for a limited number of verbs, including *mélō* 'care for, be of interest', *metamélō* 'repent', *deî* 'need', *elleípō* 'fall short of' (see Conti 2010a, b). In Classical Greek, these verbs may occasionally occur in the third person singular, and take a DatGen construction, with a dative experiencer and a genitive stimulus. However, they occur more frequently in other constructions, as shown in Conti (2010a). In particular, the verbs *mélō* is also attested in Homeric Greek with constructions that feature dative experiencers and nominative stimuli, while the verb *déō* normally occurs in the NomGen construction, and means 'miss', 'feel the need', as in (81). The impersonal form *deî* occurs only once, in (82) (see Chantraine 1977: 270).

(81) *ou   dé   ti   thumòs   edeúeto   daitòs*
     NEG PTC INDF.ACC heart.NOM need.IMPF.M/P.3SG food.GEN
     eîsēs
     abundant.GEN
     '(His) heart did not need abundant food.' (*Il.* 1.468)

(82) *tí   dè   deî   polemizémenai Trṓessin*
     INT.ACC PTC need.IMPF.3SG fight.INF.PRS Trojan.DAT.PL
     Argeíous?
     Argive.ACC.PL
     'Why did the Argives need to fight the Trojans?' (*Il.* 9.337–338)

Note that in (81) the form *deî* takes the non-finite clause as subject, and the accusative noun phrase *Argeíous* 'the Argives' is the subject of the infinitive (so-called AcI clause; see Section 3.3). I return to this verb in Section 5.2.

In constructions with nominative experiencers, stimuli can be encoded in different ways. With two-place verbs three constructions are available: NomAcc, NomDat and NomGen. None of these constructions is typical only of experiential verbs. For this reason, I will now discuss the meaning of each construction, by surveying the classes of verbs that it occurs with. I will show that two-argument constructions with nominative first arguments, which will call Nom-first constructions, are highly polysemous, as they can refer to situations involving spatial relations (both motion and static events) or other more abstract relations. I will argue that polysemy can be explained diachronically. Synchronically, different meanings of constructions are often activated by lexical features of the verbs that pair with them. In particular, I will argue that the three constructions are underspecified for spatial meaning: the latter is generally activated by the occurrence of verbal prefixes or by specific features of verbal semantics, as I will show in Section 3.2.2. Hence, as I will suggest, we should reckon with homonymous constructions, with homonymy being disambiguated by the verb's meaning, often in conjunction with the meaning of the NPs that function as fillers of the constructions.

When occurring with verbs that do not activate their spatial meaning, the three constructions show clear affinities with different verb classes. In Section 3.2.3 I discuss the frequency of the three constructions with verbs, both in terms of type and in terms of token frequency, before devoting Sections 3.2.4, 3.2.5 and 3.2.6 to an in-depth analysis of the distribution of the three constructions across verb classes. In Section 3.2.8 I provide an interim summary of the meanings of argument structure constructions with two-place verbs in Homeric Greek.

3.2.1   The Sub-system of Local Cases

Greek cases are highly polysemous morphemes. Traditionally, polysemy is explained diachronically as the outcome of case syncretism, understood here as a diachronic process that involves the merger of inflectional categories, following the definition in Bloomfield (1933: 388).

Due to case syncretism, the Greek dative results from the merger of the Indo-European dative, locative, and instrumental, while the genitive results from the merger of the Indo-European genitive and ablative. Indeed, comparative evidence shows that syncretism is well attested in the morphology of the Greek dative, whose endings variously correspond to the endings of the dative, the locative and the instrumental in other ancient Indo-European languages. For example, the dative plural shows various allomorphs, partly also within the same inflectional class, that correspond to the instrumental plural of other ancient Indo-European languages, such as *-ois* (one of the allomorphs available for the *-o-* stems) corresponding to Sanskrit *-ais*, instrumental plural ending of the *-a-* stems (note that /o/ > /a/ in Indo-Aryan), and other endings that correspond to the locative plural, like *-si* (one of the possible allomorphs for consonant stems) corresponding to Sanskrit *-su*, Old

ARGUMENT STRUCTURE CONSTRUCTIONS IN HOMERIC GREEK 59

Church Slavic -*xi*, both locative plural endings (see Schwyzer 1950; Chantraine 1973; Luraghi 2004a).

Things are somewhat different for the genitive, as a separate ablative ending can be reconstructed only for the singular of -*o*- stems in Proto-Indo-European. Elsewhere, the ablative has the same ending of the genitive in the singular, while it falls together with the dative in the plural of all inflectional classes in the Ancient Indo-European languages that attest to these cases. However, the ablative ending of the -*o*- stems is not attested in Greek nominal paradigms, as the genitive singular of -*o*- stems derives from the pronominal inflection, so the merger of the two cases can be assessed only on functional evidence (see further Meiser 1992).

As a result of case syncretism, the dative and the genitive acquired a spatial function, that of a locative and of an ablative respectively. Notably, however, in Ancient Greek the plain dative and the plain genitive could function as a locative and as an ablative to different extents. The locative NomDat construction in Homer occurs with toponyms as in (83); it can also occur with nouns that have spatial reference or refer to social location, as defined in Luraghi (2003a: 66), such as *agorêi* 'at the assembly', *trapézēi* 'at (one's) table', *makhêi* 'in battle': these are nouns that denote places or event in which social life takes place in the Homeric poems. In all these cases, prepositional phrases are always a possible option as shown in (84) (see the detailed account in Luraghi 2017).

(83) *patḕr   d'   emòs   Árgeï   násthē*
   father.NOM PTC POSS.1SG.NOM Argos.DAT abide.AOR.PASS.3SG
   'My father lived in Argos.' (*Il.* 14.119)

(84) *kaí ken en Árgei   eoûsa*
   and PTC in Argos.DAT be.PTCP.PRS.NOM
   'Then, though being in Argos, ...' (*Il.* 6.456)

Conversely, the NomGen construction has a much more restricted use as an ablative. In fact, if a NomGen construction with spatial reference occurs with a verb that does not by its meaning require a source expression, it indicates static location, in much the same way as the locative NomDat construction, as shown in (85). In addition, a genitive NP can also function independently as a locative adverbial, even if the verb has no slots for any type of spatial argument, as in (86).

(85) *ê   ouk Árgeos   éen...?*
   PTC NEG Argos.GEN be.IMPF.3SG
   'Was he not in Argos?' (*Od.* 3.251)

(86) *hína mḗ... ḕ halòs ḕ epì gês algésete*
    for   NEG   or sea.GEN or on land.GEN suffer.FUT.2PL
    'In order for you not to suffer, either at sea or on land.' (*Od.* 12.26–27)

A comparison of examples (83) and (85) shows that there is some overlap between NomDat and NomGen in the locative construction. Example (86) further shows that the locative meaning of a genitive NP is not triggered by a verb that requires a locative argument, as it is the case for the dative, which can be taken as indicating a locative only when it functions as a second argument within the NomDat construction with a specific set of verbs (see Section 3.2.2). This state of affairs is connected with the original partitive meaning of the genitive, which was very productive in Homer (see Conti and Luraghi 2014 for a full account), and also partly accounts for possible overlap of the NomDat and the NomGen construction with various types of two-place verbs, as I argue in Section 3.2.6. On the other hand, the ablative NomGen construction can only occur when its meaning is activated by the verb, that is, with verbs that take source preverbs, or with some verbs that profile the source, as shown in Section 3.2.2 (see further Luraghi 2017).

No allative case is reconstructed for Proto-Indo-European. However, the ancient Indo-European languages attest to possible use of the accusative case as an allative. This is also the case in Homeric Greek, though to a limited extent, as the allative NomAcc construction only occurs with toponyms or the word for 'home', and is most often connected with verbs that mean 'reach', 'arrive (at)' (see De Boel 1988; Luraghi 2017). Even with toponyms one most often finds prepositional phrases. Compare (87) and (88).

(87) *epeì polloì ísan anéres hēméteron*
    as   many.NOM.PL come.IMPF.3PL man.NOM.PL POSS.1PL.ACC
    dô
    home.ACC
    'As many men came to our home.' (*Od.* 1.176)

(88) *prôta mèn es Púlon elthé*
    first PTC to Pylos.ACC go.IMP.AOR.2SG
    'First go to Pylos!' (*Od.* 1.284)

Thus, the NomAcc construction has a double function in Homeric Greek: on the one hand, it occurs with transitive verbs, most typically indicating change of state, while on the other hand it has a spatial function as an allative construction. This double function was inherited from PIE, as comparative evidence suggests. As a Greek development following case syncretism, the accusative, the dative and the genitive came to constitute a three-fold subsystem of local cases, replacing the original sub-system of PIE constituted by the allative accusative, the locative and the ablative. This is partly visible with some prepositions (notably *pará*, see Luraghi 2009), but especially with two-place verbs that, due to their semantics or to the occurrence of a spatial prefix (preverb), refer to situations that involve some spatial relation, as I argue in Section 3.2.2.

3.2.2 *Argument Structure Constructions with Verbs Requiring Spatial Specifications*
The allative NomAcc construction typically occurs with motion verbs, and indicates that the first participant moves in the direction of the second participant. Inherently directional verbs are *híkō* and *hikánō* 'arrive at', 'reach', as in (89).

(89) *hē   d'   ára Kúpron   híkane*
     DEM.NOM PTC PTC Cyprus.ACC go.AOR.3SG
     'She went to Cyprus.' (*Od.* 8.362)

In general, Ancient Greek motion verbs are not deictic: the three most frequent motion verbs, *baínō*, *érkhomai* and *eîmi*, can mean 'come' or 'go' depending on the type of spatial argument they take and, most frequently, on the semantics of possible preverbs, that is, verbal satellites in terms of Talmy's (2000) typology of lexicalization patterns for motion events (see further Iacobini et al. 2017).

Preverbs constitute a peculiar word class in the Indo-European languages (Pinault 1995, Booij and Van Kemenade 2003, Zanchi 2019). In origin, they were local adverbs that could modify the verb or one of the noun phrases occurring in a sentence. In most Indo-European languages, preverbs show a two-fold development, into verbal prefixes and into adpositions, most often prepositions, and lost their function as free adverbs: this was the situation in Classical Greek. In Homeric Greek, the development was still ongoing, and the local particles could function as adverbs, preverbs or adpositions (often postposed, rather than preposed as in later Greek), with occurrences in which discriminating among the functions is hardly possible (see especially Chantraine 1981: 82–84; Luraghi 2003a: 75–76; Haug 2009 and cf. further the discussion of example (181) in Section 6.1). Hence, when combined with goal or source preverbs, motion verbs such as *baínō*, *érkhomai* and *eîmi* acquire a directional meaning, either by profiling the goal or by profiling the source, and accordingly take constructions that contain an accusative or a genitive second argument. So for example with the NomAcc construction one finds verbs such as *eisbaínō* 'go to', *eisérkhomai* 'go to' both compound with the preverb *eis/es* 'to', 'toward' (see Luraghi 2017).

The locative NomDat construction frequently occurs with posture verbs as in (77), or verbs that indicate static relations, such as *naíō* 'abide' in (83). Note however that even in these cases the referent of the dative NP is one of those described in Section 3.2.1, which indicate locative concepts. More often, the NomDat construction occurs with prefixed verbs that contain preverbs which, combining with the verbal meaning, indicate some static spatial relation, such as *éphēmai* 'be sitting upon', various compounds of *eimí* 'be', such as *éneimi* 'be in', *épeimi* 'remain', *méteimi* 'be among', *páreimi* 'be beside', *húpeimi* 'be under'. Prefixed perfect forms of *baínō* 'go', which in the perfect has the resultative meaning of 'be located', 'stand', also take the locative NomDat construction, as shown in (90), in which the perfect of the verb *parabaínō* 'walk by, walk past' means 'stand by'.

(90) *Kebriónēs   dè   Trôas   orinoménous*
Cebriones.NOM PTC Trojan.ACC.PL raise.PTCP.PRS.M/P.ACC.PL
enóēsen   Héktori   parbebaốs
perceive.AOR.3SG Hector.DAT go.PTCP.PRF.NOM
'But Cebriones perceived the Trojans rising as he stood by Hector's side.'
(*Il.* 11.521–522)

In a limited number of occurrences, the NomDat construction can also occur with some directional motion verbs, such as *pḗgnumi* 'fix in, stick' or *bállō* 'throw, cast'. With respect to the NomAcc, the NomDat construction adds the information that the second participant is not only the direction toward which the first moves, but that it represents its prospective location (Luraghi 2003a:66). Notably, this is not only true of bare cases, but it also happens with local PPs with *eis*+acc and *en*+dat (Luraghi 2003a: 83–84). While the latter typically expresses location, it can also occur with the same motion verbs as the NomDat construction. This is the so-called *constructio pregnans*, in which the dative is said to occur 'in the place' of the accusative (see Nikitina and Maslov 2013).

Similar to the NomAcc construction, the NomGen construction consistently occurs with prefixed motion verbs. In this case, we find verbs that take source preverbs such as *apo-* and *ek-*, as for example *apobaínō, apérkhomai, apeîmi* all meaning 'leave, go away from'. Notably, even a verb that profiles the source such as *pheúgō* 'flee' takes the NomGen construction when it is prefixed, while the basic verb is transitive, and takes the NomAcc construction.

ARGUMENT STRUCTURE CONSTRUCTIONS IN HOMERIC GREEK   63

In general, unprefixed verbs that take the NomGen construction can only marginally be considered verbs that require spatial specification. Rather, they are verbs that indicate some lack, and mean 'need', 'miss' or 'lack', such as *khatéō* 'need' in (91), *deúomai* 'lack, miss' in (92), *hamartánō* 'miss' in (67) and (108), and the form *khrḗ* 'need', 'ought to' in (93).

(91) *pántes   dè   theôn   khatéous'   ánthrōpoi*
     all.NOM.PL PTC god.GEN.PL need.PRS.3PL man.NOM.PL
     'All men need the gods.' (*Od.* 3. 48)

(92) *ou   gár moí   pote   bōmòs   edeúeto   daitòs*
     NEG PTC 1SG.DAT never altar.NOM lack.IMPF.M/P.3SG banquet.GEN
     eísēs   loibês   te   knísēs   te
     equal.GEN drink.GEN PTC savor.GEN PTC
     'My altar was never lacking of the equal banquet, of the drink and of the savor (*sc.* of burnt).' (*Il.* 24. 69–70).

(93) *aphraíneis   Menélae   diotrephés,   ou   dé*
     be_mad.PRS.2SG Menelaos.VOC nurtured_by_Zeus.VOC NEG PTC
     tí   se   khrḕ taútēs   aphrosúnēs
     INDF.ACC 2SG.ACC need DEM.GEN madness.GEN
     'You are mad, Menelaos, nurtured by Zeus, and this madness is of no use for you.' (*Il.* 7.109–110)

(The form *khrḗ* occurs 54 times in the Homeric poems. In Homeric Greek, it is an invariable form of nominal origin, possibly neuter, which is only attested in this form. Later it served as base for various verbal and nominal derivate Chantraine 1977: 1272–1275. As such it does not display verbal categories, and occurs in impersonal constructions most often with an AcI clause. In spite of this, it occurs with the NomGen construction in a small number of cases; see further Section 5.1.) As I argue in Section 3.2.2, these verbs provide the connection between spatial and non-spatial meanings of the NomGen construction.

To sum up, the three constructions indicate spatial relations in the vast majority of cases when they occur with prefixed verbs: for this reason, it has been assumed by some scholars that the preverb governs the case in such occurrences (see Horrocks 1981). I will not follow this approach here. Rather, from a constructionist point of view, one can view the three constructions as underspecified for spatial meaning. Verbs with spatial preverbs and a limited number of other verbs that profile a specific spatial relation add the required spatial component to the whole construction consisting of the verb itself in conjunction with a specific argument structure. Along with lexical features of the fillers, it triggers the spatial interpretation of the third argument.

Besides the meanings illustrated in this Section, the three constructions also have other meanings that are not directly connected with the function of the three cases in the local sub-system. To these I now turn in Sections 3.2.3-3.2.6.

3.2.3 *Frequency of Nom-first Constructions across Verb Classes*

In this Section I present some data concerning the frequency of specific groups of verbs with each construction, including experiential verbs. As we will see, in spite of the much higher frequency of the NomAcc construction as compared to the other two constructions, clear tendencies to occur with specific groups of verbs and exhibit different semantics depending on the meaning of the verb are detectable for all three.

As a preliminary remark, it must be pointed out that the NomAcc construction, which, as I will illustrate in Section 3.2.4, is typical of highly transitive verbs, does not only occur with verbs that indicate a change of state, but also extends to all types of verbs, regardless of their degree of transitivity. This hints to high productivity: given the high number of change-of-state verbs among two-place verbs, the construction constitutes a sort of default for two-place verbs (see Section 10.4.1). Hence, many experiential verbs, even though they are endowed with a low degree of semantic transitivity, are syntactically transitive, take the NomAcc construction, and can passivize.

The productivity of constructions is defined by Barðdal (2008: 34–57) as resulting from the inverse correlation between type frequency and semantic coherence. She represents the correlation between type frequency and semantic coherence as in Figure 6 (from Barðdal 2008: 35).

In the case of argument structure constructions, type frequency is determined by the number of verbs that take a certain construction. Notably, following this approach, constructions that are regarded as productive are not only those that rely on a high type frequency, but also those that occur in a small set of cases that are all semantically very close. Barðdal (2008: 49) also acknowledges the role of token frequency as enhancing the degree of entrenchment of constructions that are semantically coherent.

Crucial to the concept of productivity as defined above is the degree of extensibility of a construction (Barðdal 2008: 29–33). According to Baayen and Lieber (1991), Baayen (1993), one way to gauge extensibility is by the number of hapaxes, that is, items that only occur once in a corpus. A high number of hapaxes for a certain construction points to its tendency to be extended, hence to its productivity. Note however that the fact that a certain construction is a hapax in a corpus may depend on limits of the corpus or on genre or register

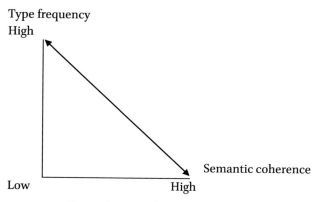

FIGURE 6　The productivity of constructions and the correlation between type frequency and semantic coherence

factors, and this criterion must be used with care when working with a limited corpus such as the Homeric poems.

In general, in a dead language and working basically on the synchronic plane it is difficult to find evidence for a construction's productivity, and this concept must be handled with care. Still, I will argue that the Homeric poems offer evidence for the extension and hence productivity of constructions. I will return to this point in Section 10.4, after having surveyed and analyzed the data. For the time being, suffice it to say that verbs that take the NomDat construction are indeed semantically quite coherent, while semantic coherence is lower for verbs that take the NomGen construction, as I illustrate further on in this Section.

Both the NomDat and the NomGen construction indicate low transitivity, but they do so in different ways. The NomDat construction is limited to verbs that do not indicate change of state. Apart from its meaning with verbs that require some spatial (locative) expression, it is crucially connected with human participants, and is especially used to denote situations in which the second participant is not only affected by the behavior of the first participant, but can potentially respond to it. The NomGen construction, instead, is not connected to any special type of participant, and it is not limited to verbs that do not indicate a change of state. Rather, it can occur with verbs denoting any type of situation, but indicates a partial participation of an entity, i.e. the second participant, in the situation.

In the first place, it is remarkable that the NomAcc construction covers over 73% of verbs, and over 80% of the occurrences with respect to the other two constructions, as shown in Table 4.

TABLE 4 Frequency of constructions

	Number of verbs	Tokens	% of verbs	% of tokens
NomAcc	1161	9829	73.53	80.18
NomDat	211	1221	13.36	9.96
NomGen	207	1208	13.1	9.85
Total	1579	12258		

The data is based on a sample of 1,411 verbs analyzed in Sausa (2015), which covers virtually all two-place verbs in the Homeric poems. The total of 1,579 is higher, because verbs that allow construction variation are counted twice or three times, depending on the number of constructions in which they can occur.

Sausa (2015) shows that over 50% of the verbs that take the NomAcc construction (685 out of 1,161) indicate change of state or change of position. More specifically, verbs of these two types are 685, that is, 59% of the verbs that instantiate the NomAcc construction and 43.38% of the total. Of the other two constructions, only the NomGen occurs with eight change-of-state verbs, while neither the NomGen nor the NomDat construction occurs with verbs that indicate change of position, which are very frequent items in terms of token frequency (*títhēmi* 'put' and *phérō* 'bring' are the third and fourth most frequent verbs with 236 and 196 occurrences respectively according to Sausa 2015). On the other hand, the most frequent bivalent verb in the Homeric poems in terms of token frequency (591 occurrences) in Sausa's (2015) sample is *ékhō* 'have', which is a stative verb and takes the NomAcc construction: this shows that the high frequency of the NomAcc construction is not only connected with the overall frequency of change-of-state or change-of-position verbs.

Verbs that take the NomDat and the NomGen construction are not among the most frequent ones in terms of token frequency. The only verb that reaches 100 occurrences is *peíthō* 'persuade' with the NomDat construction, while the most frequent verb that takes the NomGen construction is *mimnḗskomai* 'remember' with 84 occurrences (the figures refer to occurrences of the verbs mentioned with the argument structure construction overtly realized, not to their total occurrences). In spite of this, the two constructions can be regarded as being well entrenched for semantic reasons (see Sections 3.2.5, 3.2.6 and 3.2.8). As remarked above, especially in the case of the NomDat construction, which is strongly associated with humanness of the second participant and interactive character of the situations in which the participants are involved, one can detect a high degree of semantic coherence among the verbs that typically take it. This association is strengthened by the occurrence of the dative in other constructions, such as for example the NomAccDat with verbs of giving, or with other semantic roles typical of human beings, as discussed in Section 3.2.5.

The NomGen construction, on the other hand, does not show such a strong correlation with any group of verbs. However, the fact that, as I will illustrate in Section 3.2.6, the partitive genitive can occur in other constructions and in any syntactic function including subject, always indicating a reduced degree of participation of a participant in a situation, reinforces the total-partitive opposition instantiated by the possible alternation between the NomAcc and the NomGen construction with two-place verbs. With respect to the NomDat construction, the NomGen shows a distribution which is much more similar to the NomAcc, as it can also occur with change-of-state verbs, and does not show any preference for specific referential features of participants. This closer similarity is reflected in the fact that NomAcc/NomGen alternation with the same verb is frequent, while the vast majority of verbs that take the NomDat construction do not allow alternation. Moreover, the onset of the extension of the passive construction to two-place verbs with non-accusative second arguments can be detected already in Homer with verbs that take the NomGen construction, and only later affected verbs with the NomDat construction (Conti 1998, Luraghi 2010b).

The NomGen construction also shows a less complex semantics than the NomDat construction. Though being polysemous, it expresses meanings that are related through a frequent pattern of polysemy: indeed, genitive, partitive and ablative meanings are often conflated into a single morpheme (see among others Nikiforidou 1991 and several examples in Kuteva et al. 2019). On the other hand, NomDat sets of arguments seem to instantiate more loosely related constructions, one of which is connected with verbs of manipulation and partly to inanimate participants, as we will see in Section 3.2.5.

3.2.4 *The NomAcc Construction: Non-spatial Functions*
In Ancient Greek, as in all Indo-European languages, the accusative is the case of the direct object of transitive verbs, and the use of the NomAcc construction is one of the features of prototypical transitivity. With prototypically transitive verbs, this means that the accusative encodes a participant that undergoes a change of state as a consequence of an action intentionally brought about by an agent (see Kittilä 2002, Næss 2007 and the discussion in Section 2.1). Accordingly, as remarked in Section 3.2.3, change-of-state verbs feature prominently among verbs that take the NomAcc construction. According to Sausa (2015),

around 60% of two-place verbs that take this construction in Homeric Greek indicate a change of state or a change of position. In fact, according to her study, change-of-state verbs virtually only take the NomAcc construction, with a few exceptions, mainly verbs of consumption that can occasionally take the Nom-Gen construction, as I will discuss in Section 3.2.6, and account for about 3,7% of verbs that take the NomGen construction.

Change-of-state verbs do not only contribute to construing the patient as highly affected by the agent's agency, they also have the effect of construing the agent as being in full control of the situation, hence being able to fully achieve the intended effect. In other words, change-of-state verbs denote both a high degree of affectedness on the side of the patient and high degree of agency on the side of the agent (see the discussion in Sections 2.1 and 3.1.1).

Notably, the NomAcc construction also occurs with several other verbs that are not prototypically transitive, but show features of syntactic transitivity: for example, they can be passivized, and even occur with agented passives. This is not a peculiarity of Ancient Greek: in fact, transitive verbs in languages with nominative-accusative alignment do not normally only include prototypically transitive verbs. Much to the contrary, the NomAcc construction shows a high degree of productivity, and tends to extend to all types of verbs, including verbs that do not indicate a change of state. In the first place, second arguments that undergo a change of position in space are treated as those that undergo a change of state, for example with verbs such as 'take', 'move', 'bring', and so on. Verbs that encode events intentionally brought about by an agent take this construction, even if the second participant is not an affected patient, and does not undergo any changes, as with the verb 'look at'. First participants that partly share the properties of agents, notably animacy, or, more in general, participants that are especially prominent in an event tend to be encoded as agents, and trigger the occurrence of the NomAcc construction. This is especially important for the extension of the construction to numerous types of experiential predicates.

In grammatical descriptions of Ancient Greek, the NomAcc construction, being typical of prototypically transitive verbs, is considered to indicate that the second participant—the patient—is highly affected, and indeed it does, at least with change-of-state and change-of-position verbs. On the other hand, scholars have often remarked that in Ancient Greek the NomGen and the Nom-Dat construction indicate low affectedness of the second participant. In fact, while, as noted above, the NomAcc construction due to its high productivity can also occur with verbs that do not indicate a change of state, the NomDat and the NomGen construction only occur with low transitivity verbs, and not with change of state ones (except for a limited number of occurrences of the

ARGUMENT STRUCTURE CONSTRUCTIONS IN HOMERIC GREEK

NomGen construction, see Section 3.2.6). However, besides the common feature of encoding participants that do not undergo a change of state, the two constructions sport a quite different semantics, as I will show in Sections 3.2.5 and 3.2.6.

3.2.5 *The NomDat Construction: Non-spatial Functions*

In the Indo-European languages, the dative is typically associated with semantic roles taken by non-agent human participants. Besides being the case of the third argument of verbs of transfer such as 'give' (recipient), it encodes beneficiary, addressee, experiencer and possessor to a varying extent in all Indo-European languages (Delbrück 1901: 547–559). All these semantic roles can be encoded by the dative in Homeric Greek, as shown in (94)-(96) (see further Luraghi 2010c, 2019).

(94) *soì   d'   Agamémnōn   áxia   dôra*
    2SG.DAT PTC Agamemnon.NOM marvelous.ACC.PL gift.ACC.PL
    dídōsi
    give.PRS.3SG
    'Agamemnon offers you marvelous gifts.' (*Il.* 9.260–261)

(95) *all' áge   moi   tóde   eipè*
    PTC come_on 1SG.DAT DEM.ACC say.IMP.AOR.2SG
    'But come on, tell me this.' (*Od.* 1.169)

(96) *álloisin   dè   súas   siálous   antitállō   édmenai*
    other.DAT.PL PTC pig.ACC.PL fat.ACC.PL feed.PRS.1SG eat.INF.PRS
    'I feed fat pigs for others to eat.' (*Od.* 14.41–42)

In example (94), the dative second person pronoun *soì* indicates a recipient, and it is the third argument in the NomAccDat construction taken by the verb *dídōmi* 'give'. In (95) we find a dative first person pronoun, indicating the addressee of speech with the verb *eîpon* 'tell'. Example (96) contains a beneficiary dative, *álloisin* 'for (the benefit of) others'.

Human participants are versatile: even when they are not agents, they are likely to react to the action that an agent performs with some relation to them. For this reason, the dative is typical of verbs that, one way or another, indicate events in which two human participants are involved, and the one which is not assigned the agent role is still expected to be able to possibly interact in some way with the agent. In fact, aside from verbs that require a locative second argument, the NomDat construction comes almost exclusively with verbs that take human second arguments, and that indicate some sort of situation that typically involves two human beings or groups of human beings. I call these verbs 'social interaction' verbs. They account for 50.5% of the total two-place verbs that take the NomDat construction (including verbs of emotion that take human target stimuli, see Section 8.1.1) according to Sausa (2015).

Social interaction verbs include in the first place verbs indicating inherently reciprocal situations, such as meeting, as for example *antiázō* 'meet with, encounter' and *ántomai* 'meet', opposing someone, as *epórnumi* 'rise against', fighting, like *márnamai* 'fight', *mákhomai* 'fight' and *neikéō* 'quarrel'. Among these verbs, some, as for example *antiázō*, may also take the NomGen construction: most often the choice between the two constructions is based on animacy of the second participant, with inanimate participants being virtually limited to occurrences of the NomGen construction. Verbs of communication, such as, among others, *légō* 'tell', *methomiléō* 'converse with', *metaudáō* 'address', *hupokrínomai* 'reply', also indicate potentially reciprocal situations, as the participants exchange the roles of speaker and addressee during the speech event.

Social interaction verbs also include verbs that indicate an asymmetric relation between or among humans, which can be divided into two groups. In the first group we find verbs of helping and protecting, as for example *arḗgō* 'aid', *amúnō* 'defend, protect', and *arkéō* 'defend'. These verbs indicate events whose outcome is positive for the second participant, who benefits from the action of the first participant, hence sharing the features of the beneficiary role. In the second group, we find verbs whose outcome is not necessarily positive, or might even be negative for the second participant, such as verbs of ruling and commanding, as for example *anássō* 'reign', *árkhō* 'command', *hēgemoneúō* 'command', *hēgéomai* 'lead', *basileúō* 'reign'.

Verbs in the latter group typically admit construction variation, as they can take not only the NomDat construction, but also the NomGen. Note that there is some overlap between the dative and the genitive in locative expressions with toponyms and nouns that indicate spatial regions, as I have already shown in Section 3.2.1. Hence, it is not surprising that the both the NomDat and the NomGen construction can occur with inanimate nouns that indicate spatial regions, including toponyms. More in general, however, in the case of verbs of commanding, animacy constitutes a minor factor in the choice of either construction: with several verbs, alternation is frequent even with human second arguments, as for example with *kráteō* 'rule' or *hēgéomai* 'lead', as shown in (97)-(100).

ARGUMENT STRUCTURE CONSTRUCTIONS IN HOMERIC GREEK 71

(97) *méga   dè   kratéousin   Akhaiôn*
mightily PTC rule.PRS.3PL Achaean.GEN.PL
'And mightily they rule over the Achaeans.' (*Od.* 15.274)

(98) *hó   te   kaì állois   andrási   te   kratéousi*
DEM.NOM.DU PTC and other.DAT.PL man.DAT.PL PTC rule.PRS.3PL
kaì athanátoisi   theoîsi
and immortal.DAT.PL god.DAT.PL
'And they rule over the rest of the mankind as well, and the immortal gods.'
(*Od.* 16.264–265)

(99) *Mḗiosin   aû   Mésthlēs   te   kaì Ántiphos*
Maeonian.DAT.PL again Mesthles.NOM PTC and Antiphus.NOM
hēgēsásthēn
lead.AOR.MID.3DU
'Mesthles and Antiphus led the Maenionans.' (*Il.* 2. 864).

(100) *Sarpēdòn   d'   hēgḗsat'   agakleitôn   epikoúrōn*
Sarpedon.NOM PTC lead.AOR.MID.3SG glorious.GEN.PL ally.GEN.PL
'And Sarpedon led the glorious allies.' (*Il.* 12. 101)

In these examples, the two constructions profile different components of the situation: while the NomDat profiles the social relation between human participants, the NomGen, as we will see in Section 3.2.6, profiles low transitivity and no change of state of the second participant, which is construed as a possible target, in much the same way as with contact verbs of verbs that mean 'aim at' as *orégō* 'aim at' discussed in Section 3.1.1.

Remarkably, historical grammars point toward a different origin for the NomDat construction with sub-groups of verbs of social interaction, as verbs that indicate inherently reciprocal situations are said to take the dative issuing from the comitative function of the PIE instrumental (see Chantraine 1981: 74–75). However, as I argued in Section 3.2, diachronic information is crucially unavailable to speakers. Synchronically, social interaction verbs constitute a unitary group, whose distinctive feature lies in the potentially interactive character of situations that involve two human beings, neither of which is a patient undergoing a change of state. The distinctive features of this group of verbs and its entrenchment constitute an instance of constructional merger, as mentioned in Section 1.2, whereby constructions with multiple origins can give rise to a constructional network whose structure does not necessarily remain the same at all stages (Torrent 2015). In this case, two original constructions involving respectively dative and comitative/instrumental second arguments merged into a single NomDat construction, which shows features of its own, namely the interactive character of the second participant, which do not necessarily match features of the two original constructions.

In addition to verbs discussed thus far, the NomDat construction can also occur with another group of verbs, that is, verbs of manipulation that take inanimate (or non-human) second arguments. Verbs of manipulation are here intended as verbs that indicate a situation in which a participant makes some use of a (mostly inanimate or non-human) entity, without bringing about a change of state in it. This is a consequence of the ancient instrumental case having merged with the dative in Greek. The group of verbs is limited, but this meaning of the construction is relevant for its use with experiential predicates. An occurrence with a two-place verb, *keletízō* 'ride (a horse)' has been given in (75) repeated here for convenience.

(75) *hōs d'   hót'   anḕr   híppoisi   kelētízein   eù*
    as PTC when man.NOM horse.DAT.PL ride.INF.PRS well
    eidṓs
    know.PTCP.PRF.NOM
    'As a man well-skilled in riding horses.' (*Il.* 15. 679)

In (101) the verb *pímplēmi* is a three-place verb with the NomAccDat construction. It can alternate with the NomAccGen construction, as shown in (102). This construction also occurs as NomGen in the medio-passive, as in (103).

(101) *hoì   dè   iakhêi   te   phóbōi te   pásas*
     DEM.NOM.PL PTC scream.DAT PTC fear.DAT PTC all.ACC
     plêsan   hodoús
     fill.AOR.3PL street.ACC
     'And they filled all the streets with screams and fear.' (*Il.* 16.373–374)

(102) *en d'   ónthou   boéou   plêto   stóma   te*
     in PTC dung.GEN bovine.GEN fill.AOR.MID.3SG mouth.ACC PTC
     rhînás   te
     nostril.ACC PTC
     'He filled his nostrils and mouth with bovine dung.' (*Il.* 23.777)

ARGUMENT STRUCTURE CONSTRUCTIONS IN HOMERIC GREEK 73

(103) *méneos   dè   méga   phrénes   amphimélainai*
anger.GEN PTC greatly midriff.NOM.PL black.NOM.PL
pímplant'
fill.PRS.M/P.3PL
'His black heart was completely filled with anger.' (*Od.* 4.661–662)

Even though an in-depth analysis of the meaning of constructions with three-place verbs remains outside the scope of the present discussion, the alternation in (102) and (103) is relevant, as it shows that verbs of manipulation allow for alternation of constructions involving the dative and the genitive. This pattern also occurs with some verbs of bodily sensation, see Section 5.1, and of rejoicing, as discussed in Section 8.1.2.

In Sections 2.1 and 3.1.1, I have argued that the NomAcc and the NomGen construction affect in different ways the construal of the first participant, which is conceived as ranking higher on the agency hierarchy when it is the subject of verbs that take the NomAcc construction and lower with the NomGen construction. How does the agency hierarchy reflect on the NomDat construction? Notably, such verbs do not admit construction variation, with the exception of verbs of ruling and commanding discussed above. This suggests that proto-agents in the NomDat construction are all construed similarly, and indeed this is also suggested by the type of situations in which such participants are involved. Verbs that take the NomDat construction for the most part refer to situations that are intentionally brought about by a human being who is also a controller, such as fighting, communicating with or helping someone. The important feature of these situations, which is relevant for the selection of the NomDat argument structure construction, is their potentially interactive nature, which is a consequence of the fact that they imply two human participants. For this reason, even situations in which intentionality can be irrelevant, as with verbs such as 'meet' or 'encounter', are construed in the same way as other, more likely controlled situations.

Turning now to verbs of manipulation, the second participant being typically inanimate or non-human cannot obviously interact with the first participant. Still, the latter typically retains the features displayed with social interaction verbs, including control and intentionality. The second participant is then construed as being actively employed by the first participant in order to bring about an event. The NomDat construction can then be viewed as a prototypical category, whose features are variously shared by situations encoded by the verbs that take it, as shown in Figure 7 and in Figure 8.

Figure 7 contains a list of features of first and second participants of situations denoted by verbs that take the NomDat construction.

$$\text{FIRST PARTICIPANT} \begin{cases} \text{human} \\ \text{acts intentionally} \\ \text{controller} \\ \text{interacts with proto-patient} \end{cases} \quad \text{SECOND PARTICIPANT} \begin{cases} \text{human} \\ \text{interacts with proto-agent} \\ \text{profits from/is affected by the situation} \\ \text{contributes to bringing about event} \end{cases}$$

FIGURE 7   Features of participants in the NomDat construction

In Figure 8 I show how groups of verbs distantiate themselves from the prototype, though sharing some of its features.

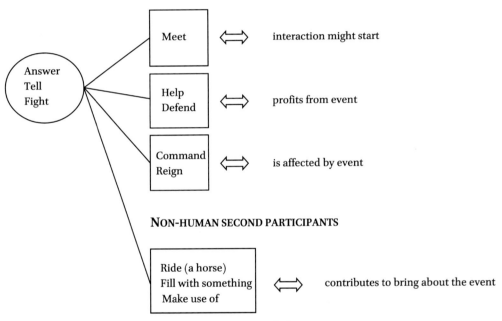

FIGURE 8   NomDat constructions as a prototypical category

Verbs that indicate inherently reciprocal situations and verbs of communication are taken as expressing the core meaning of the construction. Remarkably, such verbs indicate situations that can be brought about only by the joint action of both participants, and not by the first participant (proto-agent) alone. This means that the agency of the first particpant is somewhat limited by the necessary active involvement of the second participant (proto-patient). Even in cases in which the second participant is inanimate, it is construed as an instrument or a means necessary for the first participant to bring about an event.

Abstract referents are conceptualized as the reason that motivates the agent's reaction, extending to cause in case of uncontrolled events.

The non-spatial NomDat construction can be viewed as built up by a constructional network, which emerged partly in connection with case syncretism as the result of constructional merger (Torrent 2015, Luraghi et al. 2020). Earlier constructions involving second arguments encoded by the instrumental merged with an original NomDat construction, which, based on comparative evidence, likely only highlighted the human character of the second participant. The resulting constructional network, on the other hand, has the possible interactive character of the two participants involved in the situation as its focus.

3.2.6 The NomGen Construction: Non-spatial Functions

The genitive case in Ancient Greek, as well as in several other ancient and modern IE languages, was a partitive as its basic meaning. This indicates that an entity is construed as a whole formed by detachable parts, as shown in Figure 9 (from Conti and Luraghi 2014: 445).

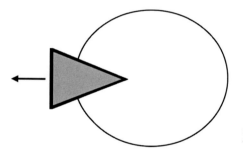

FIGURE 9
The partitive meaning of the genitive

Dedicated partitive cases exist in the Finnic languages, while in most ancient and several modern Indo-European languages the genitive can function as a partitive (see the papers collected in Luraghi and Huumo 2014, in particular Luraghi and Kittilä 2014). A peculiarity of partitive cases and of partitive genitives is that they are not associated with any specific grammatical relation. In Ancient Greek, the partitive genitive can encode most types of participants, independently of their grammatical relation, except for third arguments of three-place verbs that indicate transfer, such as 'give'.

Indeed, besides partitive second arguments, Ancient Greek also features partitive subjects, as thoroughly discussed in Conti and Luraghi (2014); see further Conti (2010a) and Luraghi (2003a: 60–62). Partitive subjects are not a prominent feature of Homeric Greek, in which one can only find a single occurrence that remains controversial (see Conti 2010c, Conti and Luraghi 2014: 455). Partitive second arguments, instead, are comparatively frequent, as I will

76   CHAPTER 3

discuss below. In addition, as I have shown in Section 3.2.1, the genitive can
function as a locative, both with verbs that require locatives, as the verb 'be'
in example (85), and as adverbial, as in (86); time adverbials are also attested,
such as *nuktós* (night.gen) 'by night', *kheímatos* (winter.gen) 'in winter time'
(Chantraine 1981: 59).

In the case of genitive second arguments in the NomGen construction, partial involvement indicates reduced participation of a participant in the situation. Reduced participation can have different facets, but it typically contrasts
with full participation: this means that several verbs that take the NomGen construction also admit variation with the NomAcc construction, based on varying
degrees of participation. Possible variation draws a sharp distinction between
the NomGen and the NomDat construction, which does not normally allow
variation with the NomAcc construction.

In the first place, reduced participation may imply that only a part of a certain referent is affected by the situation. In such cases, one finds change-of-state
verbs, most frequently verbs of consumption, as in (104)-(107).

(104) *mḗ   pṓs tis   lōtoîo   phagṑn   nóstoio*
       NEG how INDF.NOM lotus.GEN eat.PTCP.AOR.NOM return.GEN
       láthētai
       forget.SBJV.AOR.MID.3SG
       'So that nobody, having eaten some lotus, may forget the return.' (*Od.*
       9. 102)

(105) *è̄   tón   g'   en póntōi phágon   ikhthúes*
       or DEM.ACC PTC in sea.DAT eat.AOR.3PL fish.NOM.PL
       'Or in the sea, the fish have eaten him up.' (*Od.* 14.135)

(106) *tòn   pûr   kêai   ánōge   ... Menélaos*
       DEM.ACC fire.ACC kindle.INF.AOR order.PRF.3SG Menelaus.NOM
       optêsaí   te   kreôn
       roast.INF.AOR PTC meat.GEN.PL
       'Menelaus ordered him to set up a fire and roast some meat.' (*Od.* 15.97–
       98)

(107) *kréa   t'   óptōn*
       meat.ACC.PL PTC roast.IMPF.3PL
       'They were roasting the meat.' (*Od.* 3.33)

In example (104), it is said that a participant should refrain from eating some
(i.e. an unspecified quantity of) lotus in order not to lose their memories, while

ARGUMENT STRUCTURE CONSTRUCTIONS IN HOMERIC GREEK 77

in (105) Odysseus is talking about one of the Greek heroes who died, and whose corpse has perhaps been eaten up by the fish in the sea: in the first occurrence, the partitive genitive profiles the unboundedness of the quantity involved in the situation, while no such implication is relevant in the second. In (106) Agamemnon orders his companions to prepare dinner and roast a part of the meat that still has to be prepared: the genitive again profiles an unbounded quantity, contrary to the accusative in (107), in which the people of Pylos are described while preparing dinner, and roasting whatever meat is being cut.

Even though the situations referred to in sentences with the NomGen construction indicate a change of state, partial involvement of the entity that undergoes it results in a lower degree of transitivity. As Hopper and Thompson (1980: 252–253) point out, "[t]he degree to which an action is transferred to a patient is a function of how completely that patient is AFFECTED; it is done more effectively in, say, I drank up the milk than in I drank some of the milk."

The NomGen construction typically occurs with verbs that mean 'touch', 'hit', 'get hold of'. Notably, these verbs do not indicate a change of state. Tsunoda (1981, 1985) groups such contact verbs among 'verbs of effective action', but keeps them distinct from a sub-group of verbs that he calls 'resultative' (i.e. change-of-state verbs; see further Malchukov 2005: 74–75). Events of hitting and taking normally involve a part of a referent: someone who hits a thing does not hit it as a whole, but only hits a certain spot, and when one holds an object, one has a part of it in the hands. An example is the verb *tugkhánō* 'hit' in (108).

(108)   *hòs*   *mén ke*   *bálēi*   *trḗrōna*   *péleian* ...,
       REL.NOM PTC PTC hit.SBJV.AOR.3SG timid.ACC dove.ACC
       hòs   *dé ke*   *mērínthoio túkhēi*   *órnithos*
       REL.NOM PTC PTC cord.GEN   hit.SBJV.AOR.3SG bird.GEN
       hamartṓn
       miss.PTCP.AOR.NOM
       '(The man) who will hit the timorous dove (let him take up all the double axes and bear them home), and (the man) who will hit the cord, though missing the bird ...' (*Il.* 23.855–857)

In (108) we find two verbs of hitting: the first one, *bállō*, always takes the accusative, while the second one, *tugkhánō*, always takes the genitive (Chantraine 1981: 52). This alternation shows that different aspects of the same type of situation can be profiled by different verbs with specific constructions: in the first case, the NomAcc construction profiles the overall effect of an action on a patient, while in the second case the NomGen construction profiles the event of hitting a certain spot of an object. The passage also includes the verb

78   CHAPTER 3

hamartánō 'miss', which is part of another group of verbs that typically take the NomGen constructions and indicate events of missing or lacking, as those discussed in 3.2.2 (see further below).

Several verbs that mean 'take', 'hit', 'grasp' also admit variation between the NomAcc and the NomGen construction. Similar to verbs of consumption, the alternation is often connected with a lower or higher degree of involvement of the second participant in the event, as with the verb *hairéō* 'hold, get hold of' in (109) and (110).

(109)   *douròs   helṑn*
        spear.GEN take.PTCP.AOR.NOM
        'Having grabbed the spear.' (*Il.* 7. 56)

(110)   *hóte   Lésbon   euktiménēn   hélen*
        when   Lesbos.ACC well_built.ACC take.AOR.3SG
        'When he took the well-built Lesbos.' (*Il.* 9.129)

Again, the NomGen construction in (109) profiles the portion of the object that is in contact with the hand of the hero who holds the spear, while the NomAcc construction in (110) profiles the overall effect of the action of capturing.

In general, when a verb takes the NomAcc construction the degree of transitivity is higher, as the second participant is depicted as being totally affected by the action. This is also the case of construction alternation in occurrences such as (65)-(74), discussed in Section 3.1.1, in which the verb *orégomai* may mean 'aim at' or 'hit' and *epimaínomai* may mean 'try to seize' or 'touch' depending on the occurrence of the Nom Gen or the NomAcc construction.

Partial involvement and possible missing of a target provide the basis for the occurrence of the NomGen construction with verbs of missing, such as *hamartánō* in (108), and such verbs in turn provide the link with verbs of displacement that indicate motion away from a source: hence, the NomGen construction is semantically more coherent than the NomDat construction, as its spatial and non-spatial meanings are more tightly connected. The meaning of the Nom-Gen construction can be represented as in Figure 10. In Figure 10, I have also included experiential verbs, which are the matter of this book, and will be discussed extensively in Chapters 6 through 9. I have decided to anticipate them here, because they are the second largest group of verbs with the NomGen construction (30%) after verbs with ablative or elative meaning, which account for around 37% based on the verbs collected in Sausa (2015). Leaving out the latter groups of verbs, experiential predicates account for 41% of the remaining verbs. In addition, other groups of verbs listed by Sausa separately from experi-

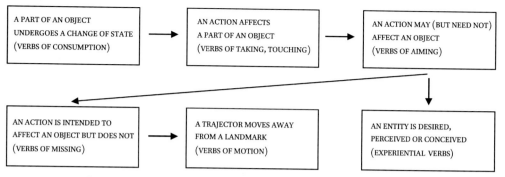

FIGURE 10   The meaning of the NomGen construction

ential verbs include verbs that mean 'need' or 'be full', 'be sated', some of which may also indicate bodily sensations, hence add to the percentage of experiential verbs.

As I have repeatedly pointed out (Sections 2.1 and 3.2.4), low transitivity is a property that affects all participants in a situation, hence not only the second participant or proto-patient, but also the first participant, or proto-agent. While the former does not undergo a change of state, the latter is construed as not being in full control of the event. This feature of the proto-agent makes the NomGen construction particularly suitable for experiential verbs, and, as we will see in the next Chapters, provides a ground for construction alternation with such verbs. Indeed, experiential verbs never indicate a change of state in the stimulus; on the other hand, however, experiencers in different types of experiential situations may be variously construed as exerting a higher or lower degree of control, or they may be conceived as acting more or less rationally, or, as I will argue in the course of the book discussing specific groups of experiential verbs, as being endowed with a higher or lower degree of awareness or of attention. Crucially, the different construals of the experiencer account for variation between the NomGen and the NomAcc construction.

3.2.7   *Two-Place Verbs with Dative Experiencers*

Dative experiencers with nominative stimuli are confined to a limited number of experiential verbs, such as *handánō* 'please', *mélō* 'be of interest' and *dokéō* 'think, seem'. The latter also takes an alternative construction with a nominative experiencer. These verbs are usually said to instantiate the DatNom construction, with the most prominent participant being the experiencer (Dahl and Fedriani 2012). However, there are occurrences in which the stimulus seems to be the more prominent participant: such cases should be regarded as instantiations of the NomDat construction, as I argue below (see further Section 8.5).

80 CHAPTER 3

The verb *handánō* 'please' mostly occurs with inanimate stimuli, often *múthos* 'speech', *boulḗ* 'plan', as in (111).

(111) *díkha dé sphisin hḗndane boulḗ*
double PTC 3PL.DAT like.IMPF.3SG opinion.NOM
'They favored two different opinions.' (*Il.* 18.510)

In (112), the stimulus is a human being.

(112) *Amphínomos ... Nísou phaídimos huiós ... málista*
Amphinomos.NOM Nisos.GEN glorious.NOM son.NOM especially
dè Pēnelopeíēi hḗndane múthoisi
PTC Penelope.DAT like.IMPF.3SG word.DAT.PL
'Amphinomos, the glorious son of Nisos, especially pleased Penelope with his speech.' (*Od.* 16.394–398)

In this and other similar occurrences that I will review in detail in Section 8.5, the stimulus is portrayed as actively and intentionally trying to please the experiencer: it shares features of agents, and it does not seem to be less prominent than the experiencer in such a situation. Similar to the case of Italian *piacere* 'like', discussed in Section 2.3, from the point of view of the construction it is not altogether clear that the dative and the nominative with this verb always instantiate a DatNom construction, and not occasionally a NomDat one, in which the most prominent participant (hence the first argument) is the stimulus.

Similar considerations also hold for *mélō* 'be of interest for': while this verb mostly occurs with inanimate stimuli, animate stimuli can be highly prominent, as in (113).

(113) *eím' Oduseùs Laertiádēs, hòs pâsi*
be.PRS.1SG Odysseus.NOM son_of_Laertes.NOM REL.NOM all.DAT.PL
dóloisin anthrṓpoisi mélō
trick.DAT.PL man.DAT.PL care.PRS.1SG
'I am Odysseus, son of Laertes, of interest to men for all types of tricks.' (*Od.* 9.19–20)

In such cases, reference is made to a situation that involves two human participants, and the argument structure instantiates the NomDat construction of verbs of social interaction, rather than a DatNom construction in which the experiencer holds the status of first argument. I return to this issue in Section

ARGUMENT STRUCTURE CONSTRUCTIONS IN HOMERIC GREEK

8.5, in which I discuss these and other verbs with dative experiencers in the wider framework of verbs of emotion.

The verb *dokéō* 'think' can take either a nominative or a dative experiencer. The first construction occurs once in the *Iliad* and once in the *Odyssey* (see Section 7.1). In example (114) it is accompanied by a sentential complement.

(114)   ô   phíloi   étoi klêros   emós,   khaírō
        oh friends.VOC.PL PTC fate.NOM POSS.1SG.NOM rejoice.PRS.1SG
        dè   kaì autòs   thumôi epeì dokéō   nikēsémen
        PTC and self.NOM soul.DAT as   think.PRS.1SG win.INF.FUT
        Héktora   dîon
        Hector.ACC god_like.ACC
        'Friends, this is my fate, and I rejoice in my soul, because I think that I
        will win god-like Hector.' (*Il* 7.191–192)

Dative experiencers come with nominative stimuli, in a much more frequent construction, in which the verb means 'seem (to somebody)', as in (115). (Similarly, other verbs of appearance may take a dative experiencer, such as *indállo-mai* 'appear, seem' and *augázomai* 'discern'.)

(115)   allà mál' hôd' érxō,   dokéei   dé   moi   eînai
        but very thus do.FUT.1SG seem.PRS.3SG PTC 1SG.DAT be.INF.PRS
        áriston
        best.ACC
        'But I will do this, and it seems to me that this is best.' (*Od.* 5.360)

The function of *dokéō* in (115) is similar to the function of another cognitive verb, *oíō* 'think'. I will return to the meaning and the distribution of the two verbs in Section 7.1.1.

3.2.8   *Summary*

In the preceding Sections, I have shown how the three constructions of two-place verbs, NomAcc, NomDat and NomGen, are distributed across verb classes. In the first place, they occur with verbs that require some sort of specification as to the spatial setting of the event. This former set of meanings associated with the three constructions is not especially relevant for their extension to experiential verbs. In addition to this, the three constructions indicate different types of involvement of the second participant or proto-patient in the event: as a fully affected entity that undergoes a change of state or a change of position (NomAcc), as a human participant that takes part in an expectedly interactive situation, and may contribute to bring it about (NomDat), as a manipulated entity, which is used by the first participant to bring about the situation or which motivates the first participant to act (NomDat), or as an entity partially affected by the event (NomGen). Finally, constructions also affect the construal of the first participant or proto-agent, which may be conceived as more or less effective in bringing about the situation. All these meanings are suitable to adapt to experiential constructions, as I will discuss at length in Chapters 5 to 8.

The NomDat construction might at first sight look similar to the NomGen construction, as both entail a lower degree of transitivity than the NomAcc construction: verbs that take the NomDat construction typically do not indicate a change of state. However, it is remarkable that the meaning of the NomGen is not connected with any particular referential feature of the second participant as is the meaning of the NomDat construction, and the former is not limited to verbs that do not indicate a change of state. Proto-agents with the NomDat constructions are construed as controllers that participate in an event in which another participant who can potentially act is also present. Even non-human second participants are conceived as having a role in bringing about the situation, either by being manipulated by the first participant, or by motivating its action. Hence, their agency is not limited by the fact that an effect is not fully achieved, or that the event is less effective than the prototypical change-of-state event, but by the fact that in order to bring it about another entity is needed: either another agent, as in inherently reciprocal events, or an inanimate entity, as with verbs of manipulation.

The DatNom construction is instantiated by a limited number of verbs, but is of special interest for the present work, as these verbs are virtually all experiential verbs. Similar to the NomDat construction with verbs of social interaction, it points to a close connection of dative encoding with humanness, as experiencers are typically human beings. Notably, human stimuli can exhibit a higher prominence than experiencers with such verbs: if this is the case, the construction should be regarded as NomDat, thus pointing toward a relational and interactive nature of the situation (see further the discussion in Section 8.5).

3.3 Complementation in Homeric Greek

In this Section, I sketch a short description of complementation in Homeric Greek, limited to constructions occurring with experiential verbs. In particular, after briefly surveying different types of finite and non-finite complement

ARGUMENT STRUCTURE CONSTRUCTIONS IN HOMERIC GREEK   83

clauses, I focus on a construction that is typical of verbs of perception and cognition, but also extends to some other groups of experiential verbs, which involve a predicative participle.

Sentential complements in Homeric Greek may be finite or non-finite. Constructions occurring with experiential predicates in the Homeric poems include: (a) infinitives; (b) participles; (c) finite complement clauses with the conjunctions *hóti* or *hōs* 'that'; (d) other types of subordinate clauses.

Some comments are in order concerning the constructions that I include under these four types. Indeed, as I am not going to give a full account of the syntax and semantics of all constructions involving some type of subordinate verb form, the four types listed above are customized to capture some peculiar features of experiential predicates. In particular, among infinitive constructions I include not only subordinate clauses, but also control infinitives (see further below). Finite subordination is more limited, and the occurrence of specific subordinating conjunctions other than *hōs* or to a more limited extent *hóti*, depends on individual verbs: for example, the verb *deídō* typically occurs with clauses introduced by the negation *mḗ* that negates non-assertive modality, as in (116).

(116) *deídō   mḗ   m'   exaûtis anarpáxasa*
       fear.PRS.1SG NEG 1SG.ACC again   carry_off.PTCP.AOR.NOM
       thúella   pónton ep' ikhthuóenta phérēi
       storm.NOM sea.ACC on fishy.ACC   carry.SBJV.PRS.3SG
       'I fear that the storm carrying me off again may bear me over the teeming sea.' (*Od.* 5.419–520)

Among experiential verbs, volition verbs take infinitive complements, as *ethélō* 'want' in (117). In the case that the verb of volition and the infinitive do not share the same subject, the subject of the latter is in the accusative, as in (118) with *boúlomai* 'wish', 'prefer'. This construction, typical of complement clauses (including declaratives) in Ancient Greek, is commonly called AcI from the Latin name *accusativus cum infinitivo* 'accusative with infinitive' (see Létoublon 1999).

(117) *ou   d'   àn   makháressi   theoîs   ethéloimi*
       NEG PTC PTC blessed.DAT.PL gods.DAT.PL want.OPT.PRS.1SG
       mákhesthai
       fight.INF.PRS.M/P
       'I would not like to fight with the blessed gods.' (*Il.* 6.141)

(118) ê   s'   àn egṓ   ge autoû bouloímēn
     PTC 2SG.ACC PTC 1SG.NOM PTC here want.OPT.PRS.M/P.1SG
     stathmôn   rhutêra   lipésthai
     shed.GEN.PL keeper.ACC remain.INF.AOR.MID
     'As for me, I would have preferred that you remain here as sheds'
     keeper.' (*Od.* 17.186–187)

Verbs of cognition, including mental activities such as 'think', 'consider', and
mental states such as 'know', allow both infinitives and subordinate clauses (see
Chantraine 1981: 288–301; Humbert 1986: 198–203). The ratio between the two
varies, but in general infinitives are more frequent, as I show in Chapter 7 (cf.
Table 10): for example, *oíō/oíomai* 'think, believe' takes infinitives in the vast
majority of cases (96 out of 131 total occurrences; occurrences of other types of
subordinate clauses are 3 see e.g. (244) in Chapter 7), while the verb *phrássomai*
'consider', 'plan' most often occurs with a finite complement (30 occurrences
out of 33 total cases in which the verb takes a sentential complement), as in
(119). Similarly, the verb *oîda* 'know' occurs with finite complementation (49
occurrences) more often than with infinitives (17 occurrences), even though
sentential complementation is relatively less frequent with this verb than with
oíō/oíomai and *phrássomai* (data from Table 10, Chapter 7). An example is
(120).

(119) phrássetai   hṓs ke néētai   epeì
     think.FUT.MID.3SG so PTC return.SBJV.PRS.M/P.3SG as
     polumḗkhanós   estin
     resourceful.NOM be.PRS.3SG
     'He will contrive to return, because he is resourceful.' (*Od.* 1.205)

(120) sápha d' ouk oîd'   ei theós   estin
     clearly PTC NEG know.PRF.1SG if god.NOM be.PRS.3SG
     'Still I'm not sure whether he is a god.' (*Il.* 5.183)

A construction that proved to be very important for experiential verbs and
which is typical in the first place of perception verbs involves a participle referring to a situation in which a participant other than the experiencer is involved.
The NP encoding this participant agrees with the participle, and is included
into the argument structure of the main verb; hence the event is construed as a
property of the participant that takes the role of the stimulus in the situation.
Let us consider (121).

ARGUMENT STRUCTURE CONSTRUCTIONS IN HOMERIC GREEK

(121) *all' étoi keînós   ge séthen   zóontos*
       but PTC DEM.NOM PTC 2SG.GEN live.PTCP.PRS.GEN
       akoúōn   khaírei   t' en thumôi
       hear.PTCP.PRS.NOM rejoice.PRS.3SG PTC in heart.DAT
       'But he, hearing that you are still alive, is happy in his heart.' (*Il.* 24.490–491)

In (121), the verb *akoúō* takes the NomGen construction, with the NP *séthen zóontos* as second argument. This NP is constituted by a Homeric form of the second singular genitive pronoun *séthen* agreeing with the participle *zóontos* 'living'. As shown in the English translation, the NP contains a secondary predication, which is syntactically constructed as an argument of the main verb. This means that the subject of the secondary predication is raised to the object of the first, and that the participant it encodes is construed as the stimulus of the experiential situation indicated by the main verb. In other words, 'you' is depicted as being the stimulus of 'hear', and the corresponding NP is marked accordingly, hence in the genitive. I will call this the Two-place plus participle construction, or Two-place+P construction, a cover for the NomAcc+P, Nom-Gen+P, and NomDat+P sub-constructions.

Cross-linguistically, similar constructions with perception verbs are not infrequent (see Noonan 2007: 85), and usually occur when the perception verb indicates direct perception, as is shown by the occurrence of present participles or past participles with resultative meaning. Remarkably, in the Homeric Greek construction in (121), it is the genitive NP that, functioning as second argument, is construed as the stimulus, hence the object of direct perception. Note however that in the situation referred to by this sentence perception cannot be direct: the sentence rather refers to the acquisition knowledge from some external source.

In Homeric Greek this construction was still on the rise (Chantraine 1981: 329). In origin, it indeed indicated direct perception, and this is still reflected in the fact that it most frequently features participles that indicate coincidence in time between the event they encode and the event in the main clause. In general, one finds present participles, as in (121): the situation encoded by the present participle *zóontos* 'being alive, living' is viewed as holding at the same time as the event of learning from hearing (more occurrences with verbs of sight and of hearing are discussed in Sections 6.1, see (172)-(174) and 6.2, see (196) and (198)). Participles from other aspectual stems are infrequent in Homeric Greek. One finds some occurrences of resultative participles, either perfect or in lexically restricted cases aorist, such as the aorist participle *thanóntos* 'having died, dead' in (227) and (300), semantically equivalent of the perfect

86   CHAPTER 3

participle *tethneóta* 'dead' in (130). Only occasionally do aorist participles that must be taken to indicate non-simultaneous events occur with verbs of hearing, as I will argue in Section 6.2 comparing two occurrences of aorist participles: (199), in which the Two-place+P construction indicates immediate perception of a state of affairs, and (202), in which it indicates acquisition of knowledge based on the reception of a propositional content about an event that precedes the event of perception (following the terminology in Dik and Hengeveld 1991: 237; see Section 2.1.2). This matter will be taken up again in detail in Section 6.4.

It is a peculiarity of Ancient Greek that the Two-place+P construction extends to other verb classes. In the first place, predicative participles may occur with cognitive verbs, as in (122).

(122) *autíka*   *d'*   *égnō*   *tòn*   *mèn*
       immediately PTC know.AOR.3SG DEM.ACC PTC
       apaínúmenon   *klutà*   *teúkhea,*   *tòn*
       pluck_off.PTCP.PRS.M/P.ACC gloroious.ACC.PL arm.ACC.PL DEM.ACC
       d'   *epì gaíēi*   *keímenon*
       PTC on earth.DAT lie.PTCP.PRS.M/P.ACC
       'At once he recognized the one stripped off of the glorious arms, the other lying on the earth.' (*Il.* 17.84–86)

In example (122), the participles *apaínúmenon* 'being stripped off' and *keímenon* 'lying' are in the accusative, and so are their subjects, the two demonstratives *tón* 'that one'. While this occurrence with *gignóskō* 'understand, recognize' is quite exceptional, more examples are available with *punthánomai* 'learn' in (300), referred to above and *oîda* 'know' in (130): Chantraine (1981: 327) lists five occurrences of each verb. In addition, the Two-place+P construction occurs with *noéō*, a verb that indicates a sudden rise of awareness often achieved through the senses, as in (236). With cognition verbs, the Two-place+P construction indicates the process of acquiring knowledge, in much the same way as with perception verbs, or it may indicate the state resulting from this process, and sometimes refers to events that are not simultaneous (see the discussion in Section 7.2.1 and 7.2.2).

Already in Homeric Greek, the construction extended to other experiential verbs. Among cognitive verbs, it can occur with *phrázomai* 'plan, devise', which complemented with the Two-place+P construction, indicates perception and means 'recognize' as in (252). Among emotion verbs (see Section 7.1.2), the Two-place+P construction occurs with *khaírō* 'rejoice' and is realized as NomDat+P constructions as in (253) and (254) (see Section 8.1.2). In these occurrences, the experiencer is referred to as rejoicing about a situation learned through direct perception. Similarly, an occurrence with *deídō* 'fear' in (394) also refers to a situation that the experiencer learns through direct perception: as I will discuss in Section 8.3.2, fear is often construed as connected with sight in Homeric Greek.

As the examples show, participles display case marking variation to the effect that they can be viewed as instantiating one of the argument structure constructions that occur with nominal second arguments. Crucially, the distribution of the two constructions reflects the distribution of the case-marked constructions before the addition of the participle. For this reason, even though participles in this construction are regarded as sentential complements (see Chantraine 1981: 326, Humbert 1986: 198), I will treat the NP constituted by the participle and its head noun as being on the same plane as other stimuli NPS with experiential verbs for the sake of the description of construction alternation in Homeric Greek.

The above description points to a peculiar distribution of complementation across verb groups, summarized in Table 5.

TABLE 5   Distribution of complements across verb groups

	Infinitive—AcI	*hōs/hóti* clause	Participle	Other finite subordinate clauses
Volitionality	+	−	−	−
Perception	+	+	++	−
Cognition	+	+	+	+
Emotion	+	+	+	+

The symbol ++ indicates that the construction involving a participle is much more frequent with perception verbs than with verbs of cognition and especially emotion, with which it remains sporadic in Homeric Greek. Concerning non-finite complementation, dependent infinites do not occur with perception verbs, which however feature a limited number of AcI clauses (see Section 6.4 for examples). Subordinate clauses of different types occur with verbs of emotion depending on the specific verb's semantics; with cognition verbs some indirect interrogative clauses occur as shown in (274) with *oîda*, but finite subordination is mostly limited to *hōs/hóti* clauses.

3.4 Discussion

In this chapter I have tackled two separate issues, that is, the meaning of argument structure constructions and their distribution across verb classes, and the types of complement clauses that occur with experiential verbs. Regarding complementation, verbs of emotion show the wider range of possibilities. This is not unexpected, as the field of emotions is the most complex one among the sub-domains of experience. On the other hand, volition verbs only allow dependent infinitive or AcI clauses, hence proving less complex than the other sub-domains. Interestingly, as I will argue in the next Chapters, these tendencies find a correspondence in the frequency and distribution of argument structure constructions. Emotion verbs are the only ones that feature the NomDat construction (Section 8.1), while verbs in the other sub-domains only feature the NomAcc and the NomGen construction, with marginal exceptions in the sub-domain of bodily sensations (Section 5.1). Conversely, volition verbs provide very limited evidence for constructions involving nominal second arguments: not only is variation limited, but, as I will show in Section 5.2, their occurrences with NPs are extremely limited not only in terms of frequency, but also of possible fillers. Perception provides a source for the conceptualization of other experiential sub-domains, and this is reflected both in the distribution of argument structure constructions, as I will argue in Sections 7.4 and 10.2, and in the extension of the Two-place+P construction, discussed in Section 3.3 (see further Section 10.4.3).

CHAPTER 4

The Ancient Greek Verb

Ancient Greek verbal categories play an important role in conveying the meaning that contributes to the conceptualization of situations. In particular, verbal tenses, in spite of being traditionally called so, indicate primarily verbal aspects, and open different perspectives on situations by construing them as ongoing or by viewing them in their globality. As we will see in Section 4.1, verbal aspect is often conditioned by the meaning of verb roots, or lexical aspect, as shown by the fact that certain verbs only inflect in some tenses.

Verbal voice in Greek displays a three-fold distinction: active, middle and passive. The middle functions as a medio-passive in most tenses, as an inflectional passive only exists in the aorist and in the future. Again, traditional labels do not reflect reality. In particular, the so-called passive functions as passive in a minority of cases, and, in the Homeric poems, never in the future (see Allan 2003). In other tenses, the medio-passive also functions as a passive to a limited extent. In the vast majority of occurrences, both the passive and the middle have a variety of other functions, as I show in Section 4.2. Among these, importantly for the subject of this study, is the function of indicating the (anti)causative alternation that will be explored in detail in Chapter 9. In addition, various verbs are *media tantum*, and have no active inflection, in spite of their meaning, which is often similar to the meaning of active verbs, sometimes even transitive ones.

4.1   Aspect and Tense

The Ancient Greek verbal system displays a peculiar pattern based on three aspectual stems, traditionally called present, aorist and perfect. This is a direct reflex of the Proto-Indo-European verbal system that has a close counterpart in some other ancient languages, most notably Indo-Aryan (see Willi 2018). The literature abounds with studies devoted to the Ancient Greek tense and aspect system (see among others Chantraine 1938, Ruiperez 1954, Ruijgh 1985, Sicking 1991, Duhoux 1992 and Napoli 2006), and in this Section I do not aim at providing a comprehensive survey but simply at giving a short overlook that can familiarize non-specialist readers with its basic features.

Before going into detail, a few remarks on my use of the term 'aspect' are in order. In this book, I follow the so-called bi-dimensional approach (Sasse

© SILVIA LURAGHI, 2021 | DOI:10.1163/9789004442528_005

2002, Tatevosov 2002), and distinguish between lexical aspect, or actionality, and verbal aspect, or simply aspect (Bertinetto and Delfitto 2000). The latter is an inflectional category that potentially applies to all verbs, and basically corresponds to the aspectual distinction between perfective and imperfective.

Following the definition in Bertinetto and Delfitto (2000: 190), aspect is "the specific perspective adopted by the speaker/writer", whereby "typically, the event may be considered from a 'global' or a 'partial' point of view": in this definition, a global point of view indicates the perfective aspect, while a partial point of view indicates the imperfective aspect. Actionality, on the other hand, is a feature of the lexical meaning of individual verb roots, and reflects distinctions based on telicity and dynamicity among states of affairs, such as, for example, those captured in Vendler's (1957) four-fold classification of events as states, activities, accomplishments and achievements. Accordingly, Bertinetto and Delfitto (2000: 190) define actionality as "the type of event, specified according to a limited number of relevant properties".

Vendler's (1957) classic classification of events is based on parameters of telicity, dynamicity and durativity. Based on these parameters, states are atelic and non-dynamic, activities are atelic and dynamic, accomplishments are telic and also have a temporal dimension (they can be gradual), while achievements are telic but do not have a temporal dimension and are not gradual. This classification is summarized as in Table 6.

TABLE 6   Vendler's classification of actionality

	States	Activities	Accomplishments	Achievements
Telicity	–	–	+	+
Dynamicity	–	+	+	+
Durativity	+	+	+	–

Not all scholars agree in keeping the notions aspect and actionality distinct, and a significant tradition exists, which views aspect as a single category encompassing the two (cf. among many others Bybee 1985, Bybee, Perkins and Pagliuca 1994, Croft 2012). On the other hand, the distinction is commonly made in Indo-European and Greek linguistics (e.g. Strunk 1994, Garcia Ramon 2002, Dahl 2010). This is possibly a consequence of the fact that the imperfective/perfective opposition has a central role in structuring the verbal system reconstructed for PIE, and is encoded in the inflectional paradigms.

There is an obvious connection between the meaning of a verb and its tendency to be inflected either in the imperfective or in the perfective aspect.

For example, verbs that denote states (stative actionality), such as *know*, cannot normally be inflected in the progressive form in English (notably, though, states can turn into non-stative events when referring to temporary states; see Chung and Timberlake 1985 and Tatevosov 2002: 348–349). However, the correspondence is far from being perfect and, notably, it cannot be generalized for verbs with similar meanings cross-linguistically, as pointed out in Tatevosov (2002). For example, in Italian both verbs *sapere* and *conoscere* 'know' indicate states as the corresponding English verb. However, contrary to English *know*, they can easily be construed as achievements, as shown in (123) and (124).

(123) *Un mese   fa   a   una festa   ho   conosciuto   la   sorella*
     a   month ago at a   party have.PRS.1SG know.PTCP the sister
    di Paolo.
    of Paul
    'A month ago I met (*knew) Paul's sister at a party.'

(124) *Sapevi   che Maria e   Giovanni si   sono*
    know.IMPF.2SG that Mary and John   REFL be.PRS.3PL
    sposati?   Sí, l'   ho   saputo   ieri
    marry.PTCP yes 3SG.ACC have.PRS.1SG know.PTCP yesterday
    'Did you know that Mary and John got married? Yes, I learned (*knew) it yesterday.'

Typically, stative verbs inflected in the perfective aspect indicate achievements as in (123) and (124), rather than accomplishments. This is because they lack a temporal dimension: states are atelic and non-dynamic events. On the other hand, accomplishments and activities, which share the characteristic of being construed as ongoing, can be viewed as the perfective and imperfective counterpart of each other, capturing the fact that both types of events are gradable, while states and achievements are not.

The possibility for verbs to refer to events that are construed differently from the verb's default construal, as in the case of Italian *sapere* and *conoscere* illustrated above, is acknowledged in discussions of aspect and actionality. Bertinetto (1986, 1991) speaks of aspectual hybridism when discussing such occurrences, and also mentions as further examples achievement verbs that are inflected in the imperfect in Italian (imperfective aspect), receive a habitual reading (the same happens in English), as in (125).

(125) *Paolo non trovava   mai le cose   che aveva*
       Paul not find.IMPF.3SG never the thing.PL that have.IMPF.3SG
       nascosto.
       hide.PTCP
       'Paul could never find the things he had hidden.'

Similarly, Croft (2012) speaks of coercion, and shows that a verb like *see* in English can be construed as a state, as in (126), or as an achievement, as in (127) (2012: 38).

(126) *I see Mount Tamalpais.*

(127) *I reached the top of the hill and saw Mount Tamalpais.*

As mentioned at the beginning of this section, the Greek verb features a three-fold aspectual distinction, with the imperfective/perfective opposition instantiated by the present and aorist stems, and the addition of the perfect. The latter has a resultative meaning, and indicates a state that results from a change of state. Hence, it comes close to a type of actionality.

Tense is intertwined with aspect in the Ancient Greek verb system (van Emde Boas et al. 2010). In fact, both tense and aspect have to do with time, the former by providing a deictic link to the moment of utterance, and the latter by indicating the choice of the speaker as to how to represent the internal temporal constituency of an event. It is generally acknowledged that there is a special link between the present tense and the imperfective aspect: the present refers to some ongoing or habitual event; hence it does not lend itself easily to depicting an event in its globality (Comrie 1976: 66). On the other hand, a past event can more easily be viewed as being either unaccomplished or accomplished, and indeed in many Indo-European languages this aspectual distinction is reflected in the verbal system.

In Ancient Greek, there is a further interaction with verbal mood, as tense distinctions are relevant only in the indicative. Thus, in the indicative the present tense has present reference, while the aorist has past reference; they are built on two different stems. In addition, there is a further tense, the imperfect, which is built on the present stem, indicates an imperfective past and does not exist in other moods. Outside the indicative mood, the present and the aorist only indicate imperfective and perfective aspect respectively.

As I have remarked above, the perfect is a resultative. In principle, it does not refer to the past: rather, it can be viewed as a present resultative, and indeed it is coupled by a past resultative, the pluperfect (Weiss 2010: 110–111). The rele-

THE ANCIENT GREEK VERB

vance of the resultative component is highlighted by the fact that stative verbs in origin did not have a perfect (Di Giovine 1990). In practice, as it implies a change from a preceding situation, the perfect often ends up functioning as a past tense, possibly an anterior, as shown in (128) (see Crellin 2020 for an exhaustive discussion of the semantics of the Ancient Greek perfect).

(128) *tô s'   aû   nûn oîō   apoteisémen hóssa*
       so 2SG.ACC again now think.PRS.1SG pay.INF.FUT REL.ACC.PL
       éorgas
       do.PRF.2SG
       'So now I think that you shall pay for all you have done.' (*Il.* 21.399).

The perfect of some verbs has lost the resultative meaning, and has become partly or fully lexicalized to indicate a state, without profiling the change of state. This is the case of *bébeka*, already discussed in Section 3.2.2 example (90), the perfect of the verb *baínō* 'go, walk' that has acquired the meaning of 'stand'. Originally, this meaning shift was based on a pragmatic inference: if someone has gone to a certain place, this person now stands in that place. Synchronically, however, the meaning brought about by the pragmatic inference has replaced the original meaning, which is no longer active.

As a result of this shift, some perfect forms have become disconnected from the original verbal paradigm. A notable case in point is the verb *oîda* 'know', whose semantic change dates back to Proto-Indo-European. This form originates from **woida*, which is the perfect of the root **wid-* 'see', and originally must have meant 'have seen', hence, by pragmatic inference, 'know from having seen'. In the Indo-European languages, the verb is variously attested, both with forms deriving from the present or from the aorist stem, such as Latin *video* 'see', or Ancient Greek *eídon* 'saw (aorist indicative)', and with forms deriving from the perfect stem, such as Sanskrit *veda* and Gothic *wait* from Proto-Germanic so-called preterite-present **wītan*, both of which mean 'know', similar to Greek *oîda*. These ancient perfect forms have dropped out of the paradigm of the verb 'see', as can be seen by the fact that in Ancient Greek *oîda* has been replaced by another perfect, *ópōpa* 'I have seen'. (The verb 'see' in Ancient Greek is suppletive, and relies on different stems and alternative forms, see Chantraine 2013 and Section 6.1.) I will discuss the meaning of *oîda* and its relation with other cognitive verbs in Section 7.2.

Napoli (2006) devotes an exhaustive study to the relation between aspect and actionality in Homeric Greek. She argues that the tendency for verbs to be inflected in a certain tense is heavily conditioned by their meaning, that is, that there is a strong correlation between aspect and actionality. This is especially true for verbs of cognition, some of which only show a single aspectual stem: among verbs of knowledge, besides *oîda* 'know' that virtually always occurs in the perfect and indicates a state, we also find *gignóskō* 'know', 'learn' that occurs in the aorist 82 out of 125 times, and has an inchoative meaning (see Section 7.2, in which I also discuss two occurrences of *oîda* in the future). However, this is not the case for all verb stems. For example, *punthánomai* 'learn' is basically inchoative and indicates a change of state, but it can also occur in the perfect. In this case, the meaning is 'have learned', 'know'. In comparison to *oîda*, the perfect of *punthánomai* preserves the resultative meaning that the lexicalized perfect had lost in Greek, even though the difference between the meanings of the two verbs can hardly be discerned in some occurrences: compare (129) and (130). Both passages contain the NomAcc construction, but while in (129) we find a stimulus NP containing a pronoun *emè* 'me' and an adjective *zōòn* 'alive', (130) features the NomAcc+P participle, with the perfect participle *tethnēóta* 'dead'.

(129) *eí ken emè zōòn pepúthoit' epì nēusìn*
      if PTC 1SG.ACC alive.ACC learn.AOR.OPT.MID.3SG on ship.DAT.PL
      Akhaiôn
      Achaean.GEN.PL
      'If he knew that I am alive on the ships of the Achaeans.' (*Il.* 10.381)

(130) *ou d' ára pṓ ti éidee Pátroklon*
      NEG PTC PTC PTC INDF.ACC know.PPF.3SG Patroclus.ACC
      tethnēóta dîos Akhilleús
      die.PTCP.PRF.ACC god_like.NOM Achilles.NOM
      'God-like Achilles did not yet know that Patroclus was dead.' (*Il.* 17.401–402)

Cognitive verbs are those that most consistently feature different lexemes in connection with different verbal aspects, and show a higher connection of aspect with actionality, as I will argue in Chapter 7. With verbs of emotion, one often finds the same verb with all three aspectual stems, whereby the aorist has an inchoative meaning, while the perfect indicates a state, as in the case of *kholóō* 'be/get angry' discussed in Section 4.2 and 8.1.1.

Among verbal tenses, the future does not belong to the original system derived from Proto-Indo-European, and accordingly it does not fit into the aspectual oppositions that hold among other tenses. In fact, even though numerous ancient Indo-European languages have a future tense, morphological differences point toward a language-specific origin of this tense. Concerning the origin of the Ancient Greek future, opinions vary as to whether it should be connected with an ancient subjunctive or an ancient desiderative (see Willi 2018: 441–445 for a recent assessment of the issue). The future most often has temporal reference, but it can also express some modal meanings (see Douhoux 1992: 441–445).

4.2 Voice

Similar to the aspectual system, the voice system of Ancient Greek also largely reflects the reconstructed system of Proto-Indo-European (Willi 2018), featuring as its cornerstone the opposition between the active and the middle voice. In addition, as an innovation, a passive was also introduced in the future and in the aorist, featuring a special suffix followed by the active endings in the aorist and most often middle endings in the future (Luraghi et al. forthc.).

In recent years, the middle voice has been the subject both of cross-linguistic research and of language specific studies devoted to Ancient Greek. Its basic function with respect to the active voice is to indicate what is generally described as a higher degree of involvement of the subject in the event. Allan (2003: 248) speaks of subject-affectedness, a notion that, as we will see especially in Chapter 6, is not completely without problems. Allan further shows that the Ancient Greek middle conforms to the description in Kemmer (1993), fulfilling all typical functions that are cross-linguistically common for the middle voice. In particular, the middle functions as a reflexive, a self-beneficiary, and, in the present and perfect stem, as a passive. In most of its functions, except that of self-beneficiary, the middle voice turns out to be an intransitivizing strategy: hence its importance for experiential verbs that, as pointed out in Chapter 2, are characterized by a low degree of transitivity.

Among the functions of the Ancient Greek middle is the encoding of the (anti)causative alternation. With verbs that indicate situations that can be construed as happening spontaneously, or as being brought about by an external agent, such as *rhḗgnumai* (middle) 'break(intr.)' vs. *rhḗgnumi* (active) 'break(tr.)', the middle voice often indicates a spontaneous event (Sausa 2016; see Haspelmath 1993 on this type of alternation). This function is likely inherited from Proto-Indo-European, and may well have been the original function of the oppositional middle, that is, of the middle of verbs that feature both voices (Luraghi 2019, Inglese 2020).

As many experiential situations can be in fact conceived as being spontaneous or externally induced, the middle/active alternation with experiential verbs may indicate the (anti)causative alternation. An example is *mimnḗsko-mai* 'remember' that I have already mentioned in Section 1.1. This verb shows middle morphology, and indicates the spontaneous event of some memory coming to one's mind. Its active counterpart, *mimnḗskō*, indicates an event induced by some external entity, and means 'remind' (see further Section 9.2).

In spite of the morphological distinction, the passive aorist in Homer has frequently the same meaning as the middle. A case in point is the verb *kholóomai* 'be/get angry (at someone)' that will be discussed at length in Section 8.1. Out of a total of 73 occurrences, 58 are middle forms and 11 passive aorists. Allan (2003: 148–150) shows that passive and middle aorist forms occur in similar contexts, and express the same meaning. In the remaining four occurrences the verb is inflected in the active voice, and means 'anger', thus embodying the (anti)causative alternation illustrated above. In three out of four occurrences, the experiencer is the subject/speaker, as in (131).

(131) *hōs emè   nûn ekhólōsen   ánax   andrôn*
       thus 1SG.ACC now anger.AOR.3SG king.NOM man.GEN.PL
       Agamémnōn
       Agamemnon.NOM
       'So now, Agamemnon, king of men, made me angry.' (*Il.* 18.111)

As I discuss in Chapter 9, the (much) higher frequency of middle forms with verbs such as *kholóomai* and *mimnḗskomai* raises the question of the original voice of some experiential verbs. Indeed, in Ancient Greek, as in other ancient Indo-European languages, a sizable number of *media tantum* exists, that is, verbs that only have middle morphology. As remarked in Allan (2003: 49–52), the Greek *media tantum* constitute a heterogeneous category; however, experiential predicates of all types and covering the whole domain of experience feature prominently among them. The semantic connection between the domain of experience and the middle voice follows quite obviously from the function of the middle to highlight the involvement of the subject in a situation. In the case of *kholóomai* both Schwyzer (1950) and Chantraine (1981: 179) argue that the middle voice is more ancient, while the active counterpart developed at a later time. This development is in fact attested for some other verbs, for example *théromai* 'be warm' that shows active morphology only after Homer (see Delbrück 1911: 410, Lazzeroni 2004: 143 with more examples). However, as I will discuss extensively in Chapter 9, not all experiential verbs featuring voice opposition in Homeric Greek can be taken as original *media tantum*, even though they may encode the (anti)causative alternation through voice, and an in-depth analysis of the individual verbs is necessary in order to gauge the original state of affairs concerning voice.

A small but semantically cohesive group of original *media tantum*, with cognates in the other Indo-European languages, is constituted by stative verbs. At first sight, this may seem at odds with the widespread tendency of the middle voice to indicate spontaneous, change-of-state events, but it is not surprising if one views lack of control as the common feature that connects the two types of events. This partly accounts for the fact that, as discussed further on in this Section, the perfect of some *media tantum* features active forms, as the perfect indicates a state.

The passive aorist mentioned above features two suffixes, *-thē* and *-ē*, which originally functioned as intransitivizers, and in other ancient Indo-European languages occur in stative verbs (Luraghi et al. forthc.). As I remarked above, passive aorist forms often do not have passive meaning in Homeric Greek: rather, they partly cover the same semantic domain of the middle voice, in particular with verbs that indicate spontaneous events, collective motion (such as 'gather') or body motion ('stand up', 'crouch down'). In a sample of 100 passive aorist forms scrutinized by Allan (2003: 127–129), out of 72 forms that do not have passive meaning, 41 indicate spontaneous events. Among them, almost half are experiential verbs ('mental processes' in the terminology of Allan 2003), and include cognitive verbs and verbs of emotion. An example is (132).

(132) *basilêi   kholōtheìs*
       king.DAT be_angry.PTCP.AOR.PASS.NOM
       'Having got upset at the king.' (*Il.* 1.9)

In the aorist, the middle voice and the passive often overlap in the case of experiential verbs, while other types of spontaneous events, featuring inanimate subjects, are characteristic of passive forms (Allan 2003: 147). Notably, the partial overlap only concerns a part of the domain of experience and, accordingly, only a part of the experiential verbs that encode it: perception verbs and verbs of volition are often *media tantum*, but they remain middle in the aorist, and do not show a tendency toward taking passive aorist forms.

As pointed out in Section 4.1, the future tense is of more recent origin than the other verbal tenses. Its relation with voice is complex. On the one hand, the future, similar to the aorist, features passive forms. On the other hand, in Homer this formation was still on the rise, and only two verbs feature *-ē-* 'passive' futures, which, however, do not have passive meaning (see Allan 2003: 181). In addition, some verbs tend to always show middle morphology in the future, with the same meaning of the active counterparts in the present tense. This especially holds for denominal verbs (Chantraine 2013: 426).

I have left the perfect out of consideration thus far, because its interaction with voice is especially complicated. As mentioned above, some original *media tantum* traditionally reconstructed for Proto-Indo-European indicated states (Delbrück 1911; Luraghi 2019). This means that there was an area of overlap between the stative middle and the perfect, the only difference between the two consisting in the resultative component of the latter (see Di Giovine 1996). In addition, at the earliest stages of the Indo-European languages, the perfect was subject-oriented, and with transitive verbs had the effect of indicating a state of the subject, similar to a passive form. Compare *pépoitha* (persuade.PRF.1SG) 'I am / have been persuaded' with the later form *pépeika* (persuade.PRF.1SG) 'I have persuaded (someone)' (Luraghi et al. 2005: 60) both from *peíthō*. Interestingly, some *media tantum* have active forms in the perfect, such as for example *gígnomai* 'become', perfect *gégona* 'I have become' with active morphology; this hold for several experiential verbs as well, as for example *élpomai* 'hope', perfect *éolpa*, again with active morphology (see Section 9.2). In Homer, middle forms of the perfect are quite frequent, and may have passive meaning, but the phonological shape often betrays a recent origin (Chantraine 2013: 417–418).

4.3 Discussion

Verbal categories play an important role in the construal of situations. Verbal aspect correlates with actionality, and the two contribute to construing a situation as a state, a change of state, or an ongoing process. Verbal voice can often indicate whether a situation comes about spontaneously or because it is externally induced.

The role of verbal categories may be different with groups of experiential verbs. For example, as I have pointed out in Section 4.2, while all types of experiential verbs, including verbs of bodily sensation, volition, perception, cognition and emotion, show an affinity with the middle voice, only the last two domains are encoded by verbs that also show passive aorist forms. According to Allan (2003: 127–128) these are *kholóomai* 'be/get angry', *mimnéskomai* 'remember', *térpomai* 'enjoy', *khaírō* 'rejoice', and the aorist root *da-* 'learn'. As the passive aorist, besides the passive function, often encodes spontaneous events typical of inanimate entities, and, being perfective, indicates a change of state, it seems to be connected with uncontrolled situations to a higher extent than the middle voice (see Allan 2003: 174–175). This seems to indicate that certain situations involving cognition and emotion are conceived as more uncontrolled than perception and volition, a conclusion that, as we will see discussing individual in the next chapters, is only partly supported by the distribution of argument structure constructions.

CHAPTER 5

At the Edges of the Experiential Domain: Bodily Sensations and Volition

In this Chapter, I undertake the discussion of the sub-domains of experience in Homeric Greek by analyzing, first, the subdomains of bodily sensations (Section 5.1) and of volition (Section 5.2). The reasons for starting with these two sub-domains and for treating them in the same Chapter are briefly explained below.

In the first place, these two subdomains are smaller than the others, partly for extra-linguistic reasons connected with the limits of the corpus (some verbs of bodily sensation are only scarcely attested), but partly also for conceptual reasons that depend on the construal of specific situations. Indeed, as has already been pointed out in Section 2.1.5, the sub-domain of volitionality largely overlaps with other sub-domains, notably emotion and cognition. Accordingly, in my description of this sub-domain, I limited the number of verbs included, and left out most verbs of desiring, which are treated in Chapter 8 among verbs of emotion, and verbs that indicate a controlled and intentional mental activity such as 'plan' that I treat in Chapter 7.

Moreover, the two sub-domains discussed in this Chapter can be seen as constituting two extremes, the opposite edges of the experiential domain: bodily sensations are the least controlled type of experiential situations, while volition, being connected with intentionality, is, at least in its core, usually conceived as implying control. From the point of view of argument structure, they are quite peculiar with respect to verbs in other subdomains, and also represent two extremes. Verbs that denote bodily sensations are often monovalent, and take nominative subjects, as mentioned in Section 3. Among them, only verbs that encode feelings concerning a state of saturation or its contrary, such as 'be hungry', 'be sated' may take a stimulus, and occur with the NomGen or, occasionally, the NomDat construction, with verbs of bodily need only taking the NomGen construction. As I pointed out in Section 2.1.5, the latter verbs are considered close to verbs of volition by some scholars. In Homeric Greek, their constructions pattern partly with verbs of bodily sensation and partly with verbs of volition, thus providing the link between the two experiential domains. In fact, verbs of bodily need also provide a conceptual link between sensation and volition. A need is based on a sensation: for example, the sensation of hunger can be understood as the feeling of a need for food, which then results in the desire to eat.

© SILVIA LURAGHI, 2021 | DOI:10.1163/9789004442528_006

BODILY SENSATIONS AND VOLITION

Verbs of volition tend to take infinitive complements, rather than an NP as their second argument. Interestingly, a limited number of occurrences in which nominal second arguments occur consistently show the NomAcc construction for verbs of all three classes (*want-* *hope-* and *wish*-class, see Noonan 2007: 132 and above, Section 2.1.5). On the other hand, verbs that indicate uncontrolled desire occur in the NomGen construction, and pattern with verbs of emotion. Accordingly, they will be only shortly discussed in this Chapter, while an in-depth analysis will be carried out in Section 8.2.1.

5.1 Bodily Sensations

Verbs of bodily sensation in Homeric Greek are scarcely attested. Among verbs that encode feelings concerning a state of saturation or lack thereof for example, *dipsáō* 'be thirsty' only occurs once in the passage quoted in (63), Section 3. The verb *peináō* 'be hungry' occurs four times, three of which are participles. In the only occurrence of an infinitive, it shows the NomGen construction and takes a stimulus in the genitive *sítou* 'food' as shown in (133).

(133) *sítou   d'   oukét' éphē   peinémenai*
       food.GEN PTC NEG   say.IMPF.3SG be_hungry.INF.PRS
       'He said that he wasn't hungry of food.' (*Od.* 20.137)

In general, alternation between the NomGen and the NomDat construction is typical of verbs of saturation, either as verb-specific or as alternating constructions. For example, the verb *adéō* 'be sated' takes the NomDat construction. It occurs four times in Book 10 of the *Iliad* in the metaphorical expression *kamátōi adēkótes* 'sated with toil' (i.e. extremely tired), as in (134). In this expression, a dative stimulus occurs, *kamátōi* 'toil', and the verb form is a perfect participle, hence it indicates a state. In a single occurrence from the *Odyssey* we find a finite verb form and a different stimulus, *deípnoi* 'dinner', also in the dative. Compare example (135).

(134) *hoi   d'   heûdon   kamátōi hadēkótes*
       DEM.NOM PTC sleep.IMPF.3PL toil.DAT be_sated.PTCP.PRF.NOM.PL
       'They slept won by weariness.' (*Il.* 10.471)

(135) *mḕ xeînos   aniētheìs   orumagdôi*
       NEG stranger.NOM annoy.PTCP.AOR.PASS.NOM noise.DAT
       deípnōi   hadéseien
       meal.DAT be_sated.OPT.AOR.3SG
       'Lest perchance that the stranger, annoyed by the noise, should refuse
       the meal.' (*Od.* 1.133–134)

The NomDat and the NomGen construction profile different aspects of the situation: while the former focuses on the instrumental function of the dative NP, the latter highlights the bodily feeling of saturation.

The verb *korénnumai* 'satiate oneself', however, only takes the NomGen construction, as in (136) and (137).

(136) *hòs   dé k' anḕr   oínoio*
       REL.NOM PTC PTC man.NOM wine.GEN
       koressámenos   kaì edōdês
       satiate.PTCP.AOR.MID.NOM and food.GEN
       'The man who had his fill of wine and food.' (*Il.* 19.167)

(137) *hōs d' hót' ónos ...   epeí t'   ekoréssato*
       as PTC when donkey.NOM as   PTC satiate.AOR.MID.3SG
       phorbês
       forage.GEN
       'As a donkey ... when it has had its fill of forage.' (*Il.* 11. 558–562)

Its active counterpart, *korénnumi* 'satiate', only occasionally is to be understood as causative. See the discussion of examples (445) and (446) in Section 9.2.

Alternation between the NomGen and the NomDat construction is attested with the verb *térpomai*. Etymologically, its meaning was 'be sated', as shown by its Vedic Sanskrit cognate *tṛp-* (Mallory and Adams 2006: 341, cf. Monier-Williams 2008 s.v.). In Homeric Greek, *térpomai* had already started shifting toward the area of emotions, and even when occurring with second arguments referring to food or drink it does not simply mean 'satiate oneself' but always implies pleasure, and means 'enjoy'. In such cases, it always takes the NomGen construction, as in (138).

(138) *epeì tárpēmen   edētúos   ēdè potêtos*
       as enjoy.AOR.1PL food.GEN and drink.GEN
       'When we had had our fill of food and drink.' (*Il.* 11.780)

BODILY SENSATIONS AND VOLITION 103

Even though examples (136) and (138) look similar, they refer to completely different situations. In (136) reference is made to the physical conditions of a generic soldier who has had enough food before a fight, and can then endure fighting without losing strength, while (138) refers to a specific situation, which is being narrated by Neleus, in which the speaker was visiting Achilles, and having food and drink in his hut, in a friendly and pleasant environment.

The difference between the two verbs is also captured by Latacz's (1966: 180–181) remark that, while *térpomai* always only takes human (or divine) subjects, *korénnumai* can also refer to animals as in (137). In fact, *térpomai* occurs with concrete second arguments only in a minority of cases: second arguments with this verb are often abstract entities referring to states, such as love or sleep. The shift away from bodily sensations and toward the domain of emotion is also indicated by the extension of the NomDat construction to this verb that shows its ongoing inclusion in the group of verbs of rejoicing. More examples will accordingly be discussed in Section 8.1.2.

A similar meaning is expressed by the verb *onínamai* 'take profit from', and in some cases 'enjoy', as in (139). This verb always takes the NomGen construction.

(139)   *daitòs   ónēso*
       dinner.GEN profit.IMP.AOR.MID.2SG
       'Enjoy the dinner!' (*Od.* 19.68)

As mentioned in Section 5, bodily needs pattern with verbs of bodily sensations in Homeric Greek: this is not surprising, considering that a state of physical need can be viewed as the opposite of a state of saturation. Several verbs that indicate bodily needs take the NomGen construction in Homeric Greek. The same holds for the invariable form *khrḗ* 'need', which often indicates a more general concept of necessity, but can also indicate physical needs. It most often takes an infinitive complement, as in (140), but it can also occasionally take the NomGen construction as in (141) (see further Section 3.2.2).

(140)   *ou   khrḕ pannúkhion   heúdein   boulēphóron ándra*
       NEG need all_night_long sleep.INF.PRS adviser.ACC man.ACC
       'There is no need for an adviser man to sleep all night long.' (*Il.* 2.61)

(141)   *autàr épeita deípnou   passámenos   muthḗseai*
       but   then   food.GEN eat.PTCP.AOR.MID.NOM say.FUT.MID.2SG
       hótteó   se   khrḗ
       INDF.GEN 2SG.ACC need
       'Then, having been refreshed by the food, you will say what you need.'
       (*Od.* 1.123–124)

104   CHAPTER 5

In fact, this type of construction does not primarily indicate bodily need: rather, it often indicates that an option is more suitable, that it better fits in a certain situation, compare (142).

(142) *oudé tí   se   khrè̀ nēleès   êtor*
       NEG INDF.ACC 2SG.ACC need ruthless.ACC heart.ACC
       ékhein
       have.INF.PRS
       'You don't need to have a ruthless heart.' (*Il.* 9.496–497)

The verb *krēízō*, a Homeric derivate based on *khrḗ*, means 'need', 'lack'. This verb is attested four times. Similar to *peináō* 'be hungry' (see example (133)) it can occur either with the NomGen construction as in (143), or without a second argument, as in (144), in which it simply indicates a state of need.

(143) *khrēízonta   kaì autòn   amúmonos iētêros*
       need.PTCP.PRS.ACC and self.ACC good.GEN   healer.GEN
       'And he himself needs a good healer.' (*Il.* 11.835)

(144) *mēdè tà   dôra   hoútō khrēízonti*
       NEG DEM.ACC.PL gift.ACC.PL so   need.PTCP.PRS.DAT
       koloúete
       cut_short.IMP.PRS.2PL
       'Do not be stingy with gifts with one who is in need.' (*Od.* 11.339–340)

Also connected with *khrḗ* is the verb *khráomai* 'need', which similarly takes the NomGen construction, as in (145).

(145) *all' állōs   komidês kekhrēménoi   ándres*
       but randomly care.GEN need.PTCP.PRF.NOM.PL man.NOM.PL
       alêtai   pseúdont'
       vagabond.NOM.PL lie.PRS.M/P.3PL
       'Vagabonds lie at random when they need care.' (*Od.* 14.124–125)

In spite of limited evidence, some interesting observations can be made. In the first place, in Ancient Greek bodily sensations that indicate saturation or temperature are lexicalized as verbs, rather than nouns or adjectives as they frequently are in English. In the second place, when a stimulus occurs with verbs of saturation it triggers the NomGen or the NomDat construction, thus conforming to the pattern described in Section 3.2.5 for the verb *pímplēmi* 'fill',

BODILY SENSATIONS AND VOLITION

see examples (101) and (102). Verbs of bodily need partly pattern after verbs of bodily sensation, as they also take the NomGen construction.

Feelings of temperature denote situations that are typically construed as not involving an additional stimulus. In Homeric Greek, they are encoded by intransitive verbs, and are indicated by verbs such as *rhigóō* 'be cold' in (146).

(146) *epeì ouk ephámēn   rhigōsémen   émpēs*
  as   NEG say.IMPF.M/P.1SG be_cold.INF.FUT alike
  'For I did not think that I should be as cold as this.' (*Od.* 14.481)

Other one-place verbs that indicate bodily states are *algéō* 'suffer' in (147)-(149) and *kámnō* 'become tired' in (150).

(147) *hò   d' ár' hézeto   tárbēsén   te,*
  DEM.NOM PTC PTC sit.IMPF.M/P.3SG shiver.AOR.3SG PTC
  algésas
  suffer.PTCP.AOR.NOM
  'He was sitting and, having suffered, he shivered with fear.' (*Il.* 2.268–269)

(148) *algésas   d' anépalto,   bélos   d' eis*
  suffer.PTCP.AOR.NOM PTC jump.AOR.MID.3SG arrow.NOM PTC to
  egképhalon dû
  brain.ACC   dive.AOR.3SG
  'He jumped out of suffering: an arrow had gone through his brain.' (*Il.* 8.85)

(149) *hína   mḗ ti   kakoppaphíēi alegeinêi è halòs*
  in_order_to NEG INDF.ACC trap.DAT   evil.DAT PTC sea.GEN
  è   epì gês   algésete   pêma   pathóntes
  PTC on land.GEN suffer.FUT.2PL pain.ACC suffer.PTCP.AOR.NOM.PL
  'In order for you not to suffer pain, having experienced any suffering for an evil trap either across the sea or across the land.' (*Od.* 12.26–27)

(150) *epeí ke kámōsin   eüxéstēis elátēisi pónton*
  as   PTC be_tired.SBJ.AOR.3PL fir.DAT.PL oar.DAT.PL sea.ACC
  elaúnontes
  drive.PTCP.NOM.PL
  'When they have grown weary of beating the sea with polished oars of fir.' (*Il.* 7.5–6)

Examples (147) and (148) contain the aorist participle *algésas*. The perfective aspect of this verb form indicates the sudden inception of a state of suffering, which has immediate bodily reflexes: starting shivering in (147) and an abrupt upright movement in (148). In (149), the future *algésete* 'you will suffer' occurs along with the aorist participle of *páskhō*, *pathóntes* 'having suffered', which takes the cognate object *pêma* 'pain, accident' and a cause adverbial in the dative *ti kakoppaphíēi alegeinēi* 'because of some evil intrigue'. Notably, the participial clause *ti kakoppaphíēi alegeinēi pêma pathóntes* 'suffering pains for an evil trap' encodes the cause for the possible inception of the state indicated by *algésete*. Similarly in (150) the cause for reaching the state of being tired is encoded by the participial clause *elátēisi pónton elaúnontes* 'beating the sea with the oars'.

Some more words need to be spent on the verb *páskhō* shown in (149), which also means 'suffer', and in the vast majority of the occurrences (106 out of 118) takes the NomAcc construction limited to second arguments such as *kaká*, *álgea*, *pêma* 'evils, pains, sufferings'. As remarked above with reference to *pêma*, such second arguments must be regarded as cognate objects. Though not etymologically related with the verb *páskhō*, they are semantically close to it, and do not add any information about a specific second participant. Commenting on the syntactic status of cognate objects, Jacquinod (1989: 138–139) argues that they do not properly fill one of the slots in the verbal valency: rather, they are added to monovalent verbs (as in this case) that remain monovalent, or to bivalent verbs that already have another object. In constructionist terms, one may view the NomAcc construction in occurrences of cognate objects as being used as default construction (it is by far the most frequent construction of two-place verbs, see Section 3.2.3), rather than on account of its specific semantic features.

5.2   Volitionality and Need

In this section, I discuss the meaning of two verbs of volition, *ethélō* 'want' and *boúlomai* 'wish', and of the verbs *élpomai* 'hope', 'expect' and *mémona* 'desire eagerly'. Both verbs *ethélō* and *boúlomai* indicate volition, but they display a different semantics and different constructions. Before going into detail, it is interesting to note that the two verbs also exhibit different morphology: while *ethélō* only inflects in the active, *boúlomai* is a *medium tantum*. Similarly, *élpomai* was originally a *medium tantum*: two active forms based on the present stem in the *Odyssey* are clearly secondary and have causative meaning (Chantraine 1977: 342 and Section 9.2). In addition, perfect and pluperfect forms are morpholog-

BODILY SENSATIONS AND VOLITION

ically active, as is sometimes the case for *media tantum* (see Chapter 4 and the pluperfect form *eólpei* in (165) below). The verb *mémona* is active, only has the perfect stem, and does not show any form built on the present and aorist stems.

As anticipated in Section 3.3, the verb *ethélō* takes an infinitive complement. Examples with the infinitive are (117) and (151). Occasionally, *ethélō* may show the NomAcc construction, as in (152), in which it occurs with an indefinite neuter pronoun that refers back to the generic object of the verb *phrázomai* 'think', 'devise'.

(151)   *ei dè   mnēstérōn   ethéleis   katadûnai   hómilon*
        if PTC suitors.GEN.PL want.PRS.2SG plunge.INF.AOR crowd.ACC
        'If you want to plunge into the crowd of the suitors.' (*Od.* 15.328)

(152)   *mál' eúkēlos   tà   phrázeai   háss'*
        very quiet.NOM DEM.ACC.PL think.PRS.M/P.2SG INDF.ACC.PL
        ethéleistha
        want.SBJV.PRS.2SG
        'You very quietly devise whatever things you wish.' (*Il.* 1.554)

Elsewhere, *ethélō* may occur without a complement, and indicate a generic state of being willing or not willing, as in (153) and (154).

(153)   *Zeùs   emé   g'   ēnógei   deûr' elthémen   ouk*
        Zeus.NOM 1SG.ACC PTC force.IMPF.3SG here come.INF.AOR NEG
        ethélonta
        want.PTCP.PRS.ACC
        'Zeus forced me to come here, but I didn't want to.' (*Od.* 5.99)

(154)   *hérxon   hópōs ethéleis*
        do.IMP.AOR.2SG as   want.PRS.2SG
        'Do what you want!' (*Il.* 4.37)

Often, will is located in the *thumós*. This word is generally translated as 'spirit', 'heart', 'mind'. This is a very important concept in Homer. The *thumós* is not only the location of will, but also the location of emotions: will and desire entertain a complex relation with intentionality, as I pointed out in Section 2.1.5, and they can be construed as being controlled and intentional or uncontrolled. In the latter case, will comes close to the field of emotions, while in the former it rather patterns with mental activities, which often involve planning and hence control.

Most often, *ethélō* and the dependent infinitive share the same subject, but this is not necessarily the case, and some AcI constructions also occur, as in (155) and (156).

(155) eí m'   ethéleis   polemízein   ēdè mákhesthai
       if 1SG.ACC want.PRS.2SG fight.INF.PRS and fight.INF.PRS.M/P
       'If you want me to fight and make war.' (*Il.* 3.67)

(156) ê   t' àn égōg'   ethéloimi   kaì autíka
       PTC PTC PTC 1SG.NOM want.OPT.PRS.1SG and immediately
       toûto   genésthai
       DEM.ACC   be.INF.AOR.MID
       'I, too, would want this to happen immediately.' (*Il.* 12.69)

The verb *ethélō* is much more frequent than *boúlomai* in Homeric Greek, with 293 occurrences against 37. Handbooks and dictionaries point out that *ethélō* indicates will more generically, while *boúlomai* indicates wish or desire but often also preference, in accordance with its etymological connection with *boulé* 'decision' and *bouleúō* 'decide', 'plan' (Chantraine 1977: 189). In such cases, it implies comparison and judgment, as in (157). As *ethélō*, *boúlomai* takes a dependent infinitive in Homer, almost always with the same subject. Examples of *boúlomai* with different subjects and an AcI clause are (117) and (157).

(157) eid' humîn   hóde   mûthos   aphandánei,   allà
       if 2PL.DAT DEM.NOM word.NOM dislike.PRS.3SG but
       bólesthe   autón   te zóein   kaì ékhein
       want.PRS.M/P.2PL DEM.ACC PTC live.INF.PRS and have.INF.PRS
       patróïa   pánta
       paternal.ACC.PL all.ACC.PL
       'If you don't like these words but want him to live and be in possession of all his paternal goods.' (*Od.* 16.387–388)

In addition, *boúlomai* may occur with a beneficiary dative in the NomAcc construction with the word *nikḗn* 'victory' as second argument, and mean 'wish victory for someone', as in (158), a construction that does not occur with *ethélō*.

(158) Apóllōn ... Tróessi   dè boúleto   nikēn
       Apollo.NOM Trojan.DAT.PL PTC want.IMPF.M/P3SG victory.ACC
       'Apollo wished victory for the Trojans' (*Il.* 7.20–21)

BODILY SENSATIONS AND VOLITION

109

I have included *mémona* in this group of verbs mainly on account of its construction. It occurs 129 times in the Homeric poems, most often with an infinitive and only four with a nominal second argument in the NomGen construction. Its semantics has given rise to discussion. Being a perfect, the verb should have a resultative meaning, and indicate a state resulting from a change of state (see Section 4.1). Etymologically, it is connected with the Proto-Indo-European root **men* 'think'. Accordingly, Bertolín Cebrián (1996) includes it among verbs of cognition. However, the meaning that one can extract from the contexts in which it occurs points to a closer connection with verbs of emotion. Compare examples (159)-(162).

(159) *mémasan   dè   kaì   hôs   husmîni   mákhesthai ...   pró*
be_eager.AOR.3PL PTC and so   battle.DAT fight.INF.PRS.M/P for
te   paídōn   kaì   prò   gunaikôn
and children.GEN.PL and for woman.GEN.PL
'(The Trojans) were eager to fight in battle for their children and their wives.' (*Il.* 8.56–57)

(160) *toû   d'   ámoton   memáasin   akouémen,   hoppót'*
DEM.GEN PTC insatiably be_eager.PRF.3PL hear.INF.PRS whenever
aeídēi
sing.SBJV.PRS.3SG
'When he sings, insatiably they are eager to hear him.' (*Od.* 17.520)

(161) *Héktora   kaì   memaôta   mákhēs*
Hector.ACC and be_eager.PTCP.PRF.ACC battle.GEN
skhésesthai   oïō
hold.INF.FUT.MID think.PRS.1SG
'I think I will stop Hector, even though he is eager for battle.' (*Il.* 9.655)

(162) *hupò   dè   zugòn   égagen   Hérē   híppous*
under PTC yoke.ACC lead.AOR.3SG Hera.NOM horses.ACC.PL
ōkúpodas,   memauî'   éridos   kaì   aütês.
fast_foot.ACC.PL be_eager.PTCP.PRF.NOM fight.GEN and shout.GEN
'Hera conducted the horses fast feet under the yoke, she was eager of fighting and of shouting.' (*Il.* 5.731–732)

The passage in (159) exemplifies a frequent context of occurrence of *mémona*, with the dependent infinitive *mákhesthai* 'fight' (17 occurrences): indeed, the feeling expressed by *mémona* is most often directed toward some type of hostile activity, and is taken to indicate eagerness. Example (160) shows one of the few occurrences in which the object of *mémona* is not fighting. In this passage, reference is made to the audience of a poet, who is eager to listen to his singing. Finally, (161) and (162) contain two of the four occurrences of the NomGen construction: in (161) the abstract noun *mákhē* 'fight' is a nominal equivalent of the infinitive *mákhesthai*; similarly, *éridos kaì aütês* 'fight and battle cry' in (162) also refer to fighting.

Bertolín Cebrián (1996: 13–47) argues that, contrary to what is normally claimed, *mémona* does not refer to a feeling of eagerness, and does not indicate a state of mind implying furious craving. Rather, she claims that in some cases the verb seems to refer to a decision that is based on reasoning: for example, in (159) the Trojans are depicted as eager to fight to defend themselves and their families, as highlighted by the occurrence of the beneficiary expression *pró te paídōn kaì prò gunaikôn* 'for their children's and their wives' sake'. According to Bertolín Cebrián, this is a consequence of the resultative meaning of the perfect: in her opinion, as the root means 'think', the perfect must mean 'having thought'. Accordingly, for (159) she proposes the translation "sie waren trotztdem entschlossen" ('they were determined', p. 27).

Still, the fact that, though infrequently, *mémona* can take the NomGen construction shows that it patterns with verbs that indicate uncontrolled desire (see Section 8.2.1). On the other hand, the resultative meaning implied by the perfect stem need not be emphasized: in fact, lexicalized or semi-lexicalized perfects, such as *oîda* 'know' (from **wid-* 'see' Section 7.2) or *bébeka* 'stand' (from *baínō* 'go', discussed in Section 4.1), synchronically denote states, and the change-of-state component can be reconstructed to explain the origin of the semantic change, but is no longer active. Hence, in the case of *mémona*, in consideration of its etymology, one may well reconstruct a semantic development such as 'desire as a consequence of having thought' > 'be in a state of intense desire'.

The verb *élpomai* occurs 61 times in the Homeric poems (plus two occurrences in the active voice with causative meaning; see Section 9.2). It means 'hope', 'expect', 'have the impression', and notably its etymology connects it closely with will, as it originates from the Proto-Indo-European root **wel-* of Latin *volo* 'want', and English *will* (Mallory and Adams 2006: 341). It may indicate an opinion, thus implying a judgment, and can be translated as 'deem', as in (163).

BODILY SENSATIONS AND VOLITION

(163) *autàr epèn hēméas élpēi*   *potì*   *dómat'*
        but when 1PL.ACC hope.SBJV.PRS.M/P.2SG toward house.ACC
        aphîkhthai
        reach.INF.PRF.M/P
        'But when you think that we have reached the house.' (*Od.* 6.297)

Similar to volition verbs, *élpomai* also takes a dependent infinitive in most
occurrences, as in (164), and also occurs with an AcI clause, as in (165), in case
of different subjects. In addition, *élpomai* occasionally takes the NomAcc construction, either with neuter pronouns, as does *ethélō*, or with the object *níkēn*
'victory' as *boúlomai* in (158); compare (166).

(164) *hòs héphath',*   *hoì*   *d'* *ekhárēsan*
        so say.IMPF.3SG REL.NOM.PL PTC rejoice.AOR.PASS.3PL
        Akhaioí   *te* *Trôés*   *te* *elpómenoi*
        Achaean.NOM.PL and Trojan.NOM.PL and hope.PTCP.PRS.M/P.NOM
        paúsasthai   *oïzuroû* *polémoio*
        end.INF.AOR.MID fatal.GEN war.GEN
        'He said so, and they rejoiced, Achaeans and Trojans, hoping to make
        the fatal war end.' (*Il.* 3.111–112)

(165) *óphra mèn humîn* *thumòs* *enì stéthessin*   *eólpei*
        until PTC 2PL.DAT soul.NOM in breast.DAT.PL hope.PPF.3SG
        nostésein   *Odusêa*   *polúphrona* *hónde* *dómonde*
        return.INF.FUT Odysseus.ACC ingenious.ACC REL.ACC homeward
        'Until your soul hoped in your breast that ingenious Odysseus would
        have returned home.' (*Od.* 20.328–329)

(166) *hò*   *dè* *phresìn*   *hêisi*   *khárē*
        REL.NOM PTC heart.DAT.PL POSS.3SG.DAT.PL rejoice.AOR.PASS.3SG
        kaì eélpeto   *níkēn*
        and hope.IMPF.M/P.3SG victory.ACC
        'He rejoiced in his heart and he hoped for the victory.' (*Il.* 13.609)

Examples (158) and (166) point toward a difference between *boúlomai*, which
means 'wish for someone else', and *élpomai*, which occurs when the wish is
directed toward the experiencer. This is an interesting distribution in view of
Noonan's (2007) distinction among classes of volition verbs. Discussing different classes of volition predicates, Noonan remarks that "*Hope*-class predicates
are the true counterparts of predicates of fearing since both types express an

emotional attitude toward a proposition whose status is, for whatever reason, unknown, but which could turn out to be true." (2007: 132). The similarity between fear and hope is also noted by Wierzbicka, who writes "*hope* implies a lack of knowledge about the future ("I don't know what will happen"), and in this (as well as in some other respects) it is parallel to *fear*." (1999: 59). Similar to fear, in Homeric Greek hope is construed as an experiencer-directed type of experience (see Section 8.3.2), as indicated by the fact that one can only hope for oneself.

As in the case of other verbs of volition, a region is often indicated in which the experiencer experiences the situation indicated by *élpomai*. Similar to *ethélō*, the location involved can be *thumós* or it can be *phrḗn*, as in (166). The latter indicates a concrete body part, the midriff, and by metonymy also the heart as seat of passions, or more in general of consciousness, see Jahn (1987) and below, Section 7.2.1.

Summing up, verbs of volition denote situations in which the stimulus is a state of affairs, often controlled by the experiencer. Accordingly, especially with *ethélō* and *boúlomai*, the dependent infinitive most often has the same subject as the governing verb, even though there are also occurrences with a different subject and an AcI clause. The verb *élpomai* can also occur with a dependent infinitive or an AcI clause with a different subject. It seems to be semantically close to *boúlomai*, in that the meaning of both verbs is connected with a judgment, which leads to a preference in the case of *boúlomai* and to an opinion in the case of *élpomai*. When indicating a wish, *élpomai* is directed toward the experiencer, while *boúlomai* can be directed toward someone else, as shown by the occurrences with *nikḗn* in (158) and (166).

Morphologically, too, *boúlomai* and *élpomai* pattern similarly, as they always show middle morphology. Only *élpomai* has an active counterpart, *élpō* 'induce hope', which occurs twice in identical passages in *Od.* 2.91 and 13.380 and, as remarked by Chantraine (1977: 342), is clearly a secondary formation (see Section 9.2), while the perfect *éolpa* with present meaning is morphologically active as in the case of several other *media tantum*, but has the same meaning as the middle (see the discussion in Section 4.2). On the other hand, *ethélō* only inflects in the active. Recall that the middle voice may indicate a lesser degree of transitivity and control than the active (Section 4.2). In the case of volition verbs, this can be related to the degree of realisness implied by different verb classes as described in Noonan (2007): *ethélō*, which instantiates the *want*-class, shows the higher degree of realisness as compared to *boúlomai* and *élpomai*, instantiating the *wish*-class and the *hope*-class respectively.

The situation indicated by *ethélō* is also the least complex type of situation, as it indicates will in a more straightforward fashion *boúlomai* and *élpomai*:

BODILY SENSATIONS AND VOLITION

indeed, as I have pointed out, both *boúlomai* and *élpomai* involve some sort of judgment prior to the wish or hope they express. This difference might be reflected in the verbal voice, as I discuss in Section 5.3.

5.3   Discussion

Verbs discussed in this Section belong to two sub-domains that are apparently far apart from one another, at least judging from possible control of the experiencer over the state of affairs. However, the two types of situations are not as disparate as they may look at first sight, as bodily needs can be viewed as providing a link between them (see Section 5).

The two sub-domains of bodily sensations and of volition display a wide variety of constructions. In the first place, several verbs of bodily sensation are monovalent, while verbs of need and volition often take dependent infinitives. Among two-place verbs taking an argument structure construction that includes two nominal arguments, verbs of bodily sensation consistently take the NomGen construction, with the exception of *adéō* 'be sated' that takes the NomDat construction as in (134) and (135), and of *térpomai* 'enjoy', which shows construction variation between the NomGen and the NomDat construction. As argued in Sections 5.1 and 8.1.2, this verb did not only indicate a feeling of satiation, but also the feeling of pleasure brought about by satiation, and the adoption of the NomDat construction indicates its shift to the domain of emotions, and inclusion among verbs of rejoicing. Another apparent exception is the verb *páskhō* 'suffer', which takes the NomAcc construction. Notably, however, the construction is limited to cognate objects that do not add information about a specific entity, but rather highlight the meaning of the verb, so the NomAcc construction here must be viewed as a default construction (see the discussion in Section 10.4).

Verbs that indicate need pattern with verbs of bodily sensation, as they take the NomGen construction in cases in which they occur with two NPs. Such cases, however, are the minority: as already pointed out, verbs of need most frequently select dependent infinitives, similar to verbs of volition. Hence, verbs of need also provide a link between the two domains in terms of types of construction.

Verbs of volition show a two-NP argument structure quite infrequently. In spite of the limited number of occurrences, however, one can spot a difference between *mémōna* and other volition verbs, whereby the former takes the Nom-Gen construction and patterns with verbs of bodily sensation, while the latter feature the NomAcc construction. As I will argue in Chapter 8, this shows a closer connection of volition verbs other than *mémōna* with verbs of emotion.

Concerning verbal voice, verbs of bodily sensation show a comparatively neat pattern, with verbs of saturation featuring both voices and encoding the (anti)causative alternation through voice (see Chapter 9). Other verbs in this group, instead, are mostly active: *dipsáō* 'be thirsty', *peináō* 'be hungry', *rhigóō* 'be cold' and *algéō* 'suffer' only feature active forms in Homeric Greek, while *kámnō* 'become tired' is mostly active (43 out of 46 occurrences). Active forms are labile, and can be either transitive or intransitive depending on the context; three middle occurrences show the same semantics as intransitive active forms.

The distribution of voice with volition verbs is partly in accordance with Allan's (2003: 64–76) characterization of the middle voice with respect to verbs that indicate, in his terms, 'mental processes'. According to Allan, the middle voice indicates subject (i.e. experiencer) affectedness, which in his view characterizes in general the relation between experiencer subjects and stimuli with verbs of volition, cognition and emotion. In the case of *ethélō* 'want' and *boúlomai* 'wish', Allan strives to demonstrate that the latter verb implies a higher degree of mental involvement, hence of affectedness, precisely because it indicates preference (2003: 236–242), as I pointed out in Section 5.2, and similar considerations can be made for *élpomai* 'hope' that Allan only mentions in passing but does not discuss. (I am leaving aside *mémona* because it only features active perfect forms, which do not provide cues on the voice of a putative present or aorist, see Section 4.2.)

CHAPTER 6

Perception

In Homeric Greek, perception verbs are unevenly attested across perception modalities: while verbs that indicate sight and hearing are frequent, other perceptual modalities are scarcely if ever referred to. In particular, smell is referred to only by a phenomenon-based verb (in the sense of Viberg (1984), see Section 2.1.2), and without the experiencer. Taste and touch are more frequent, but they also raise problems, as I will show in Section 6.3. In spite of this, and with an eye to occurrences from Classical Greek prose, one can see a common pattern for these three perception modalities, whereby they consistently take the NomGen construction.

Sight and hearing, on the other hand, are well represented by various verbs that will be reviewed in Section 6.1 and 6.2. Contrary to other perceptual modalities, verbs of sight consistently take the NomAcc construction, while verbs of hearing constitute the only group of perception verbs that shows construction variation. Verbs that refer to touch and taste only feature the NomGen construction: as I argue, this should also be considered the pattern of smell verbs, based on evidence from later authors.

At first sight, the lexicalization of different event types in the area of sight and hearing in Homeric Greek might seem to be at odds with Viberg's (1984) universals of lexicalization (see Section 2.1.2), as a distinction between 'see' and 'look at' appears to be conveyed only by construction variation (NomAcc vs. NomPP), while the distinction between 'hear' and 'listen to' is, at least in part, indicated by two different lexemes. In Section 6.2 and 6.5 I will argue that this exceptional situation is likely apparent, and might be connected with the peculiarities of the Homeric language that combines constructions from different language stages.

Following a cross-linguistically common extension, sight and hearing are the source for evidentials, as discussed in Section 6.4, especially when occurring with the Two-Place+P construction.

6.1 Visual Perception

Visual perception in Homeric Greek is indicated by several verbal roots, all of Indo-European origin and also attested in other Indo-European languages. The most frequent verb, *horáō* 'see', has only the present (imperfective) stem,

© SILVIA LURAGHI, 2021 | DOI:10.1163/9789004442528_007

and already in pre-literary times it started being used to supplement the aorist (perfective) *eîdon*. The latter is the aorist from the Proto-Indo-European root **wid-* 'see', whose perfect, *oîda*, had shifted its meaning to indicate knowledge, as discussed in Sections 1.3, 4.1 and 7.2. This semantic shift is shared by other Indo-European languages and cannot be considered a specifically Greek development. As a consequence, a third stem *op-* came to be used to supply a new perfect in Greek, *ópōpa*, which also served as base for the future, and is related to the Proto-Indo-European root **okʷ-* of Latin *oculus* 'eye' and English *eye*. The present stem *horáō* also has cognates in other Indo-European languages, but they are not directly related to sight: rather, they seem to point toward a more general concept of awareness and attention, as shown by English *aware* and Latin *vereor* 'respect', 'fear' (Chantraine 1977: 815). Even though the origin of the verbal paradigm is composite, the three stems do not seem to bring about any semantic difference apart from the aspectual features borne by each of them.

In addition to this, another verb, *dérkomai*, also means 'see'; it derives from the Proto-Indo-European root **derk-* 'see' also attested in Sanskrit *dṛś-* 'see'. Interestingly, this verb has all three aspectual stems in Homeric Greek, while in Sanskrit it only has the aorist and the perfect. The verb *sképtomai* 'look', 'watch', 'spy' also occurs three times in the Homeric poems, showing the present and the aorist stem. This verb is related to the Proto-Indo-European root **spek-* of Latin *specio* 'look' and Sanskrit *paś-* 'see', the stem that supplies the present to *dṛś-*. Finally, the denominal verb *leússō* 'look', 'gaze', 'see' is related with the root of English *light* and Latin *luceo* 'shine' and only has the present (imperfective) stem. These last two verbs are semantically more marginal, and will be discussed at the end of this Section.

This brief etymological survey shows a tendency for the verb 'see' to be lexicalized by different roots that had some inherent aspectual features. Although this is a general tendency of the Proto-Indo-European verb, which is partly reflected by other verbs as well, both in Greek and in Indo-Aryan, in the field of Homeric Greek perception verbs it is one of the features that single out sight as contrasted with other perceptual modalities.

Even though *dérkomai* is much less frequent than *horáō* and *eîdon* (13 occurrences against 109 occurrences of the stems of *horáō* and *ópōpa* combined and 439 of the aorist *eîdon*), the different verbal stems seem to occur virtually in all same types of contexts, with differences only related to aspect. In the first place, both the present of *dérkomai* and *horáō* can indicate the faculty of seeing, as in (167) and (168), in which being able to see stands for being alive.

PERCEPTION

117

(167) óphra dé ... zṓei   kaì horâi   pháos   ēelíoio
while PTC live.PRS.3SG and see.PRS.3SG light.ACC sun.GEN
'While he lives, and sees the light of the sun.' (*Il.* 18.61)

(168) emeû   zôntos   kaì epì khthonì
1SG.GEN live.PTCP.PRS.GEN and on earth.DAT
derkoménoio
see.PTCP.PRS.M/P.GEN
'While I live and have sight on the earth.' (*Il.* 1.88).

Examples (169)-(171) indicate perception of a concrete entity, animate in (169) and (170), and inanimate in (171). In (169) the form *ópsetai* is a future from the root *op-* of the perfect *ópōpa* that occurs in (170), while the form *édrakon* in (171) is an aorist. In all occurrences verbs of seeing take the NomAcc construction, irrespective of verbal aspect and of referential properties of the second participant, such as animacy.

(169) átt'   ê   toi   mèn egṑn   eîm'   es pólin,   óphra
father.VOC PTC PTC PTC 1SG.NOM go.PRS.1SG to town.ACC for
me   métēr   ópsetai
1SG.ACC mother.NOM see.FUT.MID.3SG
'Father, I will go to town in order for mother to see me.' (*Od.* 17.6–7)

(170) tòn   mèn egṑ   mála pollà   mákhei   éni ...
DEM.ACC PTC 1SG.NOM very many.ACC.PL battle.DAT in
ophthalmoîsin ópōpa
eye.DAT.PL   see.PRF.1SG
'I have seen him with (my) eyes, many times in battle.' (*Il.* 24.391–392)

(171) kapnòn   d'   enì méssei   édrakon   ophthalmoîsi dià
smoke.ACC PTC in midst.DAT see.AOR.1SG eye.DAT.PL through
drumà   puknà   kaì húlen
bush.ACC.PL thick.ACC.PL and wood.ACC
'In the midst (of the island) I saw with (my) eyes smoke through the thick bush and the wood.' (*Od.* 10.196–197)

Example (170) contains the expression *éni ophthalmoîsi(n)* 'in (one's) eyes' (also see example (174)), while its more frequent variant *ophthalmoîsi* 'with/in (one's) eyes' occurs in (171). The occurrence of the locative expression with *en* 'in' shows that body parts are conceptualized as containers in Homer (Luraghi 2004b). In particular, the eyes are containers that contain the object of sight (the *expertum* in the terms of Verhoeven (2007), see Section 1). This localistic view of visual perception is also reflected in the way in which the controlled activity of looking at something is lexicalized, as I will argue further on in this Section.

Examples (169) and (170) refer to immediate perception of an individual, in the terms of Dik and Hengeveld (1991) (see Section 2.1.2). In the next set of examples, from (172) to (174), reference is made to immediate perception of a state of affairs in which an individual is involved. In this case, the state of affairs is indicated by a participle, and we find the Two-place+P construction discussed in Section 3.3, which, in the case of verbs of sight, is always realized as NomAcc+P.

(172) *ópsesthai   phílon   huiòn   apò   Troíēthen*
      see.INF.FUT.MID dear.ACC son.ACC from   from_Troy
      iónta
      go.PTCP.PRS.ACC
      'He will see his beloved son returning from Troy.' (*Il.* 24.492)

(173) *hōs ídon   Héphaiston   dià   dṓmata*
      as see.AOR.3PL Hephaestus.ACC   through palace.ACC.PL
      poipnúonta
      puff.PTCP.PRS.ACC
      'As they saw Hephaestus puffing through the palace.' (*Il.* 1.600)

(174) *epeì oú   pō tlḗsom'*   *en ophthalmoîsin horâsthai*
      as   NEG PTC bear.FUT.MID.1SG   in eye.DAT.PL   see.INF.PRS.M/P
      marnámenon   phílon   huiòn ... Menelάoi
      fight.PTCP.PRS.M/P.ACC dear.ACC son.ACC Menelaus.DAT
      'Since I can in no wise bear to behold with my eyes my dear son doing battle with Menelaus.' (*Il.* 3.306–307)

Immediate perception of an individual or of a state of affairs through the visual channel offers a source for certain knowledge. This holds true especially for Homeric Greek, in which verbs of sight in the Two-place+P construction always only refer to direct perception of an event which is simultaneous to the event of perception. Verbs of sight can function as evidentials, and indicate the source of knowledge. Let us consider example (175).

PERCEPTION

(175) egṑ   dé   min   autòs   ópōpa,   kaì   gàr
       1SG.NOM PTC 3SG.ACC self.NOM see.PRF.1SG and PTC
       mnḗmōn   eimí
       mindful.NOM be.PRS.1SG
       'I have seen him myself, and indeed remember him.' (*Od.* 21.94–95)

In (175), Antinous is talking to the other suitors in Odysseus palace. Penelope has defied them to stretch Odysseus' bow, knowing that none of them will succeed. Antinous knows that this will be a hard enterprise, and, though thinking that he will make it, tells his comrades that he does not see among them anyone who he thinks is Odysseus' equal: he can bring direct evidence for his claim, as he himself remembers seeing him when he was still a child. As we will see in Sections 6.2 and 6.4, direct evidence gained through sight is often contrasted with the less certain evidence acquired through hearing.

Homeric Greek lexicalizes to a limited extent the distinction between the controlled situation of intentionally looking at something and the uncontrolled situation of simply perceiving by sight (activities and experiences in the terms of Viberg 1984; see Section 2.1.2). Two verbs, *sképtomai* 'watch', 'spy' (three occurrences) and *leússō* 'look at', 'gaze' (13 occurrences) are taken to indicate controlled events, but in general in the Homeric poems the same verbs that mean 'see' also mean 'look', and the distinction between the two types of situation is usually indicated by a construction that contains a prepositional phrase as its second argument (NomPP construction). This is the case in (176) and (177).

(176) ou   dé   pote Zeùs   trépsen   apò   kraterês
       NEG PTC PTC Zeus.NOM turn.AOR.3SG from fierce.GEN
       husmínēs   ósse   phaeinṓ,   allà kat' autoùs   aièn
       conflict.GEN eye.ACC.DU bright.ACC.DU but to   DEM.ACC.PL ever
       hóra
       see.IMPF.3SG
       'Nor did Zeus turn his bright eyes from the fierce conflict, but ever looked down upon them.' (*Il.* 16.644–646)

(177) hupaì dè   ídeske   katà   khthonòs   ómmata
       down PTC see.AOR.3SG downward ground.GEN eye.ACC.PL
       péxas
       fix.PTCP.AOR.NOM
       'He would look down with eyes fixed upon the ground.' (*Il.* 3.217);

In (176) Zeus is observing the fight. The prepositional phrase with *katá*+acc *kat'autoús* 'toward them' accompanies the verb form *hóra* 'he was watching'. Note that the imperfective stem of *horáō* is inflected in the imperfect and denotes an ongoing activity. In (177) Odysseus is described when speaking amid the assembly: he would stand up and fix his eyes down, looking to the ground. In this case we find the prepositional phrase with *katá*+gen *katà khthonós* 'downward toward the ground' and the iterative aorist form *ídeske* from *eîdon* with the iterative suffix *-sk-*, which indicates a sudden movement habitually repeated on similar occasions.

With *horáō* and *eîdon* the most frequent instantiation of the NomPP construction contains *eis*+acc (Nom*Eis*acc construction). The preposition *eis* (most often spelled *es* in Homeric Greek) is a Greek innovation based on *en* 'in' with the addition of a *-s* suffix (Luraghi 2003a: 82, 107). It means 'to', 'into' and indicates motion toward the interior of a landmark. Examples are (178)-(180).

(178)   *ou   dé   ti   prosphásthai   dúnamai   épos*
        NEG PTC INDF.ACC say.INF.AOR.MID can.PRS.M/P.1SG word.ACC
        ou   d'   eréesthai   ou   d'   eis   ôpa   idésthai
        NEG PTC ask.INF.PRS.M/P NEG PTC into eye.ACC see.INF.AOR.MID
        enantíon
        against
        'I cannot speak a word, or ask, or look straight at his face.' (*Od.* 23.106–107)

(179)   *ho   mèn meídēsen   idṑn   es   paîda*
        DEM.NOM PTC smile.AOR.3SG see.PTCP.AOR.NOM into child.ACC
        'Then Hector smiled, as he glanced at the child.' (*Il.* 6.404).

(180)   *mnēstêres   d'   ára pántes   es   allélous*
        suitor.NOM.PL PTC PTC all.NOM.PL into one_another.ACC.PL
        horóōntes   Tēlémakhon   eréthizon
        see.PTCP.PRS.NOM.PL Telemachus.ACC provoke.IMPF.3PL
        'All the suitors, looking at one another, tried to provoke Telemachus.'
        (*Od.* 20.373–374)

In (178) and (179) the Nom*Eis*acc construction occurs with forms of the aorist *eîdon*, while the present stem *horáō* occurs in (180). The directional preposition profiles an intentional, controlled action. This construction also highlights a localistic construal of perception, as I have already pointed out with respect to

PERCEPTION

example (174) and the expression *en ophthalmoîsi* '(see) in (one's) eyes'. It needs further to be pointed out that the occurrence of the NomEisacc construction, hence reference to an intentional activity, is not connected with voice, as the construction can occur both with middle, as in (178), and with active forms, as in (179) and (180).

Contrary to *horáō / eîdon*, *dérkomai* does not occur with the NomEisacc construction. In fact, an occurrence of the NomPP construction with this verb contains another preposition, *ek* as shown in (181).

(181) *oúté toi   oxútaton kephalês   èk   dérketai*
       NEG 2SG.DAT sharply   head.GEN out.of look.PRS.MID.3SG
       ósse
       eye.NOM.DU
       'Nor do your eyes look farther away from your head.' (*Il.* 23.477)

The passage in (181) has been analyzed in the text quoted here as containing the verb *dérkomai* with the postpositional phrase *kephalês èk* 'out of (your) head' indicating the source. Another analysis is also possible, whereby *ek* 'out of' is taken to be more strictly connected with *dérkomai* and function as a verbal prefix. Such occurrences are quite frequent in Homeric Greek, in which adpostional phrases and verbal prefixes were not fully grammaticalized yet, and adpositions could be both pre- and postposed to the noun that they modified, which in many cases could not yet be analyzed syntactically as their complements (Hewson and Bubenik 2006). Indeed, adpositions did not necessarily open a slot for a complement, as shown by the fact that, contrary to Classical Greek, they could also function as adverbs (see 3.2.2 and Chantraine 1981: 82–86, Luraghi 2003a: 75–81). For these reasons, when a preverb/adposition occurs between a verb and a noun inflected in the case that one also finds in adpositional phrases, it is sometimes impossible (and, one should add, pointless) to decide how to analyze it (cf. Haug 2009, Luraghi 2010d: 216).

Given the uncertain status of preverbs/adpositions in Homer, it is worth considering whether prefixed verbs of sight containing *es/eis* share the meaning as unprefixed verbs in the NomEis construction, that is, whether they indicate a spontaneous or a controlled event. In the case of *eisdérkomai*, the Homeric poems only preserve three occurrences. In example (182), the verb seems to indicate a spontaneous event.

(182) énth' oú   tis   tḕn   nêson   esédraken
      there NEG INDF.NOM DEM.ACC isle.ACC see.AOR.3SG
      ophthalmoîsin
      eye.DAT.PL
      'There none could see the isle with his eyes.' (*Od.* 9.146–148)

In example (183), on the other hand, the context points toward an intentional, controlled action.

(183) ê   kaì Pēnelópeian esédraken   ophthalmoîsi
      say.IMPF.3SG and Penelope.ACC see.AOR.3SG eye.DAT.PL
      'So she said, and looked at Penelope with her eyes.' (*Od.* 19.476)

In this passage, Odysseus' old housekeeper, Eurycleia, has just realized that the stranger that has been entrusted to her is her master. She would like to tell Penelope that Odysseus is back, and intentionally turns her eyes and looks at her. The third occurrence in *Il.* 24.223–224 also supports a controlled event reading.

Occurrences of other prefixed stems also allow for different interpretations concerning the intentional nature of the situation. In general, they all indicate an attentive consideration of the stimulus, sometimes accompanied by wonder, similar to English 'behold'. They can indicate a sudden perception, but most often they indicate an ongoing activity. For this reason, forms of the aorist stem *eiseîdon* are less frequent than forms from other stems: indeed, the ratio of unprefixed / prefixed verb is 25.8/1 for *eîdon* / *eiseîdon* and 1.8/1 for forms based on the present and the perfect stem.

Let us consider some examples, starting with two aorist forms in (184) and (185).

(184) éti   d' éthele   thumôi eisidéein Tróōn   kaì
      still PTC want.AOR.3SG soul.DAT see.INF.AOR Trojan.GEN.PL and
      Akhaiôn   phúlopin ainḗn
      Achaean.GEN.PL fight.ACC cruel.ACC
      'He still wished in his heart to watch the cruel fight of the Trojans and
      the Achaeans.' (*Il.* 16.255–256)

PERCEPTION 123

(185)   *autàr epeì dè speûse   ponēsámenos*
      but   as   PTC hasten.AOR.3SG work.PTCP.AOR.MID.NOM
      tà   hà   érga,   kaì tóte pûr
      DEM.ACC.PL POSS.3SG.ACC.PL work.ACC.PL and then fire.ACC
      anékaie   kaì eísiden,   eíreto   d' hēméas: "Ô
      light.IMPF.3SG and see.AOR.3SG ask.IMPF.M/P.3SG PTC 1PL.ACC oh
      xeînoi'   tínes   esté?"
      stranger.VOC.PL INT.NOM.PL be.PRS.2PL
      'After he finished doing his work, and lit up the fire, he saw us (also possible: "he looked in front of himself") and asked us: "Strangers, who are you?"' (*Od.* 9.250–252)

In (184), Achilles refrains from fighting; however, he has sent his friend Patroclus to fight against the Trojans with some other Greeks. After making offerings to Zeus, he goes out of his hut, in order to watch his comrades fighting against the enemies. The occurrence of the verb *éthele* 'he wanted/wished' supports the interpretation of a controlled activity, even though one needs to remark that even in English the same passage can be translated as 'he still wishes to see the fight', hence without profiling the controlled nature of the perception event. In (185), Odysseus and his comrades are in the Cyclops' den, still hiding in the darkness. The Cyclops is preparing his supper, and lights a fire in the den: in doing so, he suddenly sees the Greeks and addresses them. The sight is unexpected, and current translations highlight unexpectedness by adding a null object (overt in the translation). However, the verb need not refer to a spontaneous event: rather, the directional meaning of the prefix may indicate that he intentionally directed his sight in the direction where the Greeks were standing, even though he did not know beforehand that someone was there.

The more frequent *eisoráō* 'see', 'behold' shows less ambiguity as to whether the situation is construed as spontaneous or controlled, as control seems to be implied in the majority of cases, as in (186) and (187).

(186)   *all' emé   t'   eisoróōn   kaì emèn*
      but 1SG.ACC PTC watch.PTCP.PRS.NOM and POSS.1SG.ACC
      potidégmenos   hormén
      expect.PTCP.AOR.MID.NOM lead.ACC
      'Looking at me and waiting for my lead.' (*Il.* 10.123)

(187) erkhómenon   d'   anà ástu   theòn   hòs
walk.PTCP.PRS.M/P.ACC PTC up   town.ACC god.ACC as
eisoróōsin
watch.PRS.3PL
'When he goes through the town, (men) look at him as if they looked
at a god.' (*Od.* 8.173)

Another prefixed verb, *ephoráō*, occurs 13 times (only once in the aorist) and
means 'see', 'oversee', as in (188).

(188) Ēéliós   th' hòs   pánt'   ephorâis   pánt'
Sun.VOC PTC REL.NOM all.ACC.PL see.PRS.2SG all.ACC.PL
epakoúeis
hear.PRS.2SG
'And you Sun, who see and hear everything.' (*Il.* 3.277)

In example (188), the verb *ephoráō* is coordinated with *epakúō* 'hear', 'perceive by hearing', in a formulaic expression that occurs two more times in the
Odyssey, again referring to the sun. Both verbs contain the preverb *epí* 'on', 'over',
which clearly preserves its spatial meaning in this formula.

Other verbs of seeing are *leússō* 'watch', 'gaze', 'see' and *sképtomai* 'look',
'spy'. The former occurs 13 times. It is usually glossed as indicating a controlled situation (Ebeling 1885: 983, Chantraine 1977: 633); however, actual
occurrences do not rule out the meaning 'see'. It occurs eight times in the
NomAcc construction and three in the NomPP construction. Examples are
(189) and (190).

(189) égkhos   mèn tóde   keîtai   epì khthonós   ou
spear.NOM PTC DEM.ACC lie.PRS.M/P.3SG on ground.GEN NEG
dé ti   phôta   leússō
PTC INDF.ACC body.ACC see.PRS.1SG
'The spear (that I cast) does lie on the ground, but I can't see the body
(of the man that I tried to hit).' (*Il.* 20.345–346)

(190) Kuklópōn   d' es gaîan   eleússomen   eggùs
Cyclops.GEN.PL PTC to land.ACC see.IMPF.1PL nearby
eóntōn
be.PTCP.PRS.GEN.PL
'We looked to the land of the Cyclops, who lived nearby.' (*Od.* 9.166)

PERCEPTION   125

In (189) Achilles cast his spear against Aeneas, but the latter escaped thanks
to the protection of Poseidon, who confounded Achilles' sight with fog. When
the fog disappears, Achilles can only see his spear, but not the body of the
Trojan hero that he intended to kill. The context supports an uncontrolled construal of the situation. On the other hand, the occurrence of the Nom*Eis*acc
construction in (190) points toward an intentional and controlled activity.

The verb *sképtomai* occurs three times in the Homeric poems, and only once
in the NomAcc construction, as shown in (191).

(191) *hò ...   sképtet'   oïstôn   te   rhoîzon   kaì*
       DEM.NOM look.IMPF.MID.3SG arrow.GEN.PL PTC buzz.ACC and
       doûpon   akóntōn
       clash.ACC spear.GEN.PL
       'He was spying the buzz of the arrows and the clash of the spears.' (*Il.*
       16.359–361)

Summing up, the addition of a verbal prefix may indicate control, and this is a
systematic feature of the construction containing a prepositional phrase as its
second argument, in particular of the Nom*Eis*acc construction. However, it is
remarkable that, in spite of the wealth of verbal stems that indicate sight, the
distinction between the uncontrolled event of seeing and the controlled event
of looking at is not indicated by distinct lexical roots, but rather by construction
variation.

Finally, sight can provide evidence for further knowledge based on inference, as in (192) and in (193), in which the experiencer may infer information
about the social status of a person based on visual perception.

(192) *kaí kén tis   phaíē   gónon   émmenai olbíou*
       and PTC INDF.NOM say.OPT.PRS.3SG son.ACC be.INF.PRS rich.GEN
       andrós   es mégethos   kaì kállos   horómenos
       man.GEN to stature.ACC and beauty.ACC see.PTCP.PRS.M/P.NOM
       'Looking to your stature and your comeliness, one would say that you
       are the son of a prosperous man.' (*Od.* 18.218–219)

(193) *mēdè sú ...   tòn   mèn areíō   kalleípein,*
       NEG 2SG.NOM DEM.NOM PTC better.ACC leave_behind.INF.PRS
       sù   dè   kheíron'   opásseai ...   es geneèn
       2SG.NOM PTC worse.DAT take.SBJV.AOR.MID.2SG to birth.ACC
       horóōn,
       see.PTCP.PRS.NOM

'And do not leave the better man behind, and take as your comrade one that is worse, looking to birth.' (*Il.* 10.237–239)

In (192), Penelope is reproaching her son Telemachus for his childish behavior: but he is now an adult, and anyone can get clear evidence of his belonging to an upper-class family (and hence inferably being well-behaved) just by his looks. Visual perception construed as an intentional activity then triggers a mental operation, leading to comparison and judgment. The shift from sight to mental process is complete in (193), in which a judgment on the value of a man is based on consideration of his birth: in this case, no perception is implied.

In these and other similar occurrences, sight is construed as a mental activity. The close relationship between sight and cognition has already been remarked on in relation to the semantic shift of the form *oîda* 'know', originally the perfect resultative of *eîdon* 'see', and is also indicated by the evidential use of sight verbs that can indicate direct experience, as shown in Section 6.4. Further evidence from constructions will be discussed in Chapter 7.

The distribution of verbal voice deserves some additional remarks. Among the verbs surveyed above, *dérkomai* and *sképtomai* are *media tantum*, while *leússō* only features active forms. The much more frequent *horáō* and *eîdon* occur both in the active and, less frequently (176 occurrences out of 483 of the two stems combined), in the middle, while forms based on the root *ops-* are either middle or active depending on the verbal tense, with the future always featuring middle forms and the perfect always active ones. Various attempts have been made at finding semantic nuances connected with either voice, which appear to be hardly compelling. Allan (2003) following Bechert (1964) argues that "the middle voice of verbs of perception marks that the subject is mentally affected", while the active is "unmarked with respect to the feature of affectedness." (2003: 101). In the case of verbs of sight, and more in general of perception verbs, 'mental affectedness' in Allan's view equals volitionality. However, the actual distribution rather supports the traditional view that metrical factors are largely responsible for the occurrence of either voice (see Schwyzer 1950: 232 and Covini 2013 with a detailed discussion of various passages). Moreover, the fact that, even according to proponents of a meaningful distinction between voices, the active functions as an unmarked form, hence being possible in any context, makes this assumption doubtful.

Allan (2003: 99) also argues that *dérkomai* and *sképtomai* are *media tantum* because they are always volitional. However, this is hardly the case for *dérkomai* in occurrences such as (168), for example, in which the verb simply indicates the faculty of sight (see further the discussion of examples (170) and (171)). On the other hand, while it is true that *sképtomai* indicates an intentional activ-

PERCEPTION

ity, the same holds for *leússō* that only inflects in the active and indicates an intentional activity in Homeric Greek. Covini (2013) argues that seven out of 30 middle occurrences of *horáō/eîdon* analyzed in his research are possibly motivated as indirect reflexives. Still, the fact that, as stressed above, active forms can also occur in the same types of contexts makes the finding less compelling. Hence, it seems safer to conclude that voice alternation does not consistently bring about any semantic difference with verbs of sight in Homeric Greek.

6.2 Aural Perception

The morphosyntactic features of hearing verbs are quite different from those of verbs of sight, and differences also concern their semantics, as a partial distinction based on the spontaneous or controlled nature of the situation emerges in connection with different verbal roots. In addition, we do not find suppletive stems, and the distribution of aspectual stems is peculiar, as verbs of hearing in general only feature present and aorist stems but do not occur in the perfect in Homeric Greek.

The most frequent verb, *akouō* 'hear', 'listen to', is possibly related to Gothic *hausjan* 'obey, listen to' and Latin *caveo* 'take heed' (Chantraine: 1977: 50–51; Lehmann 1986: 180–181). In Homer, it features the present and the aorist stem and is virtually always active, with only three middle occurrences. It most frequently indicates the spontaneous event of hearing, but it can also, though less frequently, refer to the controlled activity of listening, without the intervention of preverbs or prepositions. The verb *klúō* 'hear', 'listen to' is cognate of Sanskrit *śru-* (same meaning). It originally only featured the aorist stem, and it is especially frequent in the imperative (48 out of 103 occurrences in Homer): this points toward a stronger tendency of this verbal stem to imply control, a tendency supported by non-imperative occurrences as well. A third verb, less frequent, is *aíō*, etymologically connected with Latin *audio* 'hear'. This verb is described in dictionaries as not only conveying the meaning of hearing but also, more in general, of perceiving. However, as we will see in Section 6.4, evidence for this broader sense is not especially compelling.

The fact that verbs of hearing feature a clearer distinction between a spontaneous perception event and a controlled 'inactive action' (Croft 2012) than verbs of sight is at odds with typological generalizations observed in the existing literature and, as I will argue, might be connected with the characteristics of the Homeric language, which often conflates lexical and grammatical features from different diachronic stages. On the other hand, it needs to be stressed that verbs of hearing do not seem to change their meaning regarding the spontaneous vs. controlled nature of the event they denote through the addition of a preverb or by means of the NomPP construction. A prepositional phrase occurs only once with *akoúō* in the passage discussed in (204) and is not related to control, while prefixed forms include one occurrence of *eisakoúō* and 12 of *epakúō* whose semantics is close to that of the unprefixed verb, as discussed further on (an additional prefixed verb *hupakúō* means 'answer' and does not belong among experiential verbs). The derivative verb *akouázomai* consistently refers to the controlled situation of listening, but evidence remains scanty, as it only occurs twice. Conversely, the verb *klúō* quite consistently indicates the controlled event of listening to. It never occurs with preverbs or prepositions and, as we will see, shows a strong connection with formulaic expressions.

Contrary to verbs of sight, verbs of hearing display construction variation, featuring both the NomAcc and the NomGen construction (with one occurrence of the NomDat construction with *akoúō*). The distribution of constructions is illustrated in Table 7.

TABLE 7   Constructions of hearing verbs

	No object	NomAcc	NomGen	NomDat	PP	Infinitive	Sub. clause	Total
akoúō	39	77	56	1	1	2	5	181
klúō	15	9	75	–	–	–	4	103
aíō	4	5	10	–	–	–	2	21
epakúō	2	7	2	–	–	–	1	12
akouázomai	–	–	2	–	–	–	–	2

Table 7 shows all possible constructions of the verbs of hearing. Even though subordinate clauses are possible with all of them, these verbs tend to feature an argument structure that includes two nominal arguments. With *klúō* and *aíō*, the NomGen construction is (much) more frequent than the NomAcc construction, which instead prevails with *akoúō* and *epakoúō*. To these, one must add the only occurrence of *eisakoúō*, which does not contain a second argument.

Focusing on the type of stimulus, one can see that animacy plays a role in triggering or at least favoring construction variation, as shown in Table 8.

In Table 8, I summarize the distribution of different argument structure constructions in relation to animacy of the stimulus. As already noted above, while the NomGen and the NomAcc construction account for almost all occurrences, *akoúō* also takes once the NomDat construction. With all verbs, the

PERCEPTION

TABLE 8   Occurrences of hearing verbs with different argument structure constructions

		Total occurrences	Animate stimuli	Inanimate stimuli
akoúō	NomGen	56	48	8
	NomAcc	77	1	76
	NomDat	1	1	–
klúō	NomGen	75	66	9
	NomAcc	9	–	9
aíō	NomGen	10	2	8
	NomAcc	5	–	5
epakúō	NomGen	2	1	1
	NomAcc	7	–	7
akouázomai	NomGen	2	1	1

NomAcc is virtually limited to inanimate stimuli, an animate stimulus only occurring once with *akoúō* (see example (200)). Remarkably, however, the genitive is not limited to animate stimuli, but can occur both with animate and with inanimate ones, though the former prevail with the exception of *aíō* (in fact the exception is only apparent, as the NomAcc construction with this verb is confined to formulaic expressions, as I will show further on in this Section). On the other hand, with *klúō*, while inanimate stimuli are much less frequent than animate ones, there is no preference for accusative encoding, as they are divided in equal parts between the two constructions. Only *akouázomai* 'listen to' does not feature construction variation, possibly on account of the limited number of occurrences, which take the NomGen construction, once (*Il.* 4.343) with an inanimate and once (*Od.* 13.9) with an animate stimulus.

Inanimate stimuli are often sounds, noises, animal calls or the human voice. With *akoúō* such stimuli are encoded either in the genitive or in the accusative with no detectable semantic difference, as shown in (194)-(196) (see Luraghi and Sausa 2019 for more examples and further discussion). The verb is in the aorist in about two thirds of the occurrences (120/181); accordingly, it most often indicates a sudden perception, and shows an inchoative meaning, rather than indicate an activity. Apart from lower frequency of inanimates with the NomGen construction, it is difficult to see any difference between this and the NomAcc construction when they occur with inanimate nouns. In some cases, the choice seems highly idiosyncratic: the word *múthos* 'word, discourse', for example, always occurs in the accusative in the singular, but a few occur-

130   CHAPTER 6

rences in the plural feature the genitive. Examples of the two constructions
with inanimate stimuli are (194)-(196).

(194) *hṑs gàr egṑ   óp'   ákousa   theôn*
       as   PTC 1SG.NOM voice.ACC hear.AOR.1SG god.GEN.PL
       aieigenetáōn
       eternal.GEN.PL
       'When I heard the voice of the eternal gods.' (*Il.* 7.53)

(195) *ou   gár pṓ sphin   akoúeto   laòs*
       NEG PTC yet 3PL.DAT.PL hear.IMPF.M/P.3SG host.NOM
       aütês
       war_cry.GEN
       'For their host could not yet hear the war cry.' (*Il.* 4.331)

(196) *mukēthmoû t'   ḗkousa   boôn   aulizomenáōn*
       lowing.GEN PTC hear.AOR.1SG cow.GEN.PL lie.PTCP.PRS.M/P.GEN.PL
       oiôn   te   blēkhḗn
       sheep.GEN.PL PTC bleating.ACC
       'I heard the lowing of the cattle lying (in the courtyard) and the bleat-
       ing of the sheep.' (*Od.* 12.265–266)

In (194), the stimulus is *ópa* 'voice' in the NomAcc construction, while in (195)
we find *aütês* 'the war cry' in the NomGen construction. The occurrence in
(196), which shows coordination of a genitive and an accusative object, both
referring to animal calls, is especially interesting in this connection. Remarkably, metrical factors, often adduced as an explanation for unexpected morphological marking in the Homeric poems, do not play a role here, as the accusative
mukēthmón would have yielded the same metrical structure as the genitive
mukēthmoû. The two objects instantiate the two constructions, and show that
they are equivalent in this context. Example (195) features one of the few occurrences of middle forms, the imperfect *akoúeto*. As remarked above, the stimulus
is inanimate and is a sound produced by human beings, while the experiencer
is an animate collective noun *laós* 'host'. In the Homeric poems, there are two
more occurrences of middle voice with this verb built from the aorist stem, both
in the *Iliad*, one featuring the NomGen+P construction and containing the genitive of an animate third person pronoun (15.199), and the other featuring the
NomAcc construction, with an accusative neuter demonstrative (15.96). As discussed in Luraghi and Sausa (2019), these three occurrences seem to indicate
that voice alternation does not convey any relevant semantic difference with
akoúō.

PERCEPTION   131

When animate participants are involved as triggers of perception, the Nom-Gen construction is normally used. Some occurrences can be described as immediate perception of an individual, as in (197), or to immediate perception of a state of affairs (types (i) and (ii) in Dik and Hengeveld 1991: 237–239, see Section 2.1.2), as in (198) and (199). In the latter case, the verb takes the Nom-Gen+P construction.

(197)   *síga*   *nûn, mḗ tís*   *seu*
        keep_silent.IMP.PRS.2SG now NEG INDF.NOM 2SG.GEN
        Akhaiôn   *állos*   *akoúsēi*
        Achaean.GEN.PL other.NOM hear.SBJV.AOR.3SG
        'Keep silent now, so that no other Achaean can hear you!' (*Od.* 14.493)

(198)   *ê   ouk otrúnontos*   *akoúete   laòn*
        PTC NEG encourage.PTCP.PRS.GEN hear.PRS.2PL army.ACC
        hápanta Héktoros...?
        all.ACC   Hector.GEN
        'Don't you hear Hector encouraging the army?' (*Il.* 15.506–507)

(199)   *allà kládxantos*   *ákousan*
        but cry.PTCP.AOR.GEN hear.AOR.3PL
        'But they heard it (*sc.* the heron) crying.' (*Il.* 10.276)

In (198), what is heard is the event of Hector encouraging the army: Hector, who is the participant responsible for bringing about the event, is encoded as the stimulus, and the event brought about by Hector is encoded by the participle *otrúnontos* thus yielding a complex NP that functions as second argument in the NomGen+P construction. In (199), the stimulus is a non-human animate (a heron), which is referred to by a null object (it occurs in the immediately preceding context), and the act of crying is encoded by the aorist participles *kládxantos*: this is one of the few occurrences in which an aorist participle occurs in the Two-place+P construction with a perception verb, but note that even though the aorist, being perfective, construes an event as concluded before the following event takes place, this does not mean that perception is indirect. Rather, the two events of crying and hearing the cry immediately follow each other in an uninterrupted sequence in time. The genitive inflection of the participle indicates that a possible overt object would also be in the genitive (see Luraghi 2003b: 169–171).

All occurrences of this type take the NomGen+P construction, except for (200), which features the only occurrence of the NomAcc+P construction with an animate stimulus.

(200) *toùs   nûn ei ptóssontas   huph' Héktori*
DEM.ACC.PL now if flee.PTCP.PRS.ACC.PL under Hector.DAT
pántas   akoúsai
all.ACC.PL hear.OPT.AOR.3SG
'If he were to hear now all of them cowering before Hector.' (*Il.* 7.129)

Example (200) contains the accusative NP *toùs pántas* 'all (of the men)', referring to the participant responsible for bringing about the event encoded by the participle *ptóssontas*, similar to (198) with the genitive.

The passage in (200) contains a conditional clause introduced by *ei* 'if' with an optative aorist *akoúsai* and is different in terms of modality from other occurrences seen thus far, as it is counterfactual. Peleus, the referent of the omitted subject of *akoúsai* is dead, and Nestor, who is addressing the Greeks, imagines what his reaction would be in case he could learn about their cowardly behavior from the underworld. For this reason, the passage cannot refer to concrete perception, but rather to reception of the propositional content of a speech act (type (iv) situation according to Dik and Hengeveld 1991, see Section 2.1.2). This type of occurrence constitutes the pathway for *akoúō* to extend to the function of an evidential. Further examples featuring the NomGen construction are (201) and (202).

(201) *eí pou   éti zóontos   akoúete   paidòs*
if somewhere still live.PTCP.PRS.GEN hear.PRS.2PL son.GEN
emoîo
POSS.1SG.GEN
'If you hear somewhere that my son is still alive.' (*Od.* 11.458)

(202) *è autèn   pothésai   kaí aphormēthéntos*
or DEM.ACC miss.INF.AOR and depart.PTCP.AOR.PASS.GEN
akoûsai
hear.INF.AOR
'Either in case that she misses (me) or learns that (I) have left.' (*Od.* 2.375)

In (201) and (202), the experiencer does not perceive the situation directly, but relies on reports heard from someone else. As observed for (200), *akoúō* no longer indicates the physical perception of hearing, but refers to the reception of the propositional content of a speech act: In this type of occurrence, *akoúō* acquires the function of hearsay evidential. The shift from direct perception to the acquisition of a propositional content from another source is

PERCEPTION

also highlighted in (202) by the fact that the event encoded in the participial clause cannot be simultaneous with the perception event.

In such occurrences, the source of information is most often not specified. As I will show in Section 6.4, it can occasionally be indicated by a genitive NP with a human referent, but this only happens with indefinites, that is, uncertain sources. Notably, the difference between genitive of source (adverbials) and genitive stimuli (second arguments) remains clear, as shown in the discussion of example (227) in Section 6.4, where two genitive NPs in the two different functions co-occur.

In example (203), the NomGen construction indicates indirect knowledge without the addition of a predicative verb form that encodes the event in which the stimulus is involved.

(203) dákru   d'   apò   blephárōn   khamádis   bále
       tear.ACC PTC from eyelid.GEN.PL to_the_ground throw.AOR.3SG
       patròs   akoúsas
       father.GEN hear.PTCP.AOR.NOM
       'Tears from his eyelids he let fall upon the ground, when he heard about his father.' (*Od.* 4.114)

The genitive NP *patrós* in (203), strictly speaking, is not the stimulus, but rather the topic that is heard about. Another topic constituent, overtly marked as such is *perì nóstou* 'about (his) return' in (204).

(204) hōs édē Odusêos   egṑ   perì   nóstou   ákousa
       so PTC Odysseus.GEN 1SG.NOM about return.GEN hear.AOR.1SG
       agkhoû, Thesprōtôn   andrôn   en píoni   démōi,
       near   Thespotrian.GEN.PL man.GEN.PL in rich.DAT land.DAT
       zōoû
       alive.GEN
       'Thus I heard, concerning his return, that Odysseus is near and alive, in the rich land of the Thesprotians.' (*Od.* 19.270–272)

As in (201) and (202), the passage refers to acquisition of knowledge. The propositional content received by the hearer concerns Odysseus' situation, and is further specified by an adjunct. Note however that the fact that Odysseus is alive here is not expressed through the NomGen+P construction, but with a predicative adjective *zōoû* 'alive' that appears to be semantically equivalent to the participle *zṓontos* 'living' in (201). Another topic constituent is the accusative *Atreídēn* in (229), discussed in Section 6.4.

As argued in Luraghi and Sausa (2019), *akoúō* may indicate the controlled activity of listening to someone or something, both with animate and with inanimate stimuli. This is especially clear when imperative forms of the verb occur, as in (205) with the genitive and (206), the only occurrence of the NomAcc construction in an order.

(205) *sù   dè   súntheo   kaí   meu*
      2SG.NOM PTC pay_attention.IMP.AOR.MID.2SG and 1SG.GEN
      ákouson
      hear.IMP.AOR.2SG
      'Pay attention and listen to me!' (*Od.* 18.129)

(206) *hêso   kaì állōn   mûthon   ákoue*
      sit.IMP.PRF.MID.2SG and other.GEN.PL word.ACC hear.IMP.PRS.2SG
      'Remain seated, and listen to the words of others.' (*Il.* 2.200)

Even with verb forms other than the imperative the context may indicate reference to a controlled activity, as in (207).

(207) *hestaótos   mèn kalòn   akoúein   oudè*
      stand.PTCP.PRF.GEN PTC good.ACC hear.INF.PRS NEG
      éoiken   hubbállein
      suit.PRF.3SG interrupt.INF.PRS
      'It is appropriate to listen to someone who is standing, and it is not becoming to interrupt.' (*Il.* 19.79–80)

In (205) the stimulus is expressed by a personal pronoun in the genitive, while in (206) the accusative encodes an inanimate stimulus. Both examples refer to immediate perception of an individual entity in the terms of Dik and Helgeveld (1991), as does example (207): the stimulus is referred to by an indefinite null object (someone), which is modified by a participle. It needs to be pointed out that the perfect participle *hestaótos* 'standing' refers to the situation in which the stimulus is involved, but this does not constitute a propositional content which is being acquired by hearing: indeed, the sentence does not mean "hear that someone is standing", but rather "listen to someone who is standing". Even though the two constructions look identical, in this case the participle does not function as a complement clause. The same holds for example (208) discussed below. (More occurrences are surveyed in Luraghi and Sausa (2019); see further Section 6.4.)

Finally, as shown in Table 2, the Homeric poems also feature one occurrence of the NomDat construction with a human stimulus in (208).

PERCEPTION   135

(208) *dúnasai*   *dè   sù*   *pántos'*   *akoúein*   *anéri*
       can.PRS.M/P.2SG PTC 2SG.NOM everywhere hear.INF.PRS man.DAT
       kēdoménōi
       care.PTCP.PRS.M/P.DAT
       'But everywhere you can listen to a man who is in distress.' (*Il.* 16.515–
       516)

As argued by Ebeling (1885: 66), the context suggests that the verb here has
another meaning, 'fulfill a prayer', a meaning by which *akoúō* could easily fit
into the group of social interaction verbs surveyed in Section 3.2.5 that typically
take the NomDat construction. The same meaning is also clear from the context
in (209), which features a mismatch between the NomGen and the NomDat
construction.

(209) *hótti hoi*   *ōk'*   *ékouse*   *mégas*   *theòs*
       that 3SG.DAT quickly hear.AOR.3SG great.NOM god.NOM
       euxaménoio
       pray.PTCP.AOR.MID.GEN
       '(And was glad) that the great god had quickly fulfilled his prayer.' (*Il.*
       16.531)

In (209), the stimulus is referred to by the predicative participle *euxaménoio*
'praying', inflected in the genitive, and by the dative third person pronoun *hoi*
'him'. Another occurrence of the participle *euxaménou* (genitive) mentioned by
Ebeling (*Il.* 1.381) features the co-referential pronoun *toîo*, also in the genitive.
To sum up, the occurrence in (208) and partly also the occurrence in (209) are
sporadic extensions of the NomDat construction, which contributes its specific
semantics. As I will argue in Section 10.4.2, this type of extension points toward
a certain degree of productivity of the NomDat construction.

   I have already mentioned above that the verb *klúō* often occurs in formulaic
expressions. More specifically, 23 out of 84 occurrences with a second argument show the pattern *hôs éphato* … (obj.) subj. *klu-* 'so s/he said … XY listened
(to him/her)' as in (210) and (211).

(210) *hôs éphath',*   *hoi*   *d'   ára toû*   *mála*
       so   speak.IMPF.M/P.3SG DEM.NOM.PL PTC PTC DEM.GEN much
       mèn klúon   *ēdè píthonto*
       PTC listen.IMPF.3PL PTC obey.AOR.MID.3PL
       'So he spoke, and they readily listened to him and obeyed.' (*Il.* 14.133
       and other six occurrences)

(211)   *hṑs éphat'*   *eukhómenos,*   *toû*   *d'*
        so   speak.IMPF.M/P.3SG pray.PTCP.PRS.M/P.NOM DEM.GEN PTC
        éklue   *Pallàs*   *Athḗnē*
        listen.IMPF.3SG Pallas.NOM Athena.NOM
        'So he spoke praying, and Pallas Athena listened to him.' (*Od.* 3.385)

In example (210), the occurrence of the verb *píthonto* 'they obeyed', coordinated with *klúon*, supports the reading 'listened' for the latter verb. Example (211) in principle can also refer to an uncontrolled event: however, the fact that *klúō* typically occurs as a reaction to a prayer, which then receives positive response, favors the interpretation 'listen to'.

In addition to this, about half of the occurrences (51/103) contain imperative verb forms, with (35 occurrences) or without (16 occurrences) a second argument, also pointing toward a controlled nature of the situation denoted by the verb. Examples are (212) and (213).

(212)   *klûthí*   *meu*
        hear.IMP.AOR.2SG 1SG.GEN
        'Listen to me!' (*Il.* 1.37 and other seven occurrences)

(213)   *kékluté*   *meu*   *muthôn*
        hear.IMP.AOR.2PL 1SG.GEN word.GEN.PL
        'Listen to my words!' (*Od.* 10.189)

In both examples, the addressee is urged to listen to the speaker, but while in (212) the latter is referred to directly with the first person pronoun *meu*, in (213) the speaker is referred to with an adnominal modifier in the complex NP *meu muthôn* 'my words'. The latter example is also interesting because it contains an imperative with an inanimate genitive stimulus, a pattern that does not occur with *akoúō*. Besides frequency in the Homeric poems, comparative evidence also attests to the formulaic nature of this type of occurrences, as they have a counterpart in Vedic Sanskrit: similar invocations in the hymns of the *Rig Veda* feature the cognate verb *śru-* 'hear', 'listen'.

As shown in Table 8, inanimate stimuli with *klúō* are on the whole much less frequent than with *akoúō*, but they are as likely to occur in the Nom-Gen construction as in the NomAcc construction. An example of the latter is (214).

PERCEPTION   137

(214) ēé tin'   aggelíēn   stratoû   ékluen
       if INDF.ACC news.ACC army.GEN hear.IMPF.3SG
       erkhoménoio   hḗn   kh'   hēmîn   sápha
       come.PTCP.PRS.M/P.GEN REL.ACC PTC 1PL.DAT clearly
       eípoi   hóte próterós ge púthoito?
       tell.OPT.AOR.3SG when first.NOM PTC learn.OPT.AOR.MID.3SG
       'Perhaps he has been listening to some news of the army returning, that
       now wants to report to us, as he first learned?' (Od. 2.30–31)

In comparison with *akoúō*, *klúō* does not only display a high number of occurrences in formulaic or semi-formulaic expressions, it also shows a more limited
range of meanings, being virtually restricted to controlled situations. In addition, it does not extend to evidentiality. Even in passages such as (214), one
of two occurrences that refer to learning some information (the other one is
Od. 3.42), the verb takes the second argument *aggelíēn* 'announcement, news',
which is then specified by an adnominal genitive, so it refers to concrete perception of a report, and not to the acquisition of its propositional content.
Rather, acquisition of the propositional content of the report is indicated in
the second part of the sentence by *púthoito* 'he learned' (see further the discussion of *punthánomai* in Section 7.2). (Note that my assumptions here are at
odds with Prévot's 1935b: 72–73 claim that the meaning of *klúō* also extends to
'understand', while the meaning of *akoúō* does not.) Apparently, the fact that
verbs of hearing show a difference between an uncontrolled and a controlled
event, that is, between experience and activity in the terms of Viberg (1984),
is apparently an exception to the Lexicalization Hierarchy, as verbs of sight do
not encode this difference through lexical means (see Section 2.1.2). However,
the formulaic nature of many of the occurrences of *klúō* point toward a different explanation, also in view of the fact that the verb disappeared after Homer.
Keeping this in mind, one can conclude that the verb had already been dis-
carded from actual usage, and survived in prefabs, in which it retained only a
limited part of its original semantics.

The verb *aíō* is the least frequent one among verbs surveyed in this Section. It
shows a semantic range similar to that of *akoúō*. It can refer to perception of an
individual as in (215)-(217) or to perception of a state of affairs, as in (218), and it
can also indicate acquisition of knowledge from hearsay, as in (230) discussed
in Section 6.4. This verb only features the present stem.

(215) hoì   d' hōs oûn áïon   ópa   khálkeon
       DEM.NOM.PL PTC as   PTC hear.IMPF.3PL voice.ACC brazen.ACC
       Aiakídao
       son_of_Aeacus.GEN
       'As they heard the brazen voice of the son of Aeacus.' (*Il.* 18.222)

(216) ouk aïeis   há   té phēsi   theà
       NEG hear.PRS.2SG DEM.ACC.PL PTC say.PRS.3SG goddess.NOM
       leukṓlenos   Hérē...?
       white_armed.NOM Hera.NOM
       'Don't you hear what the goddess Hera, white-armed, says?' (*Il.* 15.130)

(217) hoi   dè boês   aḯontes
       DEM.NOM.PL PTC battle_cry.GEN hear.PTCP.PRS.NOM.PL
       'Hearing the battle cry.' (*Od.* 9.401)

(218) núkta   phulassoménoisi   kakḗn: pedíon
       night.ACC keep_watch.PTCP.PRS.M/P.DAT.PL evil.ACC plain.ACC
       dè gàr aieì tetráphath',   hoppót' epì Trṓōn
       PTC PTC ever turn.PRF.M/P.3PL when   PREV Trojan.GEN.PL
       aḯoien   ióntōn
       hear.OPT.PRS.3PL come.PTCP.GEN.PL
       'They kept watch through the evil night; for toward the plain were
       they ever turning if they might hear the Trojans coming on.' (*Il.* 10.188–
       10.189)

Examples (215) and (216) contain inanimate stimuli in the NomAcc and a negation. This is a formulaic expression, which is most frequently instantiated with
the present indicative as in (216) (five occurrences out of a total of 21; see
Chantraine 1977: 41), and accounts for all occurrences of the NomAcc construction with *aíō*. As this formula most frequently occurs when the verb *aíō* acquires
the function of hearsay evidential, I will discuss it in Section 6.4. Example (218)
contains an animate stimulus in the NomGen+P construction. This passage
refers to the direct perception of a state of affairs, that is, the coming of the
Trojans. The genitive NP *Trṓōn* 'Trojan' is the stimulus, and the state of affairs
is encoded by the participle *epí* ... *ióntōn* 'approaching', with the same pattern
already discussed, for example (198). (Note that the preverb *epí* is anticipated
and occurs earlier in the sentence than the verb with which it belongs semantically. This patterns, known as 'tmesis', is typical of Homeric Greek, in which
preverbs still preserved a partly free status, as already remarked in Section 6.1.)

PERCEPTION 139

Concerning verbal voice, it is worth noting that, to a higher extent than verbs of sight, verbs of hearing also mostly feature active forms, with the exception of three middle occurrences of *akoúō* and of the marginally attested verb *akouázomai*, a *medium tantum*. Based on this limited number of occurrences, no semantic difference seems to be connected with voice.

6.3 Other Types of Sensory Perception

Other modalities of sensory perception are not well represented in the Homeric poems. This is an important limitation due to the size of the corpus, which can partly be overcome by surveying the behavior of semantically similar verbs (e.g. 'touch' for 'feel by touching') but also requires integrating the missing information from later sources, a practice I have striven to avoid in all other parts of the book.

According to Viberg (1984), touch is the third perceptual modality in the Modality Hierarchy represented in Figure 3 of Section 2.1.2. In Homeric Greek, the verb *háptomai* 'touch' most often indicates the action of coming in contact with something, hitting or even grasping something as in (219).

(219) *Tēlémakhos   d'   hetároisin   epotrúnas*
Telemachus.NOM PTC comrade.DAT.PL urge_on.PTCP.AOR.NOM
ekéleusen   hóplōn   háptesthai
order.AOR.3SG arm.GEN.PL take.INF.PRS.M/P
'Telemachus, urging on his comrades, ordered them to take the arms.'
(*Od.* 2.422–423)

In several occurrences it cannot be considered an experiential verb, as it takes an inanimate subject, typically *bélea* 'spears', which, by definition, cannot be an experiencer, as inanimate entities are not sentient. An occurrence in which it may be taken to mean 'feel by touching' is (220).

(220) *ou   dè   gunḕ   podòs   hápsetai*
NEG PTC woman.NOM.PL foot.GEN touch.FUT.MID.3SG
hēmetéroio, ...   ei mḗ tis   grēûs   ésti   palaiḗ, ...
POSS.1PL.GEN.SG if PTC INDF.NOM old.NOM be.PRS.3SG aged.NOM
hḗ   tis   dè   tétlēke   tósa   phresìn
DEM.NOM INDF.NOM PTC suffer.PRF.3SG many.ACC heart.DAT.PL
hóssa   t'   egṓ   per: têi   d'   ouk àn
REL.ACC.PL PTC 1SG.NOM PTC DEM.DAT PTC NEG PTC

phthonéoimi   podôn   hápsasthai   emeîo
grudge.OPT.PRS.1SG foot.GEN.PL touch.INF.AOR.MID 1SG.GEN
'No woman will touch my foot, unless there is some old servant who has suffered in her heart as many woes as I; such a one I would not grudge touching my feet.' (*Od.* 19.344–348)

In these and all other occurrences in which the verb takes a second argument, it shows the NomGen construction, and so it does in Classical Greek authors, in which it displays the same range of meaning as in Homer, and also indicates tactile perception more clearly.

Other verbs of touching listed by Viti (2017: 378) are *psáuō* and *tugkhánō*. The former occurs four times in Homer, and in three of these it takes an inanimate subject that cannot be viewed as being assigned the experiencer role, while in the fourth quoted in example (66) in Section 3.1.1 (*psaúsēi d'endínōn* 'will touch the interior(gen) [of the body]'), though taking a human subject, it refers to touching by means of a spear, hence it does not refer to a sensation. In all occurrences it shows the NomGen construction. Finally, the verb *tugkhánō* means 'hit', 'reach', rather than 'touch' or 'feel (by touching)'. It always takes the NomGen construction, and has been discussed in Section 3.2.6, see example (108).

All contact verbs mentioned in this Section belong among 'verbs of effective action' in the terms of Tsunoda (1981, 1985), distinct from 'resultative' (i.e. change-of-state) verbs, and, as argued in Section 3.2.6, typically take the NomGen construction as opposed to change-of-state verbs, which distinctively feature the NomAcc construction.

The verb *géuomai* 'taste' occurs five times in the Homeric poems and takes the NomGen construction. It means 'taste' 'make trial of', not only in reference to food, as in (221), but also metaphorically, as in (222).

(221)   *tákha dè̀   kaì   émellen   Odusseùs   aûtis ep'*
        now   PTC and be_about.IMPF.3SG Odysseus.NOM back on
        oudòn   iòn   proikòs   geúsesthai
        threshold.ACC go.PTCP.PRS.NOM gift.GEN taste.INF.FUT.MID
        Akhaiôn
        Achaean.GEN.PL
        'And now Odysseus was about to go back to the threshold, and to taste the gift of the Achaeans.' (*Od.* 17.412–413)

PERCEPTION

141

(222)   *all' áge*   *dè kaì douròs*   *akōkês*   *hēmetéroio*
but come_on PTC and spear.GEN point.GEN POSS.1PL.GEN.SG
geúsetai,   *óphra ídōmai*   *enì*
taste.SBJV.AOR.MID.3SG for   see.SBJV.AOR.MID.1SG in
phresìn   *ēdè daeíō*   *è ár' homôs kaì keîthen*
heart.DAT.PL and learn.SBJV.AOR.1SG or PTC like   and beneath
eleúsetai
come_back.FUT.MID.3SG
'Come on, let him also taste the point of our spear, that I may see
and learn in my heart whether he likewise will come back even from
beneath.' (*Il.* 21.60–62)

In (221) the stimulus *proikòs* 'gift' refers to the dinner that Odysseus is going
to taste. Example (222) contains a non-edible entity as stimulus, *douròs akōkês*
'the point of the spear': the meaning of the verb is extended from 'taste' to a
more 'feel', 'make try'.

Smell is referred to in the Homeric poems only by a phenomenon-based
(Viberg 1984) verb *ózō* in a monovalent construction with a nominative subject, as in (223).

(223)   *odmḕ*   *d'*   *hēdeîa*   *apò krētêros*   *odṓdei*
smell.NOM PTC sweet.NOM from bowl.GEN smell.PPF.3SG
'A sweet smell would rise from the mixing-bowl.' (*Od.* 9.210)

The experiencer-based verb *osphraínomai* 'smell' quoted by Viti (2017: 378)
does not occur in the Homeric poems. In Classical Greek writers, including
Herodotus whose Ionic dialect was closer to Homeric Greek than literary Attic,
it takes the NomGen construction as in (224).

(224)   *hōs ósphronto*   *tákhista tôn*   *kamḗlōn*
as smell.AOR.MID.3PL quickly ART.GEN.PL camel.GEN.PL
hoi   *híppoi*   *kaì eîdon*   *autás* ...
ART.NOM.PL horse.NOM.PL and see.AOR.3PL 3PL.ACC
'As soon as the horses smelled the camels and saw them ...' (Herodotus,
Histories 1.80.5)

Summing up, in spite of scanty attestations it seems safe to conclude that verbs
indicating perceptual modalities other than sight and hearing all consistently
take the NomGen construction. Based on the limited evidence reviewed above,
the distribution of verbal voice seems to draw a line between contact verbs

142   CHAPTER 6

that can indicate touch, which can be middle or active, and verbs of taste and smell, which are *media tantum*, even though the verb *háptomai* 'touch', which is the most likely one to actually indicate perception, is also a *medium tantum*. I will return to the distribution of voice with perception verbs in Section 6.5.

6.4 From Perception to Evidentiality

Cross-linguistically, perception verbs are a frequent source for evidentials (Aikhenvald 2004: 273–274). In Homeric Greek, this development especially concerns verbs of sight and hearing. In this Section, I review some contexts that favor the extension and show how the shift from perception to evidentiality can affect the use of verbal tense.

The evidential function of sight verbs in Homeric Greek is based on the construal of visual perception as being equal to first-hand experience, as shown in (225).

(225) *hṑs hò   mèn aûthi pesṑn   koimḗsato*
       thus DEM.NOM PTC there fall.PTCP.AOR.NOM sleep.AOR.MID.3SG
       khálkeon   húpnon ... apò ... alókhou, ... hês   oú   ti
       brazen.ACC sleep.ACC from   bride.GEN REL.GEN NEG INDF.ACC
       khárin   íde
       joy.ACC see.AOR.3SG
       'So there he fell, and slept a sleep of bronze, far from his bride of whom he had known no joy.' (*Il.* 11.241–243)

In (225), Iphidamas is being slain in battle by Agamemnon. The hero falls on the spot, and death is depicted by Homer as a bronze-thick sleep. Iphidamas has left behind his young bride before being able to have intercourse with her, and dies without ever having experienced her charms. In this occurrence the verb form *íde* 'saw' does not only refer to sight: rather, it extends to acquiring direct experience. (This semantic extension has become lexicalized with the perfect *oîda* 'know', originally from the same verbal root; see Sections 4.1, 6.1 and 7.2.)

As opposed to direct experience, evidence from hearsay does not require attending a situation, as shown in (226).

PERCEPTION

143

(226) ḕ autòs   pareṑn   ḕ állou
      or self.NOM be_present.PTCP.PRS.NOM or other.GEN
      akoúsas
      hear.PTCP.AOR.NOM
      '(As though) you had been present yourself, or had heard from some-
      one else.' (*Od.* 8.491)

Example (226) clearly indicates the difference between having direct experience of a situation (*pareṑn* 'being present') and having learned about it by some
indefinite source *állou* 'from someone else'. Note that the genitive NP here is not
the stimulus, does not indicate a specific participant, and does not belong into
the argument structure of the verb: much to the contrary, it is an indefinite
form indicating a generic but unknown source, similar to the indefinite *teu* in
(227).

(227) autàr Odussêos   talasíphronos   oú   pot' éphasken,
      but   Odysseus.GEN steadfast_heart.GEN NEG NEG say.IMPF.3SG
      zōoû   oudè thanóntos   epikhthoníōn   teu
      alive.GEN NEG die.PTCP.AOR.GEN mortal.GEN.PL INDF.GEN
      akoûsai
      hear.INF.AOR
      'Yet concerning Odysseus steadfast heart, he said he had heard from no
      man on earth, whether living or dead.' (*Od.* 17.114–115)

Occurrences in which *akoúō* takes a finite or, occasionally, non-finite subordinate clause may also refer to the reception of a propositional content,
rather than to immediate perception (type (iv) in Dik and Hengeveld 1991:
238–240 discussed in Section 2.1.2). Besides the occurrences mentioned in Section 6.2 (see (201) and (202)), examples (228) and (229) are worth considering.

(228) kaì sè   géron   tò   prìn mèn akoúomen
      and 2SG.ACC old_man.VOC DEM.ACC before PTC hear.PRS.1PL
      ólbion   eînai
      rich.ACC be.PRS.INF
      'We hear that you too, old man, were once happy.' (*Il.* 24.543)

144 CHAPTER 6

(229)   *Atreĩdēn*   *dè* *kaì* *autoì*   *akoúete,*   *nósphin*
son_of_Atreus.ACC PTC and self.NOM.PL hear.PRS.2PL away
eóntes,   *hṓs* *t'* *êlth'*   *hṓs* *t'*
be.PTCP.PRS.NOM.PL how PTC go.AOR.3SG how PTC
Aígisthos   *emḗsato*   *lugròn*   *ólethron*
Aegisthus.NOM devise.AOR.MID.3SG terrible.ACC destruction.ACC
'Concerning the son of Atreus, you too, though being far, know how he
came, and how Aegisthus devised his terrible destruction.' (*Od.* 3.193–
194)

Both (228) and (229) attest to a further step in the development of *akoúō* as evidential. Indeed, the meaning 'know by hearsay' seems to be fully acquired, as shown by the occurrence of the present tense of *akoúō* in both examples, even though the event of hearing cannot be taking place at the time of utterance. As the context makes clear, the verb cannot indicate an ongoing perception event, but must necessarily refer to some information already acquired at a time prior to the time of utterance. These occurrences can be compared with (204), which contains the aorist *ákousa*, a perfective form: in (228) and (229) a propositional content is presented as fully acquired, without reference to the event of acquisition, which is instead favored by the inchoative meaning of the perfective aorist in (204). Example (229) also contains an accusative adverbial, *Atreĩdēn*, which indicates the topic of the predication in the subordinate clause. A similar topic expression is also found with a prepositional phrase, *perì nóstou* 'about the return', in (204).

As I mentioned in Section 6.2, the verb *aíō* is sometimes glossed as meaning 'perceive' or even 'see' rather than 'hear' (see e.g. Ebeling 1885: 60, Prévot 1935b: 74). This may be partly due to its etymology, which connects it with the Classical Greek verb *aisthánomai* 'perceive', unattested in Homer. Notably, however, the evidence that supports this assumption is based on occurrences such as (230) and especially (231).

(230)   *ouk aíeis*   *hó*   *me*   *nēusìn*   *épi prúmnēsin*
NEG hear.PRS.2SG DEM.ACC 1SG.ACC ship.DAT.PL of stern.DAT.PL
Akhaiôn ...   *bálen*   *Aías?*
Achaean.GEN.PL smote.AOR.3SG Aias.NOM
'Don't you know that at the sterns of the Achaeans' ships Aias smote me?' (*Il.* 15.248–249)

PERCEPTION   145

(231)   *ouk aḯeis*   *hóti dḗ   moi   epillízousin   hápantes,*
        NEG hear.PRS.2SG that PTC 1SG.DAT wink.PRS.3PL all.NOM.PL
        helkémenai   dè   kélontai?
        drag.INF.PRS PTC bid.PRS.M/P.3PL
        'Don't you realize that all men are winking at me, and bidding me to
        drag you?' (*Od.* 18.11–12)

In order to understand these examples, one needs to note in the first place
that they both contain the expression *ouk aḯeis*, whose formulaic character
has already been pointed out in Section 6.2. The meaning shift from immediate perception to evidentiality is made clear by comparison of (230) and (231)
with (216), in which the stimulus is *há té phēsi* 'the things that (goddess Hera)
says', and reference is made to a concrete event of hearing. In (230), on the
other hand, we observe the same use of the present tense, which indicates
some knowledge acquired by hearsay rather than the time of its acquisition.
The idiomatic expression *ouk aḯeis* then extends to contexts in which the evidence is not necessarily acquired by hearing, as in (231). This passage is usually
translated as 'don't you see', as it refers to some action going on rather than to
something being told. However, this cannot be taken as evidence for a meaning 'see' of the verb *aíō*: rather, it conforms to the tendency of idioms to develop
a non-compositional meaning and to extend to contexts which would not be
suitable for their literal meaning.

It must be pointed out that sight can also be construed as providing indirect
information. Dik and Hengeveld (1991: 108) when illustrating "indirect perception" (their type (iii)) use examples such as (232).

(232)   *Mary saw that John had been drinking.*

In (232) the two events are not simultaneous: the speaker/experiencer may
acquire the information for example, because "she inferred this from how he
looked" (*ib.*). Notably, in Homeric Greek such occurrences are not available,
and perception through sight is always construed as being direct.

More in general, among Dik and Hengeveld's types of situations referred to
by perception verbs, type (iii) (the experiencer acquires knowledge through
an inference based on his/her own perception) does not occur in the Homeric
poems: even perception through hearing is never based on a personal inference
by the experiencer, and there are no occurrences such as (24) (Section 2.1.2).
In cases in which perception through hearing is not direct, only type (iv) situations occur, that is, situations in which the experiencer acquires knowledge
from a third party through reception of the propositional content of a speech
act.

6.5   Discussion

Construction variation with hearing verbs in Ancient Greek has been the matter of discussion for decades if not centuries. Crucially, the issue has always been approached in the framework of case variation, and hearing verbs have been compared with other verbs that display the genitive/accusative alternation, rather than with other verbs of perception. Traditionally, it is said that case alternation with verbs of hearing is connected with the partitive meaning of the genitive, but how this meaning can operate with such verbs is often left unexplained. Discussing a similar alternation in Indo-Aryan, Hettrich (2014) claims that even with perception verbs its function is to signal different degrees of affectedness, whereby the genitive implies that the verbal action refers to the patient in its totality but affects it only partially.

Under this assumption, however, it is hard to understand why the genitive should alternate with the accusative with such verbs, which do not really imply that the second argument is affected at all by the situation. Recall that lexemes occurring as second arguments both in the NomAcc and in the NomGen construction in Homeric Greek refer to sounds, animal calls or the human voice, and that the two constructions may even be coordinated as shown in (196). According to Dahl (2009), who also discusses Indo-Aryan data, the act of listening, for example to an invocation, might be understood in terms of ingestion of a specific amount of information. Notably, the fact that the partitive genitive may have a quantifying function with perception verbs, similar to the quantifying function it has with ingestion verbs, is stipulated, rather than supported by the data.

If one compares the argument structure of hearing verbs with the argument structures of other perception verbs, a striking distribution emerges: hearing verbs are the only group that allows for alternation, thereby taking an intermediate position between sight on the one hand and other perceptual modalities on the other, in accordance with the Modality Hierarchy illustrated in Figure 3 of Section 2.1.2. The Modality Hierarchy is based on cross-linguistic data from 53 languages surveyed in Viberg (1984) and supported by more data from later research. Thus, the distribution of argument structure constructions with perception verbs singles out sight as opposed to touch, smell and taste; in addition, it characterizes hearing as sharing features of both groups.

What can the opposition between sight on the one hand and touch, smell and taste on the other possibly tell us concerning the construal of perception modalities in Homeric Greek? A first answer comes from comparing perception verbs with verbs of bodily sensations. Indeed, by always featuring the NomGen construction, touch, smell and taste share the same pattern as the latter group of verbs. In other words, perception through touch, smell and taste is construed as very close to sensations. Sight, instead, does not show this connection. Rather, as we will see in 7.1 and 7.2, the occurrence of the NomAcc construction points toward a connection between sight and cognitive verbs that denote rational thinking, intellectual knowledge, as opposed to practical skills, and, most relevant, awareness and attention. Hence sight is construed as implying an immediate and clear apprehension of the situation, accompanied by awareness.

Importantly, by taking a construction-based approach and considering verbs with their arguments as units of meaning, one can avoid resorting to explanations that stretch the meaning of individual morphemes in a way that looks largely arbitrary. As I have argued in Section 3.1.1, different argument structure constructions do not only contribute to variation in the construal of the second participant, that is the proto-patient, but also to the construal of the first participant, or proto-agent. In the case of experiential verbs, the latter participant is always an experiencer, but with the NomAcc construction it is construed as sharing agent properties, in particular control over the situation. As perception events are basically unintentional, the feature of control is not construed as the ability to bring about a situation, as it is in the case of actions, but rather as attention directed toward a stimulus and raised by immediate perception. In other words, in the mapping of the domain of action and intentionally brought about events onto the domain of experience, in which the main participant does not act intentionally, the feature of control corresponds to attentiveness, as shown in Figure 11.

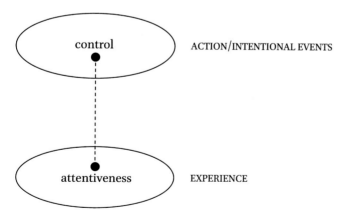

FIGURE 11 The mapping of control onto the domain of experience

A higher level of attention and consequently of awareness distinguishes sight from other perception modalities and, as we will see in Chapter 7, connects it to conscious mental activity, mental change-of-state events such as realizing, and intellectual knowledge.

In conclusion, it is true that the NomGen construction has among its meanings a lesser degree of affectedness of the second participant, but in the case of experiential verbs, with which second participants are never affected, it rather points toward a lesser degree of agency and control over the first participant. Diminished agency is construed as a lesser degree of attention and awareness by the experiencer as opposed to the full degree of awareness granted by sight.

Among perception modalities, and based on the distribution of constructions, sight shows a connection with cognition verbs while touch, taste and smell show a connection with verbs of bodily sensations, which consistently feature the NomGen construction. In this framework, hearing constitutes an in-between case, as it shows connections both with cognition and with sensation. Notably, the distribution of the NomAcc and the NomGen construction with hearing verbs is conditioned by animacy: only inanimate stimuli are allowed in the former construction. Note further that the shift toward hearsay evidential only happens with the NomGen construction. Apparently, awareness is more easily achieved even through hearing when the stimulus is inanimate, hence more easily apprehended. I will return to this peculiarity of construction distribution in Section 10.4.1, after having reviewed more verbs that allow for variation.

The way in which spontaneous events of perception are kept distinct from controlled activities through different lexicalization patterns in Homeric Greek seems to be at odds with generalizations based on cross-linguistic data. According to Viberg (1984), languages that display different lexemes for 'hear' and 'listen' also lexicalize the difference between 'see' and 'look'. This is called by Viberg Lexicalization Hierarchy and is represented in Figure 4 (Section 2.1.2). From the data surveyed in this Chapter, this prediction does not seem to be borne out. Indeed, in the field of sight the difference between the spontaneous and the controlled event is indicated either by the addition of a verbal prefix, or by the NomPP construction. On the other hand, in the field of hearing we find two distinct lexemes, *akoúō* 'hear' and *klúō* 'listen to'. I would like to argue that this exceptional distribution is only apparent. In the first place, it must be kept in mind that *akoúō* can mean both 'hear' and 'listen to', and in some cases the context clearly supports the second reading (see examples (205)-(208)), while this is not the case for *horáō/eîdon*, which consistently shows construction variation, as described above. As for *klúō*, even if it arguably refers virtually only to controlled situations, the formulaic nature of the expressions that contain it points toward an ongoing dismissal of this verb from the language (it did in fact disappear after Homer). As I have shown in Section 6.2 not only does *klúō* occur

PERCEPTION   149

23 out of 103 times in a formula, it also occurs 51 times in invocations, which are also fixed expressions. It is then plausible that *klúō* had been preserved in such formulaic context, which happened to be limited to the meaning 'listen to'. If we ignore *klúō*, the remaining distribution conforms to the Lexicalization Hierarchy. More precisely, even though we do not find different lexicalization patterns for sight, construction variation singles out this perceptual modality with respect to the others.

The distribution of voice is less straightforward. At the end of the Modality Hierarchy, verbs of taste and smell are *media tantum*. Notably, however, while hearing verbs are virtually *activa tantum* (with the exception of the marginal *medium tantum akouázomai* 'listen to'), sight offers a more complex setting, with a majority of active forms but also, in the case of the *horáō/eîdon*, a sizable group of middle forms, only partly connected with a specific verbal tense (the future of the stem *op-*), and even *media tantum*, such as *dérkomai* and *sképtomai*. For verbs of touch it is hard to make any generalizations: the verb *háptomai* means 'touch' and perhaps 'feel by touch' only in the middle voice (but it features active forms with the meaning 'tie'), while *tugkhánō* and *psaúō* are active, and do not show voice alternation. Based on this evidence, touch verbs seems to behave in a more similar way to sight and hearing verbs, but note that one might also focus only on the verb *háptomai*, the only one that possibly qualifies as a perception verb in the Homeric poems: in this latter case, hearing and sight would stand out as the only two modalities that feature active voice in the majority of occurrences, while verbs referring to other perceptual modalities would be characterized by the middle voice.

Another explanation is provided by Allan (2003). As already discussed in Section 6.1, Allan considers the middle voice with perception verbs as connected with volitionality. He argues that, while sight verbs can refer to a volitional or to a non-volitional activity, hearing verbs are typically non-volitional, hence their limitation to the active voice. In his characterization of a verb as being or not volitional, Allan follows Prévot (1935a, b), who in turn offers a cursory analysis that in some cases seems to stipulate meanings rather than extract them from contexts. In particular, Allan holds occurrences of *klúō* 'listen to' to indicate volitional activities in about half of the occurrences, without giving further details on how he reached this conclusion that, in view of the data surveyed in Section 6.2, looks doubtful. Concerning other perceptual modalities, Allan (2003: 99) claims that the meaning of *geúomai* 'taste' is 'prototypically' volitional, a view that is not supported by the Homeric occurrences (see for example (221)). In sum, the notion of subject affectedness as understood by Allan for perception verbs does not seem to be compelling in accounting for voice distribution in Homeric Greek.

CHAPTER 7

Cognition

In this Chapter, I review and discuss verbs that indicate events of cognition. These include cognitive states, such as 'know', achievements, such as 'get to know', 'learn', mental activities such as 'think', and more complex and variously construed situations, such as 'remember'. Interestingly, verbs with similar meanings often differ as to the way in which they contribute to the construal of a situation, and accordingly tend to occur in a specific aspectual stem, as shown in Table 9 (see Luraghi and Sausa 2017). Note that in Table 9 I have also included the future, which is not an aspect. This tense does not fit into the aspectual system constituted by the other tenses/aspects; hence future occurrences must be accounted for separately, and it would be wrong either to leave them out completely or to include future forms among forms of other aspectual stems.

Table 9 shows the distribution of aspectual stems across the verbs that I will discuss in this Chapter. Differences are in some cases quite striking, and point toward a precise aspectual characterization of some of the verbal roots. A remarkable distinction emerges between verbs that in various ways refer to thought and verbs that refer to knowledge or memory. The former often indicate ongoing activities, and accordingly feature the present stem: they are construed as ongoing situations unfolding over time. This holds especially for *oíō/oíomai* and *phronéō*, while *noéō* which shows a preference for the aorist stem, most often indicates an achievement. Notably, however, they never occur in the perfect, a stem that refers to a state achieved through a change of state. On the other hand, verbs that indicate knowledge and memory are more flexible. They can denote achievements and show the aorist stem when they indicate acquisition of knowledge and are frequently also construed as stative situations, hence featuring the perfect stem, while their occurrence in the present stem is on the whole less frequent.

Besides aspect, argument structure constructions add various specifications to the construal of situations. Notably, when constructed as two-place verbs, cognitive verbs do not allow for dative stimuli: they display the NomAcc and the NomGen construction, often allowing variation between the two, with the exception of the verb *dokéō* that, as anticipated in Section 3.2.7, takes either a nominative or a dative experiencer with the stimulus often encoded as a sentential complement; see the detailed description in Section 7.1.1.

When referring to an atelic activity, verbs of thinking often do not take a second argument encoding the stimulus, as for example *phronéō* 'think' in (233).

© SILVIA LURAGHI, 2021 | DOI:10.1163/9789004442528_008

COGNITION
151

TABLE 9   Distribution of aspectual stems

Verb	Meaning	Present	Aorist	Perfect	Future	Tot
oíō/oíomai	'think, believe, imagine'	121	10	–	–	131
noéō	'realize', 'become aware of'	16	112	–	12	140
phronéō	'think', 'intend'	103	–	–	–	103
dokéō	'think', 'seem to sbd'	25	2	–	–	27
phrázomai	'decide'	55	24	–	9	88
médomai	'meditate, consider, devise'	18	15	–	1	34
mētiáō/mētíomai	'have in mind, devise'	11	5	–	2	18
médomai	'take care of, think of'	14	–	–	1	15
oîda	'know', 'be skilled'	–	–	301	2	303
epístamai	'be skilled'	27	–	–	1	28
gignṓskō	'learn, recognize'	33	82	–	9	124
édaon	'learn'	–	15	5	2	22
punthánomai	'inquire, learn'	2	44	12	11	69
peúthomai	'inquire, learn'	16	–	–	–	16
mimnḗskomai	'have in mind, remember'	8	53	36	7	104
mnáomai	'have in mind, solicit'	24	–	–	–	24
lanthánomai	'forget'	19	8	4	1	32

(233) *hó   sphin   eù   phronéōn   agorḗsato*
DEM.NOM 3PL.DAT well think.PTCP.PRS.NOM address.AOR.MID.3SG
kaì   metéeipen
and speak.AOR.3SG
'He with good intent addressed them and spoke among them.' (*Od.* 2.228)

This type of construction is especially frequent with *phronéō*, a verb that often simply refers to the generic activity of thinking or reflecting. As often in the Homeric poems, in (233) the verb is accompanied by the adverb *eu* 'well', and indicates a certain mental attitude, as highlighted in the English translation.

Table 10 shows the type of construction with each of the verbs discussed in this Chapter in the Homeric poems along with the number of occurrences. It contains the possible constructions in which cognitive verbs occur. (Among subordinate complements I have included both *hōs* and *hóti* clauses and other types of subordinate clauses; see Section 3.3.) To these verbs one must add *dokéō*, which occurs 27 times in the Homeric poems, once with a nominative

152 CHAPTER 7

TABLE 10 Constructions of cognitive verbs

Verb	Meaning	Ø	GEN	ACC	INF	Sub cl	Sp	Tot
oíō/oíomai	'think, believe, imagine'	21	–	11	96	3	–	131
noéō	'realize, be aware'	37	–	94	6	3	–	140
phronéō	'mean, intend'	48	–	52	3	–	–	103
phrázomai	'consider, plan'	19	–	36	3	30	–	88
médomai	'plan, devise'	1	–	33	–	–	–	34
mētiáō/mētíomai	'meditate, plan, devise'	2	–	14	1	1	–	18
médomai	'take care of, think of'	–	13	2	–	–	–	15
oîda	'know'	46	24	167	17	49	–	303
epístamai	'be able, be skilled'	5	4	4	15	–	–	28
gignōskō	'learn, recognize'	26	2	62	3	31	–	124
édaon	'learn'	6	2	10	1	3	–	22
punthánomai	'inquire, learn'	20	19	25	–	4	1	69
peúthomai	'inquire, learn'	6	–	8	–	2	–	16
mimnḗskomai	'have in mind, remember'	4	84	7	1	6	2	104
mnáomai	'have in mind, crave'	6	3	15	–	–	–	24
lanthánomai	'forget'	2	30	–	–	–	–	32

experiencer (example (114)), while occurrences with dative experiencers are equally divided between personal (that is, with nominative stimuli) and impersonal constructions; see the examples discussed in Section 7.1.1.

In the next Sections, I discuss cognitive verbs divided into three groups: thinking (Section 7.1), knowing (Section 7.2) and remembering (Section 7.3). In Section 7.4 I discuss the findings.

7.1 Think

Thinking is typically described as an activity. As discussed in Section 2.1.2, however, other construals are possible, including stative and inchoative (see Vendler 1967: 110–111, Goddard 2003). Moreover, as argued by Fortescue (2001), verbs of thinking display complex patterns of polysemy cross-linguistically, and one cannot assume that they should necessarily pattern after English *think*.

This is true also for Homeric Greek, in which it is not easy to single out a specific verb as generically meaning 'think' and corresponding to English *think*. In general, in the Homeric poems the semantics of activity verbs ('think about something') appears to be more complex than the semantics of states ('think that') and achievements ('occur'). The latter two types of situations are expressed in Homeric Greek by *oíō/oíomai* 'think', and *noéō* 'occur', 'realize'. These two verbs are the subject of Section 7.1.1, with the addition of the verb *dokéō* 'think, have an impression, seem', which may take a dative experiencer. The latter belongs to the class of appearance verbs, which are often treated as a type of perception verbs (see for example Gisborne and Holmes 2007 on English verbs of appearance). As we will see in Section 7.1.1, this is not the only borderline case between the two sub-domains.

Bertolín Cebrián (1996) devoted an in-depth study to verbs of thinking in Ancient Greek. Besides *oíō/oíomai* and *noéō*, the book surveys nine other verbs, including *phonéō, phrázomai, mermērízō, hormaínō, mētíomai/mētiáō, médomai, médomai, bussodomeúō* and in addition *mémona* 'desire eagerly' that I have already discussed in Section 5.2. She goes through all passages in which the selected verbs occur, discusses metrical and stylistic matters, the verbs' etymology, reviews the existing literature, and finally offers a semantic characterization of each verb. The verbs *mermērízō* and *hormaínō* have a more specific meaning, 'be in doubt'. All these verbs will be discussed in Section 7.1.2.

Concerning verbal semantics, *phronéō* indicates an activity and, as already shown in example (233), it often refers to a certain disposition. It is always atelic, and accordingly only occurs in the present tense, as it never indicates a change of state (aorist) or a state (perfect). A group of verbs that indicate a more complex activity such as 'plan', 'plot' includes *phrázomai, mētíomai/mētiáō, médomai* and *bussodomeúō*. These verbs indicate controlled situations that can have a variety of constructions, as shown by the fact that they display both the present and the aorist stem. On the other hand, the verb *médomai* means 'take care of', indicates an atelic situation, and shows similarities with the constructional patterns of verbs of memory (see Section 7.3).

7.1.1 *Thought, Opinion, Awareness*

The verbs *noéō* and *oíō/oíomai* show an almost complementary distribution of aspectual stems that largely accounts for their specific meanings. They also differ in terms of their possible connections with other concepts related to thought. Indeed, while the former is a denominal verb based on *noûs* 'mind', the latter, in spite of various attempts, resists any possible etymology.

The word *noûs* refers to a concept that has been variously elaborated in the history of Greek philosophy, and studies on its meaning often concentrate on the Classical authors. Fritz (1943) sets out to determine the early meaning of *noûs* and *noéō* as attested in the Homeric poems, and argues that they both highlight an element of volitionality. Fritz further stresses the relation between *noéō* and *gignōskō*, as both verbs most frequently show the aorist stem, and indicate a mental change of state (see Section 7.2.2). Focusing on the noun *noûs*, Fritz points out a difference with respect to *thumós*, which indicates the mind as more closely connected with emotions, but also argues that it cannot be considered a purely intellectual concept, as earlier scholars have claimed based on Classical philosophical works.

In fact, a close look at the contexts in which *noéō* is used in Homer supports Fritz's latter claim, as the verb does not indicate intellectual activity, and the noun on which it is based clearly does not refer to the intellect as conceived by later philosophers. However, Fritz's assumption of an intentional component seems unwarranted, as the most important notion connected with *noéō* is a sudden onset of a state of awareness, and the noun *noûs* seems to indicate the mind as the seat of awareness. For this reason, *noéō* has sometimes been taken as a perception verb; see the discussion of examples (234) and (235). In Homeric Greek it also has two prefixed compounds, *pronoéō* 'perceive before, foresee' and *eisnoéō* 'perceive', both always inflected in the aorist, which support the interpretation of the root as indicating sudden awareness of a situation. Fritz's remark (1943: 84) that in about half of the occurrences the situation indicated by *noéō* raises a violent emotion is also in accordance with the assumption that this verb indicates a sudden change of state.

In his detailed survey of all nouns referring to the mind and the soul/spirit in Homeric Greek, Jahn (1987) argues that *noûs*, contrary to *thumós*, *phrên* and various denominations of the heart, never has a bodily connection, but indicates a purely mental concept. This difference is in fact reflected in the verbs based on *noûs* and *phrên*, *noéō*, which indicates becoming aware of something without emotional components (the latter, if present, are specified in the following context, see example (237)), and *phronéō*, which instead indicates a positive or negative attitude toward someone, as discussed in Section 7.1.2.

Let us now consider the occurrences in which *noéō* has been taken as a verb of perception, such as (234) and (235).

(234) *óphrá min   autòs   en ophthalmoîsi noḗsas*
       that   3SG.ACC self.NOM in eye.DAT.PL   realize.PTCP.AOR.NOM
       tôi   písunos   epì nêas   íēis
       DEM.DAT trusting.NOM on ship.ACC.PL go.SBJV.PRS.2SG
       Danaôn   takhupṓlōn
       Danaan.GEN.PL fast_fleeted.GEN.PL
       'Because, perceiving it (sc. the bird) with your eyes, you will trust the sign and go to the ships of the fast-mounted Danaans.' (*Il.* 24.294–295)

COGNITION

(235) *ou d' ára Tēlémakhos   íden   antíon ou   d'*
NEG PTC PTC Telemachus.NOM see.AOR.3SG before NEG PTC
enóēsen
realize.AOR.3SG
'But Telemachus didn't see or notice (her) in front of him.' (*Od.* 16.160)

Bertolín Cebrián (1996) argues that 82 occurrences out of 112 in Homer have to do with sight, hence the verb should be considered as originally having indicated this perception modality. In her understanding, both (234) and (235) provide evidence in support of this assumption. Notably, in (234) the type of perception is specified by the prepositional phrase *en ophthalmoîsi* 'in (one's) eyes', with a construction that is also frequent with verbs of sight, see for example (170). Nevertheless, in (235) the co-occurrence of the verbs *íden* 'saw' and *enóēsen* 'noticed' shows that the latter verb does not *per se* specify sight as perception modality. Rather, it indicates perception as the sudden rise of awareness, the acquisition of direct as opposed to indirect knowledge: only in this sense is it equivalent to *eîdon*, which also indicates direct knowledge secured by sight as opposed to other perceptual modalities (for example hearing, see Section 6.4). Another occurrence similar to (234) and (235) can be found in (256); see Section 7.1.2.

Another parallel between *noéō* and perception verbs is constituted by its possible occurrence with the Two-place+P construction instantiated in this case by the NomAcc+P construction, in which a predicative participle referring to the state of affair that the experiencer becomes aware of is added to the stimulus NP, as in (236) (another occurrence of this construction can also be seen in example (90)).

(236) *tòn   d' hōs oûn enóēsen   arēΐphilos*
DEM.ACC PTC as PTC realize.AOR.3SG dear_to_Ares.NOM
Menélaos   erkhómenon
Menelaos.NOM come.PTCP.PRS.M/P.ACC
'But when Menelaos, dear to Ares, realized that he was coming.' (*Il.* 3.21–22)

In (236), the stimulus is a human being, referred to by the demonstrative pronoun *tòn*. The participle *erkhómenon* 'coming' refers to the situation that Menelaos realizes, as in the case of immediate perception of a state of affairs illustrated by perception verbs. This construction is also comparatively frequent with verbs that denote acquisition of knowledge, as *punthánomai* 'learn', see Section 7.2.2.

156   CHAPTER 7

However, the situation referred to by *noéō* is not simply perception, but it also implies a mental operation. Let us consider example (237).

(237) *ho   dè   phresìn   hêisi*
       DEM.NOM PTC heart.DAT.PL POSS.3SG.DAT.PL
       noḗsas   thámbēsen   katà   thumón:
       realize.PTCP.AOR.NOM wonder.AOR.3SG around heart.ACC
       oísato   gàr theòn   eînai
       think.AOR.MID.3SG PTC god.ACC be.INF.PRS
       'He, becoming aware in his mind, wondered at his heart: he deemed
       (her) divine.' (*Od.* 1.322–323)

In (237), Telemachus meets the goddess Athena in disguise. From her words and from the feelings that she was able to raise in him, he has the unquestionable knowledge of her being divine: the sudden rise of awareness leaves him wondering, a feeling encoded by the verb *thambéō* (see Section 8.3.1), which notably occurs in the *thumós*, a complex concept translated as 'heart', 'mind' or 'soul'. The passage reflects the pattern *noéō* plus emotion verb described in Fritz (1943: 84). Telemachus' conclusion that the person he met was in fact a goddess also arises suddenly in his mind, as indicated by the verb *oísato*, one of the few occurrences of the aorist stem of the verb *oíomai* 'think, deem' that I will discuss more in detail further on in this Section. Bertolín Cebrián (1996: 59) claims that, though basically indicating sight, the meaning of *noéō* shifts to thought when the object of perception is abstract, but in so doing she misses the implication of an active mental involvement.

Realizing what the circumstances are like, being readily aware of a situation, creates a state of increased attention in the experiencer, as shown in (238) and (239).

(238) *tí   toût'   enóēsen   alḗtēs?*
       INT.ACC DEM.ACC realize.AOR.3SG vagabond.NOM
       'What has the vagabond realized?' (*Od.* 17.576)

(239) *toútou   g'   hespoménoio   kaì puròs*
       DEM.GEN PTC follow.PTCP.AOR.MID.GEN and fire.GEN
       aithoménoio   ámphō   nostḗsaimen,   ek
       blaze.PTCP.PRS.M/P.GEN both.NOM.DU return.OPT.AOR.1PL from
       epeì períoide   noêsai
       as   know_well.PRF.3S realize.INF.AOR
       'Following him, we both might return even out of blazing fire, because
       he is most capable of attention.' (*Il.* 10.246–247)

COGNITION   157

In (238), *noéō* means 'realize'. In this passage, Penelope asks why the beggar, Odysseus in disguise that she has not recognized, did not talk with her, and wonders whether he might have realized some problems that she ignores. In (239) the aorist infinitive *noêsai* depends on *períoide*, a prefixed compound of *oîda* 'know', 'know how to do something' (see Section 7.2.1 and example (277)). The context highlights the most prominent quality of Odysseus, whose prompt intelligence enables him to always be in control of the situation.

As shown in Table 9, *noéō* also shows the present stem in a limited number of occurrences. In such cases, it has a stative meaning, as typical of achievements when combined with the imperfective aspect: hence, the fact that *noéō*, when used in the present tense (imperfective aspect), indicates a state rather than an ongoing activity shows that normally, when occurring in the aorist, it indicates an achievement, rather than an accomplishment (see Napoli 2006: 162 and Sections 4.1 and 7.2.2). An example is (240).

(240) *ou   gár tis   nóon   állos   ameínona   toûde*
       NEG PTC INDF.NOM mind.ACC other.NOM better.ACC DEM.GEN
       noései   hoîon   egò   noéō   ēmèn pálai
       realize.FUT.3SG REL.ACC 1SG.NOM realize.PRS.3SG both anciently
       ēd' éti   kaì   nûn
       PTC already even now
       'No one will reach a better conclusion than the one I have reached a
       long time ago and still hold now.' (*Il.* 9.104–105)

In (240) we find two occurrences of *noéō*, the first one *noései* in the future, also featuring the cognate object *nóon* (see Bertolín Cebrián 1996: 68), and the second one, *noéō* in the present tense. In this passage, Nestor reproaches Agamemnon for his confrontation with Achilles, and says that he realized long before that Agamemnon's behavior would have brought evil to the Greeks, that he still holds the same conviction, and is sure that no other conclusion could be reached. Here the present form *noéō* indicates a state resulting from a change of state, that is, from reaching awareness of the implications of a situation. This state is steady: in fact, it is a firm persuasion. A similar meaning is expressed by the present tense in (241).

(241) *noéō   dè   kaì autòs   Héktorá   toi*
       realize.PRS.3SG PTC even self.NOM Hector.ACC 2SG.DAT
       lûsai
       release.INF.AOR
       'I, too, am minded to give Hector back to you.' (*Il.* 24.560–561)

Bertolín Cebrián (1996, 65–66) explains the shift from 'realize', 'become aware' to 'be minded', and argues that in (241) Achilles, here speaking with Priamus who is trying to persuade him to give back his son's corpse, has realized the importance of complying with this request and based on this has reached his decision.

Contrary to *noéō*, *oíō* most often occurs in the present stem (see Table 9), and indicates an atelic situation. Apart from the first person present indicative for which both an active and a middle form are available, it only features middle forms, and remains a *medium tantum* in Classical Greek; accordingly it is often lemmatized as *oíomai*. No compelling etymology is available for this verb (see the discussion in Bertolín Cebrián 1996: 251–253).

Most frequently, this verb highlights the opinion of the speaker, without specifying the source of information, with a quasi-evidential function. Out of a total of 131 occurrences, 103 are first person singular forms, of which 77 active. A typical occurrence is (242).

(242) *all', oíō,   kaì dḗthà kathḗmenos*
but think.PRS.1SG and long sit.PTCP.PRF.M/P.NOM
aggeliáōn   peúsetai   ein Ithákēi,
message.GEN.PL learn.FUT.MID.3SG in Ithaca.DAT
teléei   d' hodòn   oú pote taútēn
accomplish.FUT.3SG PTC journey.ACC NEG ever DEM.ACC
'But I think, he'll remain sitting (here) a long time, learning reports in Ithaca, and will never accomplish that journey!' (*Od.* 2.255–256)

In (242), as in many similar occurrences, the form *oíō* is used parenthetically, to point out that the speaker refers to a personal opinion, with no evidence from any specific source. Another occurrence of the first person singular, this time inflected in the middle voice, can be seen in (283), discussed in Section 7.2.2. The uncertain character of such a personal opinion is highlighted in passages in which *oíō* is contrasted with *oîda* 'know', as in (283), which contains one of the few aorist forms (another one occurs in (237), discussed earlier in this Section).

(243) *kaì sphéas ōísthēn   toùs   émmenai oudé*
and 3PL.ACC think.AOR.MID.1SG DEM.ACC.PL be.INF.PRS NEG
ti   oîda
INDF.ACC know.PRF.1SG
'And I thought it was they, but I don't know for certain.' (*Od.* 16.475)

COGNITION

Thus, *oíō* can be considered a marker of epistemic modality, which points to a low commitment of the speaker to the truth value of the propositional content of a sentence, as shown especially by this last example. The aorist adds an ingressive nuance to the meaning of the verb, as is often the case when verbs with atelic actionality inflect in a perfective aspect (see Fanning 1990: 137–138). Besides the occurrences in (237) and (243), another example is (244).

(244) *autàr egṑn   hupémeina,   oisámenos*
       but   1SG.NOM stay_behind.AOR.1SG think.PTCP.AOR.MID.NOM
       dólon   eînai
       trick.ACC be.INF.PRS
       'But I stayed behind, having spoored it a trick.' (*Od.* 10.258)

As remarked above, due to its peculiar function this verb most frequently shows first person singular forms. In (245) it occurs in the second person.

(245) *ê   toi   mèn táde   kautòs,   oíeai,*
       PTC 2SG.DAT PTC DEM.ACC.PL and+self.NOM think.PRS.M/P.2SG
       hṓs   ken etúkhthē
       how PTC hit.AOR.PASS.3SG
       'But you can imagine for yourself how it happened.' (*Od.* 3.255)

Here, Nestor promises Telemachus to tell him all the details of Agamemnon's doom: in any case, knowing how things have gone, Telemachus must already have his own opinion on the matter.

Given the uncertain nature of the opinion indicated by *oíō*, the meaning of this verb comes close to the meaning of *dokéō* 'think', 'seem'. As discussed in Section 3.2.7, this verb can occasionally take a nominative experiencer as in (114), but most often it features a dative experiencer, as in (115) and in the other examples analyzed in this Section. Similarly to *oíō*, *dokéō* also highlights the speaker's opinion, and occurs with a first person singular pronoun indicating the experiencer in 20 out of 27 occurrences. Like *oíō*, it indicates a low degree of commitment to the truth value of the propositional content of a sentence, and it specifies that the experiencer's opinion is based on an impression, rather than on clear perception.

In Section 7.1, I remarked that verbs of appearance, such as *dokéō*, are usually included among verbs of perception. The reason to include it among verbs of mental activity lies in its being semantically close to *oíō*, though differing in the types of construction in which it occurs, and having a clearer evidential func-

160   CHAPTER 7

tion. Etymologically, *dokéō* is related to Latin *decet* 'be appropriate, be fitting'
and the causative *doceo* 'teach'. In (246) it refers to uncertain visual perception.
  Let us consider examples (246) and (247).

(246) *álloi   moi   dokéousi   paróiteroi   émmenai*
       other.NOM.PL 1SG.DAT seem.PRS.3PL ahead.NOM.PL be.INF.PRS
       híppoi,   állos   d' hēníokhos   indálletai
       horses.NOM.PL other.NOM PTC charioteer.NOM seem.PRS.M/P.3SG
       'It seems to me that the horses ahead are other, and the charioteer
       seems another one.' (*Il.* 23.459–460)

Example (246) refers to a situation in which the speaker actually has an unclear
visual perception of the stimulus: here, *dokéousi* actually indicates perceptual
appearance, rather than the speaker's opinion. In this passage the stimulus is
encoded by a sentential complement with a nominative NP and a dependent
infinitive. The same construction occurs in (247).

(247) *allà mál' hôd' érdein,   dokéeis   dé moi   ouk*
       but very thus do.INF.PRS seem.PRS.2SG PTC 1SG.DAT NEG
       apinússein
       lack_understanding.INF.PRS
       'But you have to do this; you don't seem to me incapable of understand-
       ing.' (*Od.* 6.258)

Example (247) shows an evidential use of *dokéō*, in which the speaker's opinion
is no longer based on visual perception, but on a deduction from his knowledge
of his interlocutor. A further step is constituted by constructions such as those
in (115), which I repeat here for convenience.

(115) *allà mál' hôd' érxō,   dokéei   dé moi   eînai*
       but very thus do.FUT.1SG seem.PRS.3SG PTC 1SG.DAT be.INF.PRS
       áriston
       best.ACC
       'But I will do this, and it seems to me that this is best.' (*Od.* 5.360)

In (115) the verb does not take a stimulus NP, but an infinitive: it is an impersonal
construction, and indicates the speaker's evaluation concerning an action that
he is going to take.

COGNITION
161

7.1.2 *Aspects of Mental Activity*

In this Section, I discuss a set of verbs that focus on various aspects of the activity of thinking. I start with *phronéō*, whose meaning is 'think', 'mean', ' intend'. This verb only occurs in the present stem, hence pointing to an atelic activity, with participles accounting for about 80% of the occurrences (82 out of 103). The atelic character of the situation indicated by *phronéō* is further indicated by the fact that, in the vast majority of attestations, the verb occurs without an object as in (27) or with a generic one, usually *kaká* 'evil things' as in (248), while it occurs with an infinitive only in three passages, as in (249). As it mostly indicates an attitude of a participant toward another participant, *phronéō* never occurs with subordinate clauses.

(248) *kakà   phronéous'   enì thumôi*
       ill.ACC.PL think.PTCP.PRS.NOM in   heart.DAT
       'Meditating ills in his heart.' (*Od.* 10.317)

(249) *phronéō   dè diakrinthémenai   édē Argeíous   kai*
       think.PRS.1SG PTC separate.INF.AOR.PASS PTC Argive.ACC.PL and
       Trôas
       Trojan.ACC.PL
       'I think that Argives and Trojans should now be parted.' (*Il.* 3.98–99)

This verb is denominal, and is based on the noun *phrén*, which indicates the midriff, identified as the seat of passions. In fact, intention is never disjoint from emotion with this verb, as shown by the frequency of adverbs or generic objects indicating favorable or unfavorable disposition, as in (233) and (248). Besides *kaká* 'evil thoughts' other frequent second arguments are *phíla* 'friendly thoughts', *méga* 'great thoughts' or the demonstrative *tá* 'these things' used anaphorically to refer to some thoughts described in the preceding context.

The occurrences that contain an NP as second argument all show the NomAcc construction, consistently with other verbs in this group. Nevertheless, the meaningfulness of this construction with *phronéō* should not be considered on the same plane as with other cognitive verbs, as possible accusative NPs all refer to thoughts, and should better be considered cognate objects. In this respect, the constructional pattern of *phronéō* is similar to the constructional pattern of *páskhō*, discussed in Section 5.1 and example (149). A further hint in the direction of this interpretation can be seen in the correspondence between *eu phroneîn* 'have a positive attitude', which features an adverb, and *kakà phroneîn* 'have a negative attitude', with an accusative NP. In fact, the

162   CHAPTER 7

accusative *kaká* 'evils' here has exactly the same function as the adverb *eu*, and the categorial difference between the two items should not blur their substantial equivalence.

According to Chantraine (1977: 1224), *phrázomai* should also be connected with *phrḗn*, but the etymology is rejected by Berolín Cebrián (1996: 140), who highlights the semantic difference between this verb and *phronéō*. Indeed, the two verbs show a quite different behavior, and seem to indicate different types of situations. In the first place, while *phronéō* only shows the present stem, *phrázomai* also occurs in the aorist. Moreover, *phrázomai* often takes a subordinate clause, and when it occurs in the NomAcc construction it can take specific arguments, contrary to *phronéō*, which only features non-specific ones out of a limited set. This verb also has an active counterpart, only attested in the reduplicated aorist in Homeric Greek, which means 'indicate', 'explain', 'tell (in order to explain)', and the relation between the active and the middle is not easily explained, as argued by Berolín Cebrián (1996: 115–136) in her detailed analysis. In any case, voice alternation does not seem to affect verbal valency, as both the active and the middle feature the NomAcc construction.

As a verb of cognition, *phrázomai* indicates a controlled situation that most often involves planning and deciding, as shown in (152) already discussed in Section 5.2, (250) and (251).

(250)   *all' hóte dè̀ tén   ge   stugerèn   hodòn*
        but when PTC DEM.ACC PTC hateful.ACC journey.ACC
        eurúopa   Zeùs   ephrásath'
        far_sounding.NOM Zeus.NOM consider.AOR.MID.3SG
        'But when Zeus, whose voice is borne afar, devised that hateful journey.'
        (*Od.* 14.235–236)

(251)   *háma   d' ēoî   phainoménēphi*
        together PTC sunrise.DAT appear.PTCP.PRS.M/P.DAT
        phrassómeth'   ḗ   ke   neómeth'   eph'
        consider.FUT.MID.1PL whether PTC sail.SBJV.PRS.M/P.1PL to
        hēméter'   ê ke   ménōmen
        POSS.1PL.ACC.PL or PTC remain.SBJV.PRS.1PL
        'When the sunrise appears we will decide whether we should go back home or remain.' (*Il.* 9.618–619)

Examples (152), (250) and (251) feature the present tense, the aorist and the future respectively. In (152), we find the NomAcc construction with the demonstrative *tá* functioning as the antecedent of the subsequent relative pronoun

COGNITION 163

háss(a). The NomAcc also occurs in (250), this time with a specific NP as a second argument, *tḗn stugerḕn hodòn* 'that hateful journey'. Example (251) contains a subordinate clause, a comparatively frequent construction with this verb.

When occurring with an NP as second argument, *phrázomai* can occasionally take a human stimulus. In this case, it means 'realize', as in (252), with the NomAcc+P construction.

(252) tòn   dè   phrásato   prosiónta
       DEM.ACC PTC consider.AOR.MID.3SG come_forth.PTCP.PRS.ACC
       diogenḕs   Oduseús
       godly.NOM Odysseus.NOM
       'But godly Odysseus realized that he was coming forth.' (*Il.* 10.339–340)

In (252), the second argument, the demonstrative pronoun *tón*, refers to a human participant, and is modified by the participle *prosiónta* 'coming forth'. Similar to verbs of sight in (172)-(174) or verbs of hearing in (196) and (199), *phrásato* here indicates immediate perception of a situation, but contrary to specific perception verbs; here, what sensory modality enables perception is left unspecified: the situation is construed similarly to the situation construed by *noéō*, cf. example (236).

That the situation indicated by *phrázomai* is often controlled and intentional is shown by its frequent occurrence in orders, as in (253).

(253) all' íthi,   dî'   Eúmaie,   ...kaì
       but go.IMP.PRS2SG god_like.VOC Eumaeus.VOC and
       phrásai   ḗ   tis   ár'   estì
       consider.IMP.AOR.MID.2SG whether INDF.NOM PTC be.PRS.3SG
       gunaikôn   hḕ   táde   rhézei
       woman.GEN.PL REL.NOM DEM.ACC.PL do.PRS.3SG
       'But go now, god-like Eumaeus, and try to understand whether it was one of the servants who did this.' (*Od.* 22.157–158)

In (253), Telemachus orders Eumaenus to find out who helped the suitors find the weapons that Odysseus kept hidden in the palace, and uses the aorist imperative *phrásai* that indicates a mental operation, 'try to understand', 'find out'.

As I pointed out in the discussion of example (252), *phrázomai* can mean 'realize', 'sense (by immediate perception)'. The same holds for the prefixed verb *epiphrázomai*, which occurs nine times (other prefixed compounds of *phrázomai* are *amphrázomai* 'realize', *metaphrázomai* 'think of' and *periphrázomai*

164   CHAPTER 7

'consider' all occurring once, and *sumphrázomai* 'devise together' five occurrences). An example is (254).

(254)   *énth' állous*   *mèn pántas*   *elánthane*   *dákrua*
        then other.ACC.PL PTC all.ACC.PL escape.IMPF.3SG tear.ACC.PL
        leíbōn,   *Alkínoos*   *dé   min*   *oîos*
        pour.PTCP.PRS.NOM Alcinous.NOM PTC 3SG.ACC alone.NOM
        epephrásat'   *ēd' enóēsen*   *hḗmenos*
        perceive.AOR.MID.3SG PTC realize.AOR.3SG sit.PTCP.PRF.M/P.NOM
        ágkh' autoû,   *barù   dè   stenákhontos*   *ákousen*
        near   DEM.GEN heavily PTC sob.PTCP.PRS.GEN hear.AOR.3SG
        'None of the others noticed that he was crying. Only Alcinous, who was
        sitting next to him, perceived and realized, as he heard him groaning
        heavily.' (*Od.* 8.93–95)

In (254) Odysseus, who is at Alcinous' court after his shipwreck, listens to a
poet singing of the deeds of the Greek and Trojan heroes. His memories move
him: he tries to hide his tears, but his host, who is sitting next to him, hears him
groaning and understands he is crying. In this passage, *epephrásato* takes the
NomAcc construction with the second argument *min* 'him', indicating immediate perception of an individual. The verb is coordinated with *enóēsen*: together,
the two verbs denote the complex situation of becoming aware through perception. In this occurrence, the modality is further specified by *ákousen* in the
following clause, which comes with the Two-place+P construction and refers
to immediate perception of a situation indicated by the predicative participle
stenákhontos 'groaning' in the genitive (as for example in (199)).

     The verb pair *mētiáō/mētíomai* is based on the Proto-Indo-European root
**mē-* of Latin *metior* 'measure', 'weight', and attests to a frequent semantic
extension, by which thinking, intended as planning and reflecting, is conceptualized as measuring (see Fortescue 2001). The present stem is always active,
while the aorist and the future only feature middle forms. As the two stems are
slightly different, they are sometimes lemmatized as two different verbs. Examples are (255)-(257).

(255)   *hássá*   *te   mētióōsi*   *metà   sphísin*
        INDF.ACC.PL PTC devise.PRS.3PL among 3PL.DAT
        'Whatever they are planning among them.' (*Il.* 10.409 = *Il.* 10.208)

COGNITION 165

(256)   *hòn*   *d'*   *àn*   *egòn*   *apáneuthe neôn*   *hetérōthi*
       REL.ACC PTC PTC 1SG.NOM far   ship.GEN.PL elsewhere
       noésō,   *autoû hoi*   *thánaton*   *mētísomai*
       realize.FUT.1SG there 3SG.DAT death.ACC devise.FUT.MID.1SG
       'Whoever I will notice elsewhere far from the ships, I will devise his
       death on the spot.' (*Il.* 15.348–349)

(257)   *hoi*   *d'*   *hétaroi*   *méga*   *érgon*
       DEM.NOM.PL PTC comrade.NOM.PL great.ACC deed.ACC
       emētísanto
       devise.AOR.MID.3PL
       'The comrades had devised a great deed.' (*Od.* 12.373)

Examples (255)-(257) all feature the NomAcc construction. The meaning of the verb remains the same across aspectual stems, but the fact that the present stem is twice as frequent as the aorist (see Table 9) shows that the verb is basically atelic. It indicates an activity in the present, as in (255), and an accomplishment in the aorist, as in (257). The future in (256) refers to a situation that is preceded by another experiential situation, here indicated by *noésō* 'I will notice'. The two verbs differ in actionality: as highlighted in Section 7.1.1, *noéō* indicates a sudden change of state, an achievement. In the passage in (256), this is followed by the planning activity indicated by *mētísomai* 'I will devise', which will predictably unfold over time.

The verb *médomai* is semantically close to *mētiáō/mētíomai*, as example (258) shows.

(258)   *kaì*   *tóte*   *dè*   *Zeùs*   *lugròn*   *enì phresì*
       and then PTC Zeus.NOM baneful.ACC in   heart.DAT.PL
       médeto   *nóston*   *Argeíois*
       devise.IMPF.M/P.3SG return.ACC Argive.DAT.PL
       'Even then, Zeus was planning in his heart a grievous journey for the
       Argives.' (*Od.* 3.132–133)

In (258), the present stem of *médomai* indicates an ongoing, controlled and intentional activity, as does *mētiáō* in (255). The verbs *médomai* also shares the morphosyntactic behavior of *mētiáō/mētíomai*, as it inflects both in the present and in the aorist (though the relative frequency of the two stems is different), and takes the NomAcc construction.

Based on the semantic similarity highlighted above, Bertolín Cebrián (1996: 220–222) proposes an etymological connection between *mētiáō/mētíomai* and *médomai*, and does not accept the etymology given by Chantraine (1977: 675), who connects the latter verb with the Proto-Indo-European root **med-* also attested in *médomai* 'care for' and elsewhere in the Indo-European languages, as in Latin *medeor* 'care for' and *medito* 'reflect'. In fact, *médomai* and *médomai* sport a quite different semantics along with a different behavior, as shown in (259) and (260).

(259) *eû   dé   tis   hármatos   amphìs idṑn*
       well PTC INDF.NOM chariot.GEN around see.PTCP.AOR.NOM
       polémoio medésthō
       war.GEN care.IMP.PRS.M/P.3SG
       'Let everyone take care to prepare for the war, checking their chariot.'
       (*Il.* 2.384)

(260) *hṓs   k'   éndon parà Tēlemákhōi   deípnoio*
       so   PTC inside by   Telemachus.DAT dinner.GEN
       médētai   hḗmenos   en megárōi
       care.SBJV.PRS.M/P.3SG sit.PTCP.PRF.M/P.NOM in hall.DAT
       'So that he can care for his dinner, sitting in the palace by Telemachus.'
       (*Od.* 19.321–322)

Both example (259) and example (260) refer to an activity that implies some personal interest or special involvement, as is especially clear in (260). In addition, they feature the NomGen construction that never appears with *médomai*, but is typical of verbs of emotion, in particular verbs of care and affection, as well as of verbs of memory (see Sections 7.3 and 8.2.2): in fact, the notion of personal involvement indicates vicinity of *médomai* to the domain of emotions. A further difference between the two verbs is that *médomai* only inflects in the present stem. On the other hand, in two identical occurrences with the NomAcc constructions the meaning of *médomai* seems closer to the meaning of *médomai*, as shown in (261).

(261) *kakà   dè   Trṓessi   medésthēn*
       bad.ACC.PL PTC Trojan.DAT.PL devise.IMPF.M/P.3DU
       '(The two of them) were devising evil for the Trojans.' (*Il.* 4.21 = *Il.* 8.458)

In sum, construction alternation is meaningful with *médomai*, showing the pattern of verbs of thought in connection with the meaning 'plan', 'devise', and the pattern of emotion verbs in connection with the meaning 'care for' (see further Section 8.2.2).

COGNITION

167

Besides the verbs included in Table 9, three more verbs are discussed in Bertolín Cebrián (1996): *bussodomeúō* 'plan secretly', *mermērízō* 'hesitate', 'ponder', 'be in doubt' and *hormaínō* 'ponder'. The first verb is based on an unattested compound **bussodom-* and its literal meaning is 'build in the deep', hence metaphorically 'plan in disguise, secretly' (see Bertolín Cebrián 1996: 238). It is attested only in the *Odyssey*, in which it occurs seven times, always with the present stem. An example is (262).

(262) *ésthl'* *agoreúontes,* *kakà* *dè* *phresì*
   good.ACC.PL say.PTCP.PRS.NOM.PL bad.ACC.PL PTC heart.DAT.PL
   bussodómeuon
   plan_secretly.IMPF.3PL
   'Saying good words, they were deeply brooding evils in their minds.'
   (*Od.* 17.66)

In (262), *bussodomeúō* takes the NomAcc construction with the object *kaká* 'evils', as does in five more occurrences. The only occurrence with a different second argument, also showing the NomAcc construction, contains a relative pronoun that refers back to the antecedent *múthōn* 'plans'.

The verb *mermērízō* occurs 41 times, both in the present and in the aorist stem. It is connected with various other lexemes that express worry or anxiety, such as *merímna* 'worry', and, according to Pokorny (1969 s.v.), it is based on the Proto-Indo-European root **smer-* 'remember', 'worry about', 'hesitate' attested for example in Sanskrit *smar-* 'remember' and Latin *memoria* 'memory', *mora* 'hesitation'. Most frequently, it indicates a state of hesitation in taking a decision between two alternatives, and accordingly it often occurs with disjunctive clauses rather than with NPs as second arguments. When occurring with a nominal second argument, it takes the NomAcc construction: in this case, the argument structure construction typical of transitive verbs adds an intentional feature to the verb's semantics, which is then 'ponder', but also 'plan', 'devise' with a meaning close to that of *mētiáō/mētíomai*. Examples are (263)-(265).

(263) *hoí* *rh' éti mermérizon* *ephestaótes*
   DEM.NOM.PL PTC still doubt.IMPF.3PL stand.PTCP.PRF.NOM.PL
   parà *táphrōi*
   beside ditch.DAT
   'These were still divided in doubt as they stood there beside the ditch.'
   (*Il.* 12.199)

CHAPTER 7

(264)   *dîos*   *Odusseús*   *mnēstéressi*   *phónon*   *sùn*
god_like.NOM Odysseus.NOM suitor.DAT.PL death.ACC with
Athénēi   *mermērízōn*
Athena.DAT doubt.PTCP.PRS.NOM
'God-like Odysseus (was) planning the suitors' death with the help of
Athena.' (*Od.* 19.51–52)

(265)   *hóssa*   *dè*   *mermérixe*   *léōn*   *andrôn*   *en*
REL.ACC.PL PTC doubt.AOR.3SG lion.NOM man.GEN.PL in
homílōi   *deísas,*   *hoppóte min*   *dólion*   *perì*
crowd.DAT fear.PTCP.AOR.NOM when   3SG.ACC crafty.ACC around
kúklon   *ágōsi,*   *tóssa*   *hormaínousan*
circle.ACC lead.SBJV.PRS.3PL INDF.ACC.PL turn_over.PTCP.PRS.ACC
epéluthe   *nédumos*   *húpnos*
come_upon.AOR.3SG sweet.NOM sleep.NOM
'As much as a lion in a crowd of men broods anxiously with fear when
they draw their crafty circle around him, that much she was pondering
when sweet sleep came upon her.' (*Od.* 4.791–793)

In (263) the verb in the imperfect indicates an ongoing situation of doubt in a
group of people trying to reach a common line of thought. In (264) we find the
NomAcc construction with the second argument *phónon* 'killing'. The present
stem, here instantiated by a participle, again indicates an ongoing situation:
Odysseus is trying to figure out how he, counting on Athena's help, can kill
the suitors. The NomAcc construction also occurs in (265), with the accusative
hóssa 'such' correlative of *tóssa*. The aorist stem indicates the rise of an increasing state of confusion in a non-human experiencer, a lion.

The passage in (265) contains a simile: the rise of the mental state in the
lion in the first clause is contrasted with the rise of a similar mental state in
Penelope, which in turn is described by the aorist participle of the verb *hormaínō*. This points toward a similar construal of the situation depicted by the
two verbs, which accounts for the observation by Bertolín Cebrián (1996: 177)
that *hormaínō* seems to be used as a metrical variant of *mermērízō* in a sizeable number of occurrences. Similar to *mermērízō*, *hormaínō* indicates a state
of doubt and hesitation. Etymologically, it is related to *hórnumi* 'stand, leap up'
and *hormé* 'assault'. Another example is (266).

COGNITION   169

(266)   *en Lésbōi   d'   ékikhen   dolikhòn plóon*
        in Lesbos.DAT PTC reach.AOR.3SG long.ACC navigation.ACC
        hormaínontas
        turn_over.PTCP.PRS.ACC.PL
        'He reached (us) in Lesbos, while we were discussing the long journey.'
        (*Od.* 3.169)

Example (266) refers to an activity of a group of people who are trying to come
to a common decision, similar to (263). The verb *hormaínō* occurs with the second argument *dolikhòn plóon* 'the long journey', and, as all verbs in this Section,
it always takes the NomAcc construction in such cases.

7.2   Know / Learn

Verbs that indicate knowledge are clearly distinct based on their actionality
and their tendency to occur in specific aspectual stems: on the one side, we find
verbs that indicate cognitive states, here discussed in Section 7.2.1, while on the
other side are verbs that indicate acquisition of knowledge, which constitute
the subject of Section 7.2.2. As we will see, both areas show further subdivi-
sions: cognitive states can refer either to intellectual knowledge or to skills,
while acquisition of knowledge can imply understanding or learning through
perception.

7.2.1   *Cognitive States and Skills*
The most frequent verb that indicates a cognitive state and means 'know' in
Homeric Greek is *oîda*. As I have already remarked in Sections 1.3 and 4.1, *oîda*
was originally the perfect of the Proto-Indo-European verb **wid-* 'see', which
in Homeric Greek preserves the original meaning in the aorist (see Section
6.1). The perfect became an independent verb, losing connection with visual
perception at an early time, as attested by its occurrence with the meaning
'know' in several other languages, such as Sanskrit *veda*, German *wissen* and
Old Church Slavonic *vědĕti*. Two occurrences of future tense, based on the stem
eísomai (*Il.* 1.548) and *eidésō* (*Od.* 7.327), are new formations of the Homeric
language (Chantraine 2013: 406, 423).
    In Ancient Greek, *oîda* indicates knowledge as a state: the resultative mean-
ing that, in pre-Greek times, led to the semantic extension outlined above, was
no longer active synchronically (see Section 4.1), as shown by the occurrence of
perfect forms of other verbs to indicate result, such as *édaon* and *punthánomai*
'learn' with the meaning 'know as a result of having learned' (see Section 7.2.2).

170　　　　　　　　　　　　　　　　　　　　　　　　　　　CHAPTER 7

It takes both the NomAcc and the NomGen construction, with a quite consistent semantic distinction. Let us start with some passages that contain the NomAcc construction.

In the first place, *oîda* refers to intellectual knowledge as in (267).

(267)   *Kálkhas ...   hòs   éidē   tá   t'*
       Calchas.NOM REL.NOM know.PPF.3SG DEM.ACC.PL PTC
       eónta   tá   t'   essómena
       be.PTCP.PRS.ACC.PL DEM.ACC.PL PTC be.PTCP.FUT.MID.ACC.PL
       pró   t'   eónta
       before PTC be.PTCP.PRS.ACC.PL
       'Calchas ... who knew the things that were, and that were to be, and that had been before' (*Il.* 1.69–70)

Example (267) describes Calchas, according to Homer the best of all bird-diviners: he has knowledge of present, past and future events.

Most frequently, *oîda* refers to knowledge of situations and indicates a state of consciousness, as in (268) and (269). It can occur with human stimuli in cases in which it indicates knowledge about the situation in which a human participant is involved, as in example (130) discussed in Section 4.1 and repeated here for convenience. In such cases, the Two-place+P construction occurs, in which a secondary predication is encoded by a participle that depends on the NP referring to the latter participant, as with perception verbs (see Section 3.3). With *oîda* the construction is realized as NomAcc+P.

(268)   *eû   gàr   dè̄   tóde   ídmen   enì phresín*
       well PTC PTC DEM.ACC know.PRF.1PL in heart.DAT.PL
       'Indeed we know well in our hearts.' (*Il.* 2.301)

(269)   *hōs kaì   nûn Aígisthos   hupèr   móron   Atreḯdao*
       as   and now Aegisthus.NOM beyond destiny.ACC Atreides.GEN
       gêm'   álokhon mnēstḗn,   tòn   d'   éktane
       marry.AOR.3SG wife.ACC wedded.ACC DEM.ACC PTC kill.AOR.3SG
       nostḗsanta,   eidòs   aipùn
       return.PTCP.AOR.ACC know.PTCP.PRF.NOM utter.ACC
       ólethron
       destruction.ACC
       'Then Aegisthus took the legitimate wife of the son of Atreus, and he slew him on his return, though he was well conscious of utter destruction.' (*Od.* 1.35–37)

COGNITION

171

(130) *ou   d'   ára   pō   ti   éidee   Pátroklon*
       NEG PTC PTC PTC INDF.ACC know.PPF.3SG Patroclus.ACC
       tethnēóta   dîos   Akhilleús
       die.PTCP.PRF.ACC god_like.NOM Achilles.NOM
       'God-like Achilles did not know about Patroclus' death yet.' (*Il.* 17.401–402)

In (268), Odysseus is speaking to his companions, and the demonstrative *tóde* refers to the circumstances in which the Greeks find themselves in the tenth year of war. Notably here *ídmen* 'we know' co-occurs with the prepositional phrase *enì phresín* 'in our hearts', which refers to the body part in which the experience is located (cf. Section 1, and see Jahn 1987 for further discussion on the meaning of *phrḗn*, literally 'midriff' in Homer). In (269) the context suggests that *oîda* indicates a state of consciousness: Aegistus married Clytemnestra even though he understood well that this would have taken more evil upon them, and eventually led to their death. Example (130) contains an animate stimulus, which is in turn the subject of the predicative participle *tethnēóta*. Another similar occurrence is *Od.* 23.29.

In some cases, *oîda* may indicate knowledge of or acquaintance with concrete referents, as in (270).

(270) *eis hó   ke   toùs   aphíkōmai   hoì*
       to DEM.ACC PTC DEM.ACC.PL reach.SBJV.AOR.1SG REL.NOM.PL
       ouk ísasi   thálassan anéres ...   ou   d'   ára
       NEG know.PRF.3PL sea.ACC   man.NOM.PL NEG PTC PTC
       toí   g'   ísasi   néas
       DEM.NOM.PL PTC know.PRF.3PL ship.ACC.PL
       'Until I should reach men who don't know the sea, and have no knowledge of ships.' (*Od.* 23.269–271)

In (270), the verb *ísasi* does not indicate a state of consciousness, but rather means 'have knowledge of', 'know about'. This type of mental state however does not concern acquaintance with a person: the meaning 'know somebody' occurs only occasionally with indefinites and is limited to the Odyssey. An example is (271), and another occurrence is *Od.* 7.211.

(271) *tôi   oú   tina   oîda   anthrṓpōn, hoì*
       DEM.DAT NEG INDF.ACC know.PRF.1SG man.GEN.PL REL.NOM.PL
       tḗnde   pólin   kaì gaîan   ékhousin
       DEM.ACC town.ACC and land.ACC have.PRS.3PL

172   CHAPTER 7

'For this reason, I don't know any of the men who possess this town and land.' (*Od.* 7.25–26)

Finally, imperative forms of *oîda* also occur: typically, they are used in protestations, as in (272).

(272) *ístō*   *nûn tóde*   *Gaîa*   *kaì Ouranòs*
       know.IMP.PRF.3SG now DEM.ACC Earth.NOM and Heaven.NOM
       eu[rùs   *húperthe*
       broad.NOM above
       'Hereto now be Earth and the broad Heaven above my witnesses.' (*Il.* 15.36)

Passages in which *oîda* only features a nominative first participant, or in which it takes a subordinate clause, also construe the situation as involving a state of consciousness or intellectual knowledge, as shown in examples (273) and (274).

(273) *métēr*   *mén té   mé*   *phēsi*   *toû*   *émmenai,*
       mother.NOM PTC PTC 1SG.ACC tell.PRS.3SG DEM.GEN be.INF.PRS
       autàr egṓ   *ge   ouk oîd'*   *ou   gár pṓ   tis*
       but   1SG.NOM PTC NEG know.PRF.1SG NEG PTC ever INDF.NOM
       heòn   *gónon*   *autòs*   *anégnō*
       POSS.REFL.ACC parentage.ACC self.NOM know_certainly.AOR.3SG
       'My mother says that I am his (child), but I don't know, for never yet did any man of himself learn certainly about his own parentage.' (*Od.* 1.215–216)

(274) *óphr' eidéō*   *hóssoi*   *te   kaì hoí*
       for   know.SBJV.PRF.1SG how_many.NOM.PL PTC and REL.NOM.PL
       tines   *anéres*   *eisí*
       INDF.NOM.PL man.NOM.PL be.PRS.3PL
       'So that I know how many there are and what sort of men they are.' (*Od.* 16.236)

When taking the NomGen construction, *oîda* most often occurs as a participle: finite forms are only three out of 24 (*Il.* 15.412, *Il.* 12.229, *Il.* 18.192). The meaning in virtually all occurrences is 'be skilled in', 'be expert of'. Examples are (275) and (276).

COGNITION 173

(275) *hós   rhá te   páses   eû   eidêi   sophíes*
REL.NOM PTC PTC all.GEN well know.SBJV.PRF.3SG science.GEN
hupothēmosúnēisin Athénēs
counsel.DAT.PL   Athena.GEN
'Who by Athena's inspiration is a great expert of all sciences.' (*Il.* 15.411–412)

(276) *kaí hoi   Teûkros   háma   spésthō*
and 3SG.DAT Teucros.NOM together follow.IMP.AOR.MID.3SG
tóxōn   eù eidṓs
bow.GEN.PL well know.PTCP.PRF.NOM
'Let Teucros, who is an expert archer, follow him.' (*Il.* 12.350)

The passage in (275) contains one of the three occurrences of a finite form of *oîda*, while (276) shows the much more frequent pattern with a participle. Besides *tóxon* 'bow', which occurs five times, other typical objects of expertise are *aikhmḗ* 'spear', *alkḗ* 'force', *mákhē* 'fight' and *pólemos* 'war', all of which occur twice. Occurrences in which the NomAcc construction seems to refer to a skill rather than to a cognitive state are limited: one can be found in (290) discussed in Section 7.2.2, in which *oîda* is coordinated with a form of *édaon* 'learn', a verb that can indicate both acquisition of knowledge and proficiency in skills.

Other occurrences with the NomGen construction indicate skill in battle (*Il.* 7.236–237, 11.719; see Ebeling 1885: 354). This same meaning is also connected to the construction in which *oîda* takes an infinitive, as in (277).

(277) *en dé   te   têisi   nomeùs   oú pō sápha*
in PTC PTC DEM.DAT.PL herdsman.NOM NEG PTC clearly
eidṑs   thērì   makhéssasthai
know.PTCP.PRF.NOM beast.DAT fight.INF.AOR.MID
'And among them a herdsman, who is not an expert in fighting with a wild beast.' (*Il.* 15.632–633)

The verb *epístamai* 'know' also indicates a state. It always occurs in the present stem, and, similar to *oîda* with the NomGen construction, it refers to practical rather than intellectual knowledge (Chantraine 1977: 360). In contrast with *oîda*, it can occur both in the NomGen and in the NomAcc construction without a semantic difference. Notably, however, the NomAcc construction is limited to the second argument *érga*, thus showing an idiomatic character (two out of four occurrences are in a formula). Examples are (278)-(281).

174   CHAPTER 7

(278) *péri   gár sphisi   dôken   Athḗnē   érga   t'*
       about PTC 3PL.DAT give.AOR.3SG Athena.NOM work.ACC.PL PTC
       epístasthai   perikalléa
       know.INF.PRS.M/P very_beautiful.ACC.PL
       'Athena granted them skill in making beautiful works.' (*Od.* 7.110–111 =
       2.117–119)

(279) *all' ág'   emôn   okhéōn*
       but come_on POSS.1PL.GEN.PL carriage.GEN.PL
       epibéseo,   óphra ídēai
       mount.IMP.AOR.MID.2SG for   see.SBJV.AOR.MID.2SG
       hoîoi   Trṓioi   híppoi
       such.NOM.PL Trojan.NOM.PL horse.NOM.PL
       epistámenoi   pedíoio
       know.PTCP.PRS.M/P.NOM.PL plain.GEN
       'Come on, mount into my carriage, so that you may see what the Tro-
       jan horses are like, how they are expert of the plain.' (*Il.* 5.221–222 =
       Il. 8.106)

(280) *anḕr   phórmiggos epistámenos   kaì aoidês*
       man.NOM lyre.GEN   know.PTCP.PRS.M/P.NOM and singing.GEN
       'A man skilled in the lyre and in the art of singing.' (*Od.* 21.406)

(281) *allá min   oîos   epístato   pêlai*
       but 3SG.ACC alone.NOM know.IMPF.M/P.3SG wield.INF.AOR
       Akhilleùs
       Achilleus.NOM
       'But Achilles alone knew how to wield it.' (*Il.* 16.142–143)

The NomAcc construction occurs in (278); as noted above the second argument
is the generic noun *érga* 'work', 'deed'. Examples (279) and (280) feature the
NomGen construction, the former with a non-human experiencer, and the second with a human one. In both examples we find verbal participles, and (280)
in particular is especially similar to (276) with *oîda*. A finite verb form occurs
in (281), in which *epístamai* takes a dependent infinitive *pêlai* 'wield', again a
construction that this verb shares with *oîda*.
     Etymologically, *epístamai* is most likely connected with the Proto-Indo-
European root **stā-* of Greek *hístēmai* 'stand', with psylosis (deaspiration)
(Chantraine 1977: 360). The psylotic form became semantically separated from
the base verb at an early time, and a new, non-psylotic prefixed verb *ephístamai*

COGNITION
175

'stand upon', also attested in Homer, was likely created later, and preserves the semantic connection with *hístēmi*. The verb *epístamai* is stative, accordingly it only has the present stem and some future forms.

7.2.2 Learn, Understand, Recognize

In this Section, I review the use of three verbs that indicate acquisition on knowledge, hence a change of state: *gignôskō* 'learn', 'understand', 'recognize', *punthánomai* and its variant *peúthomai* 'learn', 'inquire', and the root *dae-* of *édaon* 'learn' that does not have a present stem. As has already been shown in Table 9 and Table 10, these three verbs are remarkably different concerning both the distribution of aspectual stems, and the distribution of constructions: while *gignôskō* and *daémenai* mostly feature the NomAcc construction, thus patterning after other cognitive verbs, *punthánomai* takes the NomGen construction quite frequently, and, as we will see in Table 11, it shows to some extent an animacy-based distribution partly similar to hearing verbs (Section 6.2). Differences concerning aspectual stems mainly concern the possible occurrence of perfect forms, limited to *daémenai* and *punthánomai*, and of forms based on the present stem, limited to *gignôskō* and *punthánomai/peúthomai*. However, this latter set of differences should not blur the common tendency of the three verbs to most frequently occur in the aorist. This is not surprising: as remarked above, these verbs indicate a change of state.

The verb *gignôskō* is based on the PIE root **gnō-*, which has cognates in several languages, including English *know*. In Homeric Greek, it never indicates a state. Most frequently, it occurs in the aorist and means 'get to know', 'realize' and often 'understand'. Events denoted by this verb are partly similar to events denoted by *noéō*, but, as remarked by Snell (1946), they are in fact more complex, as *gignôskō* does not only indicate that the experiencer becomes aware of a situation, but also entails processing and understanding the information. As I will argue discussing the examples, the difference in complexity between the situations encoded by *gignôskō* and by *noéō* indicates that the former verb denotes accomplishments while the latter denotes achievements. Let us consider (282) and (283).

(282) *autàr hò   égnō   hêisin   enì*
       but   DEM.NOM understand.AOR.3SG POSS.3PL.DAT.PL within
       phresì   phónēsén   te
       heart.DAT.PL speak.AOR.3SG PTC
       'But he understood the whole matter within his heart, and spoke (to them).' (*Il.* 8.446)

(283) *édē   mèn sè   kaì autòn   oíomai*
       PTC PTC 2SG.ACC and self.ACC think.PRS.M/P.1SG
       eisoróōnta   gignóskein   hóti pêma   theòs
       see.PTCP.PRS.ACC understand.INF.PRS that calamity.ACC god.NOM
       Danaoîsi   kulíndei
       Danaan.DAT.PL roll.PRS.3SG
       'Even now I think that you can understand for yourself, from watching,
       how the god is rolling calamities against the Danaans.' (*Il.* 17.687–688)

In (282) Zeus reached the council of the gods and, upon seeing Athena and
Hera sitting aside, he immediately understood that the two goddesses were
upset. Here, the aorist *égnō* indicates that the experiencer did not only notice
Athena and Hera, but also understood what their feelings were. Example (283)
contains a present infinitive *gignóskein* that depends on the present participle
eisoróōnta 'seeing', 'watching', 'considering' (see Section 6.1).

Napoli, discussing this passage (2006: 159–160), argues that the verb's actionality becomes stative when the verb is in the present stem, while the perfective
stem (aorist), in her view, indicates an achievement. However, as has been
highlighted in Luraghi and Sausa (2017), this does not seem to be the case. In
(283) the experiencer acquires knowledge and understanding of a situation by
carefully examining it: the two present forms *eisoróōnta* and *gignóskein* highlight the ongoing character of the process. Hence, when occurring in the aorist
the verbs should better be viewed as indicating an accomplishment. Note that
in (285) the aorist *égnō* occurs with the adverb *aîpsa* 'quickly'; however, this
adverb cannot be considered a diagnostic to identify achievements, as a survey of its occurrences in the Homeric poems shows that it is compatible both
with achievements and with accomplishments: for example, it occurs with
iknéomai 'reach', likely an achievement, and with *érkhomai* 'go', which indicates an accomplishment; in addition, it is gradable, as one finds *aîpsa mála*
'very quickly' with verbs such as *érkhomai* 'go' (several occurrences) and *thōrḗs-
somai* 'arm oneself', also an accomplishment in e.g. *Il.* 19.36. More evidence
for the present stem of *gignóskō* as denoting an ongoing activity is discussed
below.

Given its meaning, *gignóskō* often indicates understanding of a situation, as
in (282) and (283), which do not contain overt stimuli. NPs referring to events
may occur, as in (284), in which the stimulus is *níkēn* 'victory' and the experiencer is said to understand that it is *heteralkéa* 'inclining to the other side'. Here
and elsewhere, the verb takes the NomAcc construction.

COGNITION   177

(284) ê   mèn dè   gígnōske   mákhēs   heteralkéa
       PTC PTC PTC understand.IMPF.3SG battle.GEN alternate.ACC
       níkēn
       victory.ACC
       'He understood that the tide of the battle was turning.' (*Il.* 16.362)

It needs to be remarked that in (284) the verb *gígnōske* is an imperfect, and
it does not indicate a sudden event as an aorist would do. Here it is not said
that Hector (the omitted subject) suddenly realized that the battle was uncertain: rather, the hero is depicted resisting the enemy's assault though possibly
becoming aware of the turning outcomes of the battle. The whole passage
features various imperfect verb forms: "Now mighty Ajax was keen as ever to
hurl (*híeto* imperfect) a spear at bronze-clad Hector, but the Trojan leader,
skilled in war, protecting his broad shoulders by his ox-hide shield, watched
(*sképteto* imperfect) the whirring arrows and hurtling spears pass by. Hector
understood (*gígnōske* imperfect) that the tide of battle was turning, but held
on (*anémimne* imperfect), continued protecting (*sáō* imperfect) his loyal comrades."

However, the process indicated by *gignóskō* does not necessarily imply
acquiring information about a situation. Especially when the stimulus is a
human being, often acquiring knowledge and processing it equals to recognizing someone, that is, understanding that X is someone already known, as in
(285) with an aorist, and (286), with a present participle.

(285) égnō   d' aîps' ém'   ekeînos, epeì
       understand.AOR.3SG PTC quickly 1SG.ACC DEM.NOM as
       píen   haîma   kelainón
       drink.AOR.3SG blood.ACC dark.ACC
       'He quickly recognized me, when he had drunk my dark blood.' (*Od.*
       11.390)

(286) sperkhómenos   d' apò toîin
       haste.PTCP.PRS.M/P.NOM PTC from DEM.DAT.DU
       esúla   teúkhea   kalà
       strip_off.IMPF.3SG armor.ACC.PL beautiful.ACC.PL
       gignóskōn
       understand.PTCP.PRS.NOM
       'He hastened to unclothe them from their beautiful armors, recogniz-
       ing them.' (*Il.* 11.110–111)

178   CHAPTER 7

In (285), the aorist points to a change of state, which is said to happen quickly (*aîpsa*), while in (286) the present participle indicates an ongoing activity: again, as in (283), we find another present participle, *sperkhómenos* 'hastening', referring to the imperfect *ésula* 'stripped off'. This last action is performed in haste, but a present stem indicates an ongoing situation, which is matched by the process of recognition that is likewise accomplished gradually.

The event of recognizing usually happens between human beings; however the same meaning can also apply to inanimate, concrete stimuli, as in (287).

(287)   *íkhnia   gàr metópisthe podôn   ēdè knēmáōn   rheî'*
        track.ACC.PL PTC behind   foot.GEN.PL PTC leg.GEN.PL easily
        égnōn   apióntos
        understand.AOR.1SG leave.PTCP.PRS.GEN
        'I easily recognized the tokens behind of his feet and his legs as he went away.' (*Il.* 13.71–72)

Example (287) contains an inanimate stimulus, *íkhnia* 'footprints', which, similar to animate and abstract stimuli, appears in the NomAcc construction. The aorist participle *égnōn* indicates an accomplished event.

The NomGen construction only occurs twice in the *Odyssey* with the second argument *allélōn* 'each other' as in (288) (the other occurrence is *Od.* 23.109; see further Ebeling 1885: 115, who discusses some other possible occurrences, none of which, however, is compelling).

(288)   *ou   dè   trapézēi gnótēn   allélōn*
        NEG PTC table.DAT understand.AOR.3DU each_other.GEN.PL
        'They did not recognize each other at the table.' (*Od.* 21.35–36)

Summing up, *gignóskō* is similar to *noéō* as both verbs indicate telic events; however, occurrences of the present stem denote activities in the case of *gignóskō* and states in the case of *noéō*. This is in keeping with the greater complexity of the type of situation indicated by *gignóskō*, and may also be a reason for its tendency to occur in the present stem more frequently than *noéō*. As compared to *oîda*, which always indicates a state, *gignóskō* offers a telic counterpart when occurring in the aorist, and adds a temporal dimension to an atelic situation when occurring in the present.

The verb *gignóskō* has a number of compounds, the most frequent of which (eight occurrences) is *anagignóskō*, which means 'know certainly', 'recognize'. It indicates a change of state and always occurs in the aorist; an example can

COGNITION

179

be found in (273). The verb *diagignóskō*, which occurs three times, means 'single out', and can indicate an activity (two out of three occurrences show the present stem). Finally, the verb *agnoéō* 'fail to notice', 'fail to recognize' is also based on the root of *gignóskō* with the negative prefix *a-* and occurs seven times. All three verbs take the NomAcc construction when occurring with two nominal arguments.

The verb *édaon* 'learn' does not have the present stem in Homer (the same root also occurs in the reduplicated and suffixed verb *didáskō*, 'teach', with the aorist supplied by the reduplicated stem *dédae* 'taught'). Other stems (perfect, future, and aorist) take the NomAcc construction 11 times. The passages in (289) and (290) show that the process of acquiring knowledge denoted by this verb leads to the type of cognitive state indicated by *oîda*.

(289) *ei d'   ethéleis   kai taûta   daémenai   óphr' eù*
   if PTC wish.PRS.2SG and DEM.ACC. PL learn.INF.AOR for well
   eidêis   hēmetérēn   geneén   polloì   dé
   know.SBJV.PRF.2SG POSS.1PL.ACC lineage.ACC many.NOM.PL PTC
   min   ándres   ísasin
   3SG.ACC man.NOM.PL know.PRF.3PL
   'If you want to also learn these things, in order to know well about our
   lineage: many know about it.' (*Il.* 6.150–151 = *Il.* 20.213–214)

(290) *deûte,   phíloi,   tòn   xeînon*
   come_on friend.VOC.PL DEM.ACC stranger.ACC
   erómetha   eí tin'   áethlon   oîdé   te
   ask.SBJV.AOR.MID.1PL if INDF.ACC contest.ACC know.PRF.3SG PTC
   kai dedáēke
   and learn.PRF.3SG
   'Friends, let's ask the stranger whether he knows or has learned any
   contest.' (*Od.* 8.133–134)

In (289), learning more information leads to better knowledge. The passage features the NomAcc construction: another similar occurrence in which the process indicated by *édaon* leads to the acquisition of an intellectual content can be found in (298), which I will discuss further on in this Section. Example (290) contains the perfect form *dedáēke* 'has learned' coordinated with *oîde* 'knows'. The perfect has a resultative meaning in Homeric Greek: it indicates a state achieved as a result of a change of state. Hence, it depicts a situation which is virtually equivalent to the situation denoted by *oîda*, which, however, does not focus on the preceding change of state but, synchronically, is simply

180   CHAPTER 7

stative. (The same distinction also holds for the perfect of *punthánomai* 'learn' as opposed to *oîda*, see examples (129) and (130) discussed in Section 4.1.)

Remarkably, in (290) the forms *dedáēke* and *oîde* refer to a skill (the speaker is wondering whether Odysseus knows any type of contest activity), a possible meaning of *oîda* that is usually connected with the NomGen construction (see Section 7.2.1). In the case of *édaon*, the difference between acquiring knowledge and becoming proficient in some skill does not seem to be connected with either the NomAcc or the NomGen construction, which occurs in (291).

(291) *ei d'   ethéleis   polémoio daémenai*
       if PTC want.PRS.2SG war.GEN learn.INF.AOR
       'If you want to know the war.' (*Il.* 21.487)

Example (291) contains the NomGen construction; the stimulus is *pólemos* 'war', which also occurs twice in the same construction with *oîda* meaning 'be skilled at war' (see Section 7.2.1). The NomGen construction with *édaon* only occurs twice, but the second occurrence in (292) does not indicate the acquisition of a practical skill.

(292) *pôs gàr emeû   sú,   xeîne,   daéseai   eí*
       how PTC 1SG.GEN 2SG.NOM stranger.VOC learn.FUT.MID.3SG if
       ti   gunaikôn   alláōn   períeimi   nóon
       INDF.ACC woman.GEN.PL other.GEN.PL surpass.PRS.1SG mind.ACC
       'How can you learn about me, stranger, whether I excel other women in wit.' (*Od.* 19.325–326)

The passage in (292) contains an animate stimulus, and the context suggests the meaning 'learn about': Penelope suggests that the beggar (Odysseus in disguise) should be put in the condition to sit as a peer at her table, in order to be able to assess her qualities.

A human stimulus also occurs in (293) with the NomAcc construction.

(293) *all' ê   toí se   gunaîkas   egṑ   dedáasthai*
       but PTC PTC 2SG.ACC woman.ACC.PL 1SG.NOM learn.AOR.MID.INF
       ánōga,   haí   té s'   atimázousi
       order.PRF.1SG REL.NOM.PL PTC 2SG.ACC dishonor.PRS.3PL
       'I order you that you learn about the women, which (of them) dishonor you.' (*Od.* 16.316–317)

COGNITION 181

Note that (293) contains a middle infinitive of the reduplicated aorist, which is usually considered to supply the aorist stem to *didáskō* 'teach', a verb that takes the NomAccAcc construction (double accusative; see Luraghi and Zanchi 2018). Hence, the NomAcc construction here can be viewed as a reduction of the NomAccAcc due to valency reduction brought about by the middle voice.

A comparison of *édaon* with *gignóskō* shows some important differences. While the latter verb indicates understanding of some intellectual content about a situation or recognizing of some, mostly human, concrete referent, the former can indicate learning both with a cognitive and with a practical output. The perfect stem, which is never featured by *gignóskō*, profiles a cognitive state as the result of a process, as opposed to the stative meaning of *oîda*. Due to the relatively low number of occurrences, generalizing over the meaning of construction alternation with *édaon* would be unwarranted; in any case, one could argue that the two occurrences of the NomGen construction seem to cover a wide and disparate semantic range.

The verb *punthánomai* 'learn', 'inquire' shows all aspectual stems, even though most forms of the present stem are supplied by its metrical variant (cf. Chantraine 2013: 111) *peúthomai*. Etymologically it reflects the Proto-Indo-European root **bheudh-* 'be awake', 'wake up' which has cognates in several Indo-European languages, for example in the Indo-Aryan verb *bodhati* 'wake up', whose participle *buddha* means 'the awakened one'. It displays a similar range of constructions as hearing verbs, as shown in Table 11 (from Luraghi and Sausa 2019).

TABLE 11 Occurrences of *punthanómai* and *peúthomai* in different argument structure constructions

		Total	Animate stimulus	Inanimate stimulus
punthánomai	NomGen	19	15	4
	NomAcc	25	4	21
peúthomai	NomAcc	8	0	8

As shown in Table 11, *punthánomai/peúthomai* shows a pattern of construction variation only partly connected with animacy: the NomGen construction can occur both with animate and with inanimate stimuli but with the latter the NomAcc construction is much more frequent. Contrary to verbs of hearing, animate stimuli occasionally also occur in the NomAcc construction.

The distribution of constructions shows a close relation between *punthánomai* and perception verbs that also emerges from some of the occurrences.

182

Indeed, the verb may refer to immediate perception of an individual or an inanimate entity, and the context most often indicates that it refers to aural perception, as shown in (294) with the NomAcc construction and in (295). However, (296) and partly also (295) suggest that this is not necessarily the case.

(294) *eí pōs érga*   *ídoimi*   *brotôn*   *enopén*
       if ever work.ACC.PL see.AOR.OPT.1SG mortal.GEN.PL voice.ACC
       te   *puthoímēn*
       PTC learn.AOR.OPT.MID.1SG
       'If I ever saw works of mortals or I heard a voice.' (*Od.* 10.147)

(295) *prín* *gé* *ti* *sês*   *te* *boês*   *soû*   *th'*
       before PTC PTC POSS.2SG.GEN PTC cry.GEN 2SG.GEN PTC
       helkēthmoîo   *puthésthai*
       being_carried_off.GEN learn.INF.AOR.MID
       '(Let me be dead and covered with earth) rather than hear your cry and you being carried away.' (*Il.* 6.465)

(296) *all'* *aièn* *opíssō* *kházonth'*   *hōs* *epúthonto*
       but always backward retire.IMPF.M/P.3PL when learn.AOR.MID.3PL
       metà *Tróessin*   *Árēa*
       among Trojans.DAT.PL Ares.ACC
       'But they always gave ground backward, when they sensed Ares among the Trojans.' (*Il.* 5.701–702)

In (294), *punthánomai* indicates a type of perception triggered by the human voice, and is contrasted with *ídoimi* 'I saw', hence the implication that aural perception is involved. The human voice is also one of the stimuli in (295), which, however, contains a second stimulus, the human participant *soû* 'you'. Note that this occurrence contains the NomGen construction: a possible explanation connected with construction variation would be that only the NomAcc construction can indicate immediate perception, and that the passage in (295) should be taken as indicating indirect acquisition of knowledge (see Luraghi and Sausa 2019). In the light of other occurrences, however, this explanation must be rejected; see below the discussion of examples (299) and especially (301). Finally, (296), there is no contextual clue implying that perception modality is hearing rather than sight: rather, the choice of *punthánomai* leaves it unspecified.

   In (297) *punthánomai* contrasts both with hearing and with sight, not in terms of perceptual modality, but in terms of control.

COGNITION

(297) ouk ídon,   ou   puthómēn,   allà stónon
      NEG see.AOR.1SG NEG learn.AOR.MID.1SG but groaning.ACC
      oîon   ákousa   kteinoménōn
      alone.ACC hear.AOR.1SG slay.PTCP.PRS.M/P.GEN.PL
      'I did not see, I did not inquire; I only heard the groaning of men that
      were being slain.' (*Od.* 23.40–41)

Example (297) contrasts the event indicated by *punthánomai* with sensory perception. The speaker, Penelope's nurse Eurycleia, has not acquired knowledge
by direct visual perception, nor has she tried to acquire it from other sources:
she has evidence from hearing and knows that killing must have happened,
but cannot explain how. In this passage *punthánomai* denotes a way of acquiring information actively and intentionally: this type of activity contrasts with
sensory perception, which is uncontrolled. Hence, *punthánomai* here must be
taken as meaning 'inquire', with a semantic shift that was starting to appear in
Homeric Greek, and that will become the basic meaning of the verb in Classical
Greek (see further the discussion of examples (304)-(306)).

Other occurrences leave open the possibility of taking the event indicated
by *punthánomai* as implying perception, as (298).

(298) hóssa   d'   enì megároisi   kathḗmenos
      REL.ACC.PL PTC in palace.DAT.PL sit.PTCP.PRF.M/P.NOM
      hēmetéroisi   peúthomai ...   daéseai
      POSS.1PL.DAT.PL learn.PRS.M/P.1SG learn.FUT.2SG
      'What I have learned sitting in your palace you will know.' (*Od.* 3.186–
      3.187)

In (298) *punthánomai* features the NomAcc construction with the second argument *hóssa* 'whatever'. It occurs side by side with *édaon*: even though the two
verbs seem to have the same meaning, the possibility that *punthánomai* implies
immediate perception cannot be ruled out, as it points to a situation in which
information is acquired secretly, and can be taken to mean 'overhear'. Similarly,
in (299) with the NomGen construction the stimulus *aggelíēs* 'the announcement' can be viewed as indicating the information that is being acquired, as
well as a concrete act of speech that is being perceived.

(299) oú min   oḯomai   ou dè pepústhai
      NEG 3SG.ACC court.PRS.M/P.1SG NEG PTC learn.INF.PRF.M/P
      lugrês   aggelíēs, hóti hoi   phílos   óleth'
      sad.GEN news.GEN that 3SG.DAT dear.NOM die.AOR.MID.3SG

184 CHAPTER 7

hetaîros
comrade.NOM
'I do not think he had already known the sad news, that his dear comrade had died.' (*Il.* 17.641–642)

In some other occurrences, the pattern is the same as with perception verbs, and contains the Two-place+P construction: the verb may refer to direct perception of an event (Dik and Hengeveld's 1991 type (ii) situation) or to the acquisition of knowledge from a third party, through reception of the propositional content of a speech act (Dik and Hengeveld's 1991 type (iv) situation), depending on the context. The main participant is encoded as the stimulus, while the event is indicated by a predicative participle (cf. e.g. (173) with *eîdon* and (203) with *akoúō* among others). Examples are (300) and (301) with the NomGen+P construction.

(300)   *dúo*   *d'*   *oú*   *pō*   *phôte*   *pepústhēn*
two.NOM.DU PTC NEG PTC warrior.NOM.DU learn.PPF.M/P.2DU
anére   *kudalímō*   *Thrasumédēs*   *Antílokhos*
man.NOM.DU famous.NOM.DU Thrasymedes.NOM Antilochus.NOM
te   *Patrókloio*   *thanóntos*   *amúmonos*
PTC Patroclus.GEN die.PTCP.AOR.GEN noble.GEN
'Two men that were famous warriors, Thrasymedes and Antilochus, had not yet learned that noble Patroclus was dead.' (*Il.* 17.377–379).

(301)   *híppoi*   *d'*   *Aiakídao*   *mákhēs*
horse.NOM.PL PTC offspring_of_Aeacus.GEN battle.GEN
apáneuthen eóntes   *klaîon*   *epeì dè*   *prôta*
off   be.PTCP.PRS.NOM.PL weep.IMPF.3PL as   PTC first
puthésthēn   *hēniókhoio*   *en koníēisi*
learn.AOR.MID.3DU charioteer.GEN in dust.DAT.PL
pesóntos
fall.PTCP.AOR.GEN
'But the horses of Achilles, being apart from the battle, were weeping, since first they sensed that their charioteer had fallen in the dust.' (*Il.* 17.426–428)

Example (300) might refer to immediate perception: indeed, Thrasymedes and Antilochus have not been able to learn about Patroclus' death most likely on account of the distance and the confusion on the battle field. Following from this, (301) can only refer to immediate perception, even though the modality

COGNITION   185

is not specified. Here, Achilles' horses, which Patroclus, wearing his friend's
armor, had led in battle, are depicted weeping on the fallen hero: they learned
that he fell from the chariot, most likely because they felt him falling or because
they saw his body in the dust, and certainly not through someone else's report.

The NomAcc+P construction also occurs once in (302). Apart from the
higher frequency of the NomGen+P construction, (302) and (300) look quite
similar: in both cases the stimulus is human, and reference is made to the
acquisition of knowledge about a situation in which a participant is involved.
Note however that (302) shows irrealis modality, and that the verb arguably
refers to a cognitive process rather than to perception. Similarly, in (129) the
NomAcc construction also encodes a state that concerns the human stimulus.
This and two other similar occurrences (*Il.* 6.50 and *Il.* 11.135) contain the adjective *zōón* 'alive' rather than a participle, but apart from this they are equivalent
to occurrences with the Two-place+P construction (see Section 3.3). Example
(129) cannot refer to immediate perception: the speaker is begging his enemies
not to kill him, and in order to convince them he promises great rewards from
his father in case he learns that his son is alive.

(302) *ei gàr egṑ   puthómēn   taútēn   hodòn*
       if PTC 1SG.NOM learn.AOR.MID.1SG DEM.ACC road.ACC
       hormaínonta
       ponder.PTCP.PRS.ACC
       'If I had learned that he was pondering this journey.' (*Od.* 4.732)

(129) *eí ken emè   zōòn   pepúthoit'   epì nēusìn*
       if PTC 1SG.ACC alive.ACC learn.AOR.OPT.MID.3SG on ship.DAT.PL
       Akhaiôn
       Achean.GEN.PL
       'If he learned that I am alive by the ships of the Achaeans.' (*Il.* 10.381)

A mixture of the two constructions occurs with *peúthomai* in (303). The verb
takes the second argument *tó* 'this', thus showing the NomAcc construction.
The genitive *mētròs* could instantiate the NomGen construction, but note that
it also functions as second argument of the verb *akoúō*, which, with human
referents, always takes the NomGen construction.

(303) *polláki gàr tó   ge mētròs   epeútheto*
       often PTC DEM.ACC PTC mother.GEN learn.IMPF.M/P.3SG
       nósphin akoúōn
       far   hear.PTCP.PRS.NOM
       'He often heard this, listening to his mother secretly.' (*Il.* 17.408)

186 CHAPTER 7

In other occurrences, *punthánomai* indicates the acquisition of information about a certain topic. Again, this can involve both the NomGen construction, as in example (304), and the NomAcc construction, as in (305). In (306), instead, the stimulus is encoded in a subordinate clause. In such occurrences, the verb might point to a controlled nature of the situation, in which an experiencer/agent actively tries to inquire about someone or something. They provide bridging contexts to the meaning 'inquire', already discussed in reference to example (297) that only occurs in the *Odyssey* and that will become central for this verb in Classical Greek.

(304) *eis agorḕn   iénai,   óphra xeínoio*
to square.ACC go.INF.PRS for   guest.GEN
púthēsthe
learn.SBJV.AOR.MID.2PL
'Go to the square in order to learn about the guest.' (*Od.* 8.12)

(305) *eîmi   gàr es Spártēn   te   kaì es Púlon   ēmathóenta*
go.PRS.1SG PTC to Sparta.ACC PTC and to Pylos.ACC sandy.ACC
nóston   peusómenos   patròs   phílou   én
return.ACC learn.PTCP.FUT.MID.NOM father.GEN dear.GEN PTC
pou   akoúsō
somehow hear.SBJV.AOR.1SG
'For I am going to Sparta and to sandy Pylos trying to learn about the return of my dear father, if I may hear somehow.' (*Od.* 2.359–2.360)

(306) *dḕ   tot'   egṑn   hetárous   proḯein*
PTC then 1SG.NOM comrade.ACC.PL send.INF.PRS
peúthesthai   ióntas,   hoí   tines
learn.INF.PRS.M/P go.PTCP.PRS.ACC.PL DEM.NOM.PL INDF.NOM.PL
anéres   eîen   epì khthonì
man.NOM.PL be.OPT.PRS.3PL on land.DAT
'I sent forward my comrades to go and learn about the people who lived in that land'. (*Od.* 9.88–89 = 10.100–101)

The three verbs discussed in this Section indicate acquisition of knowledge in a quite different manner. In particular, the verb *gignóskō* means 'understand', 'realize', and also 'recognize'. It means that some new information is acquired and crucially focuses on the mental process of understanding. It provides a perfective counterpart to *oîda*, which in turn is always stative, and always refers to an intellectual operation: it does not match the meaning of *oîda* with the

COGNITION

187

NomGen construction or of *epístamai* and does not indicate acquisition of a skill. In turn, both *édaon* and *punthánomai* focus on the new character of the information that is acquired. They, too, may match *oîda*: in particular, their perfect forms add a resultative character to the stative meaning expressed by *oîda*, while in addition *édaon* may also refer to the acquisition of a skill. The verb *punthánomai* may refer to immediate perception without indicating a specific perceptual modality. Notably, among verbs of learning, *punthánomai* is the one that most frequently features the NomGen construction typical of verbs of non-visual perception, while the NomGen construction with *gignóskō* and *édaon* is limited to two occurrences each.

7.3   Remember / Forget

The Greek verb that indicates memory, *mimnéskomai*, is based on the Proto-Indo-European root **men-* that refers to thought and has reflexes in virtually all Indo-European languages: a suffixed form serves as base for the English *mind*, Latin *men-s, ment-is* 'mind'. Notably, in Ancient Greek this root is not reflected in verbs or nouns that indicate the mind or rational thought. Rather, as pointed out by Meillet (1897), it shows a connection with emotions. Several other lexemes are based on this root in Ancient Greek, which in some way indicate altered states of mind, such as *manía* 'madness', *ménos* 'passion', *mántis* 'seer', 'diviner', as well as the verb *mémona* 'desire eagerly' that I have discussed in Section 5.2.

In Homeric Greek, *mimnéskomai* can refer to all the different events of memory discussed in Section 2.1.3. It takes both the NomAcc and the NomGen construction, with the latter being much more frequent than the former, and shows all aspectual stems (see Table 9 and Table 10). Only for the present stem, a second verb is available, *mnáomai*, which shows a shift in construction selection between the *Iliad* and the *Odyssey*: while in the former poem it occurs three times in the NomGen construction, in the latter it occurs 14 times, and takes the NomAcc construction. This constructional change is accompanied by a semantic shift. In the occurrences in the *Iliad*, two of which are identical, the verb's meaning is 'think of', 'have in mind', similar to the meaning of *mimnéskomai* that I discuss further on in this Section (see e.g. (317)). An example is (307).

(307) *all' hoí   g'   ou   polémoio dusēkhéos*
       but DEM.NOM.PL PTC NEG war.GEN woeful.GEN
       emnóonto
       think.IMPF.M/P.3PL
       'But they were not thinking of woeful war.' (*Il.* 2.686)

188   CHAPTER 7

In (307) the subject *hoi* refers to the Myrmidons, who were lying idle during
the siege of Troy and did not take any initiative to fight, as there was nobody to
lead them in battle while Achilles refrained from fighting.

The 14 occurrences with the NomAcc construction in the *Odyssey*, on the
other hand, consistently show the meaning 'court', 'woo (for one's bride)', as in
(308), that anticipates the post-Homeric meaning 'sue for', 'solicit' (always with
the NomAcc construction).

(308)   *ḗdē gár se   mnôntai   aristêes   katà*
        PTC PTC 2SG.ACC court.PRS.M/P.3PL noble.NOM.PL throughout
        dêmon   pántōn   Phaiḗkōn
        country.ACC all.GEN.PL Phaeacian.GEN.PL
        'Even now, here in the country, the noblest of all Pheacians court you.'
        (*Od.* 6.34–35)

Remarkably, some dictionaries lemmatize *mimnḗskomai* and *mnáomai* under
the same lemma (see Chantraine 1977: 702), and in fact the distribution of
aspectual stems, as shown in Table 9 is remindful of the distribution of *punthánomai* and *peúthomai*, which are considered metrical variants. However, the
semantic development of *mnáomai* is not matched by any similar process for
peúthomai. It is likely that the pair *mimnḗskomai/mnáomai* started out as featuring two synonymous metrical variants, which then underwent a split when
mnáomai shifted to the meaning shown in the *Odyssey*.

Though being less frequent than the NomGen construction, the NomAcc
construction with *mimnḗskomai* does not seem to be semantically restricted,
and shows all possible construals of memory discussed in Van Valin and Wilkins
(1993: 511) (see Section 2.1.3 and examples (28)-(30)). In combination with aorist
forms of the verb, it indicates a mental change of state, as in (309), while the
perfect in (310) indicates a state.

(309)   *autàr epeì pósios   kaì edētúos   ex   éron*
        but   as   drink.GEN and food.GEN from desire.ACC
        hénto,   mnēsámenoi   dè   épeita
        release.AOR.MID.3PL remember.PTCP.AOR.MID.NOM.PL PTC then
        phílous   éklaion   hetaírous
        dear.ACC.PL cry.IMPF.3PL comrade.ACC.PL
        'After having satisfied the desire of food and drinks, they started crying
        as they remembered their beloved comrades.' (*Od.* 12.308–309)

COGNITION

189

(310) *Tudéa*   *d'* *ou* *mémnēmai,*   *epeí m'*   *éti*
Tydaeus.ACC PTC NEG remember.PRF.M/P.1SG as   1SG.ACC still
tutthòn   *eónta*   *kálliph'*
little.ACC be.PTCP.PRS.ACC leave.AOR.3SG
'I don't remember Tydaeus, as I was still a toddler when he left me.' (*Il.*
6.222–623)

Though differing as to their actionality, the two examples indicate an unconscious memory. In (309) the aorist *mnēsámenoi* refers to the sudden activation
of a conceptual content (the comrades that had died) which was present in the
experiencers' mind, but remained latent. In (310), the speaker refers to a permanent state: as he was too small when he encountered Tydaeus, he cannot
remember him.

Elsewhere, memory can be activated in a controlled fashion, as shown by the
hortatory subjunctive in (311).

(311) *allà hékēlos*   *pîne,*   *kaì álla*   *parèx*
but at_ease.NOM drink.IMP.PRS.2SG and other.ACC.PL before
memnṓmetha,   *mēdé me*   *toútōn*
remeber.SBJV.PRF.M/P.1PL NEG   1SG.ACC DEM.GEN. PL
mímnēsk'
remind.IMP.PRS.2SG
'But drink at your ease, let's think of other things, and don't remind me
of these things.' (*Od.* 14.167–169)

The passage in (311) displays a frequent meaning of *mimnḗskomai*, which, rather
than a state or a process of recollection, seems to simply indicate the activity of
thinking about something known. It also contains an occurrence of the active
counterpart *mimnḗsko*, 'remind', that I will discuss in Section 9.2.

Different aspectual stems also indicate different construals of the situation
when *mimnḗskomai* takes the NomGen construction, as in (312)-(314).

(312) *autíka*   *gàr mnḗsontai*   *Akhaioì*
immediately PTC remember.FUT.MID.3PL Achaean.NOM.PL
patrídos   *aíēs*
native.GEN land.GEN
'Straightaway the Achaeans will think of their native land.' (*Il.* 4.172)

CHAPTER 7

(313) hoi   d' aieì boúlonto   theoì
      DEM.NOM PTC ever wish.IMPF.M/P.3PL god.NOM.PL
memnêsthai   *ephetméōn*
remember.INF.PRF.M/P command.GEN.PL
'And the gods always wished that men should be mindful of their commands.' (*Od.* 4.353)

(314) *memnêsthai*   *patròs*   *kaì* *metéros*   *en*
remember.INF.PRF.M/P father.GEN and mother.GEN in
megároisin   *hōs* *nûn*
palace.DAT.PL as   now
'Be mindful of my father and my mother in the halls as you are now.'
(*Od.* 18.267–268)

Example (312), with the aorist stem, indicates the sudden inception of recollection, as highlighted by the adverb *autíka* 'suddenly'. In (313) the perfect indicates a state, as also shown by the occurrence of the adverb *aieì* 'ever', 'all the time'. The state of being remindful implies complying with some orders or regulations, as well as taking care of someone, as in (314). In these last two occurrences, the stimulus is a matter of concern for the experiencer, and *mimnéskomai* comes close to verbs of emotion that indicate care, and share the same construction, discussed in Section 8.2.2.

As with the NomAcc construction in (311), *mimnéskomai* can simply mean 'think of', 'have in mind', 'occur'. Let us consider (315) and (316).

(315) *oudé ti*   *khármēs* *Trôes*   *mimnéskonto:*
NEG INDF.ACC fight.GEN Trojan.NOM.PL remember.IMPF.M/P.3PL
suneklóneon   *gàr* *oïstoí*
confound.IMPF.3PL PTC arrow.NOM.PL
'The Trojans were no longer minding to fight, as the arrows were confounding them.' (*Il.* 13.721–722)

(316) *hoì*   *dè* *phóboio* *duskeládou*
DEM.NOM.PL PTC flight.GEN ill_sounding.GEN
mnésanto,   *láthonto*   *dè* *thoúridos*
remember.AOR.MID.3PL forget.AOR.MID.3PL PTC fighting.GEN
alkês
valor.GEN
'(The Greeks fell upon the Trojans), and they thought of ill-sounding flight, and forgot their fighting valor.' (*Il.* 16.356–357)

COGNITION

191

Example (315) with the present stem construes the situation as atelic: the Trojans, bewildered by the enemy overtaking them, gave up fighting. The situation described is not a state of forgetfulness, but rather one in which the warriors no longer cared about fighting, and is paralleled by the situation described in (316) and referred to by the verb *lanthánomai* 'forget'. The Trojans, overwhelmed by the Greeks, did not think of (*láthonto*) their usual readiness to fight: in these circumstances they could only think of fleeing. Here, the aorist *mnésanto* of *mimnéskomai* does not indicate memory, but rather the rise of a sudden thought, which in (315) and (316) is not the outcome of a rational activity, nor does it originate from realizing or understanding some new information. Rather, running away is the only reaction that occurs to the bewildered Trojans, instead of fighting as they could have been expected to do, given their previous deeds in battle. Moreover, the parallel between *mimnéskomai* in (315) and (316) and *mnáomai* with the NomGen construction in (307) must also be pointed out.

Example (317) also refers to the activation of a thought that is already present in the experiencer's mind.

(317) *nûn dè   mnēsómetha   dórpou.   kaì   gár   t'*
      now PTC remember.SBJV.AOR.MID.1PL supper.GEN even PTC PTC
      ēǔkomos   Nióbē   emnḗsato   sítou
      fair_haired.NOM Niobe.NOM remember.AOR.MID.3SG food.GEN
      'But now let us think of supper. Even the fair-haired Niobe enjoyed her
      food.' (*Il.* 24.601–602)

In (317), Achilles invites Priamus to enjoy dinner in his hut, in spite of the unpleasant circumstances of their meeting. The meaning of *mimnéskomai* here is close to the meaning of *médomai* with the NomGen construction for example in (260), as discussed in Section 7.1.2.

Memory, as the spontaneous coming up of some thought which is latent in the experiencer's mind, can also happen in dreams, as shown in (318).

(318) *toû   potè memnḗsesthai   oíomai   én*
      DEM.GEN PTC remember.INF.FUT.PRF.M/P think.PRS.M/P.1SG in
      per oneírōi
      PTC dream.DAT
      '(A palace) which, I think, I will remember even in my dreams.' (*Od.*
      21.79)

192   CHAPTER 7

In addition to occurrences with the NomAcc and the NomGen construction, *mimnéskomai* also occurs twice with prepositional phrases in (319) and (320). Moreover, the prefixed verb *epimimnéskomai* occurs four times (*Il.* 17.102, *Od.* 1.31 = 4.189, *Od.* 4.191) with the NomGen construction, always in the aorist. It means 'come to one's mind' and has an inchoative meaning.

(319) *épeita dè kaì perì pompês   mnēsómeth'*
       then   PTC and about travel.GEN remember.FUT.MID.1PL
       'We will also take care of (his) journey.' (*Od.* 7. 191–192)

(320) *kaì nûn ê   toi egṑ   memnēménos   amph'*
       and now PTC PTC 1SG.NOM remember.PTCP.PRF.M/P.NOM about
       Odusêï   mutheómēn,   hósa   keînos
       Odysseus.DAT speak.IMPF.M/P.1SG REL.ACC.PL DEM.NOM
       oïzúsas   emógēsen   amph' emoí
       suffer.PTCP.AOR.NOM toil.AOR.3SG about 1SG.DAT
       'Yes, I just spoke about Odysseus as I remembered him, all that he suffered and toiled at for my sake.' (*Od.* 4.151–153)

Examples (319) and (320) contain stimuli encoded by the prepositional phrases *peri*+gen and *amphi*+gen respectively. In (319) Alcinous, who has just met Odysseus after his shipwreck, tells his fellows about his plans: after inviting the stranger to his palace, he plans to also take care of organizing a safe trip home for him. In (320) the stimulus is the human being about whom the experiencer preserves memories that he has retrieved while talking about him (cf. Luraghi 2003a: 258).

Lexically, remembering and forgetting are not connected with each other in Homeric Greek, and also show different relations with other domains of human experience. While the verb *mimnéskomai* is connected with the PIE root **men*, which relates to the mind and to mental activities, the verb *lanthánomai* derives from a PIE root **lā* or perhaps **lāi* whose meaning is reconstructed as 'hide (intr.), be in hiding, be concealed', which is also attested in Latin *lateō* 'be absent, be missing' (Vaan 2008: 329). Accordingly, active forms of *lanthánō* mean 'escape notice'. In origin, this root did not belong to the domain of cognition, and the connection of the PIE root with the domain of human experience, if any, rather links it to perception. Hence, while remembering is construed as an event of occurring, having in mind, or bringing (back) to mind, forgetting is construed as not being able to perceive (possibly through sight).

The different connections of the PIE roots and of their Greek outcomes are especially remarkable in the light of D'Andrade's (1995) theory about the

COGNITION 193

structure of a folk model of the mind. According to D'Andrade (1995: 158–160), this model includes five major areas: perceptions, thoughts, feelings/emotions, wishes and intentions ('feelings' here refers to bodily sensations, which Andrade groups together with emotions). Notably, remembering and forgetting belong to different groups in this model, that is, thought and perception, but the connection that D'Andrade assumes (but does not discuss) is contrary to the one hinted to by the etymology of the Greek verbs: according to D'Andrade (1995: 160), it is remembering that belongs to the field of perceptions, while forgetting belongs to the field of thoughts. In spite of his contrary description, which, however, is not supported by any data, it still is interesting to notice that either type of experiential event is ascribed to one of these two fields, and that they are kept separate.

In Homeric Greek, the verb *lanthánomai* 'forget', 'have not in mind' always takes the NomGen construction. In spite of the differences pointed out above between the concepts of memory and forgetfulness and in spite of the different origins of the two lexical roots, the meaning of *lanthánomai* appears to be specular to the meaning of *mimnéskomai*: it mostly indicates that some idea did not occur to the experiencer, as already shown in example (316). Other examples are (321), (322) and (323).

(321) *mḗ pṓs tis   lōtoîo   phagṑn   nóstoio*
NEG PTC INDF.NOM lotus.GEN eat.PTCP.AOR.NOM return.GEN
láthētai
forget.SBJV.PRS.M/P.3SG
'In order for nobody to forget about their return, having tasted some lotus.' (*Od.* 9.102)

(322) *è láthet'   è   ouk enóēsen*
PTC forget.AOR.MID.3SG PTC NEG realize.AOR.3SG
'Whether he forgot (her) or didn't notice.' (*Il.* 9.537)

(323) *heúdeis,   autàr emeîo   lelasménos*
sleep.PRS.2SG but   1SG.GEN forget.PTCP.PRF.M/P.NOM
épleu   Akhilleû   ou   mén meu
become.IMPF.M/P.2SG Achilles.VOC NEG PTC 1SG.GEN
zṓontos   akḗdeis,   allà thanóntos
live.PTCP.PRS.GEN neglect.IMPF.2SG but die.PTCP.AOR.GEN
'You sleep, Achilles, and have become forgetful of me. You didn't neglect me when I was living, but (you do) after my death.' (*Il.* 23.69–70)

194   CHAPTER 7

In (321), Odysseus and his comrades are in the land of the lotus-eaters, an island covered with lotus plants, whose flower has a narcotic power: eating it induces a state of apathy, here described as forgetfulness. Those who try it lose interest even in what should be most important for them, such as the return home for the Greek heroes. Example (322) comes from a passage that reports the deeds of Oineus. He caused the wrath of Artemis, because he gave offerings to all gods except for her: either he forgot (*láthet(o)*) about her, or did not pay any attention (*ouk enóēsen*) to her. In (323) we find a human stimulus, the first person pronoun *emeîo*. Patroclus, who has been killed by Hector but still lies on the campground, appears to Achilles in a dream, and reproaches him for having forgotten him, and not having taken care of his corpse.

Forgetfulness as depicted by *lanthánomai* is a situation in which the experiencer fails to retrieve from their mind some piece of information that belongs to his or her cognitive background. This is especially clear in example (316), discussed earlier in this Section, in which the Trojans flee the enemy rather than fight back. The warriors are said to have forgotten their courage, hence behaving cowardly. Similar occurrences with *alkḗ* 'courage', 'strength' appear four other times in the *Iliad*, and refer to situations in which the experiencer, rather than being forgetful, does not focus on a certain (expected) reaction, but reacts in an uncontrolled and unexpected fashion.

7.4   Discussion

Similar to perception verbs, cognitive verbs also show a division based on the distribution of constructions. Verbs that indicate thought, opinion and awareness consistently take the NomAcc construction. This is irrespective of voice: in fact, voice does not seem to play a major role with cognitive verbs, as I will discuss further on in this Section. The only exception is the verb *médomai* 'take care of, think of', which shows alternation of the NomAcc and the NomGen construction, in connection with a clear semantic contrast: while with the former construction the verb indicates a controlled activity of planning, with the latter it means 'care about', and patterns after verbs of memory and affection (see Section 8.2.2).

Memory shows an opposite pattern of constructions that contrasts with thought, as the NomGen construction dominates. In particular, *mnáomai* shows construction alternation, but only when taking the NomGen construction does it refer to memory. Forgetfulness is always connected with the NomGen construction, the only one featured by *lanthánomai*, while *mimnḗskomai* shows construction alternation with no noticeable semantic difference, but even in the case of this verb it is remarkable that the NomGen construction is 12 times as frequent as the NomAcc construction. As I have shown in the discussion of several examples, *mimnḗskomai* can refer to the process of retrieving some (possibly long forgotten) pieces of information from memory, but most frequently it simply means 'occur to', 'have in mind', and similarly its opposite *lanthánomai* means that a certain thought did not occur to the experiencer at a given moment.

Rather than as the retrieval of information, then, one can view the situation construed by *mimnḗskomai* as the activation of some latent piece of information. In this perspective, *mimnḗskomai* can be included among verbs of thought, but it crucially also differs from verbs in this group. Indeed, it never implies the elaboration of some new mental content, as do *phronéō* and other verbs that mean 'plan', 'devise'. It also differs from a verb such as *noéō* that refers to the rise of awareness brought about by an external stimulus, or *oîomai* and *dokéō*, which refer to an opinion. Hence, in many of the passages in which it occurs *mimnḗskomai* can be taken as a verb of thought that covers an area not covered by the other verbs, that is, the area of thinking about something already known, a stimulus internal to the experiencer's mind that simply needs to be activated.

The relationship between verbs of thought and memory can be represented as in Figure 12.

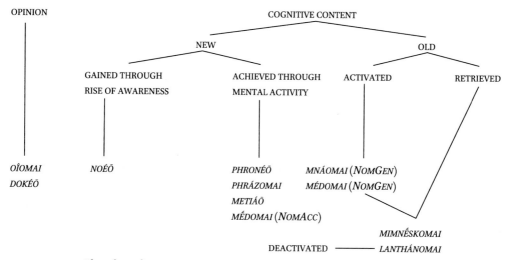

FIGURE 12 Thought and memory

Verbs that indicate knowledge show several parallels with perception verbs. Apart from the obvious etymological connection between *oîda* 'know' and *eîdon* 'see', we have seen that among verbs that indicate acquisition of knowledge *punthánomai* patterns after verbs of hearing and in fact often indicates learning through immediate perception. The distribution of constructions in this group of verbs points toward a two-fold distinction. Notably, *gignṓskō* virtually only takes the NomAcc construction (the NomGen is limited to two similar occurrences), and refers to a mental process by which the experiencer understands some type of conceptual content regarding a situation. It does not focus on the channel through which the information is acquired, as does *punthánomai*. Hence, *gignṓskō* refers to an intellectual operation, while *punthánomai* indicates a process mediated by sensation. (The verb *édaon* offers more limited evidence due to the small number of occurrences. The NomAcc construction is more frequent than the NomGen, which however, in spite of only occurring twice does not seem to be semantically restricted.)

Cognitive states are indicated by *oîda* with the NomAcc construction, which generally refers to a state of consciousness. As *oîda* only has the perfect stem, and can only denote states, *gignṓskō*, which basically refers to the same type of knowledge construed as focusing on consciousness, supplies a temporal dimension, either by indicating a change of state when occurring in the aorist, or by referring to an activity in the present. Construction variation with *oîda* is largely based on the distinction between intellectual knowledge and consciousness on one side and proficiency in skills on the other. The former type of knowledge is connected with the NomAcc construction, while the latter is connected with the NomGen construction, with only a limited number of exceptions. The verb *epístamai* always indicates practical knowledge: this is not limited to the NomGen construction, even though the NomAcc construction is restricted to generic objects.

Table 12 summarizes the discussion on different types of states and processes involving knowledge.

Verbs in Table 12 are arranged similarly to verbs in Figure 12 as to the distribution of constructions, with the NomAcc construction selected by verbs on the left, and the NomGen construction extending to the right. If we now compare the two groups of verbs, we can see that intellectual knowledge and consciousness match awareness, rational thought and opinion. All these types of cognitive situations are consistently connected with the NomAcc construction, and they match sight among perception modalities. The NomGen construction, on the other hand, is connected with low awareness (forgetfulness), the insurgence of thoughts triggered by internal, as opposed to external stimuli, and practical knowledge. Verbs in this area match lower perception modalities and bodily sensations and need (see Sections 5.1, 6.3 and 6.5). In the intermediate area, among cognitive verbs only verbs that indicate acquisition of knowledge show construction alternation disconnected from clear semantic differences.

COGNITION

TABLE 12   Cognitive states and acquisition of knowledge

	Intellectual knowledge / consciousness	Skill / perception
State	*oîda* (*NomAcc*)	*oîda* (*NomGen*)
		epístamai
		punthánomai (*Perfect*)
Change of state	*gignôskō*	*punthánomai*

In this group, *punthánomai* and perhaps *édaon* pattern in a way that is partly similar to hearing verbs (even though they do not show a clear animacy-based distribution of constructions), and allow free construction alternation, while *gignôskō*, with only sporadic occurrences of the NomGen construction, rather reflects the pattern of verbs in the area of sight, consciousness, and intellectual knowledge.

Besides the sub-domain of bodily sensations, the sub-domain of volitionality can also be compared with perception and cognition. Even though verbs that belong to this sub-domain, as discussed in Section 5.2, mostly take control infinitives or the AcI construction, verbs that indicate will and hope (*ethélō*, *boúlomai* and *élpomai*) provide some evidence for the NomAcc construction, while the verb *mémōna* 'crave', 'be eager for', may take the NomGen construction. The latter verb indicates an uncontrolled craving, rather than a controlled intention or wish, as do other verbs of volition. In this case, the NomAcc construction is connected with rationality and control, while the NomGen construction is connected with loss of control.

Summing up, perception and cognition verbs point toward the existence of two distinct areas, each connected with a specific argument structure construction: the area of sight, consciousness and rational thought, encoded by the NomAcc construction, and the area of touch, smell and taste, low awareness and internally generated thought, encoded by the NomGen construction. The latter area is rooted in bodily needs and sensations and uncontrolled craving, and shows a stronger link to the body, while the former is matched by controlled volition, and shows a link to the mind. Between these two maximally distinct areas, hearing and learning provide a bridging zone, in which bodily and intellectual processes are intermingled in bringing about experiential situations.

The distribution of experiential situation in distinct regions and of constructions across the sub-domains is represented in Figure 13.

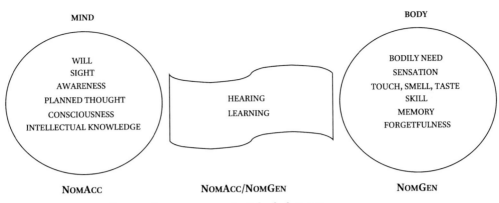

FIGURE 13   Constructions across experiential sub-domains

Crucially, construction alternation does not bring about a difference in the construal of the stimulus, for example denoting different degrees of affectedness as often suggested. Rather, construction alternation affects the construal of the experiencer. As has already been pointed out, it is not the case that alternation between the accusative and the genitive in the coding of the second participant, or proto-patient, indicates that the latter must be viewed as totally or partially affected. Verbs surveyed in this Chapter denote events that do not involve any change of state in the proto-patient, hence construction variation cannot indicate total vs. partial affectedness with such verbs.

Rather, it is the experiencer that is conceived as exerting varying degrees of control. As argued in the case of perception verbs (Section 6.5), control over experiential situations is construed as involving direct visual perception, awareness and attention, and extends to conscious mental activity and intellectual knowledge. On the other hand, the experiencer in the NomGen construction shows a diminished degree of attention, matched by situations connected with bodily sensations, uncontrolled desire, senses other than sight, and memory.

Turning now to voice, as I anticipated at the beginning of this Section, it does not seem to play a role that can be generalized over all verbs discussed in this Chapter. Verbs of thought are partly *activa* and partly *media tantum*, possibly due to morphological reasons: for example, *noéō* and *phronéō* only have active forms, but one can remark that they are both denominal verbs. In turn, *oíomai* is basically a *medium tantum*, even though the first person singular also has an active form, *oîō*. Allan (2003: 67) considers this verb a typical mental process middle, a category that he views as 'related to the passive middle. In both types, the subject passively undergoes the event.' (Notably, Allan does not mention the occurrence of the active first person singular form in Homeric Greek.)

COGNITION   199

However, it is not clear why this particular verb, which, as we have seen in Section 7.1.1, indicates the experiencer's opinion, should be closer to a passive than other verbs of cognition.

In the field of acquisition of knowledge, too, voice distribution is puzzling in view of Allan's assumptions, as *punthánomai* is a *medium tantum*, but *gignóskō* has middle forms restricted to the future, while in the present and the aorist stems it is basically an *activum tantum*. A tense-based distribution of voice also characterizes *mētiáō/mētíomai*, with present form always active and aorist and future forms always middle. Other verbs that indicate the activity of mental planning are partly active (*mermērízō, hormaínō, bussodomeúō*) and partly middle (*médomai, médomai*). Among verbs that indicate cognitive states, *oîda* is always active but this might depend on the fact that the perfect in origin only had active forms (see Chapter 4), while *epístamai* is middle because it is based on the middle *hístamai* 'stand'.

Moreover, verbs that have voice alternation do not show a uniform behavior. While with verbs of memory voice alternation affects valency, the verb *phrázomai* has an active counterpart, with a different semantics but the same valency (both the active and the middle take the NomAcc construction). Even in the field of memory, while *mimnéskomai* has the active counterpart *mimnéskō* with causative meaning, the situation is more complex for *lanthánomai*, whose active counterpart *lanthánō* means 'escape', and is not simply the causative counterpart of *lanthánomai* (see the discussion in Section 9.2).

CHAPTER 8

Emotions

Among experiential situations, emotions constitute the most variegated domain. In the first place, they are of different types not only in terms of the experiencer's evaluation, but also in terms of social evaluation, especially when they involve other human participants. In addition, the same experience can be construed differently, for example as controlled or not controlled by the experiencer.

In Homeric Greek, verbs of emotion are the only type of experiential predicate that comprises two sizeable and semantically coherent groups of verbs that consistently feature the NomDat construction. In the first place, we find verbs that denote negative feelings directed toward another person conceived as a target stimulus. As I will argue in Section 8.1.1, their constructional pattern is a direct consequence of the social dimension of emotions, as they imply an active involvement of the stimulus participant, who is typically expected to react. They do not normally allow for construction alternation. In a limited number of cases, the NomAcc construction can occur with some of the verbs in this group, and show clear semantic differences, as I argue in Section 8.4. In the second place, verbs of rejoicing also take the NomDat construction with inanimate stimuli, variously conceived as a means or more often a reason that prompts the experiencer's reaction (Section 8.1.2).

Several verbs of emotion feature the NomGen and the NomAcc construction, either as unique options or as possible alternatives. These verbs, too, are semantically quite homogeneous, and denote feelings such as love, desire, care and affection. As I discuss in Section 8.2, the effect of construction variation with this group of verbs does not bring about detectable changes in the resulting semantics. In contrast, verbs that indicate experiencer-centered, often negative feelings with source stimuli take the NomAcc construction, as shown in Section 8.3.

As anticipated in Section 3.2.7, some verbs of emotion also feature experiencer datives. These verbs take nominative stimuli that trigger verb agreement, and show coding properties of subjects. Concerning semantic and pragmatic subject properties, specific occurrences must be taken into account, as relevant properties can be variously distributed between the experiencer and the stimulus, as argued in Section 8.5.

In Section 8.6 I discuss the findings concerning different groups of emotion verbs. I show how the constructional patterns of these verbs, and in partic-

© SILVIA LURAGHI, 2021 | DOI:10.1163/9789004442528_009

EMOTIONS

ular alternation between the NomAcc and the NomGen construction, match those of verbs in other domains of experience. The wider range of constructions, also including NomDat, reflects the complexity of emotions with respect to other types of experiential situations as well as their relevance in a social setting.

8.1 Verbs of Emotion with the NomDat Construction

Verbs that take the NomDat construction may be divided into two groups, depending on animacy of the stimulus. In the first group, discussed in Section 8.1.1, we find verbs with animate stimuli, construed as the targets of some more or less controlled emotion, which is typically negative, such as envy, hate or anger. The social and interactive nature of these emotions accounts for the fact that they always occur with human stimuli. Verbs in this group most often do not allow construction alternation. Occasionally, as we will see in Section 8.4, some of these verbs can take the NomAcc construction that combines its own semantics with the verbs' meaning, so that the resulting constructions sport clear semantic differences among each other.

A second, more limited group of verbs that take the NomDat construction is constituted by verbs of rejoicing, which almost exclusively occur with inanimate stimuli. These verbs display a wider range of constructional patterns, and often occur without a stimulus. They are discussed in Section 8.1.2, in which I argue that the NomDat construction is extended from verbs of manipulation and, depending on the nature of the stimulus, may indicate a certain degree of control by the experiencer over the situation. In such cases, the stimulus is construed as a means for the experiencer to actively achieve an emotional state. Most frequently, the stimulus is construed as a reason that motivates the emotional state.

8.1.1 *NomDat Construction with Human Stimuli*
Emotion verbs that take the NomDat construction typically indicate negative emotions targeting a human being, such as envy, anger and, partly, hate. In what follows, I discuss examples of their construction.

Verbs that indicate a state of anger, or its inception, are *kholóomai* and *kotéō*; see (324)-(327) and (132).

(324) *Tudéos   huîi   kotéssato   Phoîbos*
Tydeus.GEN son.DAT be_angry.AOR.MID.3SG Phoebus.NOM
Apóllōn
Apollo.NOM
'But Phoebus Apollo got angry at Tydeus' son.' (*Il.* 23.383);

(325) *soì   d'   oú   pō mála págkhu theoì   mákares*
2SG.DAT PTC NEG yet very utterly god.NOM.PL blessed.NOM.PL
kotéousin
be_angry.PRS.3PL
'But the blessed gods are not utterly enraged at you.' (*Il.* 14.143)

(326) *ou   dé   sphōïn   idṑn   thumôi*
NEG PTC 3DU.DAT see.PTCP.AOR.NOM heart.DAT
ekholṓsato
be_angry.AOR.MID.3SG
'He did not get upset in his heart seeing them.' (*Il.* 15.155)

(327) *ou   gàr Akhilleùs   eía   márnasthai*
NEG PTC Achilles.NOM allow.IMPF.3SG fight.INF.PRS.M/P
kekholōménos   Atreïōni
be_angry.PTCP.PRF.M/P.NOM son_of_Atreus.DAT
'Achilles did not allow (us) to fight, being upset at the son of Atreus.'
(*Il.* 24.394–395)

In examples (324) and (326), aorist forms of the two verbs indicate the inchoative situation of getting angry at someone. In (325) the present tense construes a state of anger as ongoing, while the perfect participle in (327) profiles the stative character of the possible situation resulting from the emotion.

The verb *odússomai*, also a *medium tantum*, indicates a violent state of anger that borders with hate. Compare (328)-(330).

(328) *odúsanto   gàr autôi Zeús   te   kaì*
be_furious.AOR.MID.3PL PTC DEM.DAT Zeus.NOM PTC and
Ēélios: toû   gàr bóas   éktan
Helios.NOM DEM.GEN PTC cattle.ACC.PL kill.AOR.3PL
hetaîroi
comrade.NOM.PL
'Indeed Zeus and Helios got furious at him because (his) comrades had killed the cattle of Helios.' (*Od.* 19.275–276)

EMOTIONS 203

(329) kámmore, típte toi hôde Poseidáōn enosíkhthōn
troubled.VOC why 2SG.DAT such Poseidon.NOM earth_shaker.NOM
ōdúsat' ekpáglōs, hóti toi kakà
be_furious.AOR.MID.3SG terribly that 2SG.DAT evil.ACC.PL
pollà phuteúei?
many.ACC.PL prepare.PRS.3SG
'Unhappy man, how has Poseidon, the earth-shaker, conceived such a
violent anger toward you, that he prepares (so) many evils for you?'
(Od. 5.339–340)

(330) oîda gàr hṓs moi odṓdustai
know.PRF.1SG PTC that 1SG.DAT be_furious.PRF.M/P.3SG
klutòs ennosígaios
glorious.NOM earth_shaker.NOM
'I know how much the glorious Earth shaker hates me.' (Od. 5.423).

In (328) the verb is in the aorist indicative: it indicates the rise of an emotional
state of anger and evil attitude that precedes the current situation. In (330) the
perfect refers to the resulting state. In this case, it indicates a state achieved
through a change of state that can result in hate.

The verb megaírō indicates a state of resentment against someone, and
means 'grudge', 'hate', as in (331).

(331) sunékheue theòs Danaoîsi megéras
confound.AOR.3SG god.NOM Danaan.DAT.PL grudge.PTCP.AOR.NOM
'A god who hates the Danaans confounded them.' (Il. 15.473)

The etymology of megaírō is interesting: it is a denominal verb from the adjective mégas 'great', and its original meaning is 'regard as too great', hence with
a dative beneficiary 'regard as too much for someone' (Chantraine 1977: 675).
This triggers a negative inference: if someone has too much, then s/he provokes
envy in those who have less, hence the meaning illustrated above. It also points
toward a connection between hate and envy, and shows the complex nature
of negative emotions and their social dimension, as they involve comparison
against standards that are culture-dependent and connected with social evaluation.

Remarkably, however, hate cannot only be construed as a feeling that targets
another human participant, but also as an experiencer-centered negative feeling, and be connected with fear. The stimulus participant is then conceived as
threatening the experiencer, and the emotion arises out of the possible dan-

ger that it brings about. This is the case of the verb *ekhthaírō* 'hate', based on the noun *ékhthos* 'hostility', 'hate' and the adjective *ekhthrós* 'hateful'. In such occurrences, we find the NomAcc construction, as I will show in Section 8.3.2.

According to Wierzbicka (1999: 50), envy is a feeling that implies thinking about others, and realizing "that 'something good happened', but alas, it happened to someone else, and the experiencer feels 'something bad', not 'something good'". It further involves "wishing that things like this would happen to us." (*ib.* 97) This 'something' is the reason for envy, as shown in (332) with *phthonéō* 'envy', 'begrudge' and (333) with *ágamai* 'envy'.

(332)   *oúte toi   hēmiónōn   phthonéō,   tékos,   oúte teu*
        NEG 2SG.DAT mule.GEN.PL envy.PRS.1SG child.VOC NEG INDF.GEN
        állou
        other.GEN
        'I do not begrudge you the mules, my child, nor anything else.' (*Od.* 6.68)

(333)   *hoí   te   theaîs   agáasthe   par'*
        REL.NOM.PL PTC goddess.DAT.PL envy.PRS.M/P.2PL by
        andrásin   eunázesthai
        man.DAT.PL lie.INF.PRS.M/P
        'You who envy the goddesses because they lie with humans.' (*Od.* 5.119).

In (332) and (333) we find target stimuli in the dative, *toi* 'you' and *theaîs* 'the goddesses' respectively. In addition, in (332) a genitive NP, *hēmiónōn* 'mules', indicates the reason that prompts the experiencer to be envious. Similarly, in (333) a reason for envy is indicated, this time with a dependent infinitive clause *par'andrásin eunázesthai* 'lie with humans'.

Another similar occurrence features the verb *megaírō* 'grudge' that we have already seen in (331). In (334) it occurs with a genitive NP indicating the reason for the negative feeling.

(334)   *amenénōsen   dé   hoi   aikhmḕn   kuanokhaîta*
        weaken.AOR.3SG PTC 3SG.DAT spear_point.ACC dark_haired.NOM
        Poseidáōn   biótoio   megéras
        Poseidon.NOM life.GEN grudge.PTCP.AOR.NOM
        'But Poseidon, dark haired, weakened his spear, denying him his life.' (*Il.* 13.562–563)

EMOTIONS   205

As pointed out above, the etymological meaning of the verb *megaírō* is 'regard as too great (for someone)'. Here, it is said that Poseidon is causing the death of Antilochus, because he regarded his life as too long for him, i.e. he considered his life accomplished. Note that the dative constituent here is subject to argument sharing (Luraghi 2003b), a phenomenon by which when a participle (*megéras* in this case) and the governing verb (here *amenénōsen*) share the same arguments, these are overtly realized only once. In (334), the argument *hoi* 'him (dat)' occurs once as arguments of both verbal forms.

As mentioned in Section 2.2.2, several authors, including Klein and Kutscher (2002) and Verhoeven (2007) speak of split stimulus in such occurrences. Following this approach, situations such as those encoded in (332) and (333) feature a source stimulus (the reason for the emotion) and a target stimulus (the human participant targeted by the emotion). In this vein, one might regard occurrences such as (332) as featuring a three-place NomDatGen construction. As I discuss further on in this Section, a genitive NP may indicate the semantic role of cause or reason only with experiential predicates (mostly emotion verbs), and never when it functions as a syntactic adjunct. Hence, the meaning appears to be crucially dependent on the type of argument structure construction in which the genitive NPs occurs.

Note that, as shown in (333), (335) and (336) the genitive NP can be replaced by other types of cause expression. On the one hand, this may point toward a low degree of constructionalization. On the other hand, however, possible replacement by means of some other cause/reason expression, but never by means of source expressions, must not be disregarded. Indeed, it shows that the occurrence of the genitive can be explained only within a construction that is specific of emotion verbs, and does not depend on a putative ablative meaning of the genitive in isolation, as is sometimes claimed (e.g. Chantraine 1981: 65). As I have argued in Section 3.2.2, the genitive acquires an ablative meaning within the NomGen construction only when this meaning is activated by specific verbs that require it.

Moreover, as we will see in Section 8.2.2, the NomGen construction is typical of verbs that indicate care. With such verbs, the stimulus is conceived as the matter of care or concern for the experiencer, a construal that can also be triggered by verbs of memory (see Section 7.3, and example (314)). Verbs of envy and anger extend this construction when they occur with a genitive source stimulus: the matter of concern in such cases is the reason for the rise of the negative feeling directed toward some human participant (encoded in the dative).

The dative target stimulus, conversely, cannot be replaced by any other type of expression. Interestingly, as I will show below (see examples (341) and (342)),

206 CHAPTER 8

even when it is not overtly encoded in the argument structure, the target stimulus is always implied in the context, while this does not hold for the source stimulus. The possible occurrence of a reason/cause expression, whatever its syntactic status, gives us important clues to the construal of the situations indicated by verbs discussed in this Section.

Conti (1999) discusses some occurrences that also contain verbs of emotion, in which the cause or reason for the emotional state is encoded with the prepositional phrase *héneka*+genitive or with causal subordinates. Let us consider examples (335) and (336).

(335)   *Aíantos   psukhḕ... nósphin aphestḗkei*
        Ajax.GEN soul.NOM far   be_away.PPF.3SG
        kekholōménē   *heíneka níkēs,   tḗn*
        be_angry.PTCP.PRF.M/P.NOM for   victory.GEN DEM.ACC
        min   egṑ   níkēsa
        3SG.ACC 1SG.NOM win.AOR.1SG
        'The soul of Ajax stood apart, angry because of the victory that I won against him.' (*Od.* 11.543–544);

(336)   *oú   t'   ár   ho   g'   eukhōlês epimémphetai   oud'*
        NEG PTC PTC DEM.NOM PTC vow.GEN complain.PRS.M/P.3SG NEG
        hekatómbēs,   all' hének' arētéros   hòn   étímēs'
        hecatomb.GEN but for   priest.GEN REL.ACC dishonor.AOR.3SG
        Agamémnōn
        Agamemnon.NOM
        'It is not because of a vow that he complains, nor because of a hecatomb, but because of the priest whom Agamemnon dishonored.' (*Il.* 1.93–94).

In example (335), the prepositional phrase *heíneka níkēs* 'because of the victory' indicates a cause: it causes the emotion indicated by *kholóomai* 'be angry'. Note that the human participant that is targeted by the emotion is not encoded with a dative NP in the argument structure of the verb, but is nevertheless indicated in the following clause, which specifies that the speaker had defeated Ajax, thus triggering his anger. In (336) a similar prepositional phrase, *hének'arētéros* 'because of the priest', is coordinated with two genitive noun phrases, *eukhōlês* 'vow', and *hekatómbēs* 'hecatomb'. Conti (1999:297) takes coordination as evidence for functional identity, based on Dik (1968:200), and argues that the two genitive noun phrases indicate cause.

Cause or reason expressions occur with other emotion verbs that take the NomDat construction, suggesting that not only envy, but also other negative

EMOTIONS

207

feelings targeting another human participant, such as anger or hate, do not rise spontaneously and without a motivation. Rather, they constitute a matter of concern for the experiencer, as described by Wierzbicka (1999). Consider examples (337) and (338).

(337) *hós   moi   pallakídos   perikhósato*
       REL.NOM 1SG.DAT concubine.GEN be_angry.AOR.MID.3SG
       kallikómoio
       fair_haired.GEN
       'Who got angry at me because of the fair-haired concubine.' (*Il.* 9.449)

(338) *pótna   theá,   mḗ   moi   tóde*
       mistress.VOC goddess.VOC NEG 1SG.DAT DEM.ACC
       khóeo
       be_angry.IMP.PRS.M/P.2SG
       'Mighty goddess, don't be angry at me for this.' (*Od.* 5.215)

In (337) we again find a reason NP in the genitive, this time referring to a third human participant, *pallakídos kallikómoio* 'the concubine with beautiful hair', while in (338) the reason is encoded by the demonstrative *tóde* 'this', a neuter accusative. As I will argue in Section 10.4.1, neuter pronouns may occur in the accusative even in constructions that normally require another case.

Example (338) also shows another interesting feature of verbs in this group, that is, the verb occurs in the imperative, and encodes a negative order, thus providing evidence for possible control over the situation by the experiencer. More negative orders occur with *(apo)skudmaínō* 'be angry', as in (339) and (340).

(339) *Hḗrē,   mḕ   dḕ   pámpan aposkúdmaine   theoîsin*
       Hera.VOC NEG PTC utterly   be_angry.IMP.PRS.2SG god.DAT.PL
       'Hera, don't be so angry at the gods.' (*Il.* 24.65)

(340) *mḗ   moi,   Pátrokle,   skudmainémen*
       NEG 1SG.DAT Patroclus.VOC be_angry.INF.PRS
       'Don't be angry at me, Patroclus.' (*Il.* 24.592)

The occurrences reviewed above show that negative feelings directed toward a human participant are often construed as responding to some concern. The occurrences with negative imperatives indicate that, once the emotion has arisen, the experiencer might consciously try to control it: notably, however, such emotion can be the matter only of negative orders. This means that the experiencer has no control on their rise, and that, even when they are motivated, they are irrational.

Verbs that denote negative emotions discussed in this Section occur with the NomDat construction, that is, the construction of verbs of social interaction, thus pointing toward a potentially active role for the target stimulus as well. Indeed, someone who is the target of anger, envy or hate is likely to react and respond, and such emotions are likely to trigger a situation of fight or litigation between the experiencer and the reactive target stimulus. Such a complex situation typically involves only human participants, as it requires mental involvement on both sides, and, as we will see, constitutes a counterpart to feelings like love and desire that are construed as non-interactive situations.

In some cases, the verbs reviewed in this Section may occur outside the NomDat construction, with a genitive NP encoding the reason, while the target stimulus is not encoded in the argument structure. Even in such occurrences, however, the target stimulus is implied in the context, as in examples (341) and (342).

(341) *ou   dé   tí   se   khrề allotríon   phthonéein:*
       NEG PTC INDF 2SG.ACC need others.GEN.PL envy.INF.PRS
       'You have no need to be jealous for the goods of others.' (*Od.* 18.17–18)

(342) *epeì kekhólōto   daiktaménōn   aizēôn*
       as   be_angry.PRF.3SG killed_in_battle.GEN.PL young.GEN.PL
       'Because he was upset for the young men killed in battle.' (*Il.* 21.146)

Remarkably, even in cases in which the human target is not encoded in the verb's argument structure (or shared with another verb, as in (334)), it is always easily recoverable from the context. In (341), the human target stimulus is implied by the occurrence of the headless genitive *allotríon* '(the goods) of other people', which refers to the reason for jealousy. For (342) one must consider the whole passage in which the example occurs: "Achilles rushed upon him, and Asteropaeus stood forth from the river to face him, holding two spears; and courage was set in his heart by (the river) Xanthus, because he (i.e. Xanthus) was upset for the youths slain in battle, that Achilles was butchering mercilessly along (his) stream." Here, the river Xanthus is a divine being who experiences a state of anger toward Achilles, because of the fury with which the Greek hero is killing the enemies along its shore.

EMOTIONS 209

As this passage makes clear, negative feelings such as those as expressed by *phthonéō, kholómai* and other verbs treated in this Section are always construed as targeting another animate (human or divine) participant: they are negative feelings directed toward the stimulus. This is in contrast with experiencer-centered negative emotions discussed in Section 8.3.2 that take source stimuli and consistently occur with the NomAcc construction.

8.1.2 *Verbs of Rejoicing*

The second group of verbs that may take the NomDat construction is constituted by verbs of rejoicing. These verbs have received a thorough treatment in Latacz (1966), who has shown that rejoicing refers to quite diverse situations, as construction variation also shows.

In the first place, rejoicing can be construed as especially focused on the experiencer. This is the case with the verb *gēthéō* 'rejoice'. Most frequently, this verb refers to an inchoative situation, as shown by the high number of aorist forms (30/39), and does not feature voice opposition, being an *activum tantum*. It occurs 38 times in the Nom construction, that is, only with the experiencer argument, and only once with the NomAcc construction encoding a generic stimulus (*táde* 'these things'). Elsewhere, the trigger of the emotion can be found in the context, and it is connected to perception: in half of the occurrences it is something that the experiencer has seen; less frequently it may be something perceived by hearing, as shown in (343) and (344).

(343) *kaì toùs mèn gḗthēsen idṑn*
and DEM.ACC.PL PTC rejoice.AOR.3SG see.PTCP.AOR.NOM
kreíōn Agamémnōn
lord.NOM Agamemnon.NOM
'Lord Agamemnon rejoiced seeing them.' (*Il.* 4.283 = 4.311)

(344) *hṑs pháto, gḗthēsen dè polútlas*
so speak.IMPF.M/P.3SG rejoice.AOR.3SG PTC costant.NOM
îos Odusseús, khaírōn hêi
glorious.NOM Odysseus.NOM rejoice.PTCP.PRS.NOM DEM.DAT
gaíēi patrṓiēi
land.DAT home.DAT
'So she spoke: the constant and glorious Odysseus was glad, and rejoiced for his homeland.' (*Od.* 13.250)

In (343), the feeling of joy is triggered by direct perception of an individual through sight (*toùs ... idṓn* 'seeing them'); see further example (346). Example (344) contains the verse initial formula *hòs pháto, géthēse dé* + 3rd person subject 'so s/he spoke, and (Subject) rejoiced', indicating the onset of a state of joy. The situation may be further elaborated with the addition of another, more flexible verb of rejoicing, as in (344), in which the participle *khaírōn* 'rejoicing' indicates the ensuing state, and also contains the stimulus, *hêi gaíēi patróiēi* 'his homeland', in its argument structure; a similar occurrence is (346).

Also mostly used as monovalent is the verb *iaínomai*, whose original meaning is 'warm up' (Chantraine 1977: 452) or perhaps 'stir up' (Latacz 1966: 221–222), as in (345).

(345) *kaì pûr anékaie pollòn hupò trípodi megálōi:*
       and fire.ACC light.IMPF.3SG big.ACC under tripod.DAT big.DAT
       iaíneto d' húdōr
       warm.IMPF.M/P.3SG PTC water.ACC
       'He lit a big fire under a big tripod; the water was warming up/stirring.'
       (*Od.* 10.358–359)

This verb is frequently used metaphorically in Homer, indicating a feeling of physical or most often psychical relaxation. Often, the subject is not the experiencer, but the (abstract) body part in which the emotion is located, mostly *thumós* 'soul', 'spirit'. The experiencer is then encoded as a dative external possessor, as in (346).

(346) *hoi dè idóntes géthēsan, kaì*
       DEM.NOM.PL PTC see.PTC.AOR.NOM.PL rejoice.AOR.3PL and
       pâsin enì phresì thumòs iánthē
       all.DAT.PL in chest.DAT.PL heart.NOM rejoice.AOR.PASS.3SG
       'They rejoiced as they saw (her), the heart rejoiced in everyone's chest.'
       (*Od.* 15.164–165)

In (346), we again find the verb *gēthéō* which, as in (344), refers to a situation of joy, further elaborated by another verb, in this case *iánthē* the passive aorist of *iaínomai*: differently from (344) this does not specify the stimulus, but rather the body part involved in the experience. The verb *iaínomai* has an active causative counterpart, see Section 9.3.

Latacz (1966: 143) regards the verb *khaírō* 'rejoice' as the most generic verb in this semantic area. He notes that it is the only verb of rejoicing that indicates a situation in which the experiencer is not necessarily human (or divine), but can even be an animal, as in (347).

EMOTIONS

(347) *hôs te léōn ekhárē* *megálōi epì sṓmati*
as PTC lion.NOM rejoice.AOR.PASS.3SG big.DAT on carcass.DAT
'As a lion rejoices over a big carcass.' (*Il.* 3.23)

This verb occurs 105 times in the Homeric poems, and shows all aspectual stems (with only one perfect occurrence); it features a peculiar voice distribution, whereby aorist forms are middle or passive, while other forms are active. The future is mostly active with one middle occurrence. Voice alternation, being largely dependent on the verbal aspect, does not bring about any semantic difference.

When the stimulus is encoded in the verb's argument structure, the verb patterns after verbs of manipulation (see Section 3.2.5 and the discussion further on in this Section) and takes the NomDat construction in 20 occurrences. The stimulus is construed as a reason for rejoicing, as adverbial dative NPs with abstract referents discussed in Section 3.1.3. Examples are (344) and (348).

(348) *Aíant'... Akhaioì* *eis Agamémnona* *dîon*
Ajax.ACC Acheans.NOM.PL to Agamemnon.ACC divine.ACC
ágon *kekharēóta* *níkēi*
lead.IMPF.3PL rejoice.PTCP.PRF.ACC victory.DAT
'The Achaeans led Ajax, who rejoiced for the victory, to divine leader Agamemnon.' (*Il.* 7.311–312)

Rejoicing as construed by the verb *khaírō* indicates a state of joy that is motivated by a stimulus/reason, and whose rise might to some extent be controlled, as shown by the sizeable number of occurrences (22 out of 104) in the imperative, even though it must be noted that these are partly wishes or forms of address, as in (349), which also contains an ethical dative *moi*.

(349) *khaîré* *moi* *ô* *Pátrokle* *kaì* *ein*
rejoice.IMP.PRS.2SG 1SG.DAT PTC Patroclus.VOC even in
Aḯdao *dómoisi*
Hades.GEN house.DAT.PL
'Rejoice, Patroclus, even in the house of Hades.' (*Il.* 23.19)

Still, in some cases some degree of control over the emotion seems to actually be implied, as in (350).

(350) *khaîre,*   *gúnai,*   *philótēti*
       rejoice.IMP.PRS.2SG woman.VOC love.DAT
       'Rejoice, woman, for (our) love!' (*Od.* 11.248)

In (350), Poseidon raped Tyro by pretending to be Enipeus, with whom she was in love. When she realizes what happened, the god tells her that she should be glad, because she will beget glorious sons as a result of having had sex with him.

The fact that the NomDat construction is extended from verbs of manipulation with *khaírō* points toward a certain degree of control, as the dative, in this type of argument structure construction, is instrumental in origin. As I have argued in Section 3.1.3, instrumental dative adjuncts could encode various semantic roles, including cause and reason, depending on the nature of the situation. Another hint as to the partly controlled nature of the situation comes from (347), the only occurrence in which the experiencer is an animal. In this example, the stimulus is not encoded in the argument structure: rather, it is added in a local adjunct, the prepositional phrase *megáloi epì sómati* 'over a big carcass', a type of expression that indicates proximity in Homer (Luraghi 2003a: 298–302). This points to a difference between the feeling of rejoicing as experienced by a human being (i.e. a potential controller), and by an animal.

Stimuli with *khaírō* are typically inanimate. When NPs with a human referent occur as second arguments, they may appear in the Two-Place+P construction that we have seen as typical of verbs of cognition and of perception. The stimulus NP in the dative is the head of a dependent participle, as in (351).

(351) *khárē*   *d'* *ára hoi*   *prosiónti*
       rejoice.AOR.PASS.3SG PTC PTC DEM.DAT come.PTCP.PRS.DAT
       Sarpēdòn
       Sarpedon.NOM
       'Sarpedon rejoiced at his (i.e. Hector's) coming.' (*Il.* 5.682–683)

In (351), even though the second argument refers to a human participant, the trigger of the emotion is a state of affairs, that is, the coming of Hector. The Two-Place +P construction indicates that rejoicing occurs in conjunction with perception: the experiencer enters the emotional situation because he or she perceives a situation, as indicated by the occurrence of a present participle that indicates simultaneity.

Another frequent verb in this group is *térpomai* 'enjoy', occurring 91 times plus seven occurrences of the active *térpō*. As I have already mentioned in Section 5.1, this verb, whose original meaning is 'satiate oneself', patterns partly with other verbs of saturation, and partly with verbs of rejoicing. Accordingly,

EMOTIONS

it can take both the NomGen and the NomDat construction. It refers to a situation in which an experiencer achieves a pleasant state of satisfaction by exploiting a stimulus. According to Latacz (1966: 193), the NomGen construction profiles the achievement of the state of satisfaction, while the NomDat construction focuses more prominently on the pleasant feeling that derives from it.

As remarked in Section 5.1, the NomGen construction may occasionally occur with concrete stimuli, but most often it occurs with abstract ones, such as sleep, sex, or mourning. Examples are (352) and (353); the latter also contains an occurrence of the NomDat construction, as I discuss below.

(352) *epeí k' olooîo tetarpómestha góoio*
as PTC dire.GEN enjoy.PRF.M/P.1PL groan.GEN
'When we have taken our fill of dire lamenting.' (*Il.* 23.10)

(353) *tṑ d' epeì oûn philótētos etarpétēn*
DEM.DU.NOM PTC as PTC love.GEN enjoy.AOR.PASS.3DU
erateinês terpésthēn múthoisi, pròs allélous
joy.GEN enjoy.IMPF.M/P.3DU tales.DAT.PL toward other.ACC
enéponte
speech.PTCP.PRS.NOM.DU
'But when the two had their fill of the joy of love, they took delight in tales, speaking to each other.' (*Od.* 23.300–301)

The NomDat construction profiles a more active involvement of the experiencer that seems to be in control of the situation to a higher extent than with other verbs of rejoicing. Let us compare examples (353) and (354).

(354) *all' áge dḕ philótēti trapeíomen*
but come_on PTC love.DAT enjoy.SBJV.AOR.PASS.1PL
eunēthénte
lay.PTCP.AOR.PASS.NOM.DU
'Come on, let's take our joy in love lying together!' (*Il.* 3.441).

In (353) and (354), the same stimulus, love, occurs once in the NomGen (*philótētos*) and once in the NomDat (*philótēti*) construction. In the former example, Odysseus and Penelope are described as having had sex, and turning to tell each other of the adventures they had during the man's absence. The NomGen construction profiles the state of satisfaction. In the latter example, Paris tries to stop Helen who is blaming him for not having defeated her former husband Menelaus in battle. Here the NomDat construction does not profile the prospective sense of satisfaction, but rather the pleasant nature of the activity.

The same difference between the two constructions can be seen if one compares the first occurrence of *térpomai* in (353) with the second, in which the NomDat construction occurs with the stimulus *múthoisi* 'tales'. In this case as well, the focus is not on achieving satisfaction, but rather on taking pleasure in talking about past events, as also indicated by the occurrence of the imperfect form *terpésthēn*. Another similar example is (355), to be compared with (352).

(355) *metà gár te   kaì álgesi   térpetai   anér,*
       after PTC PTC also pain.DAT.PL delight.PRS.M/P.3SG man.NOM
      hós   tis   dè mála pollà   páthēi
      DEM.NOM INDF.NOM PTC very many.ACC.PL suffer.AOR.SBJV.3SG
      'A man who suffered much later takes delight even in his pains.' (*Od.* 15.400–401)

Latacz (1966: 192) rightly highlights the instrumental nature of the stimulus in such constructions, and supports his argument with example (356).

(356) *tòn   d' heûron   phréna   terpómenon*
      DEM.ACC PTC find.AOR.3PL spirit.ACC delight.PTCP.PRS.M/P.ACC
      phórmiggi ligeíēi   kalêi   daidaléēi
      lyre.DAT clear_toned.DAT beautiful.DAT shaped.DAT
      'They found him delighting his spirit with a clear-toned, beautifully shaped lyre.' (*Il.* 9.186–187)

Schwyzer (1950: 167) considers the dative here as encoding reason. Latacz, on the contrary, argues that the experiencer (Achilles) did not find pleasure in regarding the lyre, but in playing it. This implies that the experiencer has an agentive nature, and is in full control of the situation. As Latacz remarks, control here is more clearly implied than with other verbs of rejoicing: notably, lexical features of the dative NP, which has a concrete referent, support the construal of the stimulus as an instrument rather than a reason.

In Section 3.2.5 I discussed non-spatial functions of the NomDat construction. I have shown that this construction has different meaning depending on the animacy feature of the second argument. While with human second arguments it indicates interactive situations, and typically occurs with verbs of social interaction, with inanimate/non-human second arguments it profiles a situation in which the second participant functions as a means or instrument, and is typical of verbs of manipulation. Inanimate NPs in dative adjuncts

EMOTIONS   215

cannot only encode the semantic role of instrument, but also other, related
semantic roles such as means, reason, manner, cause or attendant circumstances, depending on the context in which they occur (Luraghi 2003a: 33–
38).

Contrary to reason expressions in the genitive discussed in Section 8.1.1 that
only occur with verbs of emotion, reason expressions in the dative are not
so constrained. The possible interpretation of an inanimate dative NP as an
instrument or a reason depends on various contextual factors, for example on
whether the NP refers to a manipulated entity or not (see Luraghi 2003a: 68–
72), and occur in any type of context. This indicates a different construal of the
reason role: while genitive encoding construes the reason as a matter of concern specific to emotional reactions, dative encoding construes it as a means
that, depending on its nature, may or may not be actively manipulated by the
human participant involved in the situation.

8.2   Verbs of Emotion with the NomGen Construction

Verbs of emotion that take the NomGen construction typically indicate longing, desire, or positive feelings such as love and care. Even though the stimulus
is most often human, these verbs, contrary to verbs that take the NomDat construction and indicate negative emotions such as those reviewed in Section
8.1.1, can also occur with inanimate stimuli. In addition, some of these verbs
allow variation between the NomGen and the NomAcc construction, while a
few others always take the latter construction.

Love, in much the same way as other emotions, has a culturespecific construal. As is well known, romantic love as we intend it today is a construct that
emerged in the 19th century (see Tissari 2003). Tissari (2003: 31–43) suggests
to focus on the participants of a love event, and distinguishes between love as
eros, love as affection (she further distinguishes between family love and love
for friends), love for things, and love for god. This last concept is linked to Chris-
tianity, and is not relevant for my study.

In Homeric Greek, two verbs can be singled out to indicate two different
prototypes of love: *éramai*, which denotes love as eros and will be the object of
Section 8.2.1, and *philéomai*, which denotes affection and encompasses family
love, friendliness, care and protection, and will be discussed in Section 8.2.2.
Other verbs with partly similar meanings also relate to yearning and desiring,
often construed either as feelings that can also be directed toward inanimate
objects (love for things), or as feelings of care and thoughtfulness. In the latter
case, the occurrence of an inanimate stimulus is quite exceptional.

8.2.1 *Love as (Sexual) Desire*

In this Section, I discuss verbs of longing and desiring that construe love as a passion driven by desire. Let us start with examples (357) and (358).

(357)   *tês*   *dè*   *kratùs*   *Argeiphóntēs*   *érásat'*
DEM.GEN PTC strong.NOM Argeiphontes.NOM want.AOR.MID.3SG
'The strong Argeiphontes fell in love with her.' (*Il.* 16.181–182)

(358)   *ou*   *gár*   *pố*   *poté*   *m'*   *hôdé*   *g'*   *érōs*   *phrénas*
NEG PTC PTC ever 1SG.ACC SO   PTC love.NOM midriff.ACC.PL
amphekálupsen,   ... *hốs seo*   *nûn éramai*   *kaí*   *me*
enwrap.AOR.3SG as   2SG.GEN now love.PRS.1SG and 1SG.ACC
glukùs   *hímeros*   *haireî*
sweet.NOM desire.NOM take.PRS.3SG
'Never yet has love so encompassed my heart as I now love you, and sweet desire gets hold of me.' (*Il.* 3.442–446)

The verb *éramai*, as shown in (357) and (358), means 'love', or, in the aorist, 'fall in love'. As already remarked, it does not denote affection but rather sexual desire, and indicates an uncontrolled attraction. It occurs seven times, always with the NomGen construction, and takes animate stimuli in six occurrences. It only occurs once with an inanimate stimulus, in (359).

(359)   *aphrḗtōr*   *athémistos*   *anéstiós*   *estin*   *ekeînos*
friendless.NOM lawless.NOM homeless.NOM be.PRS.3SG DEM.NOM
hos   *polémou ératai*   *epidēmíou*
REL.NOM war.GEN love.PRS.M/P.3SG among_people.GEN
okruóentos
horrible.GEN
'A man who loves the horrible war among his own people is a man who has no friends, no law, and no home.' (*Il.* 9.63–64)

In (359) a man who may possibly be attracted toward an unnatural situation such a fight with his friends is depicted as missing all normal features of human affection or social rules: hence the attraction to war.

The verb *éldomai* 'desire' occurs 17 times and shows a more flexible syntax. Similar to verbs of volitionality reviewed in Section 5.2, it may take a nominative argument, the experiencer, with the stimulus encoded in a dependent infinitive. Examples are (360)-(362).

EMOTIONS

217

(360) *himeirómenós*   *per idésthai*   *sèn*
desire.PTCP.PRS.M/P.NOM PTC see.INF.AOR.MID POSS.2SG.ACC
álokhon, tês   *aièn*   *eéldeai*   *émata*   *pánta*
wife.ACC DEM.GEN always long.PRS.M/P.2SG day.ACC.PL all.ACC.PL
'Desiring to see your wife for whom you long always day by day.' (*Od.*
5.209–210)

(361) *eéldeto*   *gár se*   *idésthai*
desire.IMPF.M/P.3SG PTC 2SG.ACC see.INF.AOR.MID
'Indeed he was eager to see you.' (*Od.* 4.162)

(362) *hòs ethélō*   *kaì eéldomai*   *émata*   *pánta*
so want.PRS.1SG and desire.PRS.M/P.1SG day.ACC.PL all.ACC.PL
oíkadé   *t'*   *elthémenai*
at_home PTC go.INF.AOR.MID
'But even so I wish and desire every day to come back to my home.' (*Od.*
5.219–220)

In (360) *éldomai* occurs in the NomGen construction with the second argument *tês*, the genitive of the feminine demonstrative referring to *álokhon* 'wife'.
This construction occurs three more times in the Homeric poems. More frequently, as in (361) and (362), *éldomai* takes dependent infinitives: *idésthai* 'see'
and *elthémenai* 'go'. In the latter example it is coordinated with *ethélō* 'want'
(see Section 5.2).

The verb *éldomai* also takes the NomAcc construction, as in (363) (three
occurrences). Accusative stimuli are always inanimate, while genitive stimuli
may be either animate or inanimate.

(363) *ktḗmata*   *pollá,*   *tà*   *t'*   *éldetai*
good.ACC.PL many.ACC.PL DEM.PL PTC desire.PRS.M/P.3SG
hós   *k'*   *epideuḗs*
REL.NOM PTC poor.NOM
'Many goods, which the poor desires.' (*Il.* 5.481)

Exceptionally, this verb occurs once in an order, as shown (364).

(364) *nûn toi*   *eeldésthō*   *pólemos kakós,*   *ei*
now 2SG.DAT desire.IMP.PRS.M/P.3SG war.NOM evil.NOM if
thoós   *essi*
valiant.NOM be.PRS.2SG
'Now you must desire the evil war, if you are valiant.' (*Il.* 16.494)

As remarked in Luraghi and Sausa (2015), the circumstances referred to in (364) are quite exceptional. Sarpedon, who has been wounded to death by Patroclus, is summoning the other warriors and urging them to fight and revenge him: this situation prompts him to order other men what their will must be. This occurrence is also exceptional for the meaning of the verbal voice. The verb *éldomai* is a *medium tantum*; accordingly, it only inflects in the middle but normally has active meaning. On the contrary, in this passage the form *eeldésthō*, a medio-passive present imperative, has passive meaning. The dative *toi* encodes the experiencer, and functions as a *dativus iudicantis*, a type of experiencer as argued in Luraghi (2003: 64): 'be war desirable for you'.

Finally, *éldomai* can occasionally refer to situations in which the experiencer is an animal, rather than a human being, as in (365). Notably, the verb still takes the NomGen construction, in spite of the fact that the experiencer is not a possible controller, contrary to what has been noted for example (347), in which the occurrence of a non-controlling experiencer triggers the occurrence of a different type of construction. This is a hint at a different construal of the experiencer, which is a potential controller with the Nom-Dat construction. Conversely, the NomGen construction indicates a diminished degree of control over a situation, as discussed in Sections 3.1.1 and 3.2.6.

(365)   *taì*   *dè*   *khthóna*   *possì*   *dateûnto*
        DEM.NOM PTC earth.ACC feet.DAT.PL divide.IMPF.M/P.3PL
        eldómenai   *pedíoio*
        desire.PTCP.PRS.M/P.NOM.PL plain.GEN
        'They (sc. the mules) tore up the earth with their feet desiring the plain.'
        (*Il.* 23.121–122)

Some other verbs that also mean 'desire', 'long for', and typically occur with inanimate stimuli, take the NomGen or dependent infinitives, such as *himeírō* in (366) and (360) and *liláiomai* in (367) and (368).

(366)   *tí*   *kakôn*   *himeírete*   *toútōn*
        why evil.GEN.PL desire.PRS.2PL DEM.GEN.PL
        'Why do you desire such evils?' (*Od.* 10.431)

(367)   *lilaiómenoi*   *biótoio*
        desire.PTCP.PRS.M/P.NOM.PL food.GEN
        'Desiring food.' (*Od.* 12.328)

EMOTIONS 219

(368) *ei nûn en philótēti lilaíeai   eunēthênai*
       if now in love.DAT desire.PRS.M/P.2SG surrender.INF.AOR.PASS
       Ídēs   en koruphêisi
       Ida.GEN on peack.DAT.PL
       'If now you desire to surrender to love on the peaks of Ida.' (*Il.* 14.331–
       332)

Both verbs can indicate a state of yearning, but *lilaíomai* can sometimes be
translated as 'feel like', as in example (367). This verb also occurs in the imperative, with the function of metadirective. Let us consider (369).

(369) *tôi   mḗ me   lilaíeo*
       for_this_reason NEG 1SG.ACC desire.IMP.PRS. M/P.2SG
       deirotomêsai
       behead.INF.AOR
       'For this reason do not cut my head!' (*Od.* 22.349)

In (369) we find the imperative form *lilaíeo*. The order, however, concerns the
action denoted by the dependent infinitive *deirotomêsai* 'behead'. This use is
called metadirective. A metadirective is a type of performative, but, rather than
taking the perspective of the speaker, it takes the perspective of the addressee.
Metadirectives occur in constructions in which a matrix clause, in the case of
(369) *mḗ lilaíeo*, is devoid from any lexical meaning (it does not mean 'be unwilling'), but rather indicates a specific illocutionary force which is relevant for the
embedded verb, in this case *deirotomêsai* 'behead'. A well-known parallel to the
Homeric Greek construction is constituted by Latin *noli / nolite*, the imperative forms of the verb *nolo* 'be unwilling', which are used precisely as markers
of negation with a scope on the verb they govern. In reference to the Latin construction, Risselada (1993: 10) defines metadirective as "a specific illocutionary
force ... explicitly expressed by means of a matrix predication. The matrix predication thus functions as a kind of illocutionary meta-expression with respect
to the embedded clause."

The verb *pothéō* also indicates yearning and desire, often implying regret for
something that has been lost, with the meaning 'pine for', 'pine away'. Unlike
the verbs reviewed thus far in the Section, it always takes the NomAcc construction, as shown in (370) and (371).

(370) *sòn   nóston   pothéōn*
       POSS.2SG.ACC return.ACC desire.PTCP.PRS.NOM
       'Desiring your return.' (*Od.* 11.196)

(371) *all' Odusê*   *pothéousa*   *phílon*
       but Odysseus.ACC desire.PTCP.PRS.NOM dear.ACC
       katatékomai   *êtor*
       melt_away.PRS.M/P.1SG heart.ACC
       'While I desire dear Odysseus (my) heart melts away.' (*Od.* 19.136)

Verbs reviewed in this Section feature the constructional pattern of contact verbs that mean 'touch', 'hit', 'get hold of', discussed in Section 3.2.6, that also show construction variation involving the NomGen and the NomAcc construction, as *hairéō* 'hold, get hold of' in (109) and (110). As has been pointed out, some contact verbs, in spite of similar meanings, always only take either the NomGen or the NomAcc construction, as do respectively *tugkhánō* and *bállō* 'hit' in example (108). It appears that the pattern of contact verbs can extend easily to verbs of yearning and desiring: in both cases a participant strives to reach and possibly get hold of another participant. Notably, the second participant need not be conceived as capable or liable of reacting as in situations indicated by verbs that take the NomDat construction. Indeed, the second participant, in spite of being often human, is conceived as inactive, and can in fact also be inanimate, depending on the type of desire denoted by the verb.

Verbs that indicate love as desire partly share the semantics of verbs of volition, and this is especially clear in the case of *mémōna* 'desire eagerly', discussed in Section 5.2, which stands out among verbs of volition for the fact of taking the NomGen construction. Remarkably, verbs of desiring never occur in orders, the only exception being (364) that features an abstract stimulus, while imperative forms of *lilaíomai* function as metadirective with orders that refer to the situation denoted by the co-occurring infinitive, as in (369). In addition, I have found no co-occurring expressions of reason with these verbs: emotions such as desire are construed as rising spontaneously with no special motivation.

8.2.2   *Love as Care and Affection*
Verbs that indicate positive feelings, such as *alégō, alegízō* 'care for', 'care about', 'take heed of', *ólophuromai* 'take pity on someone', *kédomai, perikédomai* 'care for' and *philéō* 'feel affection for', 'love', most often occur with human stimuli. Indeed, while love intended as intense desire can also be directed toward things, affection is normally understood as a feeling that is aroused in human beings by other human beings. Most of these verbs take the NomGen construction as shown in (372)-(374). Alternation with the NomAcc is also possible for some of the verbs in this group. In addition, the verb *philéō* 'love', 'feel affection', always takes the NomAcc construction.

EMOTIONS

(372) ou gàr Kúklōpes   Diòs... alégousin oudè
NEG PTC Cyclopes.NOM.PL Zeus.GEN care.PRS.3PL NEG
theôn   makárōn
god.GEN.PL blessed.GEN.PL
'The Cyclopes don't care for Zeus, nor for the blessed gods.' (*Od.* 9.275–276)

(373) emòn   d' olophúretai   êtɔr   Héktoros
POSS.1SG.NOM PTC pity.PRS.M/P.3SG heart.NOM Hector.GEN
'My heart has compassion for Hector.' (*Il.* 22.169–170)

(374) hós   seu...   méga kédetai
REL.NOM GEN.2SG much care.PRS.M/P.3SG
'Who cares much for you.' (*Il.* 24.174)

The verb *alégō* and its synonym *alegízō* 'care for', 'take heed of' only have active forms. They always occur with human stimuli in the Homeric poems as in (372), except for a single passage, in which the stimulus is inanimate and the verb takes the NomAcc construction, as shown in (375).

(375) theôn   ópin   ouk alégontes
god.GEN.PL regard.ACC NEG care.PTCP.PRS.NOM.PL
'They do not care about the regard of the gods.' (*Il.* 16.388)

The verb *ólophuromai* 'take pity on someone' is a *medium tantum*. With this verb, the stimulus is always human, and the NomGen (five occurrences) and the NomAcc (seven occurrences) constructions basically convey the same meaning. Compare (373) and (376).

(376) ei mḗ tis   me   theôn   olophúrato
if NEG INDF.NOM 1SG.ACC god.GEN.PL take_pity.AOR.M/P.3SG
'If a goddess had not taken pity on me.' (*Od.* 4.364)

The verb *kédomai* means 'care for', is another *medium tantum*, and always occurs with the NomGen construction. The stimulus is usually human, even though in the Odyssey the nouns *bíotos* 'goods' and *oíkos* 'household' also occur: notably, these nouns indicate entities that belong to the sphere of a family, so they are related with the human beings that are part of it. A negative counterpart, *akédomai*, means 'do not care for', 'neglect' and occurs twice with human stimuli in the NomGen construction; one of the occurrences can be seen in (323).

222   CHAPTER 8

The verb *kḗdomai* also has active forms, which have a causative meaning 'trouble someone', and take the NomAcc construction (see Section 9.2). In the middle, *kḗdomai* and its compounds indicate a feeling that complements the feeling indicated by *philéō* 'love', 'feel affection for', as shown by frequent coordination or use in parallel passages. Remarkably, as anticipated above, *philéō* always takes the NomAcc construction. Compare examples (377) and (378).

(377) *ei gár s'   hòs ethéloi   philéein   glaukôpis*
       if PTC 2SG.ACC so want.OPT.PRS.3SG love.INF.PRS blu_eyed.NOM
       Athḗnē   hōs tót   Odussêos   perikḗdeto
       Athena.NOM as   then Odysseus.GEN care.IMPF.M/P.3SG
       kudalímoio
       glorious.GEN
       'If blue eyed Athena wanted to care for you as much as she cared for glorious Odysseus.' (*Od.* 3.218–219)

(378) *hê moûnoi   philéous'   alókhous   merópōn*
       PTC only.NOM.PL love.PRS.3PL wife.ACC.PL mortal.GEN.PL
       anthrṓpon   Atreídai?   epeì hós   tis
       man.GEN.PL son_of_Atreus.NOM.PL as   REL.NOM.3SG INDF.NOM
       anḕr   agathòs   kaì ekhéphrōn tḕn   autoû
       man.NOM noble.NOM and wise.NOM DEM.ACC DEM.GEN
       philéei   kai kḗdetai
       love.PRS.3SG and care.PRS.M/P.3SG
       'Do only the sons of Atreus among mortals love their wives? Any noble and wise man loves and cares for his own wife.' (*Il.* 9.340–342)

In (377) the verb *perikḗdomai*, a compound of *kḗdomai*, indicates a situation which is parallel to the one indicated by *philéō*, while in (378) the latter verb is coordinated with *kḗdomai*, and shares the same stimulus argument. The prefix has an intensive meaning, and indicates a high degree of emotional involvement. Notably, this argument is realized only once, preceding *philéō*, and, as *philéō* always takes the NomAcc construction, is encoded in the accusative; *kḗdomai* has a null object, as is normal in coordinated structures (conjunction reduction; see Luraghi 2003b, 2014b).

Etymologically, *philéō* is a denominal verb from *phílos* 'friend', a concept that often refers to hospitality (see example (380)), and focuses on positive feelings. As an adjective *phílos* means 'dear' and in Homer it can also indicate possession, especially with a sub-set of inherently possessed entities such as the heart/soul or close relatives (Chantraine 1977: 1204). Semantically, it dif-

EMOTIONS   223

fers from other verbs discussed in this Section because it does not construe the
stimulus as a matter of concern. Rather, the stimulus with *philéō* simply raises
in the experiencer an emotional reaction that in some circumstances conforms
to socially expected practices, as in (380) and (384).

On the other hand, *kédomai* is connected with the noun *kêdos* 'care', 'trouble', and focuses on a feeling that prompts the experiencer to provide for the
stimulus: the stimulus is a matter of concern for the experiencer. This meaning is close to the meaning expressed by *mimnéskomai* in occurrences such as
(314), in which the latter verb always features the NomGen construction, and
partly also to the meaning of *médomai* with the NomGen construction, as in
(259) and (260). The main difference between *médomai* and *kédomai* lies in
the nature of the stimulus: while the former verb typically features inanimate
stimuli, the latter refers to situations in which other human beings are involved
beside the experiencer. In turn, *mimnéskomai* takes an intermediate position,
as it can indicate care both with human and with inanimate stimuli, compare
(314) with (317), and see the discussion in Section 7.3. Caring for someone can
also mean sharing their worries or fears: as I will argue in Section 8.4.2, this is
the reason for the occurrence of the NomGen construction with verbs denoting
empathy.

Similar to *philéō*, the verb *eleaírō* 'care for', 'take pity' only features active
forms and always takes the NomAcc construction (an example is (431), see Section 8.3.2), but can share a genitive argument when coordinated with *kédomai*
as in (379).

(379) *autàr Akhilleùs   esthlòs   eòn   Danaôn*
       but   Achilles.NOM valiant.NOM be.PTCP.PRS.NOM Greek.GEN.PL
       ou   kédetai   ou   d' eleaírei
       NEG care.PRS.M/P.3SG NEG PTC take_pity.PRS.3SG
       'Yet Achilles, valiant as he is, does not care for the Danaans, nor does
       he feel pity.' (*Il.* 11.664–665)

As shown in (377) and (378), the verb *philéō* indicates affection. It can also indicate a temporary manifestation of friendly or protective feelings, such as those
of a host toward a guest, or of a deity toward a human being, as in (380) and
(381).

(380) *khaîre,   xeîne,   par   ámmi   philéseai*
       rejoice.IMP.PRS.2SG guest.VOC among 1PL.DAT love.FUT.MID.2SG
       'Rejoice, guest; in our house you will be taken care of (or: protected).'
       (*Od.* 1.123)

(381) éxokha   gár min   ephílato   Pallàs
immensely PTC 3SG.ACC love.AOR.MID.3SG Pallas.NOM
Athénē
Athena.NOM
'Indeed Pallas Athena immensely loved him.' (*Il.* 5.61)

While (377) and (378) contain active forms of *philéō*, examples (381) and (380) also show that the middle voice with this verb can have different functions. In (381), the form *ephílato* is a middle aorist. Like other middle forms built on the aorist stem, it does not show any semantic difference with respect to the active. On the other hand, the middle future *philéseai* in (380) has passive meaning, and so does an occurrence of a passive aorist, *ephiléthen* in (382), also accompanied by the agent expression *ek Diós* 'by Zeus', whereas the middle aorist imperative *phîlai* in (383) again has active meaning.

(382) phílēthen   ek Diós
love.AOR.PASS.3PL by Zeus.GEN
'They were loved by Zeus.' (*Il.* 2.668–669)

(383) eí poté moi   kaì patrì   phíla   phronéousa
if ever 1SG.DAT and father.DAT kind.ACC.PL think.PTCP.PRS.NOM
paréstēs   dēḯōi   en polémōi, nûn aût' emè
stand.AOR.2SG merciless.DAT in battle.DAT now again 1SG.ACC
phîlai   Athénē
love.IMP.AOR.MID.2SG Athena.NOM
'If ever with kindly thought you stood by my father in merciless battle, now protect me, Athena.' (*Il.* 5.116–117)

Notably, example (383) also shows that the verb can occur in the imperative: here, Diomedes asks the goddess Athena to protect him in battle as she used to protect his father. The form *phîlai* is a middle aorist imperative, and, as noted above, has active meaning.

Finally, example (384) contains an inanimate stimulus, and the verb *philéousin* denotes a feeling of approval.

EMOTIONS   225

(384)   *ou   mèn skhétlia   èrga   theoì   mákares*
        NEG PTC evil.ACC.PL deed.ACC.PL god.NOM.PL blessed.NOM.PL
        philéousin, allà díkēn   tíousi   kaì aísima
        like.PRS.3PL but justice.ACC honor.PRS.3PL and right.ACC.PL
        érg'   anthrópōn
        deed.ACC.PL man.GEN.PL
        'Indeed the blessed gods do not like evil deeds, but honor justice and
        the right deeds of men.' (*Od.* 14.83–84)

8.3   Verbs of Emotion with the NomAcc Construction

Verbs of emotion that take the NomAcc construction and do not belong to
groups that also allow other constructions are verbs that indicate feelings such
as wonder, awe, fear, and grief. These are mostly negative feelings that typically
do not target another human participant, but are centered on the experiencer.
The stimulus with such emotions is not construed as being reactive in a situation initiated by the experiencer, nor is it conceived as something that the
experiencer tries to reach or as a generic matter of concern: rather, it is a potentially dangerous source stimulus, which can target the experiencer and bring
about an emotional state.

With verbs that take the NomAcc, the experiencer is not actively involved
in the situation: it is not an agent-like, but rather a patient-like participant, in
spite of the fact that these verbs take the construction of high transitivity verbs,
a construction which, as I have argued thus far, implies awareness and attentiveness with respect to a situation (see Figure 11). In the next Sections, I will
show how these features are construed to adapt to this type of verbs.

I start in Section 8.3.1 with verbs that indicate wonder, even though they constitute a smaller group, because, as I will argue, they show a close relation with
visual perception, which can shed light on their constructional pattern. In Section 8.3.2 I discuss verbs that denote negative feelings such as fear, shame and
grief. I argue that these are connected with verbs of wonder, as wonder may
lead to awe and then to fear.

8.3.1   *Wonder*

Verbs that mean 'wonder' in Homeric Greek are *thaumázō* (with a variant *thau-
maínō* in *Il.* 8.108) and *thambéō*. Let us start by considering examples (385) and
(386).

(385) *étoi Dardanídēs*   *Príamos*   *thaúmaz'*
PTC son_of_Dardanus.NOM Priamus.NOM wonder.IMPF.3SG
Akhilêa ...   *autàr hò*   *Dardanídēn*   *Príamon*
Achilles.ACC but   DEM.ACC son_of_Dardanus.ACC Priamus.ACC
thaúmazen   *Akhilleùs*   *eisoróōn*
wonder.IMPF.3SG Achilles.NOM see.PTCP.PRS.NOM
'Then Priamus son of Dardanus marveled at Achilles, and Achilles in his turn marveled looking at Priamus.' (*Il.* 24.629–632)

(386) *laoì*   *d' aû theēúntó*   *te*   *thámbēsán*
people.NOM.PL PTC PTC watch.IMPF.M/P.3PL PTC wonder.AOR.3PL
te
PTC
'The people were watching and were seized with wonder.' (*Il.* 23.728 = *Il.* 23.881)

The passage in (385) depicts Priamus and Achilles beholding each other, as Priamus has entered Achilles' hut trying to bring back Hector's corpse from the Greek camp. The two enemies marvel at the sight of one another. Example (386) is preceded by a battle scene that leaves the other warriors astonished. Both examples point toward a close association of wonder and marvel with sight, as shown by the occurrence of *eisoróōn* in (385), the present participle of *eisoráō* 'behold' discussed in Section 6.1 (see example (186)), and of the imperfect *theēúntó* in (386) from the verb *theáomai* 'watch'.

The latter is a verb that indicates sight that I left out of the discussion in Section 6.1 precisely because its semantics combines sight with marvel, and implies a crucial emotional component. This becomes even clearer in some passages in which the verb is accompanied by another verb of sight, as in (387).

(387) *polloì*   *d' ár' etheḗsanto*   *idóntes*
many.NOM.PL PTC PTC watch.AOR.MID.3PL see.PTCP.AOR.NOM.PL
huiòn   *Laértao*   *daḯphrona*
son.ACC Laertes.GEN wise.ACC
'And many marveled at the sight of the wise son of Laertes.' (*Od.* 8.17–18)

The state of affair triggered by *etheḗsanto* in (387) arises suddenly as indicated by the aorist, similar to the state triggered by *thámbēsán* in (386). Sight, in turn, is referred to by the participle *idóntes* 'as they saw', which makes clear that

EMOTIONS

etheēsanto does not simply refer to perception, but rather indicates an emotional state brought about by perception.

Mette (1961) discusses the semantic relation between *thaumázō* and *theáomai*, and convincingly argues that marvel arises from sight in Homeric Greek, and that the two verbs indicate sight and marvel at the same time. Indeed, the *thaumázō* and *theáomai* are also etymologically related (Chantraine 1977: 425). The possible connection of *thambéō* with the other two verbs is less compelling (see Chantraine 1977: 422, Beekes 2010: 536); nevertheless, its use clearly points toward a semantic commonalty. Also etymologically related at least with *thambéō* is the verb *téthēpa* 'be astonished', which only features the perfect, hence always indicates a state (as is highlighted by its frequent occurrence with *hístēmi* 'stand'), and never occurs with a second argument. An example is (388).

(388)   *hôs   humeîs   éstēte   tethēpótes   oudè*
        so   2PL.NOM stand.AOR.2PL be_astonished.PTCP.PRF.NOM.PL NEG
        mákhesthe
        fight.PRS.MID.2PL
        'So you stand astonished and don't fight.' (*Il.* 4.246)

According to Mette (1961: 53) frequent objects of wonder in the Homeric poems are the deeds of the gods or exceptional deeds by humans (the occurrence in (386) conforms to this description, and shows that *thambéō* is indeed equivalent to *thaumázō* and *theáomai*, even though it remains outside Mette's discussion), or the looks of especially prominent people, as in (385). An example in which a divine intervention arouses wonder is (389), while (390) shows that other possible objects can also trigger the same feeling.

(389)   *thámbēsan   d'   órnithas,   epeì ídon   ophthalmoîsin*
        wonder.AOR.3PL PTC bird.ACC.PL as   see.AOR.3PL eye.DAT.PL
        'But they were seized with wonder at the birds, as they saw (them) with (their) eyes.' (*Od.* 2.155)

(390)   *nêson   thaumázontes   edineómestha*
        island.ACC wonder.PTCP.PRS.NOM.PL roam.IMPF.M/P.1PL
        kat'   autén
        throughout DEM.ACC
        'We roamed throughout the isle marveling at it.' (*Od.* 9.153)

228   CHAPTER 8

Example (389) contains the stimulus *órnithas* 'the birds', but in fact the wider context shows that the real object of wonder is the situation in which the birds are involved, which is an omen sent by the gods. In (390), Odysseus and his comrades walk around in the island close to the land of the Cyclops that they can finally explore at dawn: the night before they had reached its harbor in the darkness. In this case, the feeling of wonder arises out of the sight of an unknown place.

Of special interest is the occurrence in (237), that I discussed in Section 7.1.1 in connection with the meaning of *noéō* and repeat here for convenience.

(237)   *ho*   *dè*   *phresìn*   *hêisi*
        DEM.NOM PTC heart.DAT.PL POSS.3PL.DAT.PL
        noésas   *thámbēsen*   *katà*   *thumón:*
        realize.PTCP.AOR.NOM wonder.AOR.3SG around heart.ACC
        oísato   *gàr theòn*   *eînai*
        think.AOR.MID.3SG PTC god.ACC be.INF.PRS
        'He, becoming aware in his mind, wondered at his heart: he deemed (her) divine.' (*Od.* 1.322–323)

In Section 7.1.1 I argued that example (237) shows that *noéō* does not simply indicate sensory perception. In this passage, Telemachus does in fact see the goddess Athena, but the awareness of her divine nature is brought about by the whole situation in which they meet, and especially in the feelings that she has arisen in him. It is an internal feeling, experienced through the *phrēn* 'midriff', one of the Homeric denominations for the mind when connected to emotions (see Jahn 1987). Accordingly, the feeling of wonder in this case is also connected with attention and with the rise of awareness, and is not simply triggered by sight.

The connection of wonder with sight has precise physical correlates. Wierzbicka (1999) argues that anthropological literature on gestures agrees in associating a rise of the brows with surprise across different cultures. For this reason, she writes that the "action [of] increasing a person's visual field can serve as a semiotic basis for the message 'I want to know more (about this)'" (1999: 203). Hence, embodiment is responsible for the association of verbs that indicate wonder with verbs of sight.

Wonder results from the sight of something that does not conform to expectations. This may lead to unpleasant feelings, as the object of wonder can even be scary: wonder may turn into awe, horror or even fear. Let us consider example (391).

EMOTIONS

(391) *hōs sé,   gúnai,   ágamaí   te   téthēpá*
       as   2SG.ACC lady.VOC marvel.PRS.M/P.1SG PTC be_amazed.PRF.1SG
       te,   deídia   d'   ainôs goúnōn   hápsasthai
       PTC fear.PRF.1SG PTC greatly knee.GEN.PL touch.INF.AOR.MID
       'As you do, lady, I marvel at you, and I am amazed, and I fear greatly to
       touch your knees.' (*Od.* 6.168–169)

In (391), Odysseus, who has come to the land of the Phaeacians as the victim
of a shipwreck, is talking to Nausicaa and is expressing his feeling of confusion at her sight. Marvel is expressed by *ágamai*, one out of a small set of verbs
that admits variation between the NomDat and the NomAcc construction, to
which I will return in Section 8.4.1. The resulting feeling is fear, indicated by
deídō: the association of wonder and unexpected appearance with fear leads
to the extension of the NomAcc construction to verbs that indicate negative
emotions centered on the experiencer, which constitute the subject of the next
Section.

8.3.2   *Fear, Shame and Grief*
Wierzbicka describes negative emotions as "associated with cognitive scenar-
ios in which something bad happened, is happening, or will happen" (1999:
60), and divides them into two groups, depending on whether they concern
past events that have actually happened, or hypothetical, mostly future ones.
The first group contains feelings such as sadness and grief, while the second
contains feelings such as fear. Other similar negative feelings are shame and
embarrassment, which, as Wierzbicka (1999: 109) points out, are also focused
on the experiencer. As I will argue in this Section, the distinctive feature of
these situations is that they are construed as involving a rise of awareness and
a high level of attention in the experiencer concerning a potential threat.

   In Homeric Greek, such negative emotions are encoded by verbs that consistently feature accusative stimuli and take the NomAcc construction. Examples
are (392) and (393).

(392) *hēmeîs   mèn pròs tḕn   ídomen*
       1PL.NOM PTC toward DEM.ACC look.AOR.1PL
       deísantes   ólethron
       fear.PTCP.AOR.NOM.PL destruction.ACC
       'So we looked toward her and feared destruction.' (*Od.* 12.244)

(393) *theôn   d' hupodeísate   mênin*
       god.GEN.PL PTC fear.IMP.AOR.2PL wrath.ACC
       'Fear the wrath of the gods!' (*Od.* 2.66)

The emotion indicated by *deídō* and its compound *hupodeídō* 'fear' in (392) and (393) exemplify 'retrospective' and 'prospective' feelings ("something bad happened" and "something bad can happen" in the terms of Wierzbicka 1999: 109). Example (392) contains an imperative: rather than an order, here, we find a warning, whereby a participant is told not to be too daring defying the gods.

In (392), fear is said to arise at the sight of the stimulus. The association of fear with direct perception is in agreement with San Roque et al.'s (2018) observation of a cross-linguistic association between sight and attention to potential danger, discussed in Section 2.1.2. In Homeric Greek, this connection is further shown by the extension to *deídō* of the Two-place+P construction (in this case NomAcc+P, as with verbs of sight), as in (394)

(394) *deídia   d'   ainôs   Aineían   epiónta*
fear.PRF.1SG PTC horribly Aeneas.ACC come.PTCP.PRS.ACC
'I am deadly scared by Aeneas coming on.' (*Il.* 13.481–482)

Fear is a feeling that can be experienced to varying degrees, and associated with other feelings, as in the case of *tarbéō* 'be afraid', 'be torn apart by fear' (based on the noun *tárbos* 'fear') in (395) and (396), and *atúzomai* 'be terrified' in (397) and (398).

(395) *méga   mèn kakòn   aí ke   phébōmai   plēthùn*
great.ACC PTC evil.ACC if PTC flee.SBJV.PRS.M/P.1SG crowd.ACC
tarbésas
fear.PTCP.AOR.NOM
'A great evil (it would be) if I flee fearing the crowd.' (*Il.* 11.404–11.405)

(396) *Héktor   tís   ké   s'   ét'   állos*
Hector.VOC INDF.NOM PTC 2SG.ACC yet other.NOM
Akhaiôn   tarbéseien?
Achaean.GEN.PL fear.OPT.AOR.3SG
'Hector, who else among the Achaeans will fear you yet?' (*Il.* 17.586)

(397) *patròs   phílou   ópsin   atukhtheìs*
father.GEN dear.GEN sight.ACC be_terrified.PTCP.AOR.PASS.NOM
'Terrified at the sight of his father.' (*Il.* 6.468)

EMOTIONS   231

(398) kteínō   dè   kaì autoùs   Argeíous ...
       kill.SBJV.PRS.1SG PTC and DEM.ACC.PL Argives.ACC.PL
       atuzoménous   hupò kapnoû
       be_terrified.PTCP.PRS.M/P.ACC.PL of   smoke.GEN
       'I (can) kill the Argives, panicked because of the smoke.' (*Il.* 8.182–8.183)

In (395) the stimulus is a collective noun *plēthùn* 'crowd', while in (396) we find
the second person pronouns *s(e)* (see further (147) without an overt stimulus).
Example (397) features an inanimate stimulus, which, however, refers to an
animate entity (*patròs phílou ópsin* 'the sight of his father'). Remarkably, the
two verbs *tarbéō* and *atúzomai* have a similar meaning, but, while one shows
active voice, the second only features present middle participles and once an
aorist passive participle. Most frequently, it occurs without an overt stimulus,
and, apart from the aorist participle in (397) that takes the NomAcc construction, the only other occurrence with a stimulus is example (398), which contains the prepositional phrase *hupò kapnoû* 'by the smoke', with *hupò*+gen. This
type of prepositional phrase expressed cause in Homer, while the interpretation as passive agent could be triggered by the context in the case of human
participants (see Luraghi 2000: 281–282; 2003a: 232–233). In later epics, the
active *atúzō* is also attested, with the meaning 'cause terror', and offers support
for considering several other active causative forms as derived from original
medium tantum, as I argue in Section 9.4.

    In (399), the Trojans are mourning, shedding tears over Hector's corpse: the
verb used to indicate mourning is *odúromai* 'mourn', with the NomAcc construction. In some occurrences, crying as the effect of mourning can stand
for the feeling, as *klaíō* 'weep' in (400), again with the NomAcc construction.

(399) Héktora   dákru   khéontes   odúronto
       Hector.ACC tears.ACC shed.PTCP.PRS.NOM.PL   mourn.IMPF.M/P.3PL
       'They mourned Hector shedding tears.' (*Il.* 24.714)

(400) tôn   dè̀ nûn héteroí   ge phílon   paîda
       DEM.GEN.PL   PTC now either.NOM.PL PTC loved.ACC son.ACC
       klaúsontai   sémeron
       weep.FUT.M/P.3PL today
       'Either of them will mourn their son today.' (*Il.* 20.210–211)

As tears are the bodily correlates of grief, trembling and shivering are among
the bodily correlates of fear, and the verbs (*hupo*)*troméō* 'tremble' and *phríssō*

'shiver' can be metonymically extended to indicate the emotion. In such cases, too, the stimulus remains in the accusative and the verbs take the NomAcc construction, as in (402).

(401) *toîon gàr hupotroméousin hápantes*
  such PTC tremble.PRS.3PL everyone.NOM.PL
  'Such as everyone trembles (in front of Achilles).' (*Il.* 22.241)

(402) *hoí té se pephríkasi léonth' hōs*
  REL.NOM.PL PTC 2SG.ACC tremble.PRF.3PL lion.ACC as
  mēkádes aîges
  bleating.NOM.PL goat.NOM.PL
  'Who tremble at you as bleating goats in front of a lion.' (*Il.* 11.383)

Notably, the verb *phríssō* 'chill', 'shiver' only occurs in metonymic expressions that indicate fear in Homeric Greek, and never refers to the bodily sensation of feeling cold. An even more advanced instance of lexicalized semantic shift is shown by the verb *stugéō* 'fear' as in (403) and (404).

(403) *stugéēi dè kaì állos îson emoì*
  fear.SBJV.PRS.3SG PTC even other.NOM equal.ACC 1SG.DAT
  phásthai
  say.INF.PRS.M/P
  'Even another should not dare declaring himself my equal.' (*Il.* 1.186-187)

(404) *tḕn dè gunaîka heûron, hósēn t'*
  DEM.ACC PTC woman.ACC find.AOR.3PL such.ACC PTC
  óreos koruphḗn, katà d' éstugon autḗn
  mountain.GEN peak.ACC PREV PTC fear.AOR.3PL DEM.ACC
  'They found a woman, high as the peak of a mountain, and were terrified by her.' (*Od.* 10.112–10.113)

The verb *stugéō* means 'fear', 'dare not' but it can also indicate a stronger feeling, such as terror, as in (404), in which the preverb *katá* (here separated from the verb) adds an intensive shade of meaning. Etymologically, the verb is connected with roots that indicate cold and frost in other Indo-European languages (Chantraine 1977: 1066), but this meaning is not attested in Greek, in which the emotion has taken the place of its bodily correlate.

  The post-Homeric semantics of *stugéō* is also interesting, because it extends to indicating hate, and points toward a close connection between fear and

EMOTIONS 233

hate, as I have anticipated in Section 8.1.1. This connection is highlighted by the meaning and the construction of the verb *ekhthaírō* 'hate', 'consider an enemy', as shown in examples (405) and (406).

(405) *epeì ou dè Menoitiádēn ékhthaire páros ge*
as NEG PTC son_of_Menoetius.ACC hate.IMPF.3SG formerly PTC
óphra zōòs eòn ... mísēsen d' ára
until alive.NOM be.PTCP.PRS.NOM hate.AOR.3SG PTC PTC
min ... kúrma genésthai
3SG.ACC prey.ACC become.INF.AOR.M/P
'For even formerly, when he was living, he did not hate the son of Menoetius, so he can't stand now that he becomes the prey (of dogs).'
(*Il.* 17.270–273)

(406) *ê sé ge laoì ekhthaírous' anà dêmon,*
PTC 2SG.ACC PTC people.NOM.PL hate.PRS.3PL in town.ACC
epispómenoi theoû omphêi
follow.PTCP.PRS.M/P.NOM.PL god.GEN response.DAT
'Or whether the people in town hate you, following the response of a god.' (*Od.* 3.214–215 = 16.95.96)

As I have already pointed out, the verb *ekhthaírō* is based on the root of the adjective *ekhthrós* 'hated', 'hateful' and of the noun *ékhthos* 'hostility', 'hate'. Etymologically, these forms are related to the root of Latin *extrā* 'outside'. According to Chantraine (1977: 391), *ekhthrós* is 'the man from outside, an alien that remains outside any social relation' ("l'homme du dehors, l'étranger extérieur à toutes relations sociales"): hence, hate and hostility are triggered by the unknown brought about by someone that it characterized as not being possibly classified among known types of individuals, and constitutes a threat. This points to a close relation of the emotion expressed by *ekhthaírō* to fear. The verb profiles a possible danger for the experiencer, rather than a possible reaction from the stimulus, as in the case of hate verbs that take the NomDat construction (see Section 8.1.1).

Example (405) also contains the only Homeric occurrence of another hate verb *miséō*, which will become the most frequent verb to express the meaning 'hate' in Classical Greek. The etymology of this verb is unknown, but dictionaries agree in pointing out that its morphological shape appears to be modeled after its semantic contrary *philéō* 'love'. Its constructional pattern, too, might reflect the pattern of *philéō* (see Section 8.2.2), or it might pattern after other hate verbs reviewed in this Section.

Especially verbs that denote feelings of sadness and grievance often occur without an overt stimulus, as *tetíēmai* in (407)

(407) *típhth' hoútō tetíēsthon*
       why   so   grieve.PRF.2DU
       'Why are you so grieved?' (*Il.* 8.447)

In (407), the verb form *tetíēsthon* is a perfect, and indicates a state of sadness resulting from preceding events. Elsewhere, this verb always only shows perfect participle forms, *tetiēménos/ tetiēménē êtor* 'grieved at heart'. The indication of the body part, concrete or abstract (the soul, the mind), which is frequent in Homer with all types of experiential predicates, features prominently in reference to situations of grievance or sorrow. Often, such situations are referred to by adjectives or by metaphorical expressions such as those briefly discussed in Section 2.3, cf. examples (18) and (62). More examples are (408)-(410).

(408) *Trôas   dè   katà   krêthen   lábe   pénthos*
       Trojan.ACC.PL PTC down from_the_head take.AOR.3SG   grief.NOM
       'Grief utterly took the Trojans.' (*Il.* 16.548)

(409) *málista gàr   álgos   hikánei   thumòn emón*
       above_all PTC   pain.NOM come.PRS.3SG   soul.ACC POSS.1SG.ACC
       'Indeed deep pain comes to my soul.' (*Il.* 3.97–98)

(410) *paidòs   gár hoi   álaston   enì phresì   pénthos*
       son.GEN PTC 3SG.DAT comfortless.NOM in heart.DAT sorrow.NOM
       ékeito
       lie.IMPF.M/P.3SG
       'Comfortless grief for his son was lying on his heart.' (*Od.* 24.423)

Examples (408) and (409) refer to inchoative situations. The inception of the emotional state, *pénthos* 'sorrow' and *álgos* 'pain', is metaphorically indicated by the verbs *lábe* 'it took' and *hikánei* 'it comes'. In (410) the emotion is again *pénthos* but the situation is a state indicated by the verb *keîmai* 'lie'. In (408) the emotion targets directly the experiencer, *Trôas* 'the Trojans', while in (409) and (410) it targets the experiencer's soul (*thumós*) or heart (*phrên*), while the experiencer is indicated in a possessive expression, the possessive pronouns *emón* 'my' in (409) and the external possessor dative *hoi* in (410).

The notion of shame is heavily conditioned by social habits and moral values; hence the construal of this emotion is more culture-dependent than oth-

EMOTIONS   235

ers. Wierzbicka (1999: 109–112), for example, argues that the concept of shame
for Modern English speakers is significantly different from the same concept as
understood in Shakespeare's works. Similar to envy, shame involves a complex
mental operation, in which not only one's feeling, but also the point of view
and possible judgment of the others are at stake (see Taylor 1985). As we will
see, the concept of shame in Homeric Greek is also quite different from ours,
and rather than shame in the modern sense it often indicates cowardice (which
was of course a matter of shame for the Homeric heroes).

Verbs that indicate shame in Homeric Greek are *aiskhúnomai* and *aidéomai*
as in (411)-(415). While the former indicates a state of embarrassment deriving from lack of courage, the feeling expressed by the latter is connected with
honor and has a crucial social dimension. Notably, the reason for shame is never
encoded as a noun phrase in the verb's argument structure, but it is either infer-
able from the context, as in (411), or expressed by a dependent infinitive, as in
(413). When the NomAcc construction occurs, the stimulus is either the gods as
in (414), or some activity connected with the human beings whose judgment
triggers shame in the experiencer, as in (412) and (415). This makes shame sym-
metrical to envy, as I discuss below.

(411)   *hē   mèn gár m'   ekéleue ...   hépesthai,*
        DEM.NOM PTC PTC 1SG.ACC invite.IMPF.3SG follow.INF.PRS.M/P
        all' egò   ouk éthelon   deísas
        but 1SG.NOM NEG want.IMPF.1SG fear.PTCP.AOR.NOM
        aiskhunómenós   te, mḗ pōs kaì soì   thumòs
        respect.PTCP.PRS.M/P.NOM PTC PTC PTC and 2SG.DAT soul.NOM
        episkússaito   idónti
        get_angry.AOR.OPT.M/P.3SG see.PTCP.AOR.DAT
        'She invited me to follow her, but I didn't want to, for respect and fear
        that your soul get angry seeing me.' (*Od.* 7.304–306)

(412)   *oú tí   se   tónd'   áxesthai*
        NEG INDF.NOM 2SG.ACC DEM.ACC marry.INF.FUT.MID
        oïómeth':   oudè éoiken: all'
        think.PRS.M/P.1PL NEG suit.INF.PRF.3SG but
        aiskhunómenoi   phátin   andrôn   ēdè
        respect.PTCP.PRS.M/P.NOM word.ACC man.GEN.PL and
        gunaikôn
        woman.GEN.PL
        'We don't think he will marry you: that's absurd; but we fear the words
        of men and women.' (*Od.* 21.322–323)

Examples (411) and (412) contain the verb *aiskhúnomai*. In (411), Odysseus explains to Alcinous that he refrained from accepting his daughter's invitation to follow her into the palace, as he feared Alcinous' reaction. Here, rather than to a feeling of shame, the participle *aiskhunómenos* refers to the fact that the hero dared not enter the home of a man who had not directly invited him as a guest. The verb is coordinated with *deídō* 'fear', which takes a complement clause with *mḗ* 'lest'. In (412) we find again a participle, *aiskhunómenoi*, this time with the NomAcc construction. Odysseus, disguised as a beggar, has entered his palace, and asked to try and string the bolt that the suitors have not been able to string yet. As Penelope insists that she wants him to try, one of the suitors answers that if a beggar proved stronger that they are, they would be exposed to scornful comments of other people. In both cases, there is a focus on a predictably negative judgment of some other participant regarding the experiencer's actions, and on the confrontational situation that might arise. This prompts the experiencer to refrain from an action that s/he thinks would be too daring.

Examples (413)-(415) contain the verb *aidéomai*.

(413) *aídesthen   mèn anḗnasthai,   deîsan*
feel_shame.AOR.PASS.3PL PTC refuse.INF.AOR.M/P fear.AOR.3PL
d'   hupodékhthai
PTC accept.INF.AOR.MID
'They felt shame for refusing, but were afraid to accept.' (*Il.* 7.93)

(414) *aideîo   theoùs*
feel_shame.OPT.PRS.2SG god.ACC.PL
'Be respectful of the gods!' (*Il.* 24.503)

(415) *ou dè theôn   ópin   ēidésat'   ou*
NEG PTC god.GEN.PL regard.ACC feel_ashamed.AOR.M/P.3SG NEG
dè trápezan, tèn   hḗn   hoi   parétheken
PTC table.ACC DEM.ACC REL.ACC 3SG.DAT laid.AOR.MID.3SG
'He was not ashamed before the gods, not in front of the table that he had laid for him.' (*Od.* 21.28–29)

In (413), the Greek heroes must decide whether or not to engage in battle with Hector. Their feelings are mixed: on the one hand, they fear their Trojan foe; on the other hand, they feel ashamed, as showing fear would dishonor them. In this case, even though standards of honor are involved that refer to an external viewpoint, the focus is rather on the experiencers' judgment of their own

EMOTIONS

237

behavior. This is even clearer in the next two examples. In (414), Priamus, who is begging Achilles to give him back Hector's corpse, invokes the gods' judgment in order to convince him. Example (415) is from a passage that tells the story of Iphitus, who was killed by Heracles in spite of having been hospitable to him. In the Homeric culture, guests were protected by the gods, and violating the norms of hospitality was an extremely sacrilegious act. Here, Heracles is depicted as not having scruples in defying the gods. In these three examples, the experiencer's state of possible dishonor is focused and construed as determined by social conventions.

The social setting in which emotions such as those expressed by *aiskhúnomai* and *aidéomai* arise accounts for their association with verbs such as *deídō* 'fear' and *ekhtaírō* 'hate (something perceived as a threat)' that I have discussed earlier in this Section. As I have pointed out, verbs of negative emotion that take the NomAcc construction construe the stimulus as a threatening entity or a threatening situation that faces the experiencer and raises the experiencer's awareness and attention. In the case of shame, it might look as though there is no danger involved: still the experiencer faces a social threat, arising from a behavior that is stigmatized within a certain community.

As remarked above, the second participant in occurrences such as (412) and (414) does not refer to a reason for shame: rather, it is the participant that might utter or conceive the judgment that would generate shame in the experiencer. Much in the same way as envy, which involves two human participants and a third entity that functions as the reason for the emotion, shame, too, involves a combination of participants and circumstances. Comparing envy with shame, Wierzbicka (1999: 46) argues that the former implies "thinking about someone else", while the latter implies "thinking about ourselves". In fact, shame appears even more complex, as it involves thinking about ourselves in the light of what others might think.

In conclusion, emotion verbs reviewed in this Section denote situations in which the experiencer has some negative feeling that does not target a stimulus participant, but is rather centered on the experiencer itself: the experiencer is construed as being aware of the threat, and being in a state of high attention. When they occur with nominal arguments, these verbs take the NomAcc construction: even though experiencers in such situations are not controllers, the feature of control still remains in the construction, and is mapped onto the domain of awareness and attention as has been shown for sight verbs in Figure 11.

8.4 Alternating Constructions

8.4.1 *NomDat / NomAcc*

A limited number of verbs display argument structure variation involving the NomDat and the NomAcc construction. Variation with such verbs brings about a semantic difference, coherently with the meaning that the two constructions express elsewhere. Let us consider examples (416)-(419).

(416)   *nûn d'*   *állōi*   *dḗmōi*   *nemesízomai*
       now PTC rest.DAT people.DAT be_upset.PRS.M/P.1SG
       'Now I am upset at the rest of the people.' (*Od.* 2.239)

(417)   *eí pér moi*   *nemesḗseai*
       if PTC 1SG.DAT be_upset.FUT.MID.2SG
       'If you will get angry at me.' (*Il.* 10.115)

(418)   *epeí rha theoùs*   *nemesízeto*   *aièn*
       as   PTC god.ACC.PL be_upset.IMPF.MID.3.SG always
       eóntas
       be.PTCP.PRS.ACC.PL
       'Because he feared the eternal gods.' (*Od.* 1.263)

(419)   *hós*   *te*   *málista nemessâtai*   *kakà*   *érga*
       REL.NOM PTC really   hate.PRS.M/P.3SG bad.ACC.PL action.ACC.PL
       'Who is greatly upset at bad actions.' (*Od.* 14.284)

The verbs *nemesízō* and *nemesáō* are based on the root of the abstract noun *némesis*, whose original meaning was 'distribution of dues', 'retribution', but that already in Homer had changed into a negative concept, referring to the punishment of the gods caused by unjust deeds. The two verbs indicate a state of anger targeting some human participant when they occur in the NomDat construction (examples (416) and (417)), as do other verbs with similar meaning treated in Section 8.1.1. When occurring without this construction, both verbs indicate a negative experiencer-centered feeling, such as fear in (418). In (419), the choice of construction is dependent on animacy: indignation is directed toward an abstract entity, thus not displaying the interactive character typical of anger situations that involve two animate participants.

A similar pattern of variation occurs with the verb *agámai* 'be/get upset' in (420) with the NomDat construction, and (421) and (391) already discussed in Section 8.3.1, with the NomAcc construction.

EMOTIONS

(420) *hòs   éphaske   Poseidáōn'   agásasthai   hēmîn*
REL.NOM say.IMPF.3SG Poseidon.ACC upset.INF.AOR.MID 1PL.DAT
'He used to say that Poseidon would get upset at us.' (*Od.* 13.173)

(421) *hoi   d'   ára pántes   akèn*
DEM.NOM.PL PTC PTC all.NOM.PL silence.ACC
egénonto   siōpêi   mûthon
become.AOR.MID.3PL silence.DAT word.ACC
agassámenoi
marvel.PTCP.AOR.MID.NOM.PL
'They all became silent, marveling at (his) word.' (*Il.* 8.28–29)

The verb indicates a state of surprise. With the NomDat construction, the verb denotes a negative feeling directed toward a target stimulus, and means 'get upset at someone' as shown in (420). The NomAcc construction indicates a feeling of wonder. In both cases, the meanings activated by the different constructions are homogeneous with the meanings of other verbs that take either construction.

8.4.2   *Constructions Expressing Empathy*
Human beings are usually considered capable of feeling empathy. Often they are depicted as sharing the emotions of other human beings, be it joy or fear and grievance. In the Homeric poems, especially negative emotions are sometimes construed as being the object of empathy. Fear for someone is indicated by the verb *perideídō*, as in (422)-(424), which takes either the NomDat or the NomGen construction: the stimulus can be encoded in the genitive, and indicate a matter of care or concern as do genitive stimuli with verbs of anger and envy surveyed in Section 8.1.1, or in the dative, construing the second participant as a potential beneficiary, profiting from the positive thoughts of the experiencer.

(422) *Aíanti   perideísantes   Akhaioì*
Ajax.DAT fear.PTCP.AOR.NOM.PL Achean.NOM.PL
'The Achaeans, fearing for Aiax.' (*Il.* 23.822)

(423) *oú   moi   ep'   ómmasi   nḗdumos   húpnos   hizánei,*
NEG 1SG.DAT upon eye.DAT.PL sweet.NOM sleep.NOM fall.PRS.3SG
allà mélei   pólemos kaì kḗde'   Akhaiôn
but trouble.PRS.3SG war.NOM and woe.NOM.PL Achean.GEN.PL

240 CHAPTER 8

> ainôs   gàr Danaôn   perideídia
> terribly for Danaans.GEN.PL fear.PRF.1SG
> 'Sweet sleep does not fall upon my eyes, but war and the woes of the
> Achaeans trouble me. I fear terribly for the Danaans.' (Il. 10.91–10.93)

(424) oú   ti   tóson   nékuos   perideídia   Patrókloio,
       NEG INDF.ACC so_much corpse.GEN fear.PRF.1SG Patroclos.GEN
       hós   ke   tákha Tróōn   koréei   kúnas   ēd'
       REL.NOM PTC soon Trojan.GEN.PL eat.FUT.3SG dog.ACC.PL and
       oiōnoús,   hósson emêi   kephalêi perideídia mḗ
       bird.ACC.PL as   POSS.1SG.DAT head.DAT fear.PRF.1SG NEG
       ti   pátheisi
       INDF.ACC suffer.SBJV.AOR.3SG
       'In no way do I fear so much for the corpse of Patroclos, which soon
       might be eaten by the dogs and the birds, as I fear for my own head
       that might suffer some evil.' (Il. 17.240–17.242)

In (422) the Achaeans are said to feel fear for Aiax. The latter participant is
encoded as a beneficiary in the dative (see Section 3.2.5). In (423), the stimulus
is again human, and refers to the Greeks, but is encoded by the genitive. As I
argued in Section 8.1.1, the genitive can indicate reason only with verbs of emotion, hence showing that it is part of a specific construction limited to these
specific verbs. The same examples also contain the verb *melō* 'trouble' with the
DatNom construction, see the discussion in Section 8.5. Finally, (424) contains
both the NomGen and the NomDat construction. Notably, the latter features
an inanimate stimulus, which, however, being a body part accompanied by a
possessive *emêi kephalêi* 'my head', can be taken as referring to the possessor,
hence as having human reference.

Empathy also means sharing sorrow with someone, or worrying about them.
This feeling is encoded by the verb *akheúomai*, most often (7 occurrences) with
the NomGen construction, while the NomDat construction is limited to three
occurrences.

(425) opsómenos   patér'   esthlón, hó   moi
       see.PTCP.FUT.MID.NOM father.ACC noble.ACC REL.NOM 1SG.DAT
       pukinôs   akákhētai
       exceedingly feel_sorry.AOR.MID.3SG
       '(I'll go) see my noble father, who is exceedingly worrying for me.'
       (Od. 23.360)

EMOTIONS

241

(426)   *tòn   mèn épeit' eíase   kaì*
DEM.ACC PTC then leave.AOR.3SG and
akhnúmenós   per hetaírou   keîsthai
feel_sorry.PTCP.PRS.M/P.NOM PTC comrade.GEN lie.INF.PRS.M/P
'He then left him lying (on the ground), though feeling sorry for his comrade'. (*Il.* 8.125–126)

(427)   *seîo   d'   Akhaioì   îson   Akhillêos   kephalêi*
2SG.GEN PTC Achaean.NOM.PL equally Achilles.GEN head.DAT
Pēlēïádao   akhnúmetha
son_of_Peleus.GEN feel_sorry.IMPF.M/P.1PL
'We Achaeans are in sorrow for your death, as we are for the head of Achilles son of Peleus.' (*Od.* 11.556–11.558)

The NomGen construction in (426) construes the stimulus as the matter of worry, in the same way as it does with verbs of care and affection and with source-like stimuli expressing reason with verbs of anger and envy. The NomDat construction in (425) construes the stimulus as a beneficiary, similar to verbs of helping and protecting, which, as I argued in Section 3.2.5, indicate events whose outcome is positive for the second participant. In (427) both constructions occur sharing the same verb.

8.5   Dative Experiencer Constructions

As I have anticipated in Section 3.2.7, a limited number of emotion verbs take dative experiencers and nominative stimuli. This construction is usually referred to as DatNom, as the experiencer is considered the most salient participant in the situation (see e.g. Dahl and Fedriani 2012; Dahl 2014c). In Section 3.2.7 I showed that this is indeed the case for the verb *handánō* 'please', at least when the stimulus is inanimate, as in example (111). More examples of this type are (428) and (429).

(428)   *all' ouk Atreḯdēi   Agamémnoni   héndane*
but NEG son_of_Atreus.DAT Agamemnon.DAT like.IMPF.3SG
thumôi
heart.DAT
'But Agamemnon, Atreus' son, didn't like (him) in his heart.' (*Il.* 1.24)

(429) *ou   gàr sphin   háde   mûthos   enì phresín*
        NEG PTC 3PL.DAT.PL like.AOR.3SG speech.NOM in heart.DAT.PL
        'They did not like the speech in their heart.' (*Od.* 24.465)

In (428) and (429), as in several other occurrences, a dative experiencer is accompanied by a locative expression, either in the plain dative or with *en*+dat indicating the body part, in this case the mind, targeted by the emotion. The mind or the heart are viewed as containers for emotions, with a frequent metaphor that also concerns all body parts in Homeric Greek (see Section 6.1 and Luraghi 2004b). Example (428) contains an imperfect, and construes the situation as ongoing, while the aorist in (429) profiles the inception of a state.

Similarly, *mélō* 'be of interest, be an object of care (for someone)' takes the DatNom construction. Especially with inanimate stimuli, the experiencer is clearly the more prominent participant, and must be considered the first argument in the argument structure constructions, as shown in example (430), in which the perfect *mémēlen* profiles a state as a permanent interest of the experiencer (another occurrence of *mélō* can be seen in example (423)).

(430) *tó   moi   oú ti   metà phresì   taûta*
        DEM.ACC 1SG.DAT NEG INDF.ACC in   heart.DAT.PL DEM.NOM
        mémēlen
        care.PRF.3SG
        'For this reason I don't care for this in my heart.' (*Il.* 19.213)

Besides *handánō* (and its compounds, cf. Dahl and Fedriani 2012) and *mélō*, verbs based on the root *ekhthrós* 'hated', 'hateful' also take the DatNom construction. Other verbs from the same root are *ékhtomai*, *apékhtomai* and *apekhthánomai* 'be(come) hateful (for someone)'; they have already been discussed in Section 8.3.2. Contrary to *handánō* and *mélō* that only have active forms, verbs that indicate hate are *media tantum*. While occurrences in the aorist point toward an inchoative nature of the event, especially with the two prefixed verbs, as in (431), the present and the imperfect indicate a state, as in (432) with the non-prefixed *ékhtomai*.

(431) *ei dé   toi   Atreḯdēs   mèn apékhtheto*
        if PTC 2SG.DAT son_of_Atreus.NOM PTC be_hateful.AOR.MID.3SG
        kēróthi mâllon ... sù   d'   állous   per Panakhaioùs ...
        too   big   2SG.NOM PTC other.ACC.PL PTC Achaean.ACC.PL
        eléaire
        take_pity.IMP.PRS.2SG

EMOTIONS

243

'But if your hate for Atreus' son is too big, have pity for all other Achaeans.' (*Il.* 9.300–302)

(432) *ê* *toi* *emoì* *khlaînai* *kaì* *rhḗgea*
indeed PTC 1SG.DAT cloak.NOM.PL and cloth.NOM.PL
sigalóenta *ḗkhtheth'*
colored.NOM.PL be_hateful.IMPF.M/P.3SG
'Indeed cloaks and bright clothes have become hateful for me (since I left Crete).' (*Od.* 19.337–338)

In (431), the dative experiencer *toi* 'you (dat)' is coreferential with the nominative *sú* 'you(nom)'. The Greeks are trying to convince Achilles to go back to fight and ask him not to forget all his other comrades in spite of his hate for Agamemnon. The latter functions as the stimulus, and, being human, is in principle also salient. However, Achilles stands out as the most prominent participant in the whole passage. The higher salience of the experiencer is even clearer in (432), which contains an inanimate stimulus, *khlaînai kaì rhḗgea sigalóenta* 'cloaks and brightly colored clothes'. Note that in spite of the subject being plural, the verb is inflected in the singular. This follows the tendency for neuter plurals (*rhḗgea sigalóenta*) to take singular agreement, which is typical of Attic Greek but is also, though less systematically, attested in Homer. The first coordinand of the complex subject is a feminine plural (*khlaînai* 'cloaks'), and conforms to the agreement pattern of the second coordinand.

In other cases, as I have argued in Section 3.2.7, the stimulus seems to have a more important status in discourse than the experiencer, as in (112) with *handánō* and in (113) with *mélō*. This also happens with *apekhthánomai*. Let us consider (433).

(433) *îson* *gár* *sphin* *pâsin*
alike.ACC PTC 3PL.DAT.PL everyone.DAT.PL
apḗkhtheto *kērì* *melaínēi*
be_hateful.AOR.MID.3SG death.DAT black.DAT
'As he was hateful to all of them as the black death.' (*Il.* 3.454)

The passage that precedes (433) describes Agamemnon looking for Paris, who had kidnapped his brother's wife Helen. The Trojans are scared: they do not know where Paris is, but at that time they would not have helped him hide, because he was exposing them to the dangers of war with the Greeks. The null subject of *apḗkhtheto* 'was hateful' here refers to Paris, who is indeed the most salient participant in the whole passage, and more individuated with respect to the experiencer *sphin pâsin* 'everyone' (compare further the Italian example in (55)).

Let us consider example (434), again with *handánō*.

(434) *énth' ế   toi   Menélaos   anốgei   pántas*
       then PTC PTC Menelaus.NOM urge.PRS.3SG all.ACC.PL
       Akhaioùs   nóstou   mimnếskesthai ...   ou   d'
       Achaean.ACC.PL return.GEN remember.INF.PRS.M/P NEG PTC
       Agamémnoni   pámpan heếndane
       Agamemnon.DAT totally   like.IMPF.3SG
       'Then Menelaus urged all the Achaeans to keep in mind their return,
       but Agamemnon was not pleased at all.' (*Od.* 3.141–143)

Similar to (112), in (434) both the experiencer and the stimulus are human. Menelaus is urging the Greeks to leave Troy immediately, but cannot convince Agamemnon, who does not want to follow his brother's advice. The NP *Menélaos* is the subject of *anógei* 'urge' in the first clause, and also governs the null subject of *handánō*. Menelaus is depicted as actively trying to push the Greeks and persuade Agamemnon: as in (112), we have to do with an agent-like stimulus in this case.

Note that, differently from (433) (but, again, similar to (112)), in (434) both the experiencer and the stimulus are highly individuated, salient participants, who are actively implicated in the situation. The pattern instantiated here is the NomDat construction of social interaction verbs: the first participant, the stimulus, tries intentionally to please the second participant, the experiencer, in order to prompt the participant's reaction.

Let us now turn again to *apekhthánomai*. As I have already remarked, this verb is *a medium tantum*, and never inflects in the active. One occurrence of the present tense shows some degree of lability, and takes a nominative experiencer. Let us consider (435).

(435) *oú   te   tí   moi   pâs   dêmos*
       NEG PTC INDF.ACC 1SG.DAT all.NOM people.NOM
       apekhthómenos   khalepaínei,   oú   te   kasignétois
       hate.PTCP.PRS.M/P.NOM threaten.PRS.3SG NEG PTC brother.DAT.PL
       epimémphomai
       blame.PRS.M/P.1SG
       'Neither do all people threaten me with their hate, nor do I blame
       brothers.' (*Od.* 16.114–115)

EMOTIONS   245

In the first sentence, the main verb is *khalepaínō* 'threaten'. This verb belongs to the group of social interaction verbs and accordingly takes the NomDat construction, with a dative second argument *moi* 'me'. The participle *apekhthómenos* here agrees with the subject *dêmos* 'the people' that clearly has the role of experiencer. Thus, it must be taken as meaning 'hating' and not 'being hateful': here the dative second argument of the governing verb is coreferential with the stimulus, which is also the second argument of *apekhthómenos* and is omitted under argument sharing (see Luraghi 2003b and Section 8.1.1).

8.6   Discussion

Verbs surveyed in this Chapter can be divided into semantically coherent groups connected to specific Nom-first constructions that feature nominative experiencers. In contrast, verbs with dative experiencers constitute a smaller and semantically incoherent group, including verbs of rejoicing (*handánō*), of caring (*mélō*) and of stimulus-oriented negative feelings (*ápekhthanomai*). (Notably, no verb denoting an experiencer-centered negative emotion such as fear takes the dative experiencer construction.) Semantic incoherence shows that the DatNom construction is a minor strategy, not well integrated into the patterns of argument structure constructions and construction variation of experiential predicates in Homeric Greek.

Verbs that take one of the Nom-first constructions belong to four groups, depending on the verb's semantics in combination with the specific semantics of the argument structure construction. Below I summarize their most important characteristics.

a)   Verbs denoting negative emotions targeted at a human stimulus. They take the NomDat construction and normally do not allow for construction alternation. In a limited number of cases, they can take the NomAcc construction that activates a different semantic interpretation of the resulting construction. The reason for the emotion can be indicated in a cause expression (a prepositional phrase or a causal clause), or it can be construed as a matter of concern for the experiencer. In such cases, a three-place construction sometimes occurs, the NomDatGen construction that results from a blend of the NomDat construction with the NomGen construction typical of verbs in group (c).

b)   Verbs of rejoicing. They take the NomDat construction. Stimuli are mostly inanimate; they can be concrete or abstract entities or states of affairs in which an animate stimulus is involved (Two-Place+P construction). These verbs generally do not allow for construction variation, except for *térpomai* that can take the NomGen construction. In the latter case, the meaning of the resulting construction focuses on the sense of satisfaction achieved by the experiencer, as do verbs of satiation in the NomGen construction.

c) Verbs of desiring, loving and caring. Stimuli are mostly human; inanimate entities may occur especially with verbs of desiring depending on the verbal meaning. These verbs take the NomGen construction, but some of them allow for construction variation with the NomAcc construction with no semantic difference. In addition, some verbs with a similar meaning always take the NomAcc construction. Verbs that indicate empathy can also be included in this group, as they mostly feature the NomGen construction, and construe the stimulus as a matter of concern (hence the feeling of empathy).

d) Verbs denoting experiencer-centered emotions. These verbs mostly indicate negative emotions, such as fear, terror, shame and grief, and take the NomAcc construction extended from verbs of visual perception through verbs of wonder. Situations referred to by these verbs are construed as involving a threat that raises the experiencer's attention. Stimuli may be animate or inanimate; occasionally they may be states of affairs involving an animate participant and be encoded through the Two-place+P construction. Construction variation is not allowed.

When comparing verbs of emotion with verbs in the other sub-domains of experience, the first peculiarity that needs to be highlighted is that these are the only verbs that can take the NomDat construction. This is in accordance with the social nature of emotions, which may imply the active involvement of more than one participant, and may depend on other people's judgment and on social evaluation. In particular, the NomDat construction indicates that two participants are potential actors in a certain situation: not only is it typical of verbs of social interaction, even with verbs of manipulation that take inanimate second arguments, but the second participant is an entity that has an instrumental nature and is involved in bringing about the situation.

Verbs that take the NomGen and the NomAcc construction can be compared to verbs in the other experiential domains. In particular, the NomGen construction with verbs of emotion has contacts both in the domain of cognition, with verbs of memory patterning in a way that is similar to verbs of care and affection, and in the domain of volition, in which the verb *mémōna* borders with verbs of desiring. With respect to perception verbs, verbs that indicate love, desire, care and affection cover the whole constructional range, with love intended as affection and friendship patterning with sight, while love intended

EMOTIONS

as sexual desire and mostly also construed as involving care and concern patterning with bodily sensations.

At the other extreme, visual perception is responsible for wonder. As wonder originates from the sight of something unexpected, it may result in awe and in fear: hence the extension of the NomAcc construction to other verbs of negative emotion. The fact that this construction is typical of highly transitive verbs that have an agent as first participant may at first sight look at odds with their extension to fearing verbs. In Chapter 6, I have argued that verbs of visual perception follow the pattern of high transitivity verbs on account of a higher degree of control afforded by sight with respect to other perceptual modalities. Note, however, that even with perception verbs control must not be understood as involving intentionality, as it does with change-of-state verbs. Rather, when mapped onto the domain of perception, control results in attention and awareness: this also accounts for the occurrence of the NomAcc construction in cognitive verbs that indicate the rise of awareness. Moreover, the connection of sight and wonder that, as I have argued in Section 8.3.1, is grounded in embodiment, provides a pathway for verbs with patient-like experiencers to also adopt this construction. In this case, control results in awareness of a potential threat facing the experiencer and capturing the experiencer's attention.

To conclude, situations construed by the three constructions with emotion verbs can be represented as in Figure 14, Figure 15 and Figure 16.

Gauging the role of voice in the field of emotion verbs is not an easy task. Verbs that take the NomDat construction with human target stimuli pattern in various ways: *kholóomai* consistently shows middle inflection, with four active occurrences expressing the causative meaning 'anger someone' (see Section 9.2), while *kotéō* occurs both in the active, as in (325), and in the middle voice, as in (324), with no appreciable semantic difference (voice is partly connected with the verbal aspect, as the aorist is always middle, while the present is almost always active, with a single exception in *Il.* 2.222). Moreover, another verb with a similar meaning, *(apo)skudmaínō*, occurs with the present stem once in the active and once in the middle voice, again without semantic differences (see examples (339) and (340)). In addition, two other verbs of anger, *khóomai* and *mēníō*, always occur in the middle and in the active voice respectively. One is then tempted to conclude that voice does not alter the semantics of verbs of anger, and that the meaningful alternation between middle *kholóomai* and active *kholóō* is likely to be secondary, as I argue in Section 9.2.

Verbs of rejoicing also show disparate patterns regarding voice. While *gēthéō* 'rejoice' is an *activum tantum*, *khaírō* 'rejoice' displays a largely tense-based voice distribution. Notably, in the case of the latter verb even Allan (2003: 209–210) admits that a semantic difference between the two voices is not detectable

NomDat

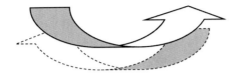

EXPERIENCER DEFIES STIMULUS - STIMULUS MAY REACT

FIGURE 14   Emotions in the NomDat construction with human stimuli

NomGen

STIMULUS TRIGGERS DESIRE IN EXPERIENCER - EXPERIENCER STRIVES TO GET HOLD OF STIMULUS

FIGURE 15   Emotions in the NomGen construction

NomAcc

STIMULUS THREATENS EXPERIENCER - EXPERIENCER IN STATE OF HIGH ATTENTION

FIGURE 16   Emotions in the NomAcc construction

(Allan does not discuss *gēthéō* in his work). On the other hand, *iaínomai* 'feel relaxed' and *térpomai* 'enjoy' are similar to *kholóomai*, in that they also have active counterparts with voice opposition encoding the (anti)causative alternation (Sections 9.2 and 9.3).

Verbs that indicate desire are mostly *media tantum*, with the exception of *pothéō* 'pine away', while verbs that indicate care and affection are partly *activa tantum*, such as *alégō, alegízō* 'care for', 'care about', 'take heed of', or *media tantum*, as *ólophuromai* 'take pity on someone'. The verb *kḗdomai*, 'care for' has meaningful voice opposition, and encodes the (anti)causative alternation, similar to *kholóomai* (Section 9.2). Finally, *philéō* 'feel affection for', 'love' offers a complex picture. As pointed out in Section 8.2.2, in some occurrences active and middle forms seem to have the same semantics, as shown in (377) and (378) (active), (381) and (383) (middle aorist). On the other hand, the middle future in (380) and the passive aorist in (382) have a passive meaning.

The verbs *thaumázō* and *thambéō*, both meaning 'wonder', are *activa tantum*, with only the single future occurrence of *thaumázō* in *Il.* 18.467 featuring the middle voice, with a tense-based distribution. Among verbs that denote experiencer-centered negative emotions, two verbs that mean 'feel ashamed', *aiskhúnomai* and *aidéomai*, show different patters: while the former also has active forms, and encodes the (anti)causative alternation through voice (see Section 9.2), the latter is a *medium tantum*. Fear verbs are mostly active: *deídō* 'fear', *tarbéō* 'be afraid', 'be torn apart by fear', and *stugéō* 'fear', 'hate' are *activa tantum*, and so is *ekhthaírō* 'hate', 'consider an enemy'. However *atúzomai* 'be terrified' is a *medium tantum* in Homer, with active forms appearing only in later epics and instantiating the (anti)causative alternation (see Sections 8.3.2 and 9.4). The fact that the causative verb *deidíssomai* 'frighten' is a *medium tantum* does not help to shed light on the semantics of voice alternation with this group of verbs.

CHAPTER 9

Causative Verbs

In this Chapter, I discuss verbs that take the NomAcc construction and feature experiencers encoded as direct objects in the accusative. More specifically, I focus on causative counterparts of non-causative verbs that have already been discussed in the preceding Chapters.

As a framework for the data treated in this Chapter, in Section 9.1 I return to the (anti)causative alternation as already briefly described in Sections 1.1 and 4.2. In the two Sections that follow, I discuss experiential verbs that encode the (anti)causative alternation through voice. Following Nichols et al (2004), I divide verbs into animate, that is, verbs that refer to events typically involving a human participant (Section 9.2), and inanimate (Section 9.3). Not surprisingly, animate verbs largely outnumber inanimate ones: after all, experiencers are necessarily animate. Still, there are also verbs whose experiential meaning is based on metonymy, but originally refer to events that involve inanimate participants. In Section 9.4 I try to assess the role of verbal voice in the linguistic encoding of the (anti)causative alternation in the experiential domain.

9.1   The (Anti)causative Alternation

In Sections 1.1 and 4.2, I have mentioned verbs that instantiate the (anti)causative alternation, that is, the possible two-fold encoding of events that can be construed as being spontaneous, or as being brought about by some external force. The alternation is typically instantiated by verb pairs. Based on a sample of 80 languages belonging to different language families, Nichols et al. (2004) observed that languages have preferred strategies for the encoding of the alternation that largely depend on morphological complexity. The authors point out that often one of the two verbs in a pair is morphologically derived from the other, which is then to be viewed as morphologically basic. In such cases, languages may rely on transitivizing strategies if the basic verb refers to a spontaneous event and is typically intransitive while its transitive counterpart is a derivate. On the other hand, if the basic verb refers to the induced event and is transitive while the intransitive verb is derived, we find a detransitivizing strategy. The different patterns are exemplified in Table 13.

© SILVIA LURAGHI, 2021 | DOI:10.1163/9789004442528_010

CAUSATIVE VERBS   251

TABLE 13   Plain-induced verb pairs in Nanai and in Russian

Plain:	'learn'	'fear'	'hide' (go into hiding)
Induced:	'teach'	'frighten, scare'	'hide' (put into hiding)
Nanai	*otoli-*	*mian-*	*siri-*
	otoli-wa:n-	*mian-bo-*	*djaja-*
Russian	*učit'-sja*	*bojat'-sja*	*prjatat'-sja*
	učit'	*pugat'*	*prjatat'*

ADAPTED FROM NICHOLS ET AL. 2004: 151

Among experiential verbs with which the alternation is morphologically encoded, the most frequent strategy in Homeric Greek is constituted by voice alternation, as anticipated in Section 4.2, with the notable exception of *deidíssomai* 'frighten', a derivate from *deídō* 'fear' illustrated below. Verbs that indicate spontaneous events have been reviewed in the preceding Chapters of the book. Here, I discuss the types of construction of their causative counterparts, and explore the semantics of voice and derivation.

With causative verbs, the subject, hence the inducer, is most often the stimulus, as with *(apo)deidíssomai* 'frighten' in (436) and (437), but in a limited number of cases we find three-place constructions, in which an agent is also added, as in (438) with the NomAccGen construction. More examples of both verbs have also been given in Section 1 (see (15) and (17)).

(436) *Pēleídē   mè dè epéessí   me   nēpútion hòs*
       son_of_Peleus.VOC NEG PTC word.DAT.PL 1SG.ACC child.ACC as
       élpeo   deidíxesthai
       hope.IMP.PRS.M/P.2SG frighten.INF.FUT.MID
       'Son of Peleus, don't hope to frighten me with words as if I were a child!'
       (*Il.* 20.200–201)

(437) *oudé hoi   híppoi   tólmōn ...*
       NEG 3SG.DAT horse.NOM.PL dare.IMPF.3PL
       ephestaótes   apò gàr deidísseto   táphros
       standing.PTCP.PRF.NOM.PL PREV PTC frighten.IMPF.3SG ditch.NOM
       eureî'
       wide.NOM
       'But his horses did not dare (jumping): they stood still as the wide trench scared them.' (*Il.* 12.50–54)

252   CHAPTER 9

In example (436) the verb *deidíssomai* in the aorist imperative takes the second argument *me* 'me(acc)': Priamus is addressing Achilles and warns him that he will not be able to frighten him with his words as if he (Priamus) were a child. The aorist adds an inceptive meaning to the verb, similar to the occurrence in (17) already discussed in Section 1. However, the verb does not necessarily refer to inchoative situations, as shown in (437) in which we find the prefixed verb *apodeidíssomai* 'scare off'. In this passage, the horses are described as not daring to jump across the ditch: rather, they are standing on its brink, frightened by its width, and the situation is stative, as shown by the occurrence of the imperfect, based on the imperfective stem of the present.

Example (438) contains the verb *mimnḗskō* 'remind', the active counterpart of *mimnḗskomai* 'remember'. Another such occurrence is (15), also discussed in Section 1.

(438) *tôn*   *s'*   *aûtis mnḗsō*   *hín'*
       DEM.GEN.PL 2SG.ACC again remind.FUT.1SG for
       apolléxeis   *apatáōn*
       leave.SBJV.AOR.2SG deception.GEN.PL
       'I will remind you again of all this, so you will give up your deceptions.'
       (*Il.* 15.31)

In (438) the first person subject indicated by the verbal inflection is the agent who will cause the addressee, here referred to by the second person pronoun *se* 'you(acc)', to remember the issues under discussion. The latter are referred to by the genitive plural demonstrative *tôn* 'these (things)'.

While, as remarked above, *deidíssomai* is a derivate of *deídō* 'fear', formed with the suffix *-iss-* (Chantraine 1977: 255), *mimnḗskō* is the active counterpart of *mimnḗskomai*. Voice alternation with the latter verb and other similar verbs raises the question whether it is the active or the middle that is morphologically basic. In fact, in the preceding Chapters, when mentioning active counterparts of middle (or passive aorist) experiential verbs I have assumed the middle to precede the active chronologically. This assumption needs to be supported by more evidence, as it is commonly thought that the active voice is basic with respect to the middle (see Allan 2003). Instead, as I will show in the course of this Section, basicness cannot be assumed for either voice once and for all for all verbs.

It must further be highlighted that while most verbs discussed in this Section share common characteristics to indicate the (anti)causative alternation through voice opposition, this function of voice alternation in Homeric Greek, though frequent, is by no means consistently displayed by all verbs indicating

CAUSATIVE VERBS

events that can be potentially conceived as spontaneous or induced. For example, as argued in Section 6.5, voice alternation does not seem to bring about any significant semantic differences with perception verbs. More significantly, voice alternation is tense-based with some emotion verbs that have similar meaning to verbs with which voice indicates the (anti)causative alternation, for example with *kotéō* 'be(come) angry' as opposed to *kholóomai* (same meaning; see Sections 8.1.1 and 8.6). This shows that verbs featuring both voices do not necessarily encode the (anti)causative alternation through voice, in spite of their semantics.

Some more words need to be spent concerning the meaning of 'basic' form. Following Nichols et al. (2004), basic verb forms are morphologically lighter and less complex than derived ones, which display extra marking. As noted above, most often it is assumed that the active voice is basic: such is considered the voice system of the only Indo-European language with an active/middle morphological opposition in Nichols et al (2004) sample, Modern Greek. But was this really the original situation in Homeric Greek? Concerning morphological complexity, this is hard to gauge. In Luraghi (2019) I have suggested that the middle is indeed morphologically more complex than the active in Homeric Greek, and that one hint to this is the extension of the nasal ending to the first person singular of the present indicative, middle *-mai* based on the active ending *-mi* (the inherited form based on Indo-European comparative data should be *-ai*, see Willi 2018: 549–550; for this origin of the middle ending see Cotticelli-Kurras & Rizza 2015). Remarkably, however, the middle voice diachronically precedes the active for some verbs, whereas for others it does not.

As I have already noted in the preceding Sections, handbooks and dictionaries consider active morphology to be an innovation with some verbs, as for example in the case of *kholóomai* 'get angry at' and *élpomai* 'hope' (see Section 4.2), as reflected in the frequency of either voice. In the next two Sections, I will argue that the verbal meaning, along with the frequency of either voice, the morphological structure of verbs and partly their etymology can shed light on the origin of voice opposition. Crucially, as I will show, this must be gauged for each verb separately.

9.2   Animate Verbs

Animate verbs in this Section belong to different experiential domains: will (*élpomai* 'hope'), bodily sensations (*korénnamai* 'satiate oneself'), cognition (*mimnéskomai* 'remember' and *lanthánomai* 'forget'), and especially emotion (*kholóomai* 'get angry', *kḗdomai* 'worry', *térpomai* 'enjoy', *aiskhúnomai* 'feel shame' in addition to *deídō* 'fear' which does not show voice alternation but has a causative derivate).

In Table 14 I show the token frequency of middle and active forms of verbs discussed in this Section (*deídō/deidíssomai* is not included as it does not encode the (anti)causative alternation through voice).

TABLE 14   Token frequency of active *vs.* middle forms

	Active		Middle	
mimnḗskō/mimnḗskomai	6		103	1 passive aorist
élpō/élpomai	2	12 perfect	49	
kholóō/kholóomai	4		58	11 passive aorist
kḗdō/kḗdomai	11		39	
aiskhúnō/aiskhúnomai	8		4	
térpō/térpomai	9		68	20 passive aorist
korénnumi/korénnamai	4	1 perfect	4	12 passive aorist
lanthánō/lanthánomai	95		36	

Let us start by analyzing active occurrences of verbs whose middle forms largely outnumber the active ones: along with *mimnḗskō* 'remind' already mentioned in (15) and (438), *élpō* 'cause to hope' (439), *térpō* 'make happy' (440), and *kholóō* 'anger somebody' (441) (see also (131)).

(439) *pántas   mén rh' élpei   kaì hupískhetai*
      all.ACC.PL PTC PTC let_hope.PRS.3SG and promise.PRS.M/P.3SG
      andrì   hekástōi
      man.DAT each.DAT
      'She induces all to hope, and has promises for each man.' (*Od.* 2.91 = 13.380)

(440) *Pátroklos ...   enì klisíēi   agapḗnoros Eurupúloio*
      Patroclus.NOM in hut.DAT kind.GEN   Eurupolus.GEN
      hêstó   te kaì tòn   éterpe   lógois
      sit.PPF.M/P.3SG PTC and DEM.ACC gladden.IMPF.3SG word.DAT.PL
      'Patroclus ... sat in the hut of kind Eurupolus, cheering him with his words.' (*Il.* 15.390–393)

CAUSATIVE VERBS

(441) deûr' áge   peirḗthétō,   epeí m'
       here lead.IMP.PRS.2.SG attempt.IMP.AOR.PASS.3SG as   1SG.ACC
       ekholṓsate   líēn
       make_angry.AOR.2PL very
       'Let him come hither and make trial, because you made me greatly
       angered.' (*Od.* 8.205)

The active forms in examples (439)-(441) all have a clear causative meaning
with respect to the corresponding non-active forms, including medio-passive
and aorist middle or passive forms, see examples (163)-(166) for *élpomai* 'hope',
(352)-(353) for *térpomai* 'enjoy', (132), (326) and (327) for *kolóomai* 'get/be angry'.
In addition, for most verbs such active forms are quite limited in number, as
shown in Table 14.

The verb *élpomai/élpō* provides a clear-cut example. As I have already remarked in Section 5.2, active forms of this verb only occur twice, in the two
identical passages from the *Odyssey* in example (439), based on the present
stem. The meaning is causative 'let hope', 'induce hope': in the passage in (439),
Antinous is speaking about Penelope, and blaming her for deceiving him and
the other suitors. In addition, the perfect *éolpa* is morphologically active, but
has the same meaning as the middle forms from the present stems (this verb
does not have an aorist stem). This fact is in accordance with the relatively
recent nature of the middle perfect (see Chapter 4): the perfect was originally
intransitive, and several Greek *media tantum* feature morphologically active
perfect forms that do not show a voice difference with respect to the middle forms of other aspectual stems (see further Willi 2018: 219–244). Hence,
as Chaintraine (1977) argues, the active-causative form in example (439) must
be considered late formations created from an original *medium tantum* on the
pattern of other verbs with which voice encoded the (anti)causative alternation.

The verb *kholóō/kholóomai* is based on the noun *khólos* 'wrath', 'hate', 'anger'.
From this noun, the verbal noun *kholōtós* 'wrathful' was created, which in turn
provided the basis for the passive and then the middle aorist that had a similar,
but inchoative meaning, as shown in (132). Notably, both passive and middle
aorists are mainly represented by participles: 7 out of 11 passive and 14 out of 22
middle forms. Besides the aorist, the middle perfect occurs 34 times in Homer,
and conveys a resultative meaning. The middle forms based on the present
stem are later: indeed, in Homer there is a single occurrence of a middle present
(*Il.* 8.421), on which the active causative forms are also based (Chantraine 1977:
1268, Beekes and Beek 2010: 1642). Occurrences of active forms are *Il.* 1.78 in
the future tense and three sigmatic aorists in *Il.* 18.111 (example (131)), *Od.* 8.205

(example (441)), and *Od.* 18.20. Note that the middle aorist forms are also sigmatic, so the active aorist could also be based on the middle aorist.

The verb *térpō/térpomai* 'please'/'enjoy' also shows a similar distribution, with middle forms largely outnumbering active ones. To these, a future middle form must be added, which, however, has causative meaning as the active forms, see example (442).

(442) *énth' horóōn*   *phréna*   *térpsomai*
        there see.PTCP.PRS.NOM heart.ACC enjoy.FUT.1SG
        'Looking from there I will make my heart glad.' (*Il.* 20.23)

This apparently odd situation must be considered in the framework of the recent character of future forms, and of their tendency to often feature only middle forms that are not semantically motivated (Chantraine 2013: 426–429).

It is also remarkable that the construction of causative *térpō* 'please' is NomAccDat as shown in (440): in other words active forms are the counterpart of middle *térpomai* 'rejoice' with the NomDat construction. However, this verb can also take the NomGen construction with the meaning 'satiate' (see Section 5.1 example (138)). The Sanskrit cognate, based on the root *tṛp-*, features the fourth and fifth class presents *tṛpyati, tṛpṇoti*. It shows active morphology but the same meaning of the Greek middle 'satiate oneself', 'rejoice' with the experiencer encoded as nominative subject, and takes both the NomGen and the NomInstr construction, the latter corresponding to Greek NomDat (see Section 3.2.5). It also has a causative counterpart with a first class present *tarpati* 'please', 'satisfy' which has been shown to be a later formation (Narten 1968). All these considerations point toward a later nature of the Greek active forms with respect to the middle.

Similar considerations can be made for *mimnéskō*, which occurs six times as active and takes the NomAccGen construction (*Il.* 15.31 quoted in example (17) and *Il.* 1.407, *Il.* 15.18, *Od.* 3.103, *Od.* 14.169, *Od.* 12.38), while the occurrences of the middle *mimnéskomai* are 103, to which one passive aorist must be added. Of course, frequency alone is not enough to support the primacy of the middle verb over its active counterpart. However, some more attention must be paid to the morphology of the verbal stem, as the present stem shows a suffix *-sk-* that indicates its relatively late formation. According to Chantraine (1977: 702–703) the oldest form was the medio-passive perfect *memnḗmai* that has a resultative meaning and has a parallel in Latin *memini* 'I remember' with present meaning but perfect form, also a *medium tantum*.

The case of *kḗdō* 'distress' is slightly different. Its middle *kḗdomai* means 'care for', examples are (374), (378), (379) and (377) with the prefixed variant *perikḗ-*

domai, in which the prefix adds an intensive meaning. It also has a negative form, *akédomai* 'not care for, neglect' shown in (323). Even though this verb, much in the same way as those discussed thus far, shows a higher frequency of the middle voice, active occurrences are comparatively numerous and, most important, they occur in a variety of different contexts. As shown in example (443), their meaning is not always exactly the causative counterpart of the meaning of the middle forms.

(443) *hòs   tóxoisin   ékēde   theoùs   hoì*
REL.NOM arrow.DAT.PL distress.IMPF.3SG god.ACC.PL REL.NOM.PL
Ólumpon   ékhousi
Olympus.ACC hold.PRS.3PL
'Who with his arrows distressed the gods who hold Olympus.' (*Il.* 5. 404)

(444) *kalón   toi sùn emoì   tòn   kédein   hós*
good.ACC PTC with 1SG.DAT DEM.ACC distress.PRS.INF REL.NOM
k'   emè   kédēi
PTC 1SG.ACC distress.SBJV.PRS.3SG
'It would be good that you trouble with me whoever troubles me.' (*Il.* 9.615)

Quantitative analysis indicates a difference in the significance of voice distribution between this and other verbs discussed thus far. A chi-square test shows that while the differences in token frequency of active and middle forms between *mimnéskō/mimnéskomai* and the other verbs are not significant, the difference between *mimnéskō/mimnéskomai* and *kédō/kédomai* is significant. The results of the chi-square statistic with Yates correction at $p < .05$ shows a p-value of .968953 for *élpō/élpomai*, of .932075 for *kholóō/kholóomai*, and of .427716 for *térpō/térpomai*. On the other hand, the result for *kédō/kédomai* shows a p-value of .004387, thus significant at $p < .05$. Note that etymologically *kédō* is connected with English *hate*, and there is no reason to reconstruct a *medium tantum* in PIE. Hence, positing a *medium tantum* that later developed into an oppositional middle in this case seems unwarranted.

The distribution of voice with *korénnumi/korénnamai* leads to similar considerations concerning the original structure of its voice system. Middle and passive aorist forms of this verb, illustrated in Section 5.1 examples (136) and (137), mean 'satiate oneself', while active forms mean 'satiate someone, feed' as in (445) and (446).

(445)   *polloùs   àn koréseien   anèr   hóde*
         many.ACC.PL PTC satiate.OPT.AOR.3SG man.NOM DEM.NOM
         'This man would satiate many.' (*Il.* 16.747)

(446)   *atàr Tróōn   koréeis   kúnas   ēd' oiōnoùs*
         but Trojan.GEN.PL satiate.FUT.2SG dog.ACC.PL and bird.ACC.PL
         dēmôi kaì sárkessi
         fat.DAT and flesh.DAT.PL
         'You will satiate the dogs and the birds of the Trojans with your fat and
         your flesh.' (*Il.* 13.831–832)

Example (445) contains the only active aorist; its meaning is 'satiate some-one' and it constitutes the causative of the middle voice occurrences discussed in Section 5.1. In (446) and in another similar occurrence (*Il.* 8.379–380), the active future features the NomAccDat construction that does not fully reflect the construction appearing with the middle voice, which features the NomGen construction. Remarkably, the noun referring to the food here does not play the role of a stimulus, but rather of an instrument: accordingly, the third argument is in the dative. The verb does not belong into the field of experience, as in this and in other occurrences with the active future it does indicate a bodily sensa-tion and does not mean 'satiate someone', 'let someone feel sated', but 'feed an animal with something'. When indicating a bodily sensation, the noun refer-ring to the food is a stimulus and it is encoded in the genitive as in (136) and (137). A fifth occurrence of an active form is a perfect, which, in the same way as I have argued for *élpomai*, has the same semantics of middle voice and features a genitive stimulus, see example (447).

(447)   *ámphō   kekorēóte   poíēs*
         both.NOM.DU satiate.PTCP.PRF.NOM.DU grass.GEN
         'Both (oxen) well fed with grass.' (*Od.* 18.372)

Even though, as Chantraine (1977: 565–566) points out, the oldest forms of this verb are constituted by the aorist, it is the future that seems to preserve the orig-inal meaning of the root 'feed (animals)', which is attested by cognates in other languages (notably Lithuanian). Possibly, in Greek the verb specialized in the meaning 'satiate', moved to the domain of bodily sensations, and for this rea-son middle and passive forms are more frequent than active ones, which mostly instantiated a meaning that had become obsolete but might well be older.

    A verb that was likely not an original *medium tantum* is *aiskhúnō* 'marr', 'make ugly', 'dishonor' as in (448)-(450).

CAUSATIVE VERBS

259

(448) *kónin ... kheúato   kàk kephalês, kharíen   d'*
       sand.ACC pour.AOR.MID.3SG over head.GEN graceful.ACC PTC
       éiskhune   prósōpon
       marr.AOR.3SG face.ACC
       'He poured sand over his head, and marred his fair face'. (*Il.* 18.23–24)

(449) *mēdè génos   patérōn   aiskhunémen*
       NEG race.ACC father.GEN.PL marr.INF.PRS
       'Not to dishonor the race of my fathers.' (*Il.* 6.209)

(450) *Tēlémakh'   hupsagórē ... poîon   éeipes   hēméas*
       Telemachus.VOC braggart.VOC INT.ACC say.AOR.2SG 1PL.ACC
       aiskhúnōn
       marr.PTCP.PRS.NOM
       'Telemachus, braggart, what did you say to bring dishonor upon us.'
       (*Od.* 2.85–86)

The verb *aiskhúnō* is a denominal derivate from *aîkhos* 'ugliness', 'shame'. Active
occurrences are equally divided between the meaning 'make ugly' and the
meaning 'dishonor', but note that even when the second argument refers to
a human participant, this does not take the role of an experiencer. The active
verb does not belong into the experiential domain, but rather refers to an objective situation that can have social consequences. This is certainly in accordance
with the construction of shame as connected with honor that I discussed in
Section 8.3.2, but it also shows that the extent to which the active can be considered the causative counterpart of the middle is limited.

An even clearer difference between the semantics of either voice surfaces
with *lanthánō* 'escape', shown in (451) and (452).

(451) *all' ou   lêthe   Diòs   pukinòn   nóon*
       but NEG escape.AOR.3SG Zeus.GEN wise.ACC mind.ACC
       'But he did not escape the wise mind of Zeus.' (*Il.* 15. 461)

(452) *all' ou   lêth'   Adámanta   tituskómenos*
       but NEG escape.AOR.3SG Adamas.ACC aim.PTCP.PRS.M/P.NOM
       kath' hómilon
       PTC throng.ACC
       'But as he was aiming amid the throng he did not escape Adamas.' (*Il.*
       13.560)

260   CHAPTER 9

The pair *lanthánō/lanthánomai* is semantically different from other verbs discussed here: indeed, the active does not normally encode the causative counterpart of *lanthánomai*, as it means 'make forget' in a single occurrence only, in (453). Its distribution relative to voice is also at odds with the other verbs, as active forms largely outnumber middle ones.

(453) *Héktora   d'   otrúnēisi   mákhēn   es Phoîbos*
       Hecotr.ACC PTC rouse.SBJV.AOR.3SG battle.ACC to Phoebus.NOM
       Apóllōn, ...   leláthēi   d'   odunáōn
       Apollo.NOM miss.SBJV.AOR.3SG PTC pain.GEN.PL
       'Let Phoebus Apollo rouse Hector to the fight, and make him forget the pains.' (*Il.* 15.59–60)

In (453), the active form *leláthēi* has a causative meaning, and features a NomAccGen construction, similar to the form *mnésō* from *mimnéskō* in (438) (note that in (453) only the genitive stimulus, *odunáōn* 'pain' overtly realized, as both the subject *Phoîbos Apóllōn* and the accusative direct object *Héktora* are shared with the preceding sentence). As the data points toward a different semantics for the active and the middle, it is tempting to take the single occurrence of the causative meaning in (453) as an innovation based on the extension of the pattern shown by *mimnéskō/mimnéskomai*. In other occurrences, the semantic difference between the two voices in not so straightforward.

Summing up, one cannot generalize as to the direction of extension of voice opposition, even though it seems reasonable to maintain that with several verb pairs active forms represent a recent development from original *media tantum*. This conclusion is indirectly supported by the state of affairs shown by the pair *deídō/deidíssomai* 'fear/frighten'. Here we have a morphologically derived verb featuring a suffix, hence the direction of derivation is clear: the basic verb is *deídō* 'fear', which indicates a spontaneous event, while the derived verb is causative *deidíssomai* 'frighten'.

Frequency also indicates that fear is most often conceptualized as rising spontaneously in the experiencer when facing the stimulus: not only does the basic verb *deídō* largely outnumber *deidíssomai* (105/8), even the metaphorical inchoative expression *déos haírei* 'fear seizes (someone)' is more frequent as it occurs 11 times (see Section 2.3) and never features any participant who can induce the emotion. If we limit our observations to verbs featuring voice opposition, one might hold that the high frequency of middle forms reflects the tendency to construe such events as spontaneous, but the fact that the same behavior is also shown by the pair *deídō/deidíssomai*, in which there is no doubt

CAUSATIVE VERBS   261

as to which form is basic and which is derived, supports the assumption that the active was indeed an innovation with some of them. Remarkably, *deidísso-mai* is not only morphologically more complex than *deídō*, it also constitutes a later formation. Hence, the innovative character of the active voice with some verbs might cast some doubts on its morphological basicness.

Assuming the recent character of the active forms with most of the verb pairs discussed above implies that voice opposition must also be viewed as a recent development. In fact, even the case of *lanthánō*, whose active occurrences largely outnumber the middle ones and are certainly ancient, the semantic extension of voice opposition to the encoding of the (anti)causative alternation seems an innovation, as in the vast majority of cases the active is not the causative counterpart of the middle. Again, support for this conclusion comes from *deídō/deidíssomai*. In this case, the spontaneous event is indicated by *deídō*, an *activum tantum*, while the causative verb *deidíssomai* is a *medium tantum*, showing that voice opposition *per se* is not connected with the (anti)causative derivation. Lack of connection is also indicated by several other experiential verbs, which may be *media* or *activa tantum* though exhibiting similar semantics, such as verbs of volition (Section 5.2), or may feature both voices without any relevant difference, such as verbs of sight (Section 6.1).

9.3   Inanimate Verbs

Verbs whose original meaning, at least in the active, indicates a state of affairs typically involving an inanimate participant are *iaínō/iaínomai* 'warm up' and *barúnō/barúnomai* 'make/grow heavy'.

The verb *iaínomai* 'feel relaxed' has been treated in Section 8.1.2 among verbs of rejoicing. The active counterpart *iaínō* is not basically an experiential verb: its meaning is 'warm up, stir up' and indicates a physical process. The middle voice denotes a positive emotion of relaxation based on a metonymic effect by which a sensation of warmth denotes wellbeing.

Let us see the distribution of the two voices. The verb occurs 20 times in the Homeric poems, 14 times in the middle and 6 in the active. While these figures seem to imply that the middle outnumbers the active by slightly more than 50%, if one considers the actual occurrences things look different. Indeed, five out of six occurrences of the active feature the direct object *thumón* 'heart'; of these four occurrences from the same book of the *Iliad* contain the formula *tá ke thumòn iénēi* 'these things comfort the heart' (*Il.* 24.119, 147, 176, 196), and only the fifth from the *Odyssey* shows a different construction, see example (454).

(454) hoîá   te   thumòn   aeì   dmóessin   iaínei
      such.NOM.PL PTC heart.ACC ever servant.DAT.PL warm_up.PRS.3SG
      'Such things always make the heart of a servant relax/grow warm.' (*Od.*
      15.379)

The concrete meaning is attested in one occurrence, also from the *Odyssey*,
with the subject *khalkós* 'iron'.

Occurrences of the middle voice and of the passive aorist, however, show a
wider variety of participants. In the first place, there are three occurrences of
concrete nouns as subjects: *kērós* 'wax', *húdōr* 'water', and *métōpon* 'forehead'
(Latacz 1966: 221 wrongly also lists *eérsē* as a possible subject with the concrete
meaning, or in his words "physicalischer Bereich", of this verb, while he keeps
métōpon separate, such as the single entry in the "physischer Bereich", as the
passage refers to the bodily process of relaxing one's forehead). Metonymical
occurrences indicating an emotion frequently feature *thumós* 'heart' (7 occurrences) or *kêr* 'heart' (3 occurrences) as in (346) and (455) as subject, but they
do not always occur in the same formula and are more evenly distributed over
the two poems.

(455) khalkón   te   khrusón   t'   apodōsomen, eis hó   ke
      bronze.ACC   PTC gold.ACC   PTC pay.FUT.1PL in DEM.NOM PTC
      sòn   kêr   ianthêi
      POSS.2SG.NOM heart.NOM heat.SBJV.AOR.PASS.3SG
      'We will pay you back in bronze and gold until your heart has warmed
      up.' (*Od.* 22.58–59)

In two cases the subject is a first or second person singular. Hence, the middle and the passive aorist seem to reflect a more lively usage than the active,
whose six occurrences should actually be counted as three, but might preserve
an older meaning and possibly an older form.

The verb *barúnō* means 'grow heavy', 'make heavy'. It occurs three times in
the active as in (456), once in the middle in (457), and twice in the passive aorist,
as in (458).

(456) bárune   dé   min   dóru   makròn
      grow_heavy.IMPF.3SG PTC 3SG.ACC spear.NOM long.NOM
      'The long spear burdened him.' (*Il.* 5.664)

CAUSATIVE VERBS

(457) allá te láthrēi guîa   barúnetai,   ēdè
but PTC secretly knee.NOM.PL grow_heavy.PRS.M/P.3SG and
kikhánei   dípsá   te kaì limós
meet.PRS.3SG thirst.NOM PTC and hunger.NOM
'But imperceptibly his knees grow heavy, and thirst and hunger come
upon him.' (Il. 19.165–166)

(458) hò   dé min   méne   kheîra
DEM.NOM PTC 3SG.ACC abide.IMPF.3SG hand.ACC
baruntheís,   prósth' horóōn
grow_heavy.PTCP.AOR.PASS.NOM before see.PTCP.PRS.NOM
thánaton
death.ACC
'He awaited him burdened by his hand, seeing death before him.' (Il.
20.480–481)

As shown in the examples, the verb always refers to a bodily sensation: indeed,
even when it features inanimate subjects with middle or passive forms, they
are always body parts, such as the knees in (457). Similarly, with active forms
the direct object-causee is always human. Hence, in Homeric Greek the verb
barúnō, which is a denominal derivate from barús 'heavy', 'grievous', does not
show any concrete meaning connected with some inanimate entity unrelated
to the human body, but always only indicates a bodily sensation.

9.4   Discussion

From the data reviewed in this Section, it is reasonable to conclude that the
extent to which the (anti)causative alternation was indicated by voice opposition in Ancient Greek was on the rise in Homer. Based on careful scrutiny of the
individual verbs, the original situation of the voice system appears quite heterogeneous. Among animate verbs, mimnḗskomai 'remember', kholóomai 'get
angry' térpomai 'enjoy' and élpomai 'hope' must be taken as original media tantum, with which the active voice was a recent development that had precisely
the function of encoding the (anti)causative alternation.

That this was an ongoing development in Greek is proven by similar post-
Homeric developments of other verbs. In particular, atúzomai 'fear' (Section
8.3.2) shows some active forms in later epics with the meaning 'frighten'. Similarly, ékhtomai 'be hateful' (Section 8.5) occurs in Classical Greek as ékhtō 'hate'.
Interestingly, in the case of the latter verb the semantics of voice opposition is

different from the semantics of other verbs mentioned thus far. Indeed, voice does not encode the (anti)causative alternation: this is because *ékhtomai* 'be hateful' shows a different type of alignment with respect to other verbs, as it takes a dative experiencer. The active counterpart, mainly attested in poetry, takes the NomAcc construction. Hence, voice opposition translates into an active/passive opposition with this verb.

With some other verbs, such as *kédomai* 'worry' and *korénnamai* 'satiate oneself', there seem to be no compelling reasons for assuming original *media tantum*, while in the case of *lanthánomai* 'forget' the evidence supports assuming the active as original voice. Notably, the semantics of voice opposition with these verbs does not always conform to the (anti)causative alternation: this is especially clear in the case of *lanthánō/ lanthánomai*, as the middle voice only occasionally seems to function as anticausative with respect to the active. On the other hand, the middle voice shows a lower degree of transitivity as indicated by the fact that it takes the NomGen construction, as opposed to the NomAcc construction taken by the active.

Inanimate verbs *iaínomai* 'warm up' and *barúnomai* 'grow heavy' have developed metaphorical meanings that connect them to the experiential domain: they denote bodily sensations typical of animate subjects. I have considered them inanimate (i.e. showing a preference for inanimate subjects) on account of their non-metaphorical meaning. Notably, however, a non-metaphorical meaning is attested only for *iaínō* 'warm up (tr.)' and only for active forms: this might point toward a primacy of the active voice for this verb, while for *barúnō/ barúnomai* things are less clear, as both voices only refer to a bodily sensation of heaviness.

If we now consider the distribution of voice with other verbs not discussed in this Section, it becomes clear that a general assessment of the role of voice opposition that can hold for all verbs displaying it is impossible. Recall that several experiential verbs have both active and middle forms that do not display any significant semantic difference. A case in point is *horáō* 'see', discussed in Sections 6.1 and 6.5. This verb features a sizable number of middle forms, but even in-depth studies devoted to the semantics of voice opposition have not been able to come up with any compelling explanation of the possible difference between the two voices. This also holds for *akoúō* 'hear', the only difference being that this verb only features a very limited number of middle forms (Sections 6.2 and 6.5).

Another interesting case is constituted by the verb *phrázō/phrázomai*, which, as remarked in Section 7.1.2, seems to have two quite different meanings in the active and in the middle: while active forms mean 'show', 'explain', middle forms indicate a planned mental activity 'ponder', 'plan', or a more spontaneous one 'realize'. Interestingly, both middle and active forms take the NomAcc construction, thus apparently showing the same degree of transitivity.

Among emotion verbs, both *media* and *activa tantum* are numerous, and even a verb that shows some clear cases in which voice has a transitivizing/detransitivizing effect such as *philéō* 'love', also features a number of occurrences in which middle forms seem to have the same semantics as active ones (see Section 8.2.2 and 10.5).

In this seemingly puzzling situation, verbs with which voice opposition encodes the (anti)causative alternation stand out as a coherent group, showing a consistent semantic difference between the two voices (usually extending to the passive aorist, which in this framework functions as the middle). This function of voice opposition is productive, as shown by the fact that Homeric Greek offers evidence for some verbs to have acquired it recently, while more verbs to developed it at later language stages.

CHAPTER 10

Concluding Remarks

We have now come to the end of our journey through the domain of experience in Homeric Greek. Construction alternation, which has long resisted a coherent explanation when tackled in reference to individual verbs, has emerged as a meaningful way to construe situations as involving varying degrees of control, awareness and attention by the experiencer. In this final Chapter, I summarize the findings and round up my argument concerning construction variation and the construal of situations. I start by outlining the semantics of construction variation with experiential verbs in Section 10.1. In Section 10.2, I highlight the crucial role of embodiment in accounting for the meaning and the distribution of constructions, while in the sub-domain of emotions the social dimension of events is also at play. Section 10.3 contains a short overview of the constructions discussed in the book, in addition to the three Nom-first constructions, and Section 10.4 addresses the issue of construction productivity, providing evidence that shows how the three Nom-first constructions are all productive, though to different extents. In Section 10.5 I address once more the issue of verbal voice with experiential verbs. Finally, in Section 10.6, I briefly discuss some open issues and indicate directions for future research.

10.1 The Meaning of Construction Variation with Experiential Verbs

The main purpose of this book was to assess the semantics of construction variation with experiential verbs in Homeric Greek, especially with regard to variation among the three Nom-first constructions, NomAcc, NomGen and NomDat. Discussing the data, I have shown that a construction based approach can shed light on semantic aspects of the three patterns that account for the construal of both the experiencer and the stimulus, partly comparing the distribution of the same constructions across other verb classes. In this Section, I pinpoint the role of construction variation with experiential verbs, based on some peculiar features of experiential situations and of their participants that I summarize below.

i) Experiential situations are characterized by a low degree of transitivity: they do not involve a change of state in the second participant.

ii) The experiencer is always necessarily animate and sentient. Even though it does not properly control the situation, it can be construed as being more or less attentive to it.

© SILVIA LURAGHI, 2021 | DOI:10.1163/9789004442528_011

CONCLUDING REMARKS

iii) As it does not undergo a change of state, the stimulus cannot be viewed as being affected to different extents.

As the three constructions behave differently regarding possible variation, I start by discussing the role of the NomAcc and the NomGen construction in Section 10.1.1. The NomDat construction, which exhibits features of its own that do not fit into the opposition between the other two constructions, is discussed in Section 10.1.2. In Section 10.1.3 I summarize the distribution of constructions across verb groups and in reference to different types of experience.

10.1.1 *The Role of the NomAcc and the NomGen Construction*

Among features of experiential situations listed in Section 10.1, especially (i) and (iii) constitute deviations from the prototypical transitive situation. As Malchukov points out "the difference in argument structure between canonical transitives and mental [i.e. experiential, SL] verbs such as 'see' and 'like' ... relate not only to properties of O [second argument, SL] but more importantly to properties of A [first argument, SL] as well ... these verbs instantiate a deviation from the agentive prototype on the part of A: the A of emotional predicates is not a controlling but rather an affected participant." (2005: 80).

Malchukov further argues that "the shift in argument structure along this dimension is also gradual, inasmuch as perception predicates of the 'see' type are arguably intermediate between 'break' and 'like' types." (*ib.*), and follows Kemmer (1993), who suggests that experiencers of perception verbs are less affected than those of other experiential situations. Kemmer writes that "perception ... involves the least degree of affectedness of the experiencer. Simply perceiving an object has a relatively small effect on the perceiver, as compared to thinking about the object or being affected by emotions aroused by it." (1993: 137).

Note that both Malchukov and Kemmer speak of the A's or the experiencer's affectedness with experiential verbs, but I prefer to speak of lower or diminished agency (see Sections 3.1.1 and 6.5), as affectedness might be viewed as implying a change of state. In fact, this may be the case with inchoative verbs, such as 'realize', 'get scared', 'fall in love', 'perceive suddenly' but this possible feature of experiential situations is indicated by the verbal aspect in Homeric Greek (see Section 4.1), and does not affect argument structure constructions. Also, affectedness is an unclear term in this framework, and does not allow generalizing across verb classes in Homeric Greek in order to account for construction variation, as I will argue below.

In Section 3.1.1, I suggested that different degrees of agency involved in the construal of the first argument, the A or proto-agent, are encoded by argument structure variation. In particular, I have argued that the NomAcc construction, which indicates high affectedness of the second argument (O, or proto-patient) with action verbs, also indicates high agency of the first argument, while the NomGen construction indicates both low affectedness of the O and low agency of the A. With change-of-state verbs this may mean, for example, that the O only partly undergoes a change of state, and that the A is not able to fully accomplish the action, as has been shown in examples (104)-(107) in Section 3.2.6. With contact verbs, variation may indicate that a target is reached or simply aimed at and that the agent has been able to reach it or not, as I have argued in the discussion of examples (65)-(69) in Section 3.1.1. Action and contact verbs show that both participants can be characterized by a full vs. diminished degree of participation in an event.

When one shifts from the domain of action or contact verbs to the domain of experiential verbs, however, the construal of the second participant, including its full vs. diminished participation, becomes much less relevant, as there is no change of state involved. On the other hand, the construal of the experiencer gains relevance: the experiencer is a human being in the vast majority of cases, and its involvement in the situation is of much greater prominence for speakers. But as the experiencer is not an agent, and it does not bring about any type of change in the second argument, how do varying degrees of agency translate when referring to the experiential domain? In Section 6.5, discussing construction variation with perception verbs, I have argued that one of the distinctive features of agency, control, which is encoded by the NomAcc construction, is construed as typical of visual perception as opposed to other perception modalities (see Figure 11).

As the occurrences of sight verbs and verbs of hearing show, sight is construed as providing first-hand, undisputed information, while hearing does not grant the same type of evidence. In this connection, it is remarkable that the Two-place+P construction takes different forms with sight verbs, with which it is instantiated by the NomAcc+P construction, and with hearing verbs. With *akoúō* 'hear' one finds the NomGen+P construction in all occurrences but one, in which the NomAcc+P construction occurs (see example (200) in Section 6.2). As the construction involves acquisition of knowledge about an event, either direct or indirect, the fact that the NomGen construction occurs is quite natural, considering that hearing is construed as a less reliable source of knowledge as opposed to sight. Notably, the Two-place+P construction also occurs in Vedic Sanskrit with the verb *śru-* 'hear' with human stimuli but it is always realized as NomAcc+P construction (Dahl 2014b, Luraghi and Biagetti 2019). Comparative evidence then supports the claim that the opposition between NomAcc and NomGen construction in terms of lower control by the experiencer is indeed the pattern that lies at the foundation of construction alternation in Homeric Greek, as the inherited construction with NomAcc is attested only marginally, and has arguably been replaced by NomGen.

Seeing something implies in the first place directing one's attention toward it, and becoming aware of it in a much clearer way than perceiving it through other perceptual modalities. Like granting awareness, perception through sight relates directly to intellectual knowledge and to thought. On the other hand, perception modalities other than sight relate to bodily sensations, rather than to mental activity, and accordingly feature the NomGen construction as verbs of bodily sensation, with hearing taking an in-between position, in accordance to typological hierarchies (see Figure 13).

Verbs of sensation are those that are viewed as featuring the most agentive type of experiencer in the literature, with verbs of emotion taking a position between sensation and perception. Tsunoda (1985) draws a distinction between cognition and perception on the one hand and emotion and sensation on the other (see Section 2.1), while according to Malchukov "sensation predicates (such as 'freeze', 'be sick') deviate arguably even further from transitivity prototype than emotion predicates, since Experiencer is their only argument, while many emotion predicates ('like', 'fear') take two arguments." (2005: 81) Based on this observation, Malchukov proposes a two-dimensional hierarchy of transitivity that separates experiential verbs from other verb classes, as shown in Figure 17 (from Malchukov 2005: 81).

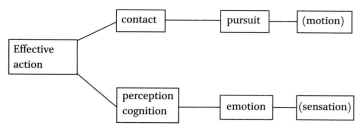

FIGURE 17   Two dimensional verb type hierarchy

Up to now, the description of the experiencer as possibly showing a more patient-like nature, hence as being affectedness, which is common to Malchukov's and to Kemmer's approach, seems to be supported by the Homeric Greek data, as experiencers with verbs of bodily sensation are certainly farther away from prototypical agents than experiencers with perception and cognition verbs. Things are, however, more complicated with verbs of emotion. Indeed, as I have shown in Chapter 8, different construals of the experiencers in the domain of emotions reflect attentiveness and awareness in a way that might look counterintuitive, if we try to match such features directly with agency.

Indeed, as I have shown in Section 8.3.2, verbs that are often thought as featuring patient-like experiencers, such as 'fear', take the NomAcc construction, and follow the pattern of sight verbs and cognitive verbs that indicate mental activity and intellectual knowledge. I have explained this seemingly odd distribution of constructions arguing that fear and other negative emotions centered on the experiencer are construed as raising a high level of attentiveness and awareness in the experiencer, which is viewed as directing their attention toward a threat.

On the other hand, emotion verbs that take the NomGen construction indicate uncontrolled states of mind that are arguably construed as obfuscating the experiencer's awareness and escaping their attention: this is typically the case of verbs that indicate yearning and uncontrolled desire. The stimulus may constitute a matter of care or concern for the experiencer, hence again disturbing its mind. Apparently, the uncontrolled nature of an emotion of this type is gradable: verbs of craving and desiring tend to take the NomGen construction with a much higher frequency than verbs that indicate care or affection. With the latter group, the default NomAcc construction is more easily available (see Section 8.2.2).

With verbs of memory, the stimulus may refer to some mental content that was temporarily absent from the experiencer's awareness and has been retrieved ('remember'), or that has moved outside ('forget'). Being viewed as a mental content that already exists in the experiencer's mind, and only needs to be activated, the stimulus in an event of remembering contrasts with the stimulus of other cognitive verbs, which refer to the elaboration of some new cognitive content: this contrast is reflected in the distribution of constructions, with NomGen characterizing memory verbs as opposed to verbs that indicate thought, realizing and intellectual knowledge, and take the NomAcc construction (see Section 7.3). Among verbs of knowledge, *oîda* 'know' shows a peculiar distribution of constructions, whereby the NomGen construction is limited to occurrences that refer to practical skills, while intellectual knowledge pairs with the NomAcc construction. This distribution reflects the consistent occurrence of the NomGen construction to encode situations that involve the body, as with bodily sensations and perception other than sight and partly hearing (see Section 7.4).

Notably, the semantic contribution of the two constructions in reference to two different types of knowledge, as well as the relevance of the pattern that pairs intellectual knowledge with mental activity and awareness and practical skill with bodily sensation, is indicated by comparative evidence. Indeed, while in Vedic Sanskrit *oîda*'s cognate verb *veda* 'know' similarly takes both the NomAcc and the NomGen construction, there is no such sharp distinction

CONCLUDING REMARKS

between intellectual knowledge and practical skills: much to the contrary, as argued in Luraghi and Biagetti (2019), both constructions occur when the verb refers to the former type of knowledge, while skills are mostly referred to when *veda* comes with the NomAcc construction.

Verbs that mean 'understand', 'realize', 'learn' take the NomAcc construction, especially if they indicate the sudden rise of awareness or conscious recognition, as do *noéō* 'realize' (Section 7.1.1) and *gignóskō* 'understand': such verbs follow the pattern of verbs of sight, as they indicate events that are often connected with direct perception. On the other hand *édaon* 'learn' and especially *punthánomai* 'learn' that indicate acquisition of knowledge from some unspecified source follow the pattern of hearing verbs, and show alternation between the NomAcc and the NomGen construction. I will elaborate further on this point in Section 10.1.3

10.1.2 *The NomDat Construction*

The NomDat construction is basically restricted to verbs of emotion. Contrary to the NomAcc and the NomGen construction, which occur with semantically related verbs and may show variation with the same verb, the NomDat construction is restricted to verbs that construe the situation as interactive, and with such verbs it does not allow for variation. In much the same way as other experiential verbs, verbs that take the NomDat construction are characterized by a low degree of transitivity, as they do not imply a change of state. However, the NomDat construction moves the focus from the diminished degree of agency of the first participant to the co-occurrence of a second participant that contributes to bringing about the situation.

The largest group of verbs that take the NomDat construction consists of verbs that denote negative feelings of the experiencer directed toward another human participant. With such verbs, the construction follows the pattern of verbs of social interaction, which similarly refer to states of affairs in which the second participant either cooperates with the first, as in the case of inherently reciprocal verbs, or can profit from the situation. Even though the second participant does not necessarily act, being human, it is still viewed as a potential agent.

Verbs of rejoicing that feature mostly inanimate stimuli also occur with this construction. They follow the pattern of verbs of manipulation, which feature a second participant that is viewed as an instrument or a means through which the agent brings about a certain state of affairs. This pattern also occurs with a verb of bodily sensation, notably *adéō* 'be sated', a verb of satiation. With verbs of rejoicing, the second participant is most often an abstract entity, construed as the reason that triggers the experiencer's reaction.

A limited number of emotion verbs surveyed in Section 8.4.1 feature variation between the NomAcc and the NomDat construction. The two constructions contribute their own semantics, and the resulting constructions built up by the verb and the two different argument structures construe different situations that conform to the construction's semantics shown elsewhere. More specifically, when the NomDat construction occurs the ensuing situation entails the co-occurrence of a human target stimulus, while the NomAcc construction denotes situations of emotions centered on the experiencer, such as wonder or fear.

Verbs that denote empathy show variation between the NomGen and the NomDat construction (see Section 8.4.2). With such verbs, the stimulus is viewed as a matter of concern for the experiencer, when they occur with the NomGen construction. The NomDat construction on the other hand construes the stimulus as a beneficiary: in this case, the stimulus is viewed as the target of positive thoughts originating from the experiencer.

10.1.3 *The Distribution of Constructions across the Experiential Domain*

Table 15 I summarize the distribution of constructions across groups of verbs. Verbs that allow for construction alternation are repeated in different groups in cases in which construction alternation entails reference to situation that belong to different parts of the experiential domain. For example, the complex built up by the verb *térpomai* with the NomGen construction indicates a state of saturation ('satiate oneself') while complex *térpomai* plus NomDat construction indicates joy. Notably, this is not simply a difference in profiling, whereby the two constructions profile different aspects of the same type of situation: rather, the two constructions with the same verb indicate situations that belong to different sub-domains of experience, that is, bodily sensation (NomGen) and emotion (NomDat). Accordingly, I have included the entry *térpomai* both in group A and in group T. Similarly, *ágamai* plus NomAcc indicates wonder, while *ágamai* plus NomDat indicates envy, and the entry appears both in group M and in group S. As construction variation with *oîda* 'know' separates intellectual knowledge (NomAcc) from practical skills (NomGen) while with *epístamai* 'know' it does not, I have divided knowledge into two sub-groups, 1a referring to the former type of knowledge and 1b referring to the latter, with *epístamai* appearing twice with both constructions.

Table 15 neatly highlights semantic affinities among verb groups that pattern in a similar way with respect to argument structure distribution. Not surprisingly, need, craving, uncontrolled desire (group C) pattern after verbs of saturation (group A): need and craving can be quenched by satiating oneself. Verbs referring to perception modalities other than sight and hearing (here labeled as

CONCLUDING REMARKS

TABLE 15   Distribution of constructions across verb groups

	NomAcc	NomGen	NomDat
A. Saturation			
adéō 'be sated'			
korénnumi 'satiate'			
térpomai 'satiate oneself'			
onínamai 'take profit from'			
B. Sensation			
háptomai 'touch'			
géuomai 'taste'			
C. Need/craving			
peináō 'be hungry'			
onínamai 'take profit from'			
khrḗ 'need'			
krēízō 'need'			
D. Desire			
mémona 'desire eagerly'			
éldomai 'desire'			
himeírō 'desire'			
liláiomai 'feel like'			
pothéō 'pine for'			
E. Care/affection			
médomai 'care'			
olophúromai 'take pity on someone'			
alégō, alegízō 'care for'			
kḗdomai 'care for'			
perikḗdomai 'care for'			
philéō 'feel affection for', 'love'			
perideídō 'fear for someone'			

TABLE 15 Distribution of constructions across verb groups (*cont.*)

	NomAcc	NomGen	NomDat
F. Memory			
mimnḗskomai 'remember' *mnáomai* 'care' *lanthánomai* 'forget'			
G. Learning			
gignṓskō 'understand' *édaon* 'learn' *punthánomai* 'learn, perceive'			
H. Hearing			
akoúō 'hear, listen to' *aíō* 'hear' *klúō* 'hear, listen to' *epakoúō* 'hear' *akouázomai* 'listen to'			
Ia. Knowledge—skills			
oîda 'be skilled' *epístamai* 'know, be skilled'			
Ib. Knowledge			
oîda 'know' *epístamai* 'know, be skilled'			
J. Sight			
horáō 'see' *eisoráō* 'behold' *leússō* 'gaze'			

CONCLUDING REMARKS

TABLE 15   Distribution of constructions across verb groups (*cont.*)

	NomAcc	NomGen	NomDat
theáomai 'watch' *sképtomai* 'look at' *dérkomai* 'see'			
K. Thought			
oíō/oíomai 'think, believe' *noéō* 'realize' *phronéō* 'think' *phrázomai* 'devise' *médomai* 'plan' *mētiáō/mētíomai* 'plan' *médomai* 'plan'			
L. Voliton			
ethélō 'want' *boúlomai* 'wish' *élpomai* 'hope'			
M. Wonder			
thaumázō 'wonder' *thambéō* wonder *ágamai* 'admire'			
N. Fear			
deídō 'fear' *hupodeídō* 'fear' *tarbéō* 'be afraid' *atúzomai* 'be terrified' *nemesízō/nemesáō* 'fear' (*hupo*)*troméō* 'tremble' *phríssō* 'shiver'			

TABLE 15   Distribution of constructions across verb groups (*cont.*)

	NomAcc	NomGen	NomDat
O. Shame			
aiskhúnomai 'feel shame' *aidéomai* 'feel shame'	▓		
P. Sadness			
odúromai 'mourn' *klaíō* 'weep'	▓		
Q. Hate			
ekhthaírō 'hate' (threat) *miséō* 'hate' *odússomai* 'hate'	▓		▓
R. Anger			
kholóomai 'be angry' *(apo)skudmaínō* 'be angry' *kotéō* 'be angry' *nemesízō/nemesáō* 'be upset'			▓
S. Envy			
megaírō 'grudge' *ágamai* 'envy'			▓
T. Joy			
térpomai 'rejoice' *khaírō* 'rejoice'			▓

CONCLUDING REMARKS

'sensation' in group B) are also constructed as verbs of saturation: these perception modalities are construed as close to bodily sensation.

As I have remarked in Section 7.4, this distribution indicates that the NomGen construction is closely connected with situations that involve the body, while the NomAcc construction points to a mental involvement that becomes more prominent (hence the occurrence of the NomAcc construction) as the level of awareness and attention increases. Alternation between the two constructions with verbs of desire and verbs of care and affection in groups D and E indicates a mental involvement of the experiencer, which, however, is partly driven by sensation, hence a lesser level of awareness than the level reached with verbs that indicate thought and volition (groups K and L).

The difference between the two types of states of affairs shows various facets: in the field of cognition, the areas of memory and acquiring new information indicate a type of mental activity that either has no external input (memory, group F), or has an external input that does reflect the rise of awareness to varying extents: recall that among the verbs in group G there are considerable differences in the frequency of the NomGen and the NomAcc construction, with *gignóskō* 'learn', 'understand' occurring twice with the NomGen construction and 62 times with the NomAcc construction, and *punthánomai/peúthomai* 'learn', 'perceive' with 19 occurrences of NomGen and 33 of NomAcc (see Table 10). As pointed out in Section 7.4, verbs of learning match verbs of hearing in the subdomain of perception (group H). Knowledge shows a partial split, reflected in the distribution of construction with the verb *oîda* 'know', between intellectual states (group Ib) and practical abilities (group Ia).

Groups J-P show a solid block of verbs patterning after sight (group J), and pointing to a high degree of awareness and attention. They include in the first place verbs that indicate rational thought and planning, such as *médomai* 'plan', the sudden rise of awareness, such as *noéō* 'realize', or an opinion, such as *oíō/oíomai* 'think, believe' (group K, see Section 7.1). As compared to verbs of memory, verbs in this group construe thought as entailing the elaboration of a new mental content, normally with an external input (see Section 7.4). Volition verbs (group L, see Section 5.2) take the NomAcc construction hence pointing to a conscious, intentional activity, as opposed to verbs that indicate uncontrolled desire and take the NomGen construction. Wonder (group M) is directly connected to sight through embodiment (see Section 8.3.1), hence to negative feelings that entail a high degree of attention as they are perceived as threats for the experiencer: fear (group N), shame (group O), and sadness (group P; see Section 8.3.2).

Hate (group Q) is the only group of verbs among which we find alternation between the NomAcc and the NomDat construction. As I argued in Sections

8.1.1 and 8.3.2, hate can be construed as targeting a potentially reactive human stimulus, or as involving an experiencer that is faced by an external threat, hence the existence of verbs that take two distinct constructions. Note, however, that none of the individual verbs admits construction variation. Other emotions involving human target stimuli, including anger and envy (groups R and S), construe the situation as potentially interactive, and do not allow for construction alternation: they can occasionally come with a three-argument construction, less entrenched than the usual two-argument one, i.e. the Nom-DatGen construction, in which an additional participant is construed as a matter of concern that prompts the emotion (Section 8.3.2; see further Section 10.3). Finally, joy is also construed as involving a stimulus that may be the means or reason for the rise of the emotion (group T).

Verbs that allow for variation between the NomDat and another construction are very few. If one leaves out *ágamai* 'wonder' (NomAcc), 'envy' (NomDat) and *térpomain* 'satiate oneself' (NomGen), 'enjoy' (NomDat) that, as I have explained at the beginning of this Section, construe different types of situations belonging to different sub-domains of experience in connection with either construction, variation is limited to a verb of saturation, *adéō* 'be sated', and to the verb *perideídō* 'fear for someone'. With the former, the NomGen construction profiles the feeling of satiation by the experiencer, while the Nom-Dat construction profiles the instrumental nature of the stimulus (Section 5.1); with the latter, the NomGen construction construes the stimulus as a matter of concern for the experiencer, while the NomDat construction construes the stimulus as receiving a potential benefit from the experiencer's worries (Section 8.4.2).

Figure 18 shows the results of a bi-dimensional correspondence analysis that matches argument structure constructions with verb groups. In Figure 18 three strong clusters emerge in correspondence with the three constructions that contain verbs not allowing for variation. In the lower part of the figure, sensation and need/craving build up a cluster in the area of the NomGen construction, with saturation slightly moved to the area of the NomDat construction on account of the behavior of *adéō* 'be sated'. In the NomDat area, we find a cluster including anger, envy and joy, with hate placed halfway toward the area of the NomAcc construction. In turn, this area contains the biggest cluster, including sight, volition, thought, knowledge, wonder, fear, shame and sadness. The most interesting area in terms of variation lies between the NomAcc and the Nom-Gen construction, and includes knowledge, learning, hearing, desire, practical skills, memory and care/affection. This last group of verbs is somewhat closer to the area of the NomDat construction on account of alternation between Nom-Gen and NomDat with *perideídō* 'fear for someone'.

CONCLUDING REMARKS 279

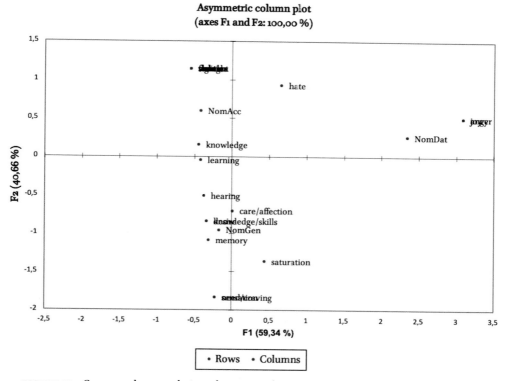

FIGURE 18   Correspondence analysis: verb groups and constructions

10.2 Embodiment and Social Setting

In Section 1.3, I pointed out that experiential verbs provide extensive evidence for embodiment. After having surveyed in detail all classes of experiential verbs in Homeric Greek, this claim can be substantiated by several factors. Table 15 pinpoints similarities across the sub-domains of experience. The first correspondence emerging already shows the crucial role of embodiment: need and craving are construed as directed to the achievement of a state of bodily satiation with food. However, in this Section I will argue that embodiment underlies the encoding of the whole domain of experience, as the sub-domain of perception provides the source for the construal of other sub-domains.

Let us then turn to the role of perception verbs. Construction variation with such verbs reflects embodiment: the NomAcc construction, which is typical of high transitivity verbs hence indicates full control by the agent on the situation, occurs with sight verbs, singling out this perception modality as granting more reliable and clearer perception of outer stimuli than other modalities.

Touch and taste (and possibly smell, based on evidence from later Greek prose, see Section 6.3), on the other hand, take the same construction as bodily sensations, and are viewed as building up a unit of experiential situations with them.

Construction distribution with perception verbs provides a common pattern for verbs in the domain of cognition. Visual perception is then mapped onto intellectual skills, such as rational thought, elaboration of new cognitive contents and intellectual knowledge, and awareness achieved through sight is viewed as corresponding to understanding and realizing something with an external input. At the opposite edge of the domain of cognition, memory and forgetfulness are construed as not involving the perception of an external stimulus or the elaboration of some new cognitive contents. Hence they generalize the construction of bodily sensations, as thoughts retrieved or lost are construed as being internal to the experiencer's cognition, rather than connected to an external input.

The extension from perception to cognition is obviously not a specific feature of Homeric Greek. Much to the contrary, it is a well-known cross-linguistic tendency, which has sometimes been explained as based on a metaphor that maps the body onto the mind (e.g. Sweetser 1990; see Section 2.1.3). Even without setting up such a metaphor, pragmatic inference can account for the mapping of different perceptual modalities on different areas of cognition. Sematic extension based on pragmatic inference can be illustrated with the evidential function of perception verbs. In Section 6.4, I have argued that hearing verbs extend to hearsay evidentials, and draw a distinction between sight, as a source of first-hand knowledge, and hearing. While knowledge acquired through sight, based on the Homeric evidence, is always direct, knowledge acquired through hearing can be direct or mediated (see Luraghi and Sausa 2019), hence the inference that having seen something means knowing it, while having heard something leaves margin to uncertainty. This difference is reflected in the distribution of constructions, with verbs of hearing most frequently occurring with the NomGen construction, including cases in which they refer to the acquisition of a propositional content from a third party (NomGen+P construction).

Embodiment also accounts for the extension of the NomAcc construction to verbs that indicate wonder, since evidence for a connection of wonder with sight has been adduced by anthropological research, as argued in Section 8.3.1. Wonder implies the rise of a state of attention in the experiencer, and may result in fear when the object of wonder is perceived as a threat. Hence the extension of the NomAcc construction not only to fear verbs, but to other verbs that indicate negative emotions centered on the experiencer and brought about by the awareness of some threat.

CONCLUDING REMARKS

Another hint at the extension of constructional patterns of perception verbs to verbs in other domains of experience is the occurrence of the Two-place+P construction across various verb classes. Indeed, this construction extends not only to cognition, which is in closer connection with perception, but occasionally also to emotion, in occurrences in which direct perception functions as the trigger of the emotion. Extension to emotion verbs also indicates the productivity of this construction, as I will argue in Section 10.4.3.

Among experiencer-centered negative emotions, shame deserves some more attention due to its socially conditioned construal. Commenting on the fact that shame verbs take the NomAcc construction, similar to fear verbs, I have argued that the connection between the two groups of verbs is provided by the rise in the experiencer of a feeling of danger in front of a potential threat. In the case of shame, this threat is not brought about by some dangerous entity. Rather, it is a socially determined risk, arising from not complying with accepted practices within the society that provides the setting for the events narrated in the Homeric poems.

The social dimension of emotions is responsible for the distribution of argument structure constructions with these as well as with other verbs. In particular, verbs of negative emotions that target a human stimulus exhibit the NomDat construction, which points toward a socially relevant type of situation. In general, the fact that emotion verbs show a wider range of constructional patterns than verbs in other domains of experience is a consequence of the social relevance of emotions. Contrary to other types of experiential situations, emotions can for example affect a social setting in a way that is not predictable: indeed, as pointed out in the Introduction, Achilles' wrath prompted him to refrain from fighting and act in an irresponsible manner, almost causing the doom of the Greeks.

10.3   The Encoding of Experiential Situations in Homeric Greek

As I have pointed out in the Introduction, the bulk of coding patterns for experiential situations in Homeric Greek consists of constructions in which the experiencer takes the subject role and appears as an NP in the nominative case, in the Nom-first construction. This construction is variously realized as NomAcc, NomGen and NomDat, depending on the coding of the stimulus. The distribution of the three constructions across verb classes points to a coherent semantic characterization of each of them, as I have argued throughout the book and have summarized in Section 10.1.

In spite of its strong tendency toward nominative alignment, Homeric Greek also provides evidence for a limited number of verbs that show a different type of alignment, with dative experiencers, and feature the DatNom construction. The DatNom construction occurs with some emotion verbs such as *handánō* 'please' and its compounds, with the verb *dokéō* 'think, have an impression, seem' and other verbs of appearance (see Sections 3.2.7, 7.1.1 and 8.5). Notably, these verbs also have alternative constructions with nominative experiencers, as is the case for *dokéō*, or may occur in contexts in which the stimulus is arguably more prominent than the experiencer, hence instantiating the NomDat construction, as I have shown for *handánō*. Taken together, they do not build a semantically coherent group, and constitute a marginal pattern in Homeric Greek. Remarkably, constructions in which neither the experiencer nor the stimulus is encoded in the nominative and in which neither argument triggers verb agreement, do not occur in the Homeric poems.

Stimuli subjects also occur in metaphorical constructions, in which the stimulus is metaphorically construed as a nominative agent-subject, actively affecting the experiencer encoded as a patient in the accusative. This typically involves the verb *hairéō* 'take, seize', with subjects such as *déos* 'fear' or *hímeros* 'lust, desire', while other verbs occur sporadically (see Section 2.3).

Three-place constructions with split stimuli occur with emotion verbs that denote negative emotions involving two human participants. In such cases, the basic pattern is constituted by the NomDat construction, with a nominative experiencer and a human target stimulus in the dative. To these, a third argument can be added, a source stimulus in the genitive, with an ensuing NomDat-Gen construction. As I pointed out in Section 8.1.1, the level of entrenchment of this construction seems to be comparatively low, as the genitive argument can be replaced by a cause/reason expression of other types. Moreover, while the target stimulus is always either overtly encoded or recoverable from the preceding context, the source stimulus occurs in a minority of cases. Still, the occurrence of the NomDatGen construction offers evidence for construction productivity, as I argue in Section 10.4. Here, it still needs to be highlighted that this construction is typical of experiential verbs, as the genitive never encodes cause/reason with verbs of other classes.

Another three-place construction occurs with causative verbs, notably *mimnéskō* 'remind', which takes the NomAccGen construction, with a nominative agent, an accusative experiencer, and a genitive stimulus. Accusative experiencers in the construction are encoded as causees in causative constructions with other verb classes.

In Section 1, I pointed out that the experiential situation is often construed as affecting a specific part of the experiencer, be it material, typically a body part, or immaterial, such as the mind or the soul. This type of construal is very frequent in Homeric Greek, in which mental activities and emotions are often

CONCLUDING REMARKS

located in the mind or in the heart, variously referred to as *thumós* 'soul, heart', *phrḗn* 'heart, midriff' (see Chapters 7 and 8). It also occurs with sight verbs, in which the expression *en ophthalmoîsi* 'in one's eyes' hints at the conceptualization of body parts as containers (Section 6.1).

10.4 Constructions' Productivity

In Section 1.2 I highlighted the role of chunking in the emergence of constructions, and introduced Perek's (2015) usage-based view of verbal valency. As I remarked, in order to adopt a usage-based perspective and gauge the entrenchment of construction, one must necessarily be able to rely on frequency data that hint at their productivity. In this Section, I argue that the Homeric poems, in spite of their limits, feature positive evidence for the productivity of various constructions, and not only, as one might have expected, for the NomAcc constructions that constitutes a default not only for experiential verbs, but across verb classes (Section 10.4.1). Indeed, evidence is available for the NomDat and the NonGen construction as well (Section 10.4.2). Besides the three Nom-first constructions, the Two-place+P construction also proves to be productive (Section 10.4.3).

10.4.1 *NomAcc as Default Construction*
As remarked in Section 3.2.3, the NomAcc construction is by far the most frequent construction of two-place verbs in Homeric Greek, accounting for over 73% of verbs, and over 80% of occurrences (data from Sausa 2015). Even though about half of the verbs that take this construction indicate change of state or change of position, it also extends to all other verb classes. Its overall frequency with semantically heterogeneous verbs offers evidence of its productivity, following the definition in Barðdal (2008) discussed in Section 3.2.3. However, the productivity of the NomAcc construction is not only shown by its overall frequency. More evidence is available, and can be seen in its distribution with specific lexical items across verb classes, including with experiential verbs.

In Sections 5.1 and 5.3, I discussed the construction of the verb *páskhō* 'suffer', which routinely takes the NomAcc construction. Given the type of fillers allowed, however, I have argued that this is not a normal two-place verb, but rather a verb that only admits cognate objects, such as *kaká, álgea, pêma* 'evils, pains, sufferings'. Such fillers do not convey any information regarding a possible second participant: rather, they highlight the meaning of the verb. As in other similar cases, cognate objects show the accusative as default case (see Jacquinod 1989: 138–139). A similar situation occurs with the verb *phronéō* 'think' discussed in Section 7.1.2. This verb is often accompanied by the expressions *eu* 'good' or by its contrary *kaká* 'evil things'. Notably, while the former is an adverb, the latter is an accusative neuter plural, but it also functions as an adverb. The two expressions refer to the experiencer's attitude, and do not properly refer to a second participant.

Discussing example (338) in Section 8.1.1 I pointed out that the demonstrative *tóde* 'this' encodes cause/reason in a construction that would normally feature a source stimulus in the genitive, and noted that neuter pronouns may occur in the accusative even in constructions that normally require another case. This peculiarity has long been known among Greek linguists, at least since Havers (1924) first called attention on it. Neuter pronouns denote low individuated entities whose roles need not be specified in detail, and in this case accusative encoding must be taken as a default occurring in contexts of underspecification.

However, it is not only the case that neuters tend to be underspecified and take the accusative. With several verbs, inanimate nouns turned out to fit more easily into the NomAcc construction than animate ones, which in turn show an affinity for the NomGen construction. The clearest example is constituted by verbs of hearing: recall the peculiar distribution illustrated in Section 6.2, whereby inanimate stimuli can occur both in the NomAcc and in the NomGen construction, while animate ones appear in the NomGen construction with a single exception to which I will return in Section 10.4.2. I argued that the occurrence of inanimate stimuli in either construction does not bring about any semantic difference: indeed, it is the same type of lexemes, referring to noises, sound, animal cries or the human voice, that function as fillers in both of them, and the two constructions may even be coordinated as shown in example (196). The alternation can then be accounted for as follows: hearing verbs normally take the NomGen construction. In cases in which the stimulus is a low individuated entity, it can be underspecified, hence inflected in the accusative.

Verbs of hearing are the most perspicuous group to show an animacy-based distribution. A different, but comparable distribution also occurs with verbs of desiring treated in Section 8.2.1. Among them, *éldomai* 'desire' takes both the NomAcc and the NomGen construction. As with hearing verbs, the latter can have both animate and inanimate fillers, while the former only features inanimate ones. Other verbs of desiring take either of the two constructions independently of animacy. In 8.2.1, I have compared this group of verbs with contact verbs, which may take either the NomAcc (*bállō* 'hit') or the NomGen construction (*tugkhánō* 'hit, touch'). Other contact verbs can also exhibit meaningful construction variation, as does *orégomai* 'aim, hit' discussed in Section 3.1.1. In such cases, the NomAcc construction indicates that a target is reached,

CONCLUDING REMARKS

while the NomGen construction does not have this implication. In the case of the verb *éldomai* 'desire' the meaning of construction variation does not imply final contact vs. lack of contact. Still, the animacy-based distribution can be explained as reflecting the fact that inanimate referents are construed as more easily apprehended than animate ones, hence they can remain underspecified.

10.4.2 *The Productivity of the NomDat and NomGen Construction*

Even though the NomDat and the NomGen construction are much less frequent both in terms of types and in terms of tokens than the NomAcc construction, some cues to their productivity are also detectable, in the first place in the semantic coherence of the verbs that take them.

The degree of semantic coherence is especially high for verbs that take the NomDat construction. Among experiential verbs, they all belong to two well-defined groups, that is, verbs of negative emotions targeting human stimuli (Section 8.1.1) and verbs of rejoicing (Section 8.1.2). These two groups of verbs in turn fit semantically into the wider set of verb classes that takes the NomDat construction, which is also divided into two groups largely depending on animacy of the second participant, that is, verbs of social interaction and verbs of manipulation. Typically, verbs of other classes that take the NomDat construction only marginally allow for variation, and if they do, it remains limited to the NomGen construction (see Section 3.2.5).

The NomGen construction, on the other hand, covers a semantically much wider range of verbs, but the fact that it constitutes an alternative to the NomAcc construction with many of them gives it a unitary status, further supported by the fact that the two constructions also alternate with other verb classes, with which the alternation is more clearly meaningful in terms of diminished participation in the event of both the first and the second participant (see Section 3.1.1).

Besides semantic coherence, evidence for the possible extension of the two constructions is also available. In the case of the NomDat construction, the extension can be seen with the verb *akoúō* 'hear' in the occurrences discussed in examples (208) and (209). This verb does not normally take the NomDat construction that can occasionally extend to it, contributing its own semantics and construing the event as similar to other situations of social interaction (Section 6.2).

Concerning the NomGen construction, a hint at its productivity can be seen in the encoding of source stimuli with verbs of negative emotion that take the NomDat construction with human target stimuli. As I pointed out in Section 8.1.1, such verbs are basically two-place verbs, with the second argument encoded in the dative and referring to the second human participant. The additional constituent that may be added, encoding the cause or reason for the emotion, can be variously encoded as a prepositional phrase or a subordinate clause. The fact that it can also be encoded by a genitive NP indicates extension of the pattern of emotion verbs that denote care and affection. The cause/reason for the emotion or source stimulus is then construed as a matter of concern for the experiencer. Note that, contrary to the dative, the genitive does not encode cause/reason with verbs of other classes, hence this construction is a trademark of experiential verbs, more precisely of verbs of emotion. The occurrence of the genitive in the Two-Place+P construction with hearing verbs also points to the productivity of the NomGen construction. Recall the the Two-Place+P construction also occurs in Vedic with hearing verbs; however, it contains the accusative (Section 6.2). In Homer, the construction is only once realized as NomAcc+P, while in all other occurrences one finds NomGen+P. This seems to point to the extension of the genitive to a construction that originally contained an accusative.

10.4.3   *The Two-Place+P Construction*

The Two-place+P construction is highly productive in Ancient Greek, as indicated by its wide extension in post-Homeric Greek. Already in Homer there are clear hints toward its rise. As remarked in Section 3.3, this construction is cross-linguistically frequent with verbs that indicate immediate perception. This is because participles usually indicate events that must necessarily be simultaneous with the event encoded by the governing verb, as remarked in Noonan (2007: 119), and shown in (459) and (460).

(459)   *Paul saw the children playing in the park.*

(460)   *The children heard Paul approaching.*

Noonan (2007: 120) further remarks that "the characteristics of the participle that make it compatible with immediate perception predicates", i.e. encoding necessarily simultaneous events, "make it unsuitable for use with most ctps [complement-taking predicates]", and argues that in English the sentence in (461) is ungrammatical precisely on account of the events not being simultaneous.

(461)   **I believe Brinck breaking his leg.*

In Homeric Greek, especially the occurrences with verbs of hearing that indicate the acquisition of a propositional content from a third source, i.e. knowl-

CONCLUDING REMARKS

edge from hearsay, can sometimes refer to non-simultaneous events, as I have argued in Section 6.2. In particular in the discussion of (202), I have shown that the event encoded by the participle precedes the event encoded by the governing verb: in other words, it is not simultaneous to the perception event. To be sure, participles are not marked for tense but only for aspect; still, an aorist participle construes an event as punctual, hence the inference that the event is accomplished at the time of the perception event and accordingly necessarily precedes it. The temporal disconnection of the two events encoded by the main verb and the participle with hearing verbs opens the path for the extension of the construction with verbs of cognition.

It needs to be remarked that extension to such verbs in Greek may also be partly connected with the fact that the verb *oîda* 'know' was in origin the perfect from the root **wid-* 'see' of the aorist *eídon* 'see', and might have been inherited from Proto-Indo-European, as the Two-place+P construction also occurs in Vedic Sanskrit with the verb *veda* 'know', cognate of Greek *oîda* (Dahl 2014b). Hence, the occurrence of the Two-place+P construction with cognitive verbs does not provide clear evidence of its productivity in Homeric Greek. Notably, however, the fact that the verb *punthánomai* 'learn, perceive' takes the Two-place+P construction is hardly inherited, as its Sanskrit cognate *budh-* 'wake up, be awake, take heed of' does not feature this construction in the oldest Vedic texts (see Grassman 1873 s.v.). Moreover, the Two-place+P also extends to *gignóskō* 'understand, realize, learn' in Homeric Greek, while its cognate *jñā-* 'know, understand, become acquainted with' does not take this construction in Vedic Sanskrit. Hence, verbs of cognition attest to its productivity.

More evidence points toward the availability of the Two-place+P construction as a possible way of encoding situations closely connected with perception events. Indeed, the construction occasionally extends to verbs of rejoicing, in particular to *khaíromai* 'rejoice' as in (351), and to fearing verbs, notably *deídō* 'fear' as in (394). In both cases, the emotion is triggered in the experiencer by direct perception through the visual channel of a situation in which the stimulus is involved, and the extension of the construction typical of sight verbs adds this information to the resulting semantics of the whole construction consisting of the emotion verb and its arguments.

10.5   Verbal Voice

As I have shown in the discussion Sections devoted to the different subdomains of experience (Sections 5.3, 6.5, 7.4 and 8.6) no clear pattern emerges from the distribution of voice that can cross-cut all classes of experiential verbs.

The only group of verbs that shows a clear pattern of voice opposition is constituted by the verbs reviewed in Chapter 9 that encode (anti)causative alternation through voice. This is, however, a comparatively small group of verbs against the totality of experiential verbs. In other cases, voice may show a tense-based distribution, difficult to explain (see Section 8.6). As experiential verbs are characterized by a low degree of transitivity, a relevant number of *media tantum* is expected; still, *activa tantum* are also quite numerous, and often *media* and *activa tantum* show similar meanings, as in the case of *medium tantum khóomai* and *activum tantum ménío*, both indicating a state of anger, or *pothéó* 'pine away', an *activum tantum* among verbs of desire, most of which are *media tantum*.

According to Allan (2003), the middle voice indicates subject affectedness, which, with most experiential verbs, he intends as a higher degree of mental involvement by the experiencer in the situation. Allan's explanation of the role of voice appears to be most compelling for volition verbs (Section 5.3), while with verbs in other sub-domains a close scrutiny of the data raised many doubts on this interpretation.

Perception verbs referring to modalities other than sight point to a peculiar distribution, whereby, as far as one can tell based on available data, verbs of touch, taste and smell are *media tantum*, while hearing verbs almost only feature active morphology, with the exception of three middle occurrences of *akoúó* 'hear' out of a total of 182. As I pointed out in Section 6.5, Allan partly acknowledges the distribution, but his claim that, for example, taste is prototypically volitional while hearing is non-volitional is not supported by the data, considering, among other things, that *akoúó* can mean both 'hear' and 'listen to', and *klúó* most often expresses the second meaning. Similarly, his distinction between volitional and non-volitional in the explanation for the distribution of active and middle forms of sight verbs often appears to be arbitrary, and does not acknowledge the fact that the NomEisacc construction, which adds an intentional meaning to the verb *horáó* 'see, look at' comes with both active and middle forms of the verb as shown in examples (178)-(180). Moreover, the verb *eisoráó* 'behold', which most often indicates a volitional activity, shows active forms in 62 out of 72 occurrences (see Section 6.1).

Allan's interpretation of the role of the middle voice with verbs referring to different sub-domains of experience also raises some coherence issues. Indeed, while with perception verbs, to his view, middle verbs "tend to express a volitional activity" (2003: 95), with cognition verbs the middle voice indicates that "the subject passively undergoes the event" (2003: 97). The latter is also the case for several emotion verbs, such as *phobéomai* 'fear', whose active counterpart *phobéó* means 'frighten'. Concerning this verb, Allan remarks that the subject

CONCLUDING REMARKS

experiences an affectedness of the emotional kind, which is certainly the case. What is doubtful, however, is the connection with the middle voice. Remarkably, *phobéomai* in Homeric Greek always only means 'flee' (with the active *phobéō* meaning 'set on flight'), and the meaning 'fear' is post-Homeric. In turn the main fear verb in Homer is *deídō* 'fear', an *activum tantum*, with a causative counterpart, the derivate *deidíssomai* 'frighten', which is a *medium tantum*. In the framework of this data the explanation loses momentum, at least for Homeric Greek.

10.6   Outlook

My main focus in this book has been on variation among argument structure constructions of two-place experiential verbs in Homeric Greek. While carrying out an exhaustive survey of the passages in which such verbs occur in the Homeric poems, I touched upon a number of other issues, some of which have remained in the background due to the limitations of this work.

The most important issue that, to my view, remains unsettled is raised by the semantics of voice, as I have discussed in Section 10.5. My survey has not allowed me to pinpoint clear patterns for all verb classes and all sub-domains of experience. A more in-depth analysis is needed that takes into account every single occurrence of individual verbs.

The role of verbal aspect in the construal of situations and its distribution across verbs also deserves a more detailed investigation. For example, a striking fact is that hearing verbs do not have perfect forms in Homeric Greek, but feature the present and the aorist stem (see Section 6.2). The perfect of the verb *akoúō* 'hear' occurs in Attic-Ionic starting with Herodotus, but is not attested in Homer and in later epics. On the other hand, sight verbs do feature perfect forms, attested both for *dérkomai* 'see' and *horáō* 'see'. As hearing may indicate a cognitive process of acquiring information, the distribution of aspectual stems can be matched against the distribution featured by other verbs of similar meaning. Among verbs of learning, *gignóskō* 'learn, understand', does not feature a perfect stem either. Similar to *akoúō*, a perfect of this verb appears after Homer. Of course, the cognitive state of having knowledge about something is denoted by *oîda* 'know', a stative verb based on a perfect stem that can be viewed as supplying the perfect to *gignóskō*. On the other hand, *punthánomai* 'learn, perceive' features all three aspectual stems, including the perfect. It would certainly be worth investigating further this and other peculiarities of the distribution of aspectual stems and their contribution to the construal of situations.

Constructions other than the three Nom-first constructions that were at the center of my study also offer a fruitful field for further research. In particular, constructions involving body parts, both material and immaterial such as the mind, deserve a detailed investigation that accounts for all their occurrences and their peculiarities. Metaphorical expressions such as those discussed in Section 2.3 are also worth being analyzed in detail. Among other things, the occurrences of similar metaphors in fields other than experience could shed light on the construal of specific situations: for example, *kikhánō* 'meet' is occasionally used in reference to the rise of bodily sensations, but more frequently it occurs in reference to death, while another verbs that may refer to death, *amphikalúptō* 'enwrap', when used in the experiential domain, refers to sexual pleasure. The verb that I found most frequently used in metaphors referring to various types of experience, including fear, anger and desire, *hairéō* 'seize', in turn, never refers to death. This peculiar distribution would certainly deserve being pursued further.

Turning back to the main subject of my research, more insights on construction variation could be gained from diachrony. A broader view that encompasses later stages of the Greek language would certainly help gauging construction productivity, as it would indicate which constructions do extend and how far. Moreover, comparative data from other ancient Indo-European languages, if brought into the picture, would also provide more evidence in this respect. In Section 10.1.1 I showed how Sanskrit cognates of the verbs *klúō* 'hear' and *oîda* 'know' feature construction variation between the same constructions as the two Greek verbs, but pattern differently concerning their semantic contribution to the ensuing construction. I have taken this difference as evidence for the productivity of the Greek patterns within Homeric Greek, as they contribute to producing a coherent picture of construction variation across experiential verbs.

In conclusion, I hope that this book will show the interested reader some paths that may lead to answers to various open questions, while in the meantime raising more question and prompting other researchers to find more new answers.

References

Aikhenvald, Alexandra Y. 2004. *Evidentiality*. Oxford: Oxford University Press

Aldai, Gontzal and Søren Wichmann. 2018. Statistical observations on hierarchies of transitivity. *Folia Linguistica* 52(2): 249–281

Allan, Rutger. 2003. *The middle voice in Ancient Greek*. Amsterdam: Gieben.

Amberber, Mengistu. 2007. Introduction. The Language of Memory, in: Mengistu Amberber (ed.) *The language of memory in crosslinguistic perspective*, pp. 1–12. Amsterdam: John Benjamins.

Athanasiadou, Angeliki and Elżbieta Tabakowska eds. 2010. *Speaking of Emotions. Conceptualisation and Expression*. Berlin: Mouton de Gruyter.

Bakker, Egbert. 1988. *Linguistics and Formulas in Homer*. Amsterdam: John Benjamins.

Barðdal, Jóhanna. 2008. *Productivity: Evidence from Case and Argument Structure in Icelandic*. Amsterdam: John Benjamins.

Barðdal, Jóhanna, Elena Smirnova, Lotte Sommerer and Spike Gildea (eds.) 2015. *Diachronic Construction Grammar*. Amsterdam: John Benjamins.

Baayen, Harald R. 1993. On frequency, transparency and productivity, in: Geert Booij and Jaap van Marle (eds.), *Yearbook of morphology 1992*, pp. 181–208. Dordrecht: Kluwer.

Baayen, Harald. R. and Rochelle Lieber. 1991. Productivity and English derivation: A corpus-based study. *Linguistics* 29(5). 801–843.

Bechert, Johannes. 1964. *Die Diathesen von ideîn und horân bei Homer*, vols. I–II. München: Kitzinger.

Beekes, Robert and Lucien van Beek. 2010. *Etymological Dictionary of Greek*. Leiden: Brill.

Bergs, Alexander and Gabriele Diewald (eds.) 2008. *Constructions and Language Change*. Berlin: Mouton de Gruyter.

Bergs, Alexander and Gabriele Diewald (eds.) 2009. *Contexts and Constructions*. Amsterdam: John Benjamins.

Bertinetto, Pier Marco. 1986. *Tempo, aspetto e azione nel verbo italiano*. Firenze: Accademia della Crusca.

Bertinetto, Pier Marco and Denis Delfitto. 2000. Aspect vs. Actionality why they should be kept apart, in: Oesten Dahl (ed.) *Tense and Aspect in the Languages of Europe*, pp. 189–226. Berlin: Mouton de Gruyter.

Bertinetto, Pier Marco. 1991. Il Verbo, in: Renzi Lorenzo and Salvi Giampaolo (eds.) *Grande Grammatica Italiana di Consultazione*, vol. II, pp. 13–162. Bologna: il Mulino.

Bertolín Cebrián, Reyes. 1996. *Die Verben des Denkens Bei Homer*. Innsbruck: Verlag des Institutes der Sprachwissenschaft der Universität Innsbruck.

Blansitt, Edward. 1978. Stimulus as a semantic role, in W. Abraham (ed.), *Valence, semantic case and grammatical relations*, pp. 311–325. Amsterdam: John Benjamins.

Bloomfield, Leonard. 1933. *Language*. New York: Henry Holt.

Boas, Hans C. 2013. Cognitive Construction Grammar, in: Thomas Hoffmann and Graeme Trousdale (eds.) *The Oxford Handbook of Construction. Grammar.* pp. 233–254. Oxford: Oxford University Press.

Boel, Gunnar de. 1988. *Goal Accusative and Object Accusative in Homer: a Contribution to the Theory of Transitivity.* Brussel: AWLSK.

Booij, Geert E. and Ans van Kemenade. 2003. Preverbs: An introduction, in: Geert E. Booij and Jaap van Marle (eds.), *Yearbook of Morphology 2003*, 1–12. Dordrecht: Kluwer.

Bossong, George. 1998. Le Marquage de l'Expérient dans les Langues d'Europe, in: Jack Feuillet (ed.) *Actance et Valence dans les Langues d'Europe*, 259–294. Berlin: Mouton de Gruyter.

Bozzone, Chiara. 2010. New Perspectives on Formularity, in: Stephanie W. Jamison, H. Craig Melchert and Brent Vine (eds.) *Proceedings of the 21st Annual UCLA Indo-European Conference*, pp. 27–44. Bremen: Hempen.

Bozzone, Chiara. 2016. The Mind of the Poet: Linguistic and Cognitive Perspectives, in: C. Gallo (ed.) *Omero: quaestiones disputatae*. Milano-Roma: Bulzoni, 79–105

Broccias, Cristiano. 2013. Cognitive Grammar, in: Thomas Hoffmann and Graeme Trousdale (eds.) *The Oxford Handbook of Construction Grammar*, pp. 191–210. Oxford: Oxford University Press.

Bybee, Joan, L. Revere Perkins and William Pagliuca. 1994. *The evolution of grammar: Tense, aspect and modality in the languages of the world.* Chicago: University of Chicago Press.

Bybee, Joan L. 2010. *Language: Usage and Cognition*. Cambridge: Cambridge University Press.

Chantraine, Pierre. 1938. Remarques sur les rapports entre les modes et les aspects en grec. *Bulletin de la Société de Linguistique de Paris* 40: 69–79.

Chantraine, Pierre. 1973. *Morphologie Historique du Grec.* Paris: Klincksieck.

Chantraine, Pierre. 1977. *Dictionnaire Étymologique de la Langue Grecque.* Paris: Klincksieck.

Chantraine, Pierre. 1981. *Grammaire Homérique* II: *Syntaxe.* Paris: Klincksieck.

Chantraine, Pierre. 2013. *Grammaire Homérique* I: *Phonétique et Morphologie.* Paris: Klincksieck

Chung, Sandra and Alan Timberlake. 1985. Tense, Aspect and Mood, in: Timothy Shopen (ed.) *Language typology and syntactic description*, pp. 241–258. Cambridge: Cambridge University Press.

Comrie, Bernard. 1976. *Aspect*. Cambridge: Cambridge University Press.

Conti, Luz. 1998. Zum Passiv von Griechischen Verben mit Gen. bzw. Dat. als Zweitem Komplement. *Münchener Studien zur Sprachwissenschaft* 58: 13–50.

Conti, Luz. 1999. La Expresión de la Causa en Homero con Referentes Humanos. *Emerita—Revista de Linguistica y Filologia Clásica* 77(2): 295–313.

REFERENCES

Conti, Luz. 2010a. Synchronie und Diacronie del Altgriechischen Genitivs als Semisubjekt. *Historische Sprachforschungen* 121. 2008(2010): 94–113.

Conti, Luz. 2010b. Weiteres zum Genitiv als Semisubjekt im Altgriechischen: Analyse des Kasus bei Impersonalen Konstruktionen. *Historische Sprachforschungen* 122: 182–207.

Conti, Luz. 2010c. Análisis del Dativo en Construcciones Impersonales: los Conceptos de Sujeto y de Semisujeto en Griego Antiguo. *Emerita—Revista de Linguistica y Filologia Clásica* 78(2): 249–273.

Conti, Luz and Silvia Luraghi. 2014. The Ancient Greek Partitive Genitive in Typological Perspective, in: Silvia Luraghi and Tuomas Huumo (eds.). *Partitive Case and Related Categories*, pp. 443–476. Berlin: Mouton de Gruyter.

Cotticelli-Kurras, Paola and Alfredo Rizza. 2015. Zur Entstehung der Medialendungen: Überlegungen zu einigen Bildungsstrategien, in: Thomas Krisch und Stefan Niederreiter (eds.) *Diachronie und Sprachvergleich*, pp. 45–55. Innsbruck: IBS.

Covini, Andrea. 2013. *Il cosiddetto medio dinamico. Studio sincronico e diacronico da Omero*. Unpublished MA thesis, Università Cattolica, Milano.

Crellin, Robert. 2020. The perfect system in Ancient Greek, in: Robert Crellin and Thomas Jugel (eds.) *Perfects in Indo-European Languages and Beyond*, pp. 436–481. Amsterdam: John Benjamins

Croft, William. 1991. *Syntactic Categories and Grammatical Relations*. Chicago: Chicago University Press.

Croft, William. 1993. Case Marking and the Semantics of Mental Verbs, in: James Pustejovsky (ed.) *Semantics and the Lexicon*, pp. 55–72. Dordrecht: Kluwer Academic Publishers.

Croft, William. 2012. *Verbs: Aspect and Causal Structure*. Oxford: Oxford University Press.

Croft, William. 2001. *Radical Construction Grammar: Syntactic Theory in Typological Perspective*. Oxford: University Press.

D'Andrade, Roy G. 1995. *The Development of Cognitive Anthropology*. Cambridge: Cambridge University Press.

Dahl, Eystein. 2009. Some semantic and pragmatic aspects of object alternation in Early Vedic, in: Jóhanna Barðdal and Shobhana L. Chelliah (eds.) *The role of semantic, pragmatic and discourse factors in the development of case*, pp. 23–55. Amsterdam: John Benjamins

Dahl, Eystein. 2010. *Time, tense and aspect in early Vedic grammar: exploring inflectional semantics in the Rigveda*. Leiden: Brill

Dahl, Eystein. 2014a. The Morphosyntax of the Experiencer in Early Vedic, in: Silvia Luraghi and Heiko Narrog (eds.) *Perspectives on semantic roles*, pp. 181–204. Amsterdam: John Benjamins.

Dahl, Eystein. 2014b. Partitive Subjects and Objects in Indo-Iranian and beyond, in: Silvia Luraghi and Tuomas Huumo (eds.) *Partitive Case and Related Categories*, pp. 417–441. Berlin: Mouton de Gruyter.

Dahl, Eystein. 2014c. Experiential Constructions, in: Giorgios K. Giannakis (ed.) *Encyclopedia of Ancient Greek, Language and Linguistic*, Vol. 1 pp. 585–588. Leiden: Brill.

Dahl, Eystein and Chiara Fedriani. 2012. The Argument Structure of Experience: Experiential Construction in Early Vedie, Homeric Greek and Old Latin. *Transactions of the Philological Society* 110(3): 342–362.

Daniel, Michael. 2014. Against the addressee of speech—Recipient metaphor: Evidence from East Caucasian, in: Silvia Luraghi and Heiko Narrog (eds.) *Perspectives on semantic roles*, pp. 207–242. Amsterdam: John Benjamins.

De Boel, Gunnar. 1988. The Homeric accusative of limit of motion revisited, in: Albert Rijskbaron, Hotze Mulder and Gerri Wakker (eds.) *In the Footsteps of Raphael Kühner*, pp. 53–65. Amsterdam: Gieben.

De la Villa, Jesús. 1989. Caractérisation fonctionelle du datif grec. *Glotta* 67: 20–40.

De la Villa, J. 2004. Aspectos del Aspecto en Griego, in: Usobiaga Begoña and Quetglas Pere Joan (eds.) *Ciencia, Didàctica i Funció Social dels Estudis Clàssics*, pp. 97–124. Barcelona: Secció Catalana de la SEEC.

Delbrück, Bertold. 1911. *Vergleichende Syntax der Indogermanischen Sprachen*. Strassburg.

Di Giovine, Paolo. 1990. *Studio sul Perfetto Indoeuropeo*, parte 1: *La Funzione del Perfetto Studiata nella Documentazione delle Lingue Storiche*. Roma: Herder.

Di Giovine, Paolo. 1996. *Studio sul Perfetto Indoeuropeo*, parte 2: *La Posizione del Perfetto all'Interno del Sistema Verbale Indoeuropeo*. Roma: Il Calamo.

Dik, Simon Cornelis. 1968. *Coordination: its Implications for the Theory of General Linguistics*. Amsterdam: North-Holland.

Dik, Simon Cornelis. 1997. *The Theory of Functional Grammar: The Structure of the Clause*. Kees Hengeveld. (ed.). Berlin: Mouton de Gruyter.

Dik, Simon Cornelis and Kees Hengeveld. 1991. The Hierarchical Structure of the Clause and the Typology of Perception-verb Complements. *Linguistics* 29: 231–259.

Dirven, René. 1993. Dividing up Physical and Mental Spaces into Conceptual Categories by Means of English Prepositions, in: Cornelia Zelinsky-Wibbelt (ed.) *The semantics of prepositions: from mental processing to natural language processing*, pp. 73–97. Berlin: Mouton De Gryuter.

Dirven, René. 1997. Emotions as cause and the cause of emotions, in: S. Niemeier and R. Dirven (eds.), *The Language of Emotions: Conceptualization, Expression, and Theoretical Foundation*, pp. 55–83. Amsterdam: John Benjamins

Duhoux, Yves. 1992. *Le verbe en grec ancien*. Louvain-La-Neuve: Peeters.

Ebeling, Heinrich. 1885. *Lexicon Homericum*. 2 vols. Leipzig: Teubner.

van Emde Boas, Evert, Albert Rijksbaron, Luuk Huitink and Mathieu de Bakker. 2010. *The Cambridge grammar of classical Greek*. Cambridge: Cambridge University Press.

REFERENCES

Evans, Nicholas and David Wilkins. 2000. In the Mind's Ear: the Semantic Extension of Perception verbs in Australian Languages. *Language* 76(3): 546–592.

Evans, Nicholas. 2010. Semantic Typology, in: Jae Jung Song (ed.) *The Oxford handbook of linguistic typology.* Oxford: Oxford University Press.

Fanning, Buist. 1990. *Verbal Aspect in New Testament Greek.* Oxford: Clarendon Press.

Fedriani, Chiara. 2014. *Experiential Constructions in Latin.* Leiden and Boston: Brill.

Fillmore, Charles J. 1971. *Santa Cruz Lectures on Deixis.* Bloomington: Indiana university linguistics club.

Fortescue, Michael. 2001. Thoughts about thought. *Cognitive Linguistics* 12(1): 15–45.

Fritz, Kurt von. 1943. NOOS and NOEIN in the Homeric Poems. *Classical Philology* 37: 79–93.

Garcia Ramon, José Luis. 2002. Zu Verbalcharakter, morphologischer Aktionsart und Aspekt in der indogermanischen Rekonstruktion, in: Heinrich Hettrich (ed.) *Indogermanische Syntax. Fragen und Perspektiven,* pp. 105–136. Wiesbaden: Reichert.

Gehring, Augustus. 1891. *Index Homericus.* Leipzig: Teubner.

Gisborne, Nikolas and Jasper Holmes. 2007. A history of English evidential verbs of appearance. *English Language and Linguistics* 11(1): 1–29.

Goddard, Cliff. 2003. Thinking Across Languages and Cultures: Six Dimensions of Variation. *Cognitive Linguistics* 14(2–3): 109–140.

Goddard, Cliff. 2010. Semantic primitives (primes), in: Patrick Colm Hogan (ed.), *The Cambridge Encyclopedia of Language Sciences,* pp. 740–741. Cambridge: Cambridge University Press.

Goddard, Cliff. 2012. Semantic Primes, Semantic Molecules, Semantic Templates: Key Concepts in the NSM Approach to Lexical Typology. *Linguistics* 50(3): 711–743.

Goldberg, Adele. 1995. *Constructions: A Construction Grammar Approach to Argument Structure.* Chicago & London: The University of Chicago Press.

Goldberg, Adele. 2006. *Constructions at Work: the Nature of Generalization in Language.* Oxford: Oxford University Press.

Grassman, H.G. 1873. *Worterbuch zum Rig-veda.* Wiesbaden: Harrassowitz.

Grimshaw, Jane Barbara. 1990. *Argument structure.* Cambridge, Mass.: The MIT Press.

Hackstein, Olav. 2010. The Greek of Epic, in: Egbert J. Bakker (ed.) *A Companion to the Ancient Greek Language,* pp. 401–423. Malden, MA: Wiley-Blackwell.

Halliday, M.A.K. 2004. *An Introduction to Functional Grammar.* Christian Matthiessen (ed.) Third Edition. London: Arnold.

Harkins, Jean and Anna Wierzbicka (eds). 2001. *Emotions in Crosslinguistic Perspective.* Berlin: Mouton de Gruyter.

Haspelmath, Martin. 1993. More on the typology of inchoative/causative verb alternations, in: Bernard Comrie and Maria Polinsky (eds.) *Causatives and transitivity,* pp. 87–120. Amsterdam: John Benjamins.

Haspelmath, Martin. 2001. Non-canonical marking of core arguments in European languages, in: Alexandra Y. Aikhenvald, R.M.W. Dixon and Masayuki Onishi (eds.) *Non-canonical marking of subjects and objects*, pp. 53–83. Amsterdam: John Benjamins

Haspelmath, Martin. 2003. The geometry of grammatical meaning: Semantic maps and cross-linguistic comparison, in: Michael Tomasello (ed.) *The new psychology of language*, vol. 2, pp. 211–242. Mahwah, NJ: Lawrence Erlbaum.

Haug, Dag. 2009. Does Homeric Greek have prepositions? Or local adverbs? (And what's the difference anyway?), in: Vit Bubenik and John Hewson (eds.) *Grammatical Change in Indo-European Languages*, pp. 103–102. Amsterdam: John Benjamins.

Havers, Wilhelm. 1924. Eine syntaktische Sonderstellung griechischer und lateinischer Neutra. *Glotta* 13(3): 171–189

Hettrich, Heinrich. 2014. Some remarks on the adverbal genitive in Ṛigvedic Sanskrit, in: Jared Klein and Elizabeth Tucker (eds.) *Vedic and Sanskrit Historical Linguistics*, pp. 129–152. New Delhi: Motilal Banarshidas

Hewson, John and Vit Bubenik. *From case to adposition*. Amsterdam: John Benjamins.

Hilpert, Martin. 2013. *Constructional Change in English: Developments in Allomorphy, Word Formation, and Syntax*. Cambridge: Cambridge University Press.

Hilpert, Martin. 2014. *Construction Grammar and its Application to English*. Edinburgh: Edinburgh University Press.

Holvoet, Axel and Nicole Nau. 2014. Argument marking and grammatical relations in Baltic: An overview, in: Axel Holvoet and Nicole Nau (eds.) *Grammatical Relations and their Non-Canonical Encoding in Baltic*, pp. 1–41. Amsterdam: John Benjamins.

Hopper, Paul J. and Sandra A. Thompson. 1980. Transitivity in Grammar and Discourse. *Language* 56(2): 251–299.

Horrocks, Geoffrey C. 1981. *Space and Time in Homer. Prepositional and Adverbial Particles in the Greek Epic*. New York: Arno Press.

Horrocks, Geoffrey C. 1997. *A History of the Language and its Speakers*. London & New York: Longman.

Humbert, Jean. 1986. *Syntaxe Grecque*. Paris: Klincksieck.

Iacobini, Claudio, Luisa Corona, Noemi De Pasquale and A. Buoniconto. 2017. How should a "classical" Satellite-Framed Language behave? Path encoding asymmetries in Ancient Greek and Latin, in: Silvia Luraghi, Tatiana Nikitina and Chiara Zanchi (eds.) *Space in diachrony*, pp. 95–118. Amsterdam: John Benjamins.

Inglese, Guglielmo. 2020. *The Hittite middle voice*. Synchrony, diachrony, typology. Leiden: Brill.

Jacquinod, Bernard. 1989. *Le double accusatif en grec d'Homere a la fin du Ve siècle avant J.-C.* Louvain-la-Neuve: Peeters

Jahn, Tomas van. 1987. *Zum Wortfeld 'Seele-Geist' in der Sprache Homers*. Munich: C.H. Bech.

Johnson, Mark. 1987. *The Body in the Mind: The Bodily Basis of Meaning, Imagination, and Reason*. Chicago: University of Chicago Press.

REFERENCES

Johnson, Mark and Tim Rohrer. 2007. We are live creatures: Embodiment, American Pragmatism and the cognitive organism, in: Jordan Zlatev, Tom Ziemke, Roz Frank and René Dirven, *Body, Language and Mind. Vol. 1: Embodiment*, pp. 17–54. Berlin: Mouton de Gruyter.

Kemmer, Suzanne. 1993. *The Middle Voice*. Amsterdam: John Benjamins

Kittilä, Seppo. 2002. *Transitivity: Towards a Comprehensive Typology*. Turku: University of Turku.

Kittilä, Seppo, Katja Västi and Jussi Ylikoski (eds). 2011. *Case, Animacy and Semantic Roles*. Amsterdam: John Benjamins.

Klein, Katarina and Silvia Kutscher. 2002. *Psych-verbs and Lexical Economy*. Düsseldorf: Universität Düsseldorf.

Koptjevskaja-Tamm, Maria. 2015. Introducing "The linguistics of temperature", in: Maria Koptjevskaja-Tamm (ed.), *Linguistics of temperature*, pp. 1–40. Amsterdam: John Benjamins.

Kövecses, Zoltan. 1990. *Emotion Concepts*. Berlin: Springer.

Kuteva, Tania Bernd Heine, Bo Hong, Haiping Long, Heiko Narrog and Seongha Rhee. 2019. *World Lexicon of Grammaticalization. Second, extensively revised and updated edition*. Cambridge: Cambridge University Press.

Lakoff, George. 1993. The contemporary theory of metaphor, in: A. Ortony (ed.) *Metaphor and thought*, pp. 202–251. Cambridge: Cambridge University Press.

Lakoff George and Mark Johnson. 1980. *Metaphors We Live By*. Chicago: The University Chicago Press.

Langacker, Ronald W. 1987. *Foundations of Cognitive Grammar*, vol. 1. Stanford: Stanford University.

Langacker, Ronald W. 1999. *Grammar and Conceptualization*. Berlin: Mouton de Gruyter

Latacz, Joachim. 1966. *Zum Wortfeld "Freude" in der Sprache Homers*. Heidelberg: Winter.

Lazzeroni, Romano. 2004. Inaccusatività indoeuropea e alternanza causativa vedica. *Archivio Glottologico Italiano* 89: 1–28.

Lehmann, Winfred P. 1986. *A Gothic Etymological Dictionary*. Leiden: Brill.

Levin, Beth. 1985. Lexical Semantics in Review: An Introduction, in: Beth Levin (ed.) *Lexical Semantics in Review, Lexicon Project Working Papers 1*, pp. 1–62. Cambridge, Mass: Center for Cognitive Science, MIT.

Létoublon, Françoise 1999. Le problème de la proposition infinitive chez Homère, in: Bernard Jacquinod (ed.) *Les complétives en grec ancien*, pp. 191–198. Saint-Étienne: Centre Jean-Palerne.

Lord, Albert. 2000. *The singer of tales*. 2nd edn, Stephen Arthur Mitchell and Gregory Nagy (eds.). Cambridge, Mass.: Harvard University Press.

Luraghi, Silvia. 1989. Cause and Instrument expressions in Classical Greek. *Mnemosyne* 43: 294–308.

Luraghi, Silvia. 1996. *Studi su casi e preposizioni nel greco antico*. Milano: Franco Angeli.

Luraghi, Silvia. 2000. Spatial metaphors and agenthood in Ancient Greek, in: Christian Zinko and Michaela Offisch (eds.) *125 Jahre Indogermanistik in Graz*, pp. 283–298. Graz: Leykam.

Luraghi, Silvia. 2003a. *On the Meaning of Cases and Prepositions*. Amsterdam and Philadelphia: John Benjamins.

Luraghi, Silvia. 2003b. Definite Referential Null Objects in Ancient Greek. *Indogermanische Forschungen* 108: 169–196.

Luraghi, Silvia. 2004a. The evolution of the Greek nominal paradigms: economy and case syncretism from Mycenaean to Modern Greek. *Classica et Mediaevalia* 55: 361–379.

Luraghi, Silvia. 2004b. The container schema in Homeric Greek, in: A. Soares de Silva, A. Torres, M. Gonçalves (eds.) *Linguagem, cultura e cognição: Estudos de Linguística Cognitiva*, pp. 25–41. Braga: Almedina.

Luraghi, Silvia. 2009. The Evolution of Local Cases and their Grammatical Equivalent in Greek and Latin, in: Johanna Barðdal and Shobhana L. Celliah. (eds.) *The Role of Semantics and Pragmatics in the Development of Case*, pp. 283–305. Amsterdam: John Benjamins.

Luraghi, Silvia. 2010a. Experiencer Predicates in Hittite, in: Ronald I. Kim, Norbert Oettinger, Elisabeth Rieken and Michael Weiss (eds.) *Ex Anatolia Lux*, pp. 249–264. Ann Arbor: Beech Stave Press.

Luraghi, Silvia. 2010b. The Extension of the Transitive Construction in Ancient Greek. *Acta Linguistica Hafniensia* 42(1): 60–74.

Luraghi, Silvia. 2010c. Where do beneficiaries come from and how do they come about? in: Kathryn Allan, Heli Tissari and Margaret Winters (eds.) *Historical Cognitive Linguistics*, pp. 93–131. Berlin: Mouton de Gruyter.

Luraghi, Silvia. 2010d. The rise (and possible downfall) of configurationality, in: Silvia Luraghi and Vit Bubenik (eds.) *The Continuum companion to historical linguistics*, pp. 212–229. London/New York: Continuum

Luraghi, Silvia. 2012. The spatial meaning of *diá* with the accusative in Homeric Greek. *Mnemosyne* 65(3): 357–386.

Luraghi, Silvia. 2014a. Plotting Diachronic Semantic Maps: the Role of Metaphor, in: Silvia Luraghi and Heiko Narrog (eds.) *Perspectives on Semantic Roles*, pp. 101–152. Amsterdam: John Benjamins.

Luraghi, Silvia. 2014b. Conjunction reduction, in: Georgios K. Giannakis, Vit Bubenik, Emilio Crespo, Chris Golston, Alexandra Lianeri, Silvia Luraghi and Stephanos Matthaios (eds.) *The Encyclopedia of Greek Language and Linguistics*, vol. 1, pp. 362–363. Leiden: Brill.

Luraghi, Silvia. 2015. Asymmetries in Italian temperature terminology, in: Maria Koptjevskaja-Tamm (ed.), *Linguistics of temperature*, Amsterdam: John Benjamins, 334–353.

REFERENCES

Luraghi, Silvia. 2017. Differential Goal marking vs. differential Source marking in Ancient Greek, in: Silvia Luraghi, Tatiana Nikitina and Chiara Zanchi (eds.) *Space in diachrony*, pp. 119–145. Amsterdam: John Benjamins.

Luraghi, Silvia. 2019. Basic valency orientation, the anticausative alternation, and voice in PIE, in: Melanie Malzahn (ed.) *Akten der 16th Fachtagung der Indogermanischen Gesellschaft*, pp. 259–274. Wiesbaden: Reichert.

Luraghi, Silvia and Erica Biagetti. 2019. Comparing argument structure variation in Homeric Greek and Early Vedic: The case of *oîda* and *veda*. Paper read at the *52nd Annual Meeting of the Societas Linguistica Europaea*, Leipzig, 21st–24th August 2019.

Luraghi, Silvia and Tuomas Huumo. 2014. Introduction, in: Silvia Luraghi and Tuomas Huumo (eds.) *Partitive cases and related categories*, pp. 1–13. Berlin: Mouton de Gruyter.

Luraghi, Silvia, Guglielmo Inglese and Daniel Kölligan. Forthcoming. The passive in Indo-European. *Folia Linguistica Historica* 42.

Luraghi, Silvia and Seppo Kittilä. 2014. Typology and Diachrony of Partitive Case Markers, in: Silvia Luraghi and Tuomas Huumo (eds.) *Partitive Cases and Related Categories*, pp. 17–62. Berlin: Mouton de Gruyter.

Luraghi, Silvia, Maria Chiara Naccarato and Erica Pinelli. 2020. The *u*+gen construction in Modern Standard Russian. *Cognitive Linguistics* 31(1): 149–183.

Luraghi Silvia and Heiko Narrog. 2014. Perspectives on semantic roles. An introduction, in: Silvia Luraghi and Heiko Narrog (eds.) *Perspectives on Semantic Roles*, pp. 1–21. Amsterdam: John Benjamins.

Luraghi, Silvia, Anna Pompei and Stavros Skopeteas. 2005. *Ancient Greek*. München/New Castle: Lincom Europa.

Luraghi, Silvia and Eleonora Sausa. 2015. Hate and Anger, Love and Desire: the Construal of Emotions in Homeric Greek, in: Dag T.T. Haug (ed.) *Historical Linguistics 2013*, pp. 233–255. Amsterdam: John Benjamins.

Luraghi, Silvia and Eleonora Sausa. 2017. Pensare, sapere, ricordare: i verbi di attività mentale in greco omerico, in: Felicia Logozzo and Paolo Poccetti (eds.) *Ancient Greek Linguistics: New approaches, insights, perspectives*, pp. 745–774. Berlin: Mouton De Gruyter.

Luraghi, Silvia and Eleonora Sausa. 2019. Aspects of aural perception in Homeric Greek, in: Egle Mocciaro and William Short (eds.) *The Embodied Basis of Constructions in Greek and Latin*, pp. 149–175. Berlin: Mouton De Gruyter.

Luraghi, Silvia and Chiara Zanchi. 2018. Double accusative constructions and ditransitives in Ancient Greek, in: Agnes Korn and Andrej Malchukov (eds.) *Ditransitive constructions in a cross-linguistic perspective*, pp. 13–35. Wiesbaden: Reichert.

Malchukov, Andrej. 2005. Case Pattern Splits, Verb Types and Construction Competition, in: Mengistu Amberber and Helen de Hoop (eds.) *Competition and variation in natural languages: The case for case*, pp. 73–117. Amsterdam: Elsevier.

Malchukov, Andrej. 2008. Split intransitives, experiencer objects and transimpersonal constructions: (re-) establishing the connection, in: Mark Donohue and Soren Wichmann (eds.) *The Typology of Semantic Alignment*, pp. 76–101. Oxford: Oxford University Press.

Mallory, James and Douglas Quentin Adams. 2006. *The Oxford Introduction to Proto-Indo-European and the Proto-Indo-European World*. Oxford: Oxford University Press.

Meillet, Antoine. 1897. *De Indo-Europaea Radice *Men-"Mente Agitare"*. Paris: E. Bauilla.

Meiser, Gerhard. 1992. Syncretism in Indo-European languages—Motives, process and results. *Transactions of the Philological Society* 90(2): 187–218.

Mette, Hans Joachim. 1961. 'Schauen' und 'Staunen'. *Glotta* 39: 49–71.

Monier-Williams, M. 2008. *Sanskrit-English Dictionary*. Varanasi: Indica Books.

Næss, Åshild. 2007. *Prototypical Transitivity*. Amsterdam: John Benjamins.

Nagy, Gregory. 2010. Language and Meter, in: Egbert J. Bakker (ed.) *A Companion to the Ancient Greek Language*, pp. 370–386. Malden, MA: Wiley-Blackwell.

Napoli, Maria. 2006. *Aspect and Actionality in Homeric Greek. A contrastive Analysis*. Milano: Franco Angeli.

Nichols, Johanna, David Peterson and Jonathan Barnes. 2004. Transitivising and detransitivising languages. *Linguistic Typology* 8(2): 149–211.

Nikiforidou, Kiki. 1991. The Meanings of the Genitive: a Case Study in Semantic Structure and Semantic Change. *Cognitive Linguistics* 2: 149–205.

Nikitina, Tatiana and Boris Maslov. 2013. Redefining Constructio Praegnans: On the Variation between Allative and Locative Expressions in Ancient Greek. *Journal of Greek Linguistics* 13: 105–142.

Nishimura, Yoshiki. 1993. Agentivity in Cognitive Grammar, in: Richard A. Geiger and Brygida Rudzka-Ostyn (eds.) *Conceptualization and Mental Processing in Language*, pp. 488–530. Berlin: Mouton de Gruyter.

Noonan, Michael. 2007. Complementation, in: Timothy Shopen (ed.) *Language Typology and Syntactic Description*, pp. 52–150. Cambridge: Cambridge University Press.

Onishi, Masayuki. 2001. Non-canonically marked subjects and objects: Parameters and properties, in: Alexandra Y. Aikhenvald, R.M.W. Dixon and Masayuki Onishi (eds.) *Non-Canonical Marking of Subjects and Objects*, pp. 1–52. Amsterdam: John Benjamins.

Parry, Milman. 1971. *The Making of Homeric Verse: the Collected Papers*. Adam Parry (ed.). Oxford: Clarendon Press

Perek, Florent. 2015. *Argument structure in usage-based construction grammar: Experimental and corpus-based perspectives*. Amsterdam: John Benjamins

Pinault, George. 1995. Le problème du préverbe en indo-européen, in: André Rousseau (ed.) *Les préverbe dans les langues d'Europe*, pp. 35–59. Lille: Presses Universitaires du Septentrion.

Pinelli, Erica. 2015. *A Corpus-Based Approach to the Conceptualization of Emotions*. Roma: Aracne.

REFERENCES

Pokorny, Julius. 1969 [1887]. *Indogermanisches Etymologisches Wörterbuch*. Bern: Francke.

Prévot, André. 1935a. L'expression en grec ancien de la notion 'entendre'. *Revue des Études Grecques* 48: 70–78

Prévot, André. 1935b. Verbes Grecs relatifs à la vision et noms de l'eoils. *Revue de Philologie* 9: 233–279.

Primus, Beatrice. 2011. Case, grammatical relations, and semantic roles, in: Andrej Malchukov and Andrew Spencer (eds.) *The Oxford Handbook of Case*, pp. 261–275. Oxford: Oxford University Press.

Radden, Günter. 1989. Semantic roles, in: René Dirven and R.A. Geiger (eds.) *A User's Grammar of English*, pp. 421–471. Frankfurt am Mein: Peter Lang.

Reh, Mechthild and Christiane Simon. 1998. Experiens-Konstruktionen in Mande Sprachen, in: Mechthild Reh, Christiane Simon and Katrin Koops (eds.) *Experiens-Kodierung in afrikanischen Sprachen typologisch gesehen: Formen und ihre Motivierungen*, pp. 41–88. Hamburg: Institut für Afrikanistik und Äthiopistik.

Risselada, Rodie. 1993. *Imperatives and Other Directive Expressions in Latin: A Study in the Pragmatics of a Dead Language*. Amsterdam: Gieben

Rijksbaron, Albert. 2002. *The Syntax and Semantics of the Verb in Classical Greek*. Chicago: University of Chicago Press.

Ruijgh, Cornelis J. 1985. L'emploi 'inceptif' du thème du présent du verbe grec. *Mnemosyne* 38: 1–61.

Ruiperez Martín S. 1954. *Estructura del sistema de aspectos y tiempos del verbo griego*. Salamanca: Consejo Superior de Investigaciones Cientificas.

San Roque, Lila, Kobin H. Kendrick, Elisabeth Norcliffe and Asifa Majid. 2018. Universal meaning extensions of perception verbs are grounded in interaction. *Cognitive Linguistics* 29(3): 371–406.

Sasse, Hans-Jürgen. 2002. Recent activity in the theory of aspect: Accomplishments, achievements, or just non-progressive state? *Linguistic Typology* 6(2): 199–217.

Sausa, Eleonora. 2015. *Argument Structure Construction in Homeric Greek. A Study on Bivalent verbs*. PhD thesis. University of Pavia.

Sausa, Eleonora. 2016. Basic valency orientation in Homeric Greek. *Folia Linguistica Historica* 37: 205–238.

Schlesinger, Izchak M. 1989. Instruments as Agents: On the Nature of Semantic Relations. *Journal of Linguistics* 25: 189–210.

Schwyzer, Eduard. 1950. *Syntax und Syntaktische Stilistik*. Albert Debrunner (ed.). München: Beck.

Sicking, C.M.J. 1991. The Distribution of Aorist and Present Tense Stem Forms in Greek, Especially in the Imperative. *Glotta* 69: 14–43; 154–170.

Snell, Bruno. 1946. *Die Entdeckung des Geistes. Studien zur Entstehung des europäischen Denkens bei den Griechen*. Hamburg: Claassen & Goverts.

Stefanowitsch, Anatol and Thomas Herbst. 2011. Argument Structure—Valency and/or Constructions? *Zeitschrift für Anglistik und Amerikanistik* 59(4): 315–316.

Strunk, Klaus. 1994. Relative Chronology and Indo-European Verb-System: The Case of Present- and Aorist-Stems. *Journal of Indo-European Studies* 22(3–4): 417–434.

Sweetser, Eve. 1990. *From Etymology to Pragmatics: Metaphorical and Cultural Aspects of Language*. Cambridge: Cambridge University Press.

Tatevosov, Sergej. 2002. The parameter of actionality. *Linguistic Typology* 6(3): 317–401.

Thompson, Sandra A. and Paul J. Hopper. 2001. Transitivity, Clause Structure, and Argument Structure: Evidence from Conversation, in: Joan Bybee, Paul J. Hopper (eds.) *Frequency and the Emergence of Linguistic Structure*, pp. 27–60. Amsterdam: John Benjamins.

Tissari, Heli. 2003. *LOVEscapes: Changes in Prototypical Senses and Cognitive Metaphors Since 1500*. Helsinki: Société Néophilologique.

Torrent, Tiago T. 2015. On the relation between inheritance and change. The Constructional Convergence and the Construction Network Reconfiguration Hypotheses, in: Jóhanna Barðdal, Elena Smirnova, Lotte Sommerer and Spike Gildea (eds.), *Diachronic Construction Grammar*, 173–212. Amsterdam: John Benjamins.

Traugott, Elizabeth C. and Graeme Trousdale. 2013. *Constructionalization and Constructional Changes*. Oxford: Oxford University Press.

Tsunoda, Tasaku. 1981. Split Case-marking Patterns in Verb-types and Tense/Aspect/Mood. *Linguistics* 19: 389–438.

Tsunoda, Tasaku. 1985. Remarks on Transitivity. *Journal of linguistic* 21: 385–396.

Vaan, Michiel de. 2008. *Etymological Dictionary of Latin and the other Italic Languages*. Leiden: Brill.

Valin, Robert van and David Wilkins. 1993. Predicting Syntactic Structure from Semantic Representations: Remember in English and its Equivalents in Mparntwe Arrernte, in: Robert van Valin (ed.) *Advances in Role and Reference Grammar*, pp. 499–534. Amsterdam: John Benjamins.

Vendler, Zeno. 1957. Verbs and Times. *The Philosophical Review* 66(2): 143–160.

Verhoeven, Elisabeth. 2007. *Experiential Constructions in Yucatec Maya*. Amsterdam: John Benjamins.

Viberg, Åke. 1984. The Verbs of Perception: a Typological Study. *Linguistics* 21: 123–162.

Viti, Carlotta. 2017. Semantic and Cognitive Factors of Argument Marking in Ancient Indo-European Languages. *Diachronica* 34: 368–419.

Weiss, Michael. 2010. Morphology and Word Formation, in: Egbert J. Bakker (ed.) *A Companion to the Ancient Greek Language*, pp. 104–119. Malden, MASS: Wiley-Blackwell

Wierzbicka, Anna. 1972. *Semantic Primitives*. Frankfurt: Athenäum

Wierzbicka, Anna. 1981. Case marking and human nature. *Australian Journal of Linguistics* 1: 43–80.

REFERENCES

Wierzbicka, Anna. 1988. *The Semantics of Grammar*. Amsterdam: John Benjamins Publishing.

Wierzbicka, Anna. 1992: *Semantics, Culture, and Cognition. Universal Human Concepts in Culture-Specific Configurations*. Oxford: Oxford University Press.

Wierzbicka, Anna. 1999. *Emotions Across Languages and Cultures: Diversity and Universals*. Cambridge: Cambridge University Press.

Wierzbicka, Anna. 1999. *Emotions Across Languages and Cultures: Diversity and Universals*. Cambridge: Cambridge University Press.

Wierzbicka, Anna. 2007. Bodies and their Parts: A NSM Approach to Semantic Typology. *Language Sciences* 29: 14–65.

Willi, Andreas. 2018. *Origins of the Greek Verb*. Cambridge: Cambridge University Press.

Zalizniak, Anna. 2007. The conceptualisation of remembering and forgetting in Russian, in: Mengistu Amberber (ed.) *The language of memory in crosslinguistic perspective*, pp. 7–118. Amsterdam: John Benjamins

Zanchi, Chiara. 2019. *Multiple Preverbs in Ancient Indo-European Languages*. Tübingen: Narr.

Index of Greek Verbs

adéō 101, 113, 271, 273, 278
ágamai 204, 229, 272, 275, 276, 278
agnoéō 179
aidéomai 235–237, 249, 276
aiskhúnō 254, 258, 259
aiskhúnomai 235–237, 249, 276
aisthánomai 144
aíō 127–129, 137, 138, 144, 145, 274
akédomai 221, 257
akheúomai 240
akouázomai 128, 129, 139, 149, 274
akoúō 85, 128–130, 132, 134–137, 139, 143, 144, 148, 184, 185, 264, 268, 274, 285, 288, 289
alegízō 220, 221, 249, 273
alégō 220, 221, 249, 273
algéō 105, 114
amphikalúptō 46, 290
amphrázomai 163
amúnō 70
anagignóskō 178
anássō 70
antiázō 70
ántomai 70
apeîmi 62
apekhthánomai 242–244
apékhtomai 242
apérkhomai 62
apobaínō 62
(apo)deidíssomai 5, 249, 251, 252, 254, 260, 261, 289
(apo)skudmaínō 207, 248, 276
arégō 70
arkéō 70
árkhō 70
atúzō 231
atúzomai 230, 231, 249, 263, 275
augázomai 81

baínō 61, 62, 93, 110
bállō 62, 77, 220, 284
barúnō 261–264
barúnomai 261, 264
basileúō 70
bébeka 93, 110
boúlomai 83, 106, 108, 111–113, 197, 275
bussodomeúō 153, 167, 199

deî 57
deidíssomai 52, 249, 251, 252, 254, 260, 261, 289
deídō 5, 83, 86, 229, 230, 236, 237, 249, 251, 252, 254, 260, 261, 275, 287, 288
dérkomai 116, 121, 126, 149, 189, 275
deúomai 63
déō 57
diagignóskō 179
didáskō 179, 181
dídōmi 69
dipsáō 48, 101, 114
dokéō 37, 79, 81, 150, 151, 153, 159, 160, 195, 282

édaon 151, 152, 169, 173, 175, 179–181, 183, 187, 196, 197, 271, 274
eîdon 116, 120–122, 126, 127, 141, 148, 149, 155, 184, 196
eimí 62
eîmi 61
eîpon 69
eisakoúō 128
eisbaínō 62
eisdérkomai 121
eiseîdon 122
eisérkhomai 62
eisoráō 123, 226, 274, 288
ékhō 66
ekhthaírō 237
ékhtomai 242, 263, 264
éldomai 216–218, 273, 284, 285
eleaírō 223
elleípō 87
élpō 112, 254, 255, 257
élpomai 98, 106, 110, 111–114, 197, 253, 255, 257, 258, 263, 275
éneimi 62
epakúō 124, 128, 129
épeimi 62
ephḗmai 62
ephoráō 124
epimaíomai 51, 52, 78
epimimnéskomai 192
epístamai 151, 152, 173–175, 187, 196, 197, 199, 272, 274

INDEX OF GREEK VERBS

305

epórnumi 70
éramai 215, 216
érkhomai 61, 176
ethélō 34, 106–108, 111, 112, 114, 197, 217, 275

gēthéō 209, 210, 249
géuomai 140, 273
gígnomai 98
gignóskō 31, 86, 94, 151, 152, 154, 175–179, 181, 186, 187, 196, 197, 199, 271, 274, 287, 289

hairéō 45, 46, 78, 220, 282, 290
hamartánō 52, 63, 78
handánō 41, 43, 79, 80, 241, 242, 244, 245, 282
háptomai 139, 149, 273
hēgemoneúō 70
hēgéomai 70
hikánō 61
híkō 61
hístēmai 174
hístēmi 54, 175, 227
horáō 115, 116, 120, 121, 126, 127, 148, 149, 264, 274, 288, 289
hormaínō 153, 167–169, 199
hórnumi 168
hupakúō 128
húpeimi 62
hupodeídō 230, 275
hupokrínomai 70
(*hupo*)*troméō* 231, 232, 275

iaínō 261, 264
iaínomai 210, 249, 261, 264
indállomai 81

kámnō 105, 114
kḗdō 254, 256, 257
kḗdomai 220–223, 249, 254, 256, 257, 264, 273
keîmai 234
keletízō 72
khaírō 86, 98, 210–212, 248, 276
khatéō 63
kholóō 94, 248, 254, 255, 257
kholóomai 96, 98, 201, 206, 209, 247–249, 253, 254, 255, 257, 263, 276
khráomai 104
khrḗ 63, 103, 104, 273

kikhánō 46, 290
klaíō 231, 276
klúō 127–129, 135–137, 148, 149, 274, 288, 290
korénnamai 253, 254, 257, 264
korénnumi 102, 254, 257, 273
kotéō 201, 247, 253, 276
kráteō 70
krēízō 104, 273

lanthánō 192, 199, 254, 259–261, 264
lanthánomai 151, 152, 191–195, 199, 253, 254, 260, 264, 274
légō 70
leússō 116, 119, 124, 126, 127, 274
lilaíomai 219, 220

mákhomai 55, 56, 70
márnamai 70
médomai 151–153, 166, 191, 194, 199, 223, 273, 275
médomai 151–153, 165, 166, 199, 275, 277
megaírō 203–205, 276
mélō 37, 57, 79, 80, 242, 243
mémona 106, 107, 109, 110, 114, 153, 187, 273
mermērízō 153, 167, 168, 199
metamélō 57
metaphrázomai 163
metaudáō 70
méteimi 62
methomiléō 70
mētiáō/mētíomai 151–153, 164, 165, 167, 199, 275
mimnḗskō 4, 18, 48, 96, 189, 252, 254, 256, 257, 260, 282
mimnḗskomai 18, 66, 96, 98, 151, 152, 187–195, 199, 223, 252–254, 256, 257, 260, 263, 274
miséō 233, 276
mnáomai 151, 152, 187, 188, 191, 194, 274

naíō 62
neikéō 70
nemesáō 238, 275, 276
nemesízō 238, 275, 276
noéō 86, 150–158, 163, 165, 175, 178, 195, 198, 228, 271, 275, 277

odúromai 231, 276
odússomai 202, 276

306   INDEX OF GREEK VERBS

oîda 12, 31, 84, 86, 87, 93, 94, 110, 116, 126, 142, 151, 152, 157, 158, 169–174, 178–181, 186, 187, 195–197, 199, 270, 272, 274, 277, 287, 289, 290

oíō/oíomai 84, 150–153, 156, 158, 198, 275, 277

ólophuromai 220, 221, 249

onínamai 103, 273

orégomai 49, 52, 53, 78, 284

osphraínomai 141

ózō 141

parabaínō 62

páreimi 62

páskhō 106, 113, 161, 283

pégnumi 62

peináō 101, 104, 114, 273

peíthō 66, 98

perideídō 239, 273, 278

perikédomai 220, 222, 256, 273

periphrázomai 163

peúthomai 151, 152, 175, 181, 185, 188, 277

phérō 66

pheúgō 62

philéomai 215

phobéō 288

phobéomai 288

phrássomai 84

phrázō 264

phrázomai 86, 107, 151–153, 162–164, 199, 264, 275

phríssō 13, 231, 232, 275

phronéō 30, 150–154, 161, 162, 195, 198, 275, 283

phthonéō 209

pímplēmi 72, 104

pothéō 219, 249, 273, 288

psáuō 149

punthánomai 86, 94, 137, 151, 152, 155, 169, 175, 180–183, 186, 187, 196, 197, 199, 271, 274, 277, 287, 289

rhégnumai 95

rhégnumi 95

rhigóō 105, 114

sképtomai 116, 119, 124–126, 149, 275

stugéō 232, 249

sumphrázomai 164

tarbéō 230, 231, 249, 275

térpō 212, 254, 256, 257

térpomai 98, 102, 103, 113, 212, 214, 246, 249, 254–257, 263, 272, 273, 276, 278

téthēpa 227

tetíēmai 234

thambéō 156, 225, 227, 249, 275

thaumázō 225, 227, 249, 275

theáomai 226, 227, 275

théromai 96

títhēmi 66

tugkhánō 77, 140, 149, 220, 284

Author Index

Adams, Quentin   102, 110
Aikhenvald, Alexandra Y.   12, 26, 142
Aldai, Gontzal   10, 22, 23
Allan, Rutger   89, 95–98, 114, 126, 149, 198, 199, 248, 252, 288
Amberber, Mengistu   31
Athanasiadou, Angeliki   33

Bakker, Egbert   13, 15
Barðdal, Jóhanna   9, 64, 283
Baayen, Harald R.   64
Bechert, Johannes   126
Beek, Lucien van   255
Beekes, Robert   227, 255
Bergs, Alexander   9
Bertinetto, Pier Marco   90, 91
Bertolín Cebrián, Reyes   14, 109, 110, 153, 155–158, 165, 167, 168
Biagetti, Erica   268, 271
Blansitt, Edward   2, 39
Bloomfield, Leonard   58
Boas, Hans C.   7, 92
Boel, Gunnar de   60
Booij, Geert E.   61
Bossong, George   21, 23
Bozzone, Chiara   14
Broccias, Cristiano   7, 11
Bubenik, Vit   121
Bybee, Joan L.   8, 10, 11, 14, 90

Chantraine, Pierre   56, 57, 59, 61, 63, 71, 75, 77, 84–87, 89, 93, 96, 98, 106, 108, 112, 116, 121, 124, 127, 138, 162, 166, 169, 173, 174, 181, 188, 203, 205, 210, 222, 227, 232, 233, 252, 255, 256, 258
Chung, Sandra   91
Comrie, Bernard   92
Conti, Luz   57, 60, 67, 75, 177, 206
Cotticelli-Kurras, Paola   253
Covini, Andrea   126, 127
Crellin, Robert   93
Croft, William   3, 7, 25, 39, 42, 90, 92

D'Andrade, Roy   36, 192, 193
Dahl, Eystein   21, 45, 79, 90, 146, 241, 242, 268, 287

Daniel, Michael   35
De La Villa, Jesús   56
Delbrück, Bertold   69
Delfitto, Denis   90
Di Giovine, Paolo   93, 98
Diewald, Gabriele   9
Dik, Simon Cornelis   25, 27, 28, 86, 118, 131, 132, 134, 143, 145, 184, 206
Dirven, René   33, 39
Duhoux, Yves   89

Ebeling, Heinrich   124, 135, 144, 173, 178
Evans, Nicholas   26

Fanning, Buist   159
Fedriani, Chiara   21, 35, 42, 79, 241, 242
Fillmore, Charles J.   2
Fortescue, Michael   29–31, 152, 164
Fritz, von Kurt   153, 154, 156

Garcia Ramon, José Luis   90
Gisborne, Nikolas   153
Goddard, Cliff   29–31, 152
Goldberg, Adele   7–10, 49, 52, 53
Grassman, H.G.   287
Grimshaw, Jane Barbara   40

Hackstein, Olav   13
Halliday, M.A.K.   29
Harkins, Jean   33
Haspelmath, Martin   5, 22, 35, 95
Haug, Dag   61, 121
Havers, Wilhelm   284
Hengeveld, Kees   27, 28, 86, 118, 131, 132, 143, 145, 184
Herbst, Thomas   10
Hettrich, Heinrich   146
Hewson, John   121
Hilpert, Martin   7, 9, 11
Hopper, Paul J.   1, 21, 77
Horrocks, Geoffrey C.   13, 63
Humbert, Jean   84, 87
Huumo, Tuomas   75

Iacobini, Claudio   61
Inglese, Guglielmo   95

AUTHOR INDEX

Jacquinod, Bernard   106, 283
Jahn, Tomas van   112, 154, 171, 228
Johnson, Mark   11, 55

Kemenade, Ans van   61
Kemmer, Suzanne   95, 267, 269
Kittilä, Seppo   21, 35, 67, 75
Klein, Katarina   40, 205
Koptjevsaja-Tamm, Maria   12
Kövecses, Zoltan   13
Kuteva, Tania   67
Kutscher, Silvia   40, 205

Lakoff, George   44, 55
Langacker, Ronald W.   3, 11
Latacz, Joachim   103, 209, 210, 213, 214, 262
Lehmann, Winfred P.   127
Levin, Beth   8, 49
Létoublon, Françoise   83
Lord, Albert   14
Luraghi, Silvia   9, 12, 15, 28, 35, 37, 38, 44, 45,
   55, 56, 59, 60–62, 67, 69, 75, 95, 97, 98,
   118, 120, 121, 129–131, 134, 150, 176, 181,
   182, 192, 205, 215, 218, 222, 231, 242, 245,
   253, 268, 271, 280

Mallory, James   102, 110
Maslov, Boris   62
Meillet, Antoine   187
Meiser, Gerhard   59
Mette, Hans J.   227
Monier-Williams, M.   102

Næss, Åshild   21, 67
Nagy, Gregory   13
Napoli, Maria   89, 93, 157, 176
Narrog, Heiko   37
Nau, Nicole   43
Nichols, Johanna   250, 251, 253
Nikiforidou, Kiki   67
Nikitina, Tatiana   62
Nishimura, Yoshiki   35
Noonan, Michael   34, 85, 101, 111, 112, 286

Onishi, Masayuki   23

Parry, Milman   13
Perek, Florent   10, 283
Pinault, George   61

Pinelli, Erica   13
Pokorny, Julius   167
Prévot, André   137, 144, 149
Primus, Beatrice   35, 43, 47

Radden, Günter   35
Reh, Mechthild   34
Risselada, Rodie   219
Rizza, Alfredo   253
Rohrer, Tim   11
Ruijgh, Cornelis J.   89
Ruiperez, Martín S.   89

San Roque, Lila   26, 27, 230
Sasse, Hans-Jürgen   89
Sausa, Eleonora   12, 66, 67, 70, 78, 95, 129,
   130, 134, 150, 176, 181, 182, 218, 280, 283
Schlesinger, Izchak M.   35
Schwyzer, Eduard   89, 96, 126, 214
Sicking, C.M.J.   89
Simon, Christiane   34
Snell, Bruno   175
Stefanowitsch, Anatol   10
Strunk, Klaus   90
Sweetser, Eve   12, 26, 280

Tabakowska, Elżbieta   33
Tatevosov, Sergej   90, 91
Thompson, Sandra A.   1, 21
Timberlake, Alan   91
Tissari, Heli   215
Torrent, Tiago T.   71, 75
Traugott, Elizabeth C.   9
Trousdale, Graeme   9
Tsunoda, Tasaku   21, 77, 140, 269

Vaan, Michiel de   192
Van Valin, Robert   32, 188
Vendler, Zeno   29, 90, 152
Verhoeven, Elisabeth.   1, 2, 6, 12, 20, 23, 34–
   36, 40, 118, 205
Viberg, Åke   17, 24, 25, 115, 119, 137, 139, 141,
   146, 148
Viti, Carlotta   45, 46, 57, 140, 141

Weiss, Michael   92
Wichmann, Søren.   10
Wierzbicka, Anna   1, 12, 23, 30–33, 112, 204,
   207, 228–230, 235, 237

AUTHOR INDEX

Wilkins, David   26, 32, 188
Willi, Andreas   89, 95, 253, 255

Zalizniak, Anna   32
Zanchi, Chiara   61, 181

Index of Subjects

ablative 58–61, 67, 78, 205
actionality 25, 90–94, 98, 159, 165, 169, 176, 189
activity 4, 20, 21, 24, 25, 28, 29, 32, 24, 46, 55, 90, 110, 118, 119–123, 125–127, 129, 134, 137, 148–154, 157, 159, 161, 165, 166, 169, 176, 178–180, 183, 189, 191, 194, 196–199, 214, 235, 264, 277, 288
    mental 30, 31, 36, 37, 84, 100, 107, 126, 147, 150, 161, 192, 269, 270, 277, 282
affectedness 23, 36–38, 52, 53, 68, 95, 114, 126, 146, 147, 149, 198, 267–269, 288
agency 22, 36, 68, 73, 74, 82, 147, 267–269, 271
allative 60, 61
anger 29, 201–203, 205–208, 238, 239, 241, 248, 276, 278, 288, 290
(anti)causative alternation 5, 18, 89, 95, 96, 114, 249, 250, 252–255, 263, 264, 287
aspect
    imperfective 90–92, 115, 120, 157, 252
    perfective 90–92, 98, 106, 116, 131, 144, 159, 176
atelic 4, 20, 21, 25, 90, 91, 150, 153, 158, 159, 161, 165, 178, 191
attention 18, 26, 27, 40, 53, 79, 116, 147, 156, 198, 228–230, 237, 246, 247, 266, 269, 270, 277, 280
awareness 18, 29, 36, 53, 79, 86, 116, 147, 148, 154–157, 194–198, 225, 228, 229, 237, 247, 266, 269–271, 277, 280

bodily sensation(s) 1, 2, 11, 15–18, 20, 21, 23, 24, 34–36, 41, 46, 48, 73, 79, 88, 100, 101, 103–105, 113, 114, 146, 148, 193, 196–198, 232, 247, 253, 258, 263, 264, 269–272, 277, 280, 290

case syncretism 54, 58, 59, 61, 75
change-of-state verb 22, 52, 60, 64, 66–68, 76, 77, 97, 110, 148, 247, 268
cognition 1, 12, 15, 17, 20, 21, 26–29, 32–34, 36, 39, 48, 83, 84, 86, 87, 94, 98–100, 109, 114, 126, 148, 150, 162, 192, 197, 199, 212, 246, 253, 269, 277, 280, 281, 287, 288

comitative 71, 72
control 7, 12, 13, 16, 17, 20, 21, 25, 34, 36, 38, 53, 68, 73, 79, 97, 100, 107, 112, 113, 123, 125, 127, 128, 147, 148, 157, 182, 197, 198, 201, 207, 208, 211, 212–214, 218, 237, 247, 266, 268, 279
    infinitive(s) 83, 197
craving 18, 110, 197, 270, 272, 273, 278, 279

desire 34, 36, 52, 101, 107, 108, 110, 198, 200, 208, 215, 216, 219, 220, 246, 247, 249, 270, 272, 273, 277, 278, 288, 290

embodiment 11–13, 18, 36, 228, 247, 266, 277, 279, 280
empathy 223, 239, 240, 246, 272
envy 33, 36, 38, 39–41, 201, 203–206, 208, 235, 237, 239, 241, 272, 276, 278
evidentiality 12, 26, 28, 137, 142, 145

fear, fearing 5, 13, 18, 22, 24, 29, 33, 36, 44–46, 50, 86, 87, 111, 112, 116, 168, 203, 223, 225, 228–233, 235–240, 245–247, 249, 251, 252, 254, 260, 263, 269, 270, 272, 273, 275, 277, 278, 280–282, 287, 288, 290
forgetfulness 17, 191, 193, 194, 196, 280
formula(s), formulaic expression 10, 11, 14, 15, 124, 128, 129, 135, 137, 138, 148, 173, 210, 261, 262
frighten 5, 249, 251, 252, 260, 263, 288, 289

grief 225, 229, 231, 246

hate 30, 33, 44, 201, 202–204, 207, 208, 232, 233, 237, 242, 243, 249, 255, 257, 263, 276–278
hearing 12, 17, 24, 26–28, 32, 85, 86, 115, 119, 124, 127–129, 131, 132, 134, 137, 139, 141, 142, 144–149, 155, 163, 175, 181–183, 195, 197, 209, 268–272, 274, 277, 278, 280, 284, 286–289
homonymy 9, 10, 29, 30, 49, 53, 54, 58
hope 29, 34, 98, 101, 106, 110, 111–114, 197, 253, 255, 263, 275

INDEX OF SUBJECTS

inchoative 4, 21, 23, 32, 33, 37, 94, 129, 144, 152, 192, 209, 234, 242, 252, 255, 260, 267

instrumental 41, 54–56, 58, 71, 72, 75, 102, 212, 214, 246, 278

intentionality 17, 20, 34, 36, 73, 100, 107, 247

learning 17, 31, 33, 85, 137, 169, 179, 181, 187, 195, 197, 274, 277, 278, 289

locative 44, 54, 58–62, 65, 69, 70, 76, 117, 242

love 4, 18, 20, 21, 30, 39, 44, 46, 103, 200, 208, 213, 215, 216, 220, 246, 267, 273

memory 17, 31, 32, 96, 150, 153, 166, 187–189, 191, 193–196, 199, 205, 246, 270, 274, 277, 278, 280

merger 54, 58, 59

  constructional 9, 71, 75

need 18, 23, 34, 35, 63, 79, 100, 103, 104, 113, 196, 197, 272, 273, 278, 279

non-canonical

  construction 22, 23

  subject 41

polysemy 8, 9, 16, 24, 29–31, 49, 53, 54, 58, 67, 152

productivity 18, 64, 65, 68, 135, 266, 282, 283, 285, 287, 290

proto-agent 22, 46, 47, 51, 53, 74, 79, 82, 147, 267

proto-patient 22, 46, 47, 52, 53, 74, 79, 81, 147, 198, 268

rationality 36, 197

rejoicing 14, 56, 73, 86, 103, 113, 200, 201, 209–214, 245, 248, 261, 271, 285, 287

shame 13, 225, 229, 234–237, 246, 254, 259, 276–278, 281

sight 12, 17, 18, 24, 26, 27, 85, 87, 115, 116, 118, 119, 121, 123, 125–128, 137, 139, 141, 142, 145–149, 155, 156, 163, 182, 192, 196–198, 209, 226–228, 230, 231, 246, 247, 261, 268–272, 274, 277–280, 283, 287–289

skill (practical) 147, 151, 152, 169, 172, 173, 180, 186, 187, 196, 197, 270–272, 274, 278, 280

smell 17, 24, 115, 141, 142, 146, 148, 149, 197, 280, 288

social interaction 55, 70, 71, 80, 135, 214, 244–246, 271, 285

state 2, 4, 18, 25, 29, 32, 34, 90–94, 97, 98, 100, 101, 103–107, 109, 110, 150, 153, 156, 157, 173, 175, 178, 179, 185, 187, 188–191, 194, 195, 196, 197, 202, 206, 208, 210, 211, 213, 219, 225–227, 234, 235, 237–239, 242, 270, 272, 279, 280, 288

  bodily 23, 36, 44, 105

  cognitive 150, 169, 173, 179, 181, 195, 197

  emotional 20, 201, 203, 225, 227, 234

  mental 12, 31, 40, 84, 168, 171

taste 17, 24, 31, 115, 140–142, 146, 147, 149, 197, 273, 280, 288

telic 4, 20, 31, 90, 178

touch 17, 24, 77, 78, 115, 139, 140, 142, 146, 148, 149, 197, 220, 273, 280, 284, 288

valency 9, 10, 106, 162, 181, 199, 283

volition, volitionality 1, 15–18, 34–36, 38, 48, 83, 87, 88, 97–101, 106, 111–114, 149, 153, 197, 216, 220, 246, 261, 277, 278, 288

wish 34, 83, 101, 106, 108, 111–114, 123, 193, 197, 211, 275

wonder 18, 122, 156, 225–229, 239, 246, 247, 249, 272, 275, 277, 278, 280

Printed in the United States
By Bookmasters